MW01128018

CPSIA information can be obtained
at www.ICGtesting.com
Printed in the USA
BVHW080957060922
646306BV00006B/80

9 780901 905178

Remembering THE REVOLUTION

A VOLUME IN THE SERIES

Public History in Historical Perspective

Edited by Marla R. Miller

Remembering THE REVOLUTION

Memory, History, and Nation Making from Independence to the Civil War

EDITED BY

Michael A. McDonnell
Clare Corbould
Frances M. Clarke
and
W. Fitzhugh Brundage

University of Massachusetts Press
Amherst and Boston

Printed in the United States of America

ISBN 978-1-62534-033-7 (paper) 032-0 (cloth)

Designed by Sally Nichols
Set in Bauer Bodoni and Filosofia
Printed and bound by IBT/Hamilton, Inc.

Library of Congress Cataloging-in-Publication Data

Remembering the Revolution : memory, history, and nation making
from independence to the Civil War / edited by Michael A. McDonnell,
Clare Corbould, Frances M. Clarke, and W. Fitzhugh Brundage.
pages cm. — (Public history in historical perspective)
Includes bibliographical references and index.
ISBN 978-1-62534-033-7 (pbk. : alk. paper) — ISBN 978-1-62534-032-0 (hardcover :
alk. paper) 1. United States—History—Revolution, 1775–1783—Influence. I.
McDonnell, Michael A.
E209.R39 2013
973.3—dc23
2013028726

British Library Cataloguing-in-Publication Data
A catalogue record for this book is available from the British Library.

An earlier version of William Huntting Howell's essay appeared as "'Starving
Memory': Joseph Plumb Martin Un-Tells the Story of the American Revolution"
in *Common-place* 10.2 (January 2010).

Publication of this book and other titles in the series Public History in Historical
Perspective is supported by the Office of the Dean, College of Humanities and
Fine Arts, University of Massachusetts Amherst.

In memory of Rhys Isaac

Contents

Acknowledgments
xi

Introduction
The Revolution in American Life from 1776 to the Civil War
Michael A. McDonnell, Clare Corbould, Frances Clarke, and W. Fitzhugh Brundage
1

Part I
The Revolutionary Generation Remembers

War and Nationhood
Founding Myths and Historical Realities
Michael A. McDonnell
19

"A Natural & Unalienable Right"
New England Revolutionary Petitions and African American Identity
Daniel R. Mandell
41

Forgotten Founder
Revolutionary Memory and John Dickinson's Reputation
Peter Bastian
58

The Graveyard Aesthetics of Revolutionary Elegiac Verse
Remembering the Revolution as a Sacred Cause
Evert Jan van Leeuwen
75

"Starving Memory"
Antinarrating the American Revolution
William Huntting Howell
93

Public Memories, Private Lives
The First Greatest Generation Remembers the Revolutionary War
Caroline Cox
110

Part II
Transmitting Memories

"More Than Ordinary Patriotism"
Living History in the Memory Work of George Washington Parke Custis
Seth C. Bruggeman
127

Plagiarism in Pursuit of Historical Truth
George Chalmers and the Patriotic Legacy of Loyalist History
Eileen Ka-May Cheng
144

Emma Willard's "True Mnemonic of History"
America's First Textbooks, Proto-Feminism, and the Memory of the Revolution
Keith Beutler
162

Remembering and Forgetting
War, Memory, and Identity in the Post-Revolutionary Mohawk Valley
James Paxton
179

"Lie There My Darling, While I Avenge Ye!"
Anecdotes, Collective Memory, and the Legend of Molly Pitcher
Emily Lewis Butterfield
198

Part III
Dividing Memories

Forgetting History
Antebellum American Peace Reformers and the Specter of the Revolution
Carolyn Eastman
217

"Of Course We Claim to Be Americans"
Revolution, Memory, and Race in Up-Country Georgia Baptist Churches, 1772–1849
Daryl Black
234

"A Strange and Crowded History"
Transnational Revolution and Empire in George Lippard's Washington and His Generals
Tara Deshpande
249

"The Sacred Ashes of the First of Men"
Edward Everett, the Mount Vernon Ladies Association of the Union, and Late Antebellum Unionism
Matthew Mason
265

Martyred Blood and Avenging Spirits
Revolutionary Martyrs and Heroes as Inspiration for the U.S. Civil War
Sarah J. Purcell
280

Old-Fashioned Tea Parties
Revolutionary Memory in Civil War Sanitary Fairs
Frances M. Clarke
294

Notes on Contributors
313

Index
319

Acknowledgments

The editors gratefully acknowledge the financial support of the Australian Research Council, the University of Sydney, Monash University, and the University of North Carolina at Chapel Hill in bringing this collection to fruition. We also thank Marla Miller and Clark Dougan for their encouragement and advice, David Waldstreicher and the other anonymous reader of the manuscript, and the efficient and patient staff at the University of Massachusetts Press. At the University of Sydney, Robert Aldrich played an important role as we formulated the project. We were extremely fortunate when Briony Neilson signed on as a research assistant in 2011. We have long appreciated her expertise in collating essays, communicating with authors, copyediting, and indexing. Our great thanks as well to all the contributors, with whom it has been a pleasure to work.

Finally, the volume is dedicated to the memory of Rhys Isaac, who died while we were still assembling the collection. Rhys was an enthusiastic supporter of this project from the start, and he looked forward to contributing to it himself. His influence over American history in Australia especially, and us, has been immeasurable; he is sorely missed.

MM, CC, FC, and WFB

Remembering THE REVOLUTION

INTRODUCTION

The Revolution in American Life from 1776 to the Civil War

Michael A. McDonnell,
Clare Corbould, Frances M. Clarke,
and W. Fitzhugh Brundage

The American Revolution today is alive and well. Celebrated and revered, it is at the heart of American life. It drives the Tea Party movement and fuels history book publishing. It is central to the heritage industry and is represented in themed amusement parks. People from television celebrities to Supreme Court judges wonder aloud what the so-called founders would think about contemporary issues, while living-history actors and amateur reenactors bring to life the Revolution on historic battlefields across the eastern seaboard. Politicians from all parties draw upon stories of what is commonly referred to as the founding era to animate and legitimize diverse agendas. Almost every president since George Washington has cited the importance of the Revolution. George W. Bush noted the enduring legacy of the Revolution in his 2005 inaugural address. Bush observed that when "the Liberty Bell was [first] sounded in celebration, a witness said, 'It rang as if it meant something.' In our time it means something still," Bush concluded.[1]

For most Americans the meaning of the Revolution stems from how the event is remembered and invoked in the present. Although historians often lament their students' ignorance of history, when it comes to the Revolution everyone is a historian; everyone remembers "something."[2] Today Americans most often recall tales of a Revolution led by a group of "demigods" who towered above their fellow colonists, led them into a war against tyranny, and established a democratic nation dedicated to the proposition that all men were endowed by their creator with equal rights to life, liberty, and the pursuit of happiness. In these stories a unity of purpose is emphasized over division. Good triumphed over evil as a small group of men overthrew a tyrannical monarchy and replaced it with a republican government, enshrined in one of the world's first written constitutions. In this telling the American Revolution is a timeless story of the defense of freedom and the rights of all humankind. Above all, it is the story of the founding of a nation.

Yet the American Revolution was not always remembered this way. Those who survived the chaotic and complicated events of 1763–89 struggled to make sense of the momentous changes that had transformed the original thirteen colonies. Having just lived through eight years of war, white colonists could not help but recall the uncertain, halting, and painful movements toward separation from Britain. They remembered, or tried to forget, the betrayal of neighbors and family, the many divisions that split communities, and the bloodshed and losses endured in what was really America's first civil war. As the years passed, many strove to reconcile their own fragmented and traumatic memories of the war with the grand narratives of liberty spun with increasing frequency by political leaders. Others—especially women, Native Americans, and African Americans—mused on the unfulfilled promises and dashed hopes of the era.

As the Revolutionary generation passed away, and especially starting in the 1820s, accounts of the Revolution that appeared in print increasingly featured common themes, individuals, and tropes, although their meaning varied between audiences. In the meantime alternative stories were kept alive by word of mouth. Individuals, communities, regions, and eventually different sections of the country told their own stories about the Revolution and emphasized new memories and meanings. By the eve of the Civil War there was still no consensus as to the principles over which the Revolution had been fought or its outcomes. Had the founders supported slavery or its demise? What did equality and liberty really mean? What aspects of the past ought to be celebrated, and whose memory mattered? Without agreement on some of these critical questions, Americans struggled to remain united. They once again went to war with one another, still unable to agree on how to remember the Revolution.

This collection gives depth and complexity to the long history of remembering the Revolutionary era by looking at how the first few generations of Americans recalled and invoked the Revolution between 1776 and 1865. Despite the centrality of this era to the nation's history and contemporary politics, there have been few efforts to analyze and understand the place of the Revolution in evolving ideas of the American past—to map out the varied ways and means by which Americans have recalled the Revolutionary era to make sense of the present. The chapters in this volume seek to comprehend exactly how, why, and when the Revolution was remembered or forgotten by different communities at different times. Our goal is to begin the task of gathering a more inclusive social, cultural, and political history of these varied memories to specify how such remembrances have influenced the past and continue to shape the present.

In bringing this collection together, we have heeded the call of historian Michael Kammen, who remains the only person to have attempted a comprehensive study of the place of the founding era in Americans' memories. In his landmark 1978 book, *A Season of Youth: The American Revolution and the Historical Imagination,* Kammen demonstrated that the Revolution has long provided a centripetal force for those seeking to define what makes the United States unique. But he limited his account to the more formal aspects of remembering and commemoration, focusing on how political elites, historical societies, and well-known white, male writers used Revolutionary memory to suit their own, usually conservative, ends. Kammen himself recognized the limits of his analysis and called, even then, for more work to be done on the topic, especially focusing on the memories of ordinary Americans.[3]

The time is long overdue for a reexamination of this question. Several important historiographical advances since Kammen's publication have facilitated a reconsideration of this topic. An explosion of literature in the field of memory studies has enriched our understanding of how memories are formed, the language of remembrance, and the importance of commemorations in building a collective sense of the past.[4] Scholars have looked at parades, festivals, and the celebration of important days or events, such as Independence Day, in creating a public culture of remembering. Others have examined the commemoration of Revolutionary battles and the creation and history of new monuments, museums, and, national parks.[5] Drawing on some of these earlier insights, historians have also recognized the need for, and begun, a massive project of uncovering a social history of memory. Their endeavors have produced studies of returning veterans, prisoners of war, popular festivals, and victims of trauma, which raise questions about the development of a simple, linear, and consensual memory in the early national period.[6]

Indeed, scholars in general have drawn attention to contested memories and complicated our ideas about the relationship between individual and collective memories.[7] As W. Fitzhugh Brundage has noted, it is insufficient to focus on public commemorations and symbols, for it is individuals who remember. Rather than locating collective memory in society, we need to situate shared memories in individual experience and posit collective memory as the aggregation of individual experience.[8] This distinction is particularly important when dealing with "alternative" or "dissenting" memories, such as those of African Americans during the early national period. Commemorative symbols and rituals acquire and retain significance, after all, only if individuals acknowledge and utilize them. The literature on memory studies, then, helps inform and enrich our larger aim of writing a social and cultural history of the diverse ways and means by which Americans remembered at the time—and later invoked—the Revolution. In particular, it compels us to revisit the Revolutionary era to try and comprehend how Americans who lived through the tumultuous events of the period understood their place in it.

While new work on memory has pushed us to rethink the relationship between individual and collective memories, a burgeoning literature on nationalism compels us to explore how these remembrances were shaped and challenged by emerging narratives about the founding of the nation. At least since the publication of Benedict Anderson's *Imagined Communities*, historians have been well aware that nations are imagined into existence as much as they have been enacted, legislated, or even declared into being.[9] Memory and history play a crucial role in that act of imagination. It is only by sharing memories and a sense of history that individuals create a common narrative that builds community and enables a collective vision of the future. For many of the Revolutionary generation, the War for Independence seemed to create this common ground, as it produced a stock of memorable stories, images, and, later, commemorative sites and statues. But as scholars have shown in other contexts, the creation of communal memory is a highly contested, conflicted, and politicized process, in which nonelites play an important role and forgetting becomes as essential as remembering. The American Revolution was no exception: as nonwhite and nonelite Americans began to toil to extend the bounty of democratic nationalism, they called on particular recollections of the Revolution.[10]

This book began with an international call for pieces on the subject of the Revolution in American life. We received more than seventy proposals from around the world, from which we chose seventeen to create a collection covering the critical period from the Revolution to the Civil War. Writing from four different countries and introducing multi- and interdisciplinary approaches, the contributors—including many prizewinning authors—bring a special international perspective to bear on the role of the Revolution in American life.[11]

The chapters have been grouped into three roughly chronological parts. Part I, "The Revolutionary Generation Remembers," explores how those who lived through the tumultuous Revolutionary period remembered and forgot their experiences. The collection opens with a salutary reminder from Michael A. McDonnell that the War for Independence could equally be remembered as a civil war. Although the trauma of a long, divisive, and bloody war has since been largely erased from the collective memory, the other chapters in this section show that participants could not forget these events so easily. Some were scarred enough by them to know that shared membership in a newly federated republic was insufficient to overcome long-standing fissures and disputes. Politicians, former military officers, and key cultural figures therefore toiled vigorously to transform the memory of the Revolution into a glorious war fought to unite disparate peoples and forge an exemplary new nation. In doing so, they met with resistance at all turns. Indeed, many individuals and groups, soldiers in particular, presented alternative accounts of their experiences, while outsiders like African Americans sought to mobilize elite rhetoric for their own ends. These chapters suggest the diverse ways that individual Americans experienced the conflict and shaped their postwar memories in unique, and often personal, ways. They also raise important questions about the nature of a unified collective memory in the early years of the new republic.

Tensions inherent in the way that the founding generation remembered the Revolutionary era were only partly moderated by the passage of time. Part II, "Transmitting Memories," traces the transfer, diffusion, and evolution of ideas about the Revolution between generations. Truly staggering changes took place in this era, as further wars fought between Native Americans, the British, and then Mexico cleared the way for the nation to double and then quadruple in size, finally reaching all the way to the Pacific Ocean. Waves of new immigrants arrived to crowd into cities that seemed to mushroom overnight, built on the proceeds of a new industrial order and an expanding slave-based cotton economy. At the same time, a mass democratic culture increasingly challenged the leadership of traditional political elites. Could memories of the Revolution unite citizens in such a disparate and far-flung country? As the living connections to the Revolution began to pass away, this question became an urgent one. The chapters in this section demonstrate the furious work done by the post-Revolutionary generation as its members tried to forge unity and consensus out of the bitter divisions of the past.

If the chapters in part II point to an embryonic collective memory of the Revolution in the antebellum period, those in part III, "Dividing Memories," show just how tentative and fragile it was. Here, the chapters highlight the ways in which memories and recollections of the Revolution divided communities, regions, and, ultimately, the nation. As these chapters show, there was far from universal agreement on the meaning of the Revolution for most of the antebellum period, even among members of the same local constituencies. Indeed, the search for a usable past for a new nation had filtered an increasingly generic memory of the Revolution that could be stretched for different purposes. Sectional, ethnic, racial, gendered, class, and political differences created new inflections of increasingly elastic memories and ideas, even while some groups struggled to convince people to forget the Revolution. Ultimately any semblance of a national identity forged by the Revolutionary War proved to be a veneer in the run-up to the Civil War. Though we now tend to think of the American Revolution as a unifying event, these chapters show that contests over the meaning of the Revolutionary past could and did divide Americans, ultimately helping to drive the nation into a devastating civil war.

Taken chronologically, the chapters in this collection chart the halting and arguably unsuccessful attempts of the first few generations of Americans to forge a nation in the face of an uncertain beginning, and through a period of momentous changes. Yet across the collection, several important themes emerge as well. While it is impossible to do justice to the numerous issues raised and the conceptual subtlety displayed by each author, there are at least three key themes worth highlighting.

By focusing on a specific event and how it was remembered over time and by different people, these chapters make a timely contribution to our understanding of how memory works. Many authors, for example, concern themselves with how both individual and collective memories are formed, transmitted, changed, and sometimes discarded. Chapters by Michael A. McDonnell, William Huntting Howell, Caroline Cox, and Peter Bastian all speak to the strenuous effort of participants to frame their experiences in ways that would be recognizable to us today. Howell and Cox show that veterans struggled to make sense of their traumatic experience long after the immediate crisis. They show that ordinary Americans experienced the conflict and shaped their postwar memories in often idiosyncratic ways. Against this, as Bastian's chapter on John Dickinson reveals, many of the now-celebrated Founding Fathers engaged in an energetic effort to remember and rewrite a Revolution—and their own parts in it—that was free of opposition and controversy. A lack of structure in the initial accounts of the Revolution gave subsequent generations plenty of freedom to construct new narratives from the recalled past. Thus, stories of the Revolution could and did arise from diverse sources—loyalist accounts, anecdotes and rumors, early living-history actors, local historians, or even graveyard elegies. But because of these diverse origins, a unified memory of the Revolution was slow to form and inherently tenuous. There was, in short, no clear collective memory of the Revolution.

Together, the chapters also underscore the need to historicize Revolutionary memory. Rather than assuming that memories are made and transmitted in the same way from generation to generation, the authors focus on the particular contexts in which memories were created. Thus, as Evert Jan van Leeuwen notes, the emotive power of eighteenth-century literary aesthetics was quickly yoked to the cause of creating a collective memory of the Revolution as sacred. His chapter highlights the power of emotion and sentiment in literary circles in the late eighteenth century. Seth C. Bruggeman's chapter on George Washington Parke Custis's efforts to preserve and promote the memory of his stepgrandfather demonstrates the need to be sensitive to the tools available at the time to shape memory. Indeed, as Keith Beutler notes, Custis's efforts were part of a resurgence of "physicalist" conceptions of memory in the early nineteenth century. The coincidence of the physicalist "turn" with the passing of the Revolutionary generation produced an intense interest in the few living relics of the war and a new desire to create sacred sites and monuments to the past. These chapters help to clarify the sudden appeal of the Revolution around the time of Lafayette's visit to the United States in 1824–25. The prominent French general rekindled memories of the Revolution at the very moment when the physical evidence of the war—and especially veterans—was disappearing.

Perhaps not surprisingly, many of the chapters dealing with the post-1825 period illuminate the increasing importance of print in creating a collective memory of the past. James Paxton explores the way local historians in upstate New York in the 1820s and 1830s wrote histories that rendered complicated stories of the past in simpler terms. Emily Lewis Butterfield tackles the issue of the transmission of memories from a slightly different angle by tracing the accretion of local folklore, anecdotes, reports, and rumors that would eventually cohere into a consistent and nationally appealing story of Molly Pitcher. Eileen Ka-May Cheng, in her careful look at early nationalist historians, shows how their work enmeshed history as a discipline and craft with the project of nation making.

The second key theme to emerge from these chapters is the constitutive nature of collective memory and its relationship to community. Among the confusion of memories forged by two and a half million people living in thirteen different states with different histories, societies, religions, and cultures, there was space in which nonelites could actively reimagine themselves into the story of the Revolution. African Americans in Revolutionary Massachusetts, as Daniel R. Mandell shows in his chapter, exploited the multistranded rhetoric of resistance to Britain to promulgate a new memory of their African origins and to legitimate their claims to transatlantic rights. To do so, they wrote themselves into a story of the Revolution that could encompass their claims for freedom. Unfortunately, many of these claims ran headlong into alternative efforts to remember a more contained narrative of the period. As Bastian and Bruggeman show, men such as John Adams and later George Washington Parke Custis also worked hard to erase memories of dissent and create new celebratory narratives in which they played prominent roles. More complicated and challenging stories such as those of John Dickinson, Joseph Plumb Martin, and Prince Hall had no place in these early elite narratives, a point driven home by Revolutionary poets who immediately began to memorialize and glorify only prominent heroes and martyrs of the war.

In turn, the creation of a collective memory of the Revolution, as Emily Lewis Butterfield's chapter on Molly Pitcher demonstrates, involved standardizing narrative accounts by erasing their inconsistencies. But in the process much was forgotten, as individual memories clashed or merged with local stories, which were often in tension with an emerging national narrative or elite-driven attempts to create a more seamless, consensual rendition of the past. These tensions were eventually elided by a more homogenous national narrative that emphasized ideas and ideals over specific events and promoted consensus over conflict. Thus, local historians, such as those in New York discussed by Paxton, had to forget as much as they remembered in their histories, even as Native Americans continued to contest that vision.

A similar impulse was conspicuous in the surprising borrowings that nationalist historians made from the work of loyalist historian George Chalmers. As Cheng explains, patriot elites had more in common with loyalist elites than they did with fellow patriots, and therefore the struggle for social order within the new nation was far more important in their histories than was the fight against tyranny without. In their histories of the Revolutionary past, early national historians used claims of "truthfulness" to legitimize narratives of stability and order and borrowed passages from Chalmers to advance their work. Perhaps this evolution should not be surprising. As Alon Confino has written, national memory demands compromise and requires adulteration. Rather than consistency, memory is "constituted by different, often opposing, memories that, in spite of their rivalries, construct common denominators that overcome on a symbolic level real social and political differences."[12]

Finally, a third theme running through these chapters is the role played by memory in the politics of making—and unmaking—the nation. The way in which these different kinds of memories clashed, and an understanding of what was suppressed as much as celebrated, reminds us that the business of memory is inherently a political project. People made choices about what they remembered, whether consciously or unconsciously. As Bruggeman notes, George Washington Parke Custis's living-history "performances" were, "in the context of early nineteenth-century politics, feverishly political, vehemently anti-Republican, and blatantly anti-Jefferson." A few groups, such as Carolyn Eastman's peace reformers, who could not easily reconcile the memorialized Revolution with their political project, labored to convince people to forget the Revolution. Others were keen to harness their own idea of the Revolution to particular political causes. They often expressed these in terms of the future they envisioned, which could range from Joseph Plumb Martin's longing for a future free from hunger and deprivation to John Dickinson's quest for a more tranquil, simple agrarian life to black Georgia Baptists envisioning a truly equal polity. As Daryl Black's chapter on this last group shows, that yearning to hew a better future from the past would continue to be a pervasive theme in American history.

Yet yoking the Revolution to political causes in any sort of nuanced way became increasingly difficult by the antebellum era, as Matthew Mason's chapter on Edward Everett and Tara Deshpande's account of George Lippard reveal. Everett and Lippard both desperately wanted a usable past to steer a new way forward, but the contradictions of that past combined with too little agreement on its meaning rendered their efforts futile. Ultimately, as Sarah J. Purcell argues, any semblance of a national identity forged by the Revolutionary War came undone in the period preceding the Civil War. The same symbols, the same traditions of Revolutionary heroism and martyrdom that had once seemingly held Americans together, helped to split the nation apart, as both Northerners and Southerners invoked the Revolution to animate sectionalist military fervor. In turn, that conflict began a new era in remembering the Revolution. Confronted with the dramatic limits of a shared sense of the Revolutionary past to keep the nation together, some Americans began thinking of new origin stories. As Frances M. Clarke concludes, the Civil War marked the point at which the status of the Revolution as *the* nation-building event was finally brought into question. Trumpeting the importance of their own military victories, Northerners began to conceive of the Revolution as ancient history—a distant prologue for grander achievements yet to come.

In exploring these themes, the chapters in the collection assay the memories of individuals, families, communities, and regions. They challenge what we know about familiar figures such as George Washington, George Bancroft, Molly Pitcher, and Joseph Plumb Martin, while also introducing us to less well-known or now-forgotten Americans such as Prince Hall, John and Mary Dickinson, Emma Willard, George Lippard, and antebellum peace reformers. Importantly, nonelites, whether whites, Native Americans, African Americans, or women, take their place alongside the so-called Founding Fathers, who currently dominate public memories of the Revolution. The collection aims to prompt reflection on the memory work of all Americans and the way their memories diverged or intersected with the ongoing creation of a more public memory of the past by the "guardians of tradition."

At the same time, and in keeping with this more expansive view of the making of a collective memory, the collection highlights diverse places as sites of memory. Thus, the Mohawk Valley, Maine, and Piedmont, Georgia, are added to more familiar sites of memory such as Boston, Washington, and Philadelphia. Likewise, graveyards, poll booths, schoolrooms, sanitary fairs, and slave quarters take their place alongside so-called sacred sites, such as Mount Vernon, and popular tourist attractions, such as Colonial Williamsburg.

Finally, the chapters in this collection challenge us to think about the transmission of memories and the ways in which collective memories have been forged. For too long scholars have focused on the means employed by the guardians of tradition in communicating collective memory—the preservation of archives and printed historical records, for example. But these chapters explore the role of anecdote, emotions, early living-history enactments, children's literature, mnemonics in and out of the classroom, kinship, graveyard poetry, and popular historical fiction, as well as traditional history writing, to explore the multivalent creation of collective memory. In examining these different media of memory and the ways in which they changed over time, the chapters also help to historicize the concept of memory itself.

In the end, we hope this collection reinvigorates debate about the

Revolution and its meanings. Although the Revolution is everywhere today, it exists as a kind of artifact—a one-dimensional object, sitting proudly on the shelf of memory—ready to be shown off to anyone who might disagree with a particular and often preconceived notion of the past. As Clarke's chapter on the Tea Partiers of yesteryear foreshadows, Revolutionary memory has become reified and petrified—transformed into a sacred relic that provokes veneration and deference rather than investigation. As historians from the left and right agree, we need to challenge the static, simplistic, and ahistorical nature of current popular understandings of the founding era.

By reminding readers of the constructed nature of the Revolution and its multiple meanings to a diverse population and different generations, we hope to make the Revolution come alive again. To do this, we first need to see it as a historical event like any other—one that was complicated and contingent, not linear or predestined. Just like every other lived and remembered time, it was a complex era that left a contested legacy. Rather than asking, what did the founding generation think?—as if that generation was of a single mind—we need to start questioning how and why certain memories of the Revolution won out over others and to what effect. After all, skepticism, not slavish devotion, is a far more fitting stance to adopt toward a generation that fomented revolt.

NOTES

1. George W. Bush, "Second Inaugural Address," January 20, 2005, www.bartleby.com/124/pres67.html.
2. See, for example, the article and notes by Sam Wineburg and Chauncey Monte-Sano, "'Famous Americans': The Changing Pantheon of American Heroes," *Journal of American History* 94, no. 4 (March 2008): 1186–1202, wherein these authors had to *exclude* the Founding Fathers from their survey to glean what else students remembered.
3. Michael Kammen, *A Season of Youth: The American Revolution and the Historical Imagination* (New York: Knopf, 1978).
4. We have drawn heavily on the conceptual insights and critical review of more traditional studies of memory and history in Alon Confino, "Collective Memory and Cultural History: Problems of Method," *American Historical Review* 102, no. 5 (December 1997): 1386–1403. In addition to Confino, we are indebted to the major works on memory and history, including, among others, Paul Ricoeur, *Memory, History, Forgetting*, trans. Kathleen Blamey and David Pellauer (Chicago:

University of Chicago Press, 2004); Maurice Halbwachs, *The Collective Memory*, trans. F. J. Ditter (New York: Harper & Row, 1980); Eric Hobsbawm and Terence Ranger, eds., *The Invention of Tradition* (Cambridge: Cambridge University Press, 1983); Natalie Zemon Davis and Randolph Starn, eds., "Memory and Counter-Memory," *Representations* 26 (Spring 1989); and especially Pierre Nora, "Between Memory and History: *Les Lieux de Mémoire*," *Representations* 26, (Spring 1989): 7–24; Nora, *Realms of Memory: The Construction of the French Past*, ed. Lawrence D. Kritzman, trans. Arthur Goldhammer, 3 vols. (New York: Columbia University Press, 1996–98); Yael Zerubavel, *Recovered Roots: Collective Memory and the Making of Israeli National Tradition* (Chicago: University of Chicago Press, 1995); John R. Gillis, ed., *Commemorations: The Politics of National Identity* (Princeton: Princeton University Press, 1994); and Klaus Neumann, *Shifting Memories: The Nazi Past in the New Germany* (Ann Arbor: University of Michigan Press, 2000). For the United States in particular, see John Bodnar, *Remaking America: Public Memory, Commemoration, and Patriotism in the Twentieth Century* (Princeton: Princeton University Press, 1992); David Glassberg, *American Historical Pageantry: The Uses of Tradition in the Early Twentieth Century* (Chapel Hill: University of North Carolina Press, 1990); Roy Rosenzweig and David Thelen, *The Presence of the Past: Popular Uses of History in American Life* (New York: Columbia University Press, 1998); and Karal Ann Marling, *George Washington Slept Here: Colonial Revivals and American Culture, 1876–1986* (Cambridge: Harvard University Press, 1988).

5. These studies have tended to focus on the more formal *lieux de mémoire* and often emphasize a kind of unfolding linear narrative of a developing collective memory guided by "the guardians of tradition" that presupposes the primary importance of the Revolutionary era and an already calcified story of that event. J. H. Plumb suggested years ago that these guardians of tradition were usually most interested in "confirmatory history"—a "narration of events of particular people, nations or communities in order to justify authority, to create confidence and to secure stability." *The Death of the Past* (Boston: Houghton Mifflin, 1969), 38–40. Michael Kammen's works are most germane to this project, but his research has mainly focused on these guardians of tradition. See especially his *Season of Youth* and *Mystic Chords of Memory: The Transformation of Tradition in American Culture* (New York: Knopf, 1991). For examples of the kind of isolated studies that have been published, of which there are many in diverse fields, see Matthew Dennis, *Red, White, and Blue Letter Days: An American Calendar* (Ithaca, N.Y.: Cornell University Press, 2002); Lorett Treese, *Valley Forge: Making and Remaking a National Symbol* (University Park: Pennsylvania State University Press, 1995); and Sarah J. Purcell, *Sealed with Blood: War, Sacrifice and Memory in Revolutionary America* (Philadelphia: University of Pennsylvania Press, 2002).

6. George B. Forgie, *Patricide in the House Divided: A Psychological Interpretation of Lincoln and His Age* (New York: Norton, 1979); Alfred F. Young, "George Robert Twelves Hewes (1742–1840): A Boston Shoemaker and the Memory of the American Revolution," *William and Mary Quarterly* 38 (1981): 562–623; Young, *The Shoemaker and the Tea Party: Memory and the American Revolution* (Boston: Beacon, 1999); David Lowenthal, *The Past Is a Foreign Country* (Cambridge:

Cambridge University Press, 1986); Marling, *George Washington Slept Here;* Kurt G. Piehler, *Remembering War the American Way* (Washington, D.C.: Smithsonian Institution Press, 1995); Purcell, *Sealed with Blood;* François Furstenberg, *In the Name of the Father: Washington's Legacy, Slavery, and the Making of a Nation* (New York: Penguin, 2006); Scott E. Casper, *Sarah Johnson's Mount Vernon: The Forgotten History of an American Shrine* (New York: Hill & Wang, 2008).

7. Halbwachs, *Collective Memory;* Alistair Thomson, *Anzac Memories: Living with the Legend* (Melbourne: Oxford University Press, 1994); Confino, "Collective Memory and Cultural History," 1386–1403.
8. W. Fitzhugh Brundage, *Where These Memories Grow: History, Memory, and Southern Identity* (Chapel Hill: University of North Carolina Press, 2000).
9. Benedict Anderson, *Imagined Communities: Reflections on the Origin and Spread of Nationalism* (London: Verso, 1983); Hobsbawm and Ranger, *Invention of Tradition;* Homi K. Bhabha, *Nation and Narration* (London: Routledge, 1990).
10. Ernst Renan, *Qu'est-ce qu'une nation? Conférence faite en Sorbonne, le 22 mars 1882*, 2nd ed. (Paris: Calman-Lévy, 1882), 7–8; Henry Rousso, *The Vichy Syndrome: History and Memory in France since 1944*, trans. Arthur Goldhammer (Cambridge: Harvard University Press, 1991); Thomson, *Anzac Memories;* Ali Behdad, *A Forgetful Nation: On Immigration and Cultural Identity in the United States* (Durham, N.C.: Duke University Press, 2005); Marilyn Lake et al., *What's Wrong with ANZAC? The Militarisation of Australian History* (Sydney: University of New South Wales Press, 2010); Hester Lessard, Rebecca Johnson, and Jeremy Webber, eds., *Storied Communities: Narratives of Contact and Arrival in Constituting Political Community* (Vancouver: University of British Columbia Press, 2011).
11. The editors asked contributors to reflect on the following six themes: (1) The historicization of memory itself: How have Americans remembered their past? How have different Americans remembered their past? Do race, gender, class, religion, or regional differences matter? How has this changed over time? How have these changes affected the way that Americans remember their founding moment? (2) Individual versus collective memory: What is the relationship between individual and collective memories? At what point do individual memories become co-opted or replaced by a collective memory? How do different memories and remembrances of the past combine or conflict to create a collective memory? (3) The multiplicity of memory: What place did or does the American Revolution have in the minds of Americans at any given moment? What memories have competed with the Revolution? Does or did the Revolution have a primary place in the remembering of the past? (4) Representations of the past versus the reception of those representations: How and why have different groups represented the Revolution? How have they tried to communicate those representations? What roles have monuments, art, film, the stage, or museums played in these representations? How successful have these different kinds of representations been? Why do some representations come to dominate? (5) Remembering and forgetting: What are the visible signs of remembrance? What do silences, omissions, and gaps in memories tell us about the place of the Revolution in American memories? How have different groups

remembered an alternative, dissenting past? Have these replaced a memory of the Revolution? and (6) Myth and history and the "founding moment": To what extent is the memory of the Revolution dominated by the idea of it being a "founding moment"? To what extent is the memory of the Revolution wedded to the creation of a nation? Has this obscured or enriched our view of the Revolutionary period as a historical event? Have historians been complicit in this mythmaking?

12. Confino, "Collective Memory and Cultural History," 1399–1400.

Part I

The Revolutionary Generation Remembers

War and Nationhood

Founding Myths and Historical Realities

Michael A. McDonnell

In his much-anticipated inaugural address in January 2009, President Barack H. Obama invoked the country's founding moment—the American Revolution—no fewer than four separate times in charting a proposed path through the difficult years to come. Concluding with a call to action, Obama recalled a nation-defining moment during the Revolutionary War: "In the year of America's birth, in the coldest of months, a small band of patriots huddled by dying campfires on the shores of an icy river," he began. "The capital was abandoned. The enemy was advancing. The snow was stained with blood. At a moment when the outcome of our revolution was most in doubt, the father of our nation ordered these words be read to the people: 'Let it be told to the future world . . . that in the depth of winter, when nothing but hope and virtue could survive . . . that the city and the country, alarmed at one common danger, came forth to meet . . . it.'" "America," Obama concluded, "in the face of our common dangers, in this winter of our hardship, let us remember these timeless words."[1]

In conjuring a memory of the Revolution as a nation-building event, Obama was following a well-worn path. Only four years previously, George W. Bush invoked the Revolution in his inaugural address to shore up support for the so-called War on Terror.[2] Obama and Bush knew what buttons to push. Presidents, of course, try to manipulate the emotions of their listeners by appealing to what they imagine their audiences find compelling. And surveys consistently reveal that if Americans remember anything about their past, it is usually something about the American Revolution. The era of the American Revolution has come to provide a rich seam of memorable events that can be mined to invoke, impart, and inspire. Whether it be iconic images or memorable stories of Valley Forge, the Boston Tea Party, the Founding Fathers, Washington's tearful Farewell Address, or knowledge of the "sacred" texts that lie enshrined under bombproof glass in a vault at the National Archives—the Declaration of Independence, the Constitution, and the Bill of Rights—most Americans do indeed seem to remember something about their Revolution.[3]

Central to these memories is an idea of the Revolutionary War as a nation-building event—perhaps *the* nation-building event. Obama was not the first to link the War for Independence with the creation of a new nation. The most memorable images and tales of the war—including stories, engravings, paintings, legends, myths, and now Hollywood movies—all connect the long and arduous conflict between the thirteen original colonies and Britain with the founding, or birth, of a new nation. And Americans today most often recall tales of a Revolutionary War that privilege unity over division, simple stories of the triumph of good over evil, and memories of a hard-fought victory that ended with the overthrow of a tyrannical monarchy and its replacement with a republican government. As the Valley Forge National Historic Park website notes, sites such as theirs "are tangible links to one of the most defining events in our nation's history." Few places "evoke the spirit of patriotism and independence, represent individual and collective sacrifice, or demonstrate the resolve, tenacity and determination of the people of the United States to be free as does Valley Forge."[4]

This powerful collective memory of the Revolutionary War as a nation-building event has been reinforced by historical accounts. Most American history textbooks, for example, make this link clear. George Brown Tindall and David Emory Shi in *America: A Narrative History* begin the second part of their textbook, titled "Building a Nation," with the Revolutionary War. The conflict, they argue, "not only secured American independence" but "generated a new sense of nationalism."[5] For Paul Boyer and his colleagues in *The Enduring Vision: A History of the American People*, the war was the seminal event in the birth of the nation. They begin their section on "The Forge of Nationhood, 1776–1788" with a chapter on the conflict, asserting that well-documented friendships like the one that developed between Virginian George Washington and Henry Knox from Massachusetts became equally commonplace among ordinary men and women during the war. Localism, which was "well entrenched at the start of the war," was overcome as "the Revolution gave northerners and southerners their first real chance to learn what they had in common, and they soon developed mutual admiration." *The Enduring Vision* is most sanguine about the national legacy of the War for Independence: "In July 1776 the thirteen colonies had out of desperation declared independence and established a new nation. But only as a result of the collective hardships experienced during eight years of terrible fighting did the inhabitants of the thirteen states cease to see themselves simply as military allies and begin to accept each other as fellow citizens."[6]

This collective memory of the Revolutionary War as a nation-building event stands in marked contrast to the historical realities of the War for Independence. Lasting eight years, the war was one of the longest and bloodiest wars in America's history. The per capita equivalent of the number of casualties in the Revolution would today mean the death of perhaps as many as three million Americans. Yet it was not such an extended and bloody war simply because the might of the British armed forces was brought to bear on the hapless colonists. As historians have been rediscovering of late, the Revolution went on so long because of the many divisions among colonists themselves over whether to fight, what to fight for, and who would do the fighting. The War for Independence was by any measure the first American Civil War.[7]

Though historians have searched hard for signs of unity, the origins of a common identity, and the roots of American nationalism amid the chaos of this conflict, they have met with little success.[8] Indeed, everywhere they have looked closely they have instead found divisions, conflicts, and sentiments that would militate *against* the creation of a new national identity during the war. Such tensions often lay along older colonial fault lines between and within the diverse colonies; others emerged under the pressure of war.[9] Leaving aside the most obvious internal conflicts between slave owners and their workers, and between Native Americans and the colonists, these tensions can be roughly grouped into four categories: a persistent localism, animosity between the colonies and new states, antipathy toward new Continental officials, and a lack of attachment more generally to the patriot cause. Though a full examination of these conflicts is beyond the scope of this chapter, a brief review of each should be sufficient to raise questions about the link between the War for Independence and the creation of a nation. In turn, the chapter concludes by raising a new question: if the roots of a new national identity cannot be found in the War for Independence, where should we start looking?[10]

In July 1776 thirteen colonies came together to declare independence. But it was largely a union of self-defense. There was, of course, no nation in 1775 when the conflict began, and older colonial attachments remained preeminent. New citizens who supported independence fought for "country"—and most people's sense of their country extended no farther than the boundaries of their own local communities, or at best their own state. While many could see a necessity for common defense and unity of purpose, most ordinary Americans were unwilling to sacrifice their own, more local, common defense for some vague idea of a greater good or larger nation. Even in the heat of the most critical moment, in May 1775, volunteers in Williamsburg, Virginia, pledged themselves to "march, on the smallest warning, to any part of the continent, where the general cause of American liberty may demand their attendance," but only if, they added, "they do not by such step leave their *own country* in a defenseless state."[11] Their counterparts in Botetourt County in western Virginia were not even that sure, for it was rumored at the same time that the Independent Company of Volunteers in that county had registered their protest "about going out of the Colony" at all.[12]

Such local feelings grew rather than diminished through the war. Thousands of white Virginians refused to take a loyalty oath when it became mandatory in the spring of 1777, because they believed they would then "be compelled to go to the northward whenever the Governor pleased to order them." The following year, an entire county secretly circulated a "Subscripsion" binding themselves "to stand by each other and oppose any attempt that may be made to march them out of this State."[13] Militia in Delaware disrupted elections in 1777 because they believed if the Whigs got into the Assembly, they would be "drafted and obliged to go to camp" northward. Later in the war, and in the face of military reverses in the South, militia rarely rallied to the Continental cause. When the British threatened Charleston, South Carolina, in the spring of 1780, the governor of Virginia ordered the militia there to go southward. Yet many rebelled at the thought of leaving home for so long (three months) to risk their lives in another state. The orders to march gave "very great & general discontent" and many who were ordered to march "staid behind." In several counties there were violent mutinies.[14]

There were important reasons why militia wanted to stay local. Pennsylvania farmers who had joined the army, for example, were incensed to find themselves attached to Washington's army in the east after they had been promised they would be used only to protect the frontier. Both officers and men had "understood they were raised for the defense of the western frontiers," and the fact that "their families and substance [were] to be left in so defenseless a situation in their absence, seems to give sensible trouble." A little later in the war, militia from the Pennsylvania backcountry county of Northumberland refused to obey a call to march eastward to help defend Philadelphia against Howe's invasion because, "at the present time, the inhabitants of this country are afraid of the Indians coming down upon our frontiers." In other words, the main priority of the militia was the safety of their homes, families, and local communities.[15]

This is not to say that these same farmers refused to fight at all. When they were called on to fight locally, in defense of "families and substance," thousands of Americans did fight. John Burgoyne learned this lesson when he invaded down the Champlain Valley in the summer of 1777. Faced with an actual invasion and spurred on by the unpunished "murder" of Jane McCrea at the hands of Burgoyne's Native American allies, hundreds of New England militia rushed to arms and helped seal the fate of Burgoyne and his troops at Saratoga.[16] Likewise, when the British invaded Virginia in 1780 and again in 1781, it was reported that the "Malitia Generally turn out Spirited." Indeed, in early 1781 James Madison's father told his son that "upon the Approach of Cornwallis, no Time, not even the Year 75 ever exhibited a more hearty Zeal in the common Cause. Old Men, who had long laid aside the Musket, even half Tories caught the Flame, and I believe had he crossed the Dan [River] his Fate w[oul]d have been glorious for Am[eric]a."[17] But even these men, who had shown so much enthusiasm, "cool in ardor in proportion as they retire from the line of the State, & grow impatient."[18] As the examples of these and other numerous communities show, it was for local defense that most people fought and died. In times of war at least, the "imagined community" rarely extended beyond the boundaries of the state, if that far, for a majority of Americans.[19]

Even among those who did cross state borders to work together in the common cause, it is questionable to what extent any kind of national feeling developed. Those who entered the Continental Army, for example—men most likely to have begun thinking continentally, given that they traveled afar and sometimes formed the kind of new relationships enjoyed by Knox and Washington—were generally not citizen-soldiers fighting for love of country. They were most often the poor, the landless, the young, and the foreign-born, looking for a wage and individual advancement, whether in the form of bounty in money, land, slaves, or even a new set of clothes.

Although some of these soldiers may have forged new and harmonious continental ties with their southern or northern compatriots, many, it seems, had their existing prejudices and suspicions reinforced. New England soldiers, for example, showed such little trust in New York general Philip Schuyler that he "virtually lost the ability to command." In turn, a captain Alexander Graydon of Pennsylvania reported that his soldiers thought the eastern troops were "contemptible in the extreme." A Maryland officer was acquitted of showing disrespect to a New England general because New Englanders were held in "so contemptible a light . . . that it was scarcely held possible to conceive a case, which could be construed into a reprehensible disrespect of them."[20] A popular and regional marching song of the New England soldiers, titled "Chester," irritated Virginians and others:

> Let tyrants shake their iron rod,
> and slavery clank her galling chains.
> We fear them not, we trust in God.
> *New England's* God forever reigns.[21]

One study that followed the fortunes of a Maryland regiment throughout the war, focusing on the very men that should have developed the most fervent nationalism—Continental soldiers—shows that a nascent *sectionalism* rather than *nationalism* developed among these southern troops. When mixing with other regiments, they quickly found they had much more in common with Virginians and Carolinians than New Englanders and those from the middle colonies.[22]

After the conflict turned southward around 1778, the strength of sectionalism intensified. Whereas before 1780 elite Virginians had looked inward and blamed themselves and their neighbors for their own military unreadiness, after 1780 and under the weight of repeated invasions by the British, some southerners—including patriot leaders—began to redirect their anger northward. John Banister, for example, called his fellow Virginians "self-interested," "venal," and lacking in "patriotism" when they refused to join the Continental Army in numbers in 1778. Yet by 1781 he thought the Virginians were "entirely unanimous . . . but I think the rest of the continent have totally abandoned us." David Jameson also concluded in 1781 that "Virginia has done her all" and that when the state's white citizens "reflect that the brethren to the North & East of them have free & open trade, free from invasion, and living in ease, & affluence—and will afford no assistance; their sufferings become more grievous. Virginia freely contributed when her sister States were in distress—why is she left not only to struggle for her self under many difficulties, but required to bear the burthen of the whole Southern War?" Such feelings reached a climax in a "Battery . . . against the Northern States," which the Virginia Assembly drew up in March 1781 for presentation to Congress. It publicly—and justifiably—condemned the northern states, "who in time of their own need, used the affectionate appellation of Brethren, but appear now to have forgotten the duties of such a relationship."[23]

If any glimmer of continental unity had survived to 1781, it took another beating as each state looked for a scapegoat for their woes. One Virginia planter reported in May 1781, for example, that "Our people—[Virginians]—are made very angry by a Report that the Pennsylvania[ns], instead of forwarding their Troops with that celerity, which their duty and the situation of things demanded, were throwing out Insulting speeches that Virginia was too grand—let her be humbled by the Enemy, and such like—What consequences this may produce, I know not." When the Pennsylvania troops finally did arrive, they forcefully seized supplies from Virginia farmers and committed "other Excesses." The marquis de Lafayette thought tensions were high enough to keep the troops moving through to North Carolina. "The Pennsylvanians and Virginians have never agreed," Lafayette wrote, "but at the present time it is worse than ever." "Every day the troops remain here adds to the danger," he concluded.[24] That Lafayette—never one to exaggerate—thought his troops more in danger from fellow colonists than the British, underscores the level of antipathy that existed during the war.

Anti-union feelings existed not only in disagreements and antipathy between citizens of different states but also in relations between citizens and the Continental Congress. Ironically, many came to the view that Congress was equally (if not more) demanding and overbearing than the British. The new Congress intruded most immediately in people's lives through constant, onerous, and invidious requisitions for men and supplies. The most common form of conflict—at least the most violent manifestation of anti-Continental feeling—was over conscription into the army. In Virginia, for example, resistance to compulsory drafts for the Continental armed services resulted every time the state tried to force men into service. The repeated confrontations culminated in violent rioting in 1781 across Virginia. In one county as many as seven hundred men assembled to stand in opposition to conscription, and in another, hundreds more gathered at the courthouse with clubs to prevent the draft from taking place.[25]

Baron von Steuben, a Continental officer, summed up mobilization problems in 1781 when he wrote with disgust, "the opposition made to the law in some counties, the entire neglect of it in others, and an unhappy disposition to evade the fair execution of it in all afford a very melancholy prospect."[26] Resistance to serving and draft protests crippled the war effort not just in Virginia—where less than a quarter of the men needed in 1781 were raised—but throughout the states. When Washington called for an additional 2,200 men from Connecticut in 1781 to guard the Highlands, for example, he got fewer than 800, or about 40 percent of the call. Even if drafts did take place, the results were the same. Again in Connecticut in 1780, of 158 men drafted or "detached" for six months' service, 130 refused to go or absconded. Mobilization problems were not isolated to specific communities. They existed everywhere. The Continental Army was chronically undermanned throughout the war.[27]

Perhaps worse than the resistance itself, as von Steuben's comments indicate, such anti-Revolutionary activity was aided and abetted by local inhabitants, local officials, and sometimes the very militia officers in charge of implementing the laws. When Connecticut towns were again asked to draft men from their militia for the Continental Army in 1780, there was widespread disobedience. One sergeant, after being ordered to draft a man, told his captain that his "orders are not worthy of my notice." Another captain refused to comply because he said the Assembly had set an unfair quota for his town. Militia also elected officers who were openly disaffected, while local officials' reluctance to "doom" delinquent divisions of militia when they failed to produce recruits showed a general and growing antipathy toward patriot service. Civilian officials in Braintree, Massachusetts, went further when they voted to indemnify their militia officers if they were ever fined for failing to carry out state and Continental levies of men, particularly drafts.[28]

Thousands more Americans resisted Continental patriot efforts when they refused to offer supplies or submit to impressments ordered by Congress or army officers. When Congress pushed the Connecticut Assembly to requisition grain from each town in 1779 for the supply of the militia supporting the French admiral d'Estaing, not one bushel was ever collected, even though local officials were given summary power to collect from individuals as they saw fit. None wanted to risk popular opposition. Tax resistance also helped cripple the patriot war effort. Evidence indicates that tax resistance levels were high in every state, and violence was avoided only because local tax collectors refused to apply pressure on their neighbors. In Connecticut, for example, locally elected selectmen in each town had a discretionary power to abate taxes where they felt there was a need or good cause. Though custom put the proportion of abated taxes at about 5 percent, it rose to 20 percent in the first years of the war and up to 25 percent in the latter years. Uncollected taxes had a direct effect on mobilization, as taxes were most often used to pay for recruiting. A tax of two shillings and six pence laid in 1781 by the Connecticut Assembly to fulfill their congressional quota for new recruits and supplies was supposed to raise £288,223 in specie. Abatement of up to 20 percent reduced this figure to £231,017. Tax collectors sent the government only £160,792, but of this, £120,260 came in as orders on the treasury for goods and services already supplied. Thus the government ultimately received only about £40,000, or just 14 percent of the original request.[29]

Contact with government officials who represented the Continental Congress seemed only to exacerbate anti-Continental feelings rather than broaden horizons and create new friendships. When local militia were forced farther afield and compelled to rub shoulders with Continental officials, especially officers, they often found the experience distasteful. As early as 1775 Pennsylvania riflemen from the backcountry, for example, felt compelled to desert to the enemy after marching all the way to Cambridge when some of their own men were court-martialed by officers in the new Continental Army. Localism, combined with a nascent antiauthoritarianism nurtured by resistance to the British, could produce a lasting enmity. Militia from Caroline County, Virginia, had originally turned out with the "greatest alacrity" when the British threatened in late 1780, but they returned "with the most rivited [*sic*] disgust" because of their experience with a Continental officer. Eight of their number had died through sickness, which they attributed to the "Brutal behaviour of a Major McGill, a Regular Officer." Complaining about the "forced Marches and too Strict Attention to Order," the returning militia had spread the word through the rest of the county "so that it is announced in all Companies, that they will die rather than stir Again."[30] Experiences like these made for lasting memories in the minds of ordinary Americans, whose only common experience seemed to be conflict with a central power, much like the one from which they had just declared independence. Indeed, antiauthoritarianism seemed far more pervasive during the war than pro-Continental feeling.

Finally, even those who did join the army were often treated badly by the Continental Congress. They could and might have blamed their fellow countrymen who were withholding the supplies that would feed them and fueling the inflation that made their wages worthless—as Charles Royster has suggested—but more often than not their animosity was directed against the Continental government. When one Connecticut brigade mutinied as early as December 1778, for example, it was mainly because they were being paid in rapidly depreciating currency. The anger of Continental soldiers climaxed at the end of the war, when most were sent home without the promised pay and land certificates for which they had sacrificed themselves. Soldiers from Pennsylvania and the South marched on Philadelphia in June 1783, surrounded the State House where both Congress and the Pennsylvania assembly met, and demanded immediate compensation for their efforts. Their actions initiated a precipitous flight of the delegates to Princeton, New Jersey. Even hardened Continental veteran Joseph Plumb Martin, years after the war and certainly long after the creation of a nation, could write with bitterness about his treatment at the hands of the Continental Congress: "The country was rigorous in exacting my compliance to *my* engagements to a punctilio, but equally careless in performing her contracts with me, and why so? The reason was because she had all the power in her own hands and I had none." He also thought the "country had drained the last drop of service it could screw out of the poor soldiers," and it now "turned [them] adrift like old worn-out horses, and nothing said about land to pasture them upon."[31]

If it is difficult to identify a new Continental unity, let alone a new nationalism among the most active supporters of the Revolutionary cause, the task is made much harder when we take into account the presence and activities of large numbers of loyalists throughout the Revolutionary War. Unpersuaded by arguments for independence, individuals and groups of active loyalists could be found throughout the new states and only grew in number as the war raged around them. More colonists fought one another than they did the British. Some areas, like the Georgia backcountry, Carolina Piedmont, Long Island, and the Eastern Shore, were plagued by chronic and persistent internal violence and strife. But everywhere the British went, they were aided in some degree by local residents. Such support encouraged the British and prolonged the war.

The numbers of those who left the colonies give us some idea of how broad-based and crippling loyalist support was to the war effort. Scholars suggest that between 60,000 and 80,000 people fled the colonies during the conflict. Even if we accept the lower figure of 60,000 refugees, this number amounts to as much as 2.4 percent of the total colonial population, or the per capita equivalent of 7,440,000 fleeing American shores today.[32] And these were colonists who had the means and/or were desperate enough to leave. Historians estimate that between one-third and one-fifth of the colonial population actively supported the British during the War for Independence. Yet while colonial historians have long emphasized the attachment most colonists felt toward Britain, Revolutionary historians—especially those keen to explain nationhood—have a harder time comprehending the persistence of royalist sentiment beyond independence and incorporating loyalists into their narratives.

Yet active supporters of the Crown were merely the tip of the iceberg. Tens of thousands of colonists may have supported the British but kept their heads down and their mouths shut. Individuals facing a barrel of boiling tar and feathers at the hands of their hotheaded neighbors knew enough to stay quiet. Once the war began thousands more continued to steer a neutral course, either by tacking between support for the new state governments and the British or simply lying low. They ignored calls to turn out in the militia. They refused to pay taxes. They harbored deserters. They made the best terms they could with whatever side made demands of them. Some even fought to stay neutral. One man from Brookhaven, New York, who was charged with raising a loyalist volunteer group, told his patriot accusers that on the contrary, "all the Combinations & Inlistments were for the purpose of Neutrality & call'd them a Club of Sivility that intended to fight on nither side."[33]

The numbers of apparent neutrals only swelled during the conflict, as those disillusioned with the patriot cause joined pro-British sympathizers on the sidelines. Many lower-class colonists, for example, abandoned the cause when it became clear who would have to do the fighting. In Virginia thousands of patriot farmers refused to fight when they learned slave owners could exempt themselves from military service. Thousands more turned away in anger when new draft laws targeted the poor and vulnerable. Former patriot supporters were quick to turn their backs on the cause when they realized "the Rich wanted the Poor to fight for them, to defend there [*sic*] property, whilst they refused to fight for themselves."[34]

Estimates of the number of neutrals in the conflict generally run anywhere between 40 and 60 percent of the population. The percentage varied according to locality and the intensity and nature of preexisting conflicts; it also varied at different times during the run-up to independence and later in the war. Despite these numbers, historians have yet to unravel the extent, motivation, and full implications of the presence of this large and important group both during and after the Revolutionary War.[35] But it is clear that overt and tacit resistance to the war effort crippled mobilization throughout all the new states, prolonging the conflict and making it far more divisive, bloody, messy, and more complicated than it might have been—and certainly more so than many patriot leaders had initially envisioned. Moreover, at several critical moments patriots almost lost the war. Good fortune, the endurance of a small group of Continental soldiers, British ineptitude, and, most important, French help were the keys to the patriots winning (or not losing) the Revolutionary War.

Historians have only begun the process of piecing together the full story of a Revolution divided against itself.[36] Until we do so, it will be difficult to measure the full impact of that long war on the hundreds of thousands of ordinary Americans who left few records of their experiences, let alone their immediate memories of the conflict. Yet several lines of study are suggestive. As Sung Bok Kim has noted of war-torn Westchester County in New York, by the end of the conflict the inhabitants there were "almost desolate," "exhausted," "debilitated," "truly deplorable," and "almost incredible," according to contemporary observers. In a region previously noted for its prosperity, by the end of the war many were "now reduced to indiscriminate poverty." Even "good Whigs" were "determined" to do nothing for the cause.[37] We can only speculate as to how the Revolutionary memories of these new citizens shaped their conduct in the new republic, but the chances are that few felt themselves to be a proud part of a new nation.

At the same time, though, many others around the new states began to invoke their wartime service and sacrifices as a shield against the unrelenting and unprecedented tax burdens imposed on them during the 1780s. Petitioners from Pittsylvania County in Virginia, for example, complained about high taxes in the fall of 1787. They noted the huge amount already collected "from the people" to pay for the war. They had not objected to it at first, as they had been assured it would be used to pay the soldiers "who Shed their blood in the field of Battle for us." But now it was clear that speculators had bought up the soldiers' certificates, and the taxes were flowing into the hands of a "few Individuals in Luxery [*sic*]" who had "perhaps never shed one Drop of blood on our behalf." This was truly "distressing" to "we a free people . . . who fought for freedom and Liberty and gained the Day."[38]

These developments, in turn, did not escape the notice of many frustrated political leaders who were busy shaping their own recollections of the war and its aftermath. Whereas at the start of the conflict patriot leaders had time and again used words such as "glorious," "sacred," and "providential" to describe the cause, by the middle of the war most described it as "calamitous," "costly," and "ruinous." Many blamed their countrymen. As one patriot leader in South Carolina noted in 1779, "a spirit of money-making has eaten up our patriotism. Our morals are more depreciated than our currency." Another regretted in 1782 that the "public spirit of our people" seems to have "vanished." As Sung Bok Kim has noted, almost every American leader bemoaned the perceived decline in public virtue by the end of the war.[39]

Indeed, for many patriot leaders the Revolutionary War only confirmed and increased their worst fears. For all their earlier rhetoric of unity, many were distinctly uneasy about the prospect for solidarity from the start. In the absence of public virtue, only the presence of the British army and the threat it imposed kept the states together. After the war and in the midst of the postwar disunity, Jeremy Belknap questioned, "if an union could not be formed until we were driven to it by external oppression and tyranny, is it likely that such an union will hold when that pressure is removed?" Even the normally sanguine Thomas Jefferson believed the lack of a common enemy would soon render unity precarious.[40] The secretary to Congress, Charles Thomson, who had been in that post since 1774, also doubted that the union could survive without British military pressure to keep it tenuously together. Thomson's fears were provoked by the mutiny of the Continental troops in June 1783, when he was forced to flee Philadelphia, along with the rest of the Continental Congress. The event haunted him.[41]

Others shared Thomson's worries, and from the chaos of the war and postwar period there emerged a small group of committed nationalists. These men were generally those who had occupied important positions—but mainly outside their own states—during the Revolution and included men like James Madison, Alexander Hamilton, John Jay, James Duane, Robert Morris, and Gouverneur Morris. Significantly, one of the core groups constituting this nationalist cadre were Continental Army officers such as George Washington and Henry Knox, the very men who had been most frustrated by the divisions and conflicts that had plagued the war effort. Almost every general in the Continental Army supported moves to strengthen the powers of the federal government.[42]

Negotiating a now well-documented deceit, this small group of distinguished elites met in Philadelphia and, without any authorization, drafted a radically different plan of government to the Articles of Confederation. Careful planning put the document into effect after only nine states ratified the plan and after the new Constitution had "almost been defeated by popularly chosen conventions in nearly every large state." Even among the small states there was considerable opposition in New Hampshire and Rhode Island. After adding to this the number of people who did not vote, there was indeed only a minority who voted *for* the ratification of the Constitution.[43]

The Constitution, then, really was a "roof without walls," as John

Murrin put it in his essay on the dilemma of American national identity in 1787. It was not, after all, the logical culmination of the process of war and peace that had been set into motion by the declaration of independence. To be sure, the war did create an embryonic national identity among many elite patriots. Moreover, it offered important political lessons for nationalist-minded men who sought to strengthen the federal government in the face of weak or even nonexistent support. Finally, the institutions created to meet the exigencies of war—the Continental Congress, in particular—did provide an embryonic national government that made it much easier for some Americans to devise national reforms in 1787. But the war did not create a widespread popular political attachment to any national (or protonational) government or its leaders, nor did it create any kind of common identity among the vast majority of the citizens of the newly formed states. Instead, the Constitution that was hammered out and adopted was erected in the face of, and because of, popular and widespread forces and feelings that were opposed to it. This process, of course, also helped undermine many future moves toward a national identity.[44]

Given these precarious origins, it is no wonder that the Founding Fathers looked ahead, rather than to history, to rally support for the new nation. As the Constitutional Convention convened, for example, Benjamin Rush urged his countrymen to forget the war. The American Revolution was only just beginning, he said, and it had to start with a new government.[45] Most supporters of the Constitution saw it as a fresh start, one that gave Americans an opportunity to begin the world anew. And because history provided few soothing stories, most early efforts at crafting a national narrative focused on the importance of the civic texts of the Revolution and the one person who seemed most likely to unify rather than divide—George Washington. It was not Washington's Revolutionary War career that took center stage in these celebrations, however, but rather his earlier life and his Farewell Address. Political leaders of the founding generation would struggle mightily to instill loyalty among citizens of the new nation over its first decade or two, and the striving to do so documented by François Furstenberg and others must be seen in this light.[46] Only when memories of the Revolutionary War began to fade, beginning with a new war in 1812, did these new narratives begin to gain traction.[47] Many of the following chapters in this collection testify to this slow, halting, and often uncertain process.

Perhaps this should not be so surprising. As Ernst Renan long ago noted, "forgetting . . . is a crucial factor in the creation of a nation." Though he was referring to more recent events in the nineteenth century, Renan's arguments are equally apt for the American experiment. He argued that the political project of founding a nation often entails forgetting the originary violence. To create a homogenous community, dissidence and dissent have to be eliminated, and their violent eradication is often forgotten.[48] Forgetting, then, was a political project and it took time. Today, in a new era when the American Revolution is often held out to be exceptional in the apparently seamless transition from colonies to a new nation and invoked as a model for others, we would do well to remember.

NOTES

1. Barack H. Obama, "Inaugural Address," January 20, 2009, www.bartleby.com/124/pres68.html.
2. George W. Bush, "Second Inaugural Address," January 20, 2005, www.bartleby.com /124/pres67.html. Significantly, only a handful of the presidential inaugural addresses since George Washington failed to reference the Revolution in some way. Very few other historical events were invoked at all. Momentous epochs such as European settlement, western expansion, industrialization, the Civil War, the two World Wars, and immigration were rarely mentioned. See Louisa MacDonald Hall, "'The Heirs of That First Revolution': Remembering and Forgetting America's Founding Era in Presidential Inaugural Addresses, 1789–2005" (honors thesis, University of Sydney, 2008).
3. See, for example, the article and notes by Sam Wineburg and Chauncey Monte-Sano: "'Famous Americans': The Changing Pantheon of American Heroes," *Journal of American History* 94, no. 4 (March 2008): 1186–1202, wherein the authors had to *exclude* the Founding Fathers from their survey to understand what else students remembered. In an important sense, too, the outpouring of biographies of significant Founding Fathers, celebratory narratives of the Revolution by popular and academic writers, and the rise of movements such as the Tea Party both tap this apparent familiarity with the Revolution and encourage it.
4. "History and Culture," Valley Forge National Historic Park, last modified August 22, 2012, www.nps.gov/vafo/historyculture/index.htm.
5. George Brown Tindall and David Emory Shi, *America: A Narrative History*, brief, 4th ed. (New York: Norton, 1997), 152. In their conclusion to the section on the War for Independence, they note that "the Revolution generated a budding sense of common nationality. The Revolution taught many Americans to think 'continentally,' as Alexander Hamilton put it" (184).
6. Paul Boyer et al., *The Enduring Vision: A History of the American People*, 3rd ed. (Lexington, Mass.: Houghton Mifflin, 1996), 163, 164. Sometimes more special-

ized works have helped substantiate these claims. Harry M. Ward, for example, begins his book, *The War for Independence and the Transformation of American Society*, by stating forcefully that "the Revolutionary War established a nation and confirmed American identity" (London: University College Press, 1991), ix.

7. See, for example, Michael A. McDonnell, *The Politics of War: Race, Class, and Conflict in Revolutionary Virginia* (Chapel Hill: University of North Carolina Press, 2007); Allan Kulikoff, "Revolutionary Violence and the Origins of American Democracy," *Journal of the Historical Society* 2, no. 2 (Spring 2002): 229–60; and Kulikoff, "The War in the Countryside," in *Oxford Handbook of the American Revolution*, ed. Edward Gray and Jane Kamensky (New York: Oxford University Press, 2012). As Michael Kammen first noted, American historical literature lacks "a sense of the tragic" (Kammen, "The American Revolution as a *Crise de Conscience*," in *Society, Freedom, and Conscience: The American Revolution in Virginia, Massachusetts, and New York*, ed. Jack P. Greene, Richard L. Bushman, and Michael Kammen [New York: Norton, 1976], 188). Literature on the Revolution has often focused on the more positive outcomes of the movement for independence and the Revolutionary War. Both these events are often portrayed as a contest of ideas—loyalism versus patriotism—or as vehicles for the development of republican, democratic, and individualistic ideology or of social radicalism. Historians on the left and the right have generally ignored the destructive, the divisive, and the tragic effects of a contest in which might often meant right, and hundreds of thousands of people found themselves caught up in a conflict not of their making, fighting for their lives. On this see especially Sung Bok Kim, "The Limits of Politicization in the American Revolution: The Experience of Westchester County, New York," *Journal of American History* 88 (December 1993): 868.
8. David Waldstreicher, for example, placed the origins of American nationalism in the years of war. Yet he could only argue that celebrations of Independence Day and other "nationally" observed fetes were an effort to overcome immediate local prejudices, differences, and divisions by envisioning a national *future*. *In the Midst of Perpetual Fetes: The Making of American Nationalism, 1776–1820* (Chapel Hill: University of North Carolina Press, 1997), chap. 1. At least for the war years, Waldstreicher's otherwise fine work seems to be more about what elites hoped for than what ordinary Americans actually thought. For an insightful critique of Waldstreicher's work along these lines, see Andrew R. L. Cayton's review essay, "We Are All Nationalists, We Are All Localists," *Journal of the Early Republic* 18, no. 3 (Fall 1998): 521–28. Simon Newman viewed the years of resistance and war as a "struggle to create an independent nation," even as he struggled to explain the "resurgence of provincialism in the aftermath of the success in the war," which "weakened the move toward a national discourse of popular politics and political activity." Such a resurgence of provincialism, he suggests, was a "temporary" aberration from the "centralizing impulses that *culminated* in the Federal Constitution." *Parades and the Politics of the Street: Festive Culture in the Early American Republic* (Philadelphia: University of Pennsylvania Press, 1997), 12; emphasis added. Once beyond the similarities in streets protests and popular rites of resistance during the prewar years, Newman seems hard-pressed to find any evidence for a national popular political culture and evidence of precisely the opposite in the immediate postwar period (see especially 33–39).

There is, of course, little doubt that the war was *later* used to substantiate claims to nationhood and the origins of a national culture in the way Newman, Waldstreicher, and others suggest.

9. Colonial historians now generally agree that the colonies had more in common with Britain than they did with one another. For the clearest statement of this, see John Murrin, "Roof without Walls: The Dilemma of American National Identity," in *Beyond Confederation: Origins of the Constitution and American National Identity*, ed. Richard Beeman, Stephen Botein, and Edward C. Carter II (Chapel Hill: University of North Carolina Press, 1987). For an iteration of this disjuncture, see Jack P. Greene, "State and National Identities in the Era of the American Revolution," in *Nationalism in the New World*, ed. Don H. Doyle and Marco Antonio Pamplona (Athens: University of Georgia Press, 2006), 61–79.
10. This chapter, then, attempts to address the crucial question asked by John W. Shy: To what extent did the long military struggle we know as the war for American independence contribute to the creation of a new national identity? See "The Legacy of the Revolutionary War," in *A People Numerous and Armed: Reflections on the Military Struggle for American Independence*, ed. John W. Shy (Ann Arbor: University of Michigan Press, 1990), 263.
11. *Virginia Gazette* (Pinkney), May 25, 1775, in *Revolutionary Virginia: The Road to Independence*, ed. William J. van Schreeven et al., 7 vols. (Charlottesville: University Press of Virginia, 1973–83), 3:170; emphasis added.
12. Botetourt County Committee Proceedings, June 26, 1775, in van Schreeven et al., *Revolutionary Virginia*, 3:230.
13. *Virginia Gazette* (Dixon and Hunter), September 19, 1777. John Augustine Washington to R. H. Lee, June 20, 1778, in *Lee Family Papers, 1742–1795*, ed. Paul Hoffman, University of Virginia Library, Charlottesville, 1966, microfilm; McDonnell, *Politics of War*, 340–41.
14. Ronald Hoffman, "The 'Disaffected' in the Revolutionary South," in *The American Revolution: Explorations in the History of American Radicalism*, ed. Alfred F. Young (Dekalb: Northern Illinois University Press, 1976), 289; Diary of Robert Honyman, August 31, 1780, and September 8, 1780, Alderman Library, University of Virginia, microfilm, 426, 428. Of course, the dangers of leaving home in the slave societies of the South were exacerbated by the presence of potential rebels in their own homes and communities. See, for example, Northampton County Committee to Continental Congress, November 17, 1775, in "Virginia Legislative Petitions," *Virginia Magazine of History and Biography* 14 (1906): 252–54; Accomack County Committee to 4th Virginia Convention, November 30, 1775, in *Virginia Magazine of History and Biography* 14 (1906): 257–59. Many communities that found themselves in the middle of hostilities clearly cultivated a more survivalist—and localistic—instinct. See Kim, "Limits of Politicization," 883, 887.
15. Quoted in Gregory T. Knouff, "'An Arduous Service': The Pennsylvania Backcountry Soldiers' Revolution," *Pennsylvania History* 61 (January 1994): 50, 52, 53.
16. See James Kirby Martin and Mark Edward Lender, *A Respectable Army: The Military Origins of the Republic, 1763–1789* (Arlington Heights, Ill.: Davidson, 1982), 83–87.

17. Joel Watkins to Thomas Read, November 9, 1780, Hugh Blair Grigsby Papers, Virginia Historical Society, Richmond; Reverend James Madison to James Madison Jr., March 9, 1781, in *The Papers of James Madison*, ed. William T. Hutchinson and William M. E. Rachal, vol. 3 (Chicago: University of Chicago Press, 1962), 10, 11–12n.
18. Edmund Pendleton to James Madison, March 19, 1781, in Hutchinson and Rachal, *Papers of James Madison*, 3:26.
19. Indeed, as Jonathan Clark's study of Revolutionary Poughkeepsie, New York, reveals, citizens there "were as intent on saving their town as on saving their country. The destruction of their community, as they knew it, was not a price they would pay for victory." "The Problem of Allegiance in Revolutionary Poughkeepsie," in *Saints and Revolutionaries: Essays in Early American History*, ed. David D. Hall, John M. Murrin, and Thad W. Tate (New York: Norton, 1984), 285–317. The phrase "imagined community," of course, comes from Benedict Anderson's influential book, *Imagined Communities: Reflections on the Origin and Spread of Nationalism* (New York: Verso, 1991).
20. Quoted in Murrin, "Roof without Walls," in Beeman, Botein, and Carter, *Beyond Confederation*, 344.
21. Quoted in Boyer et al., *Enduring Vision*, 163.
22. Mark Tacyn, "Strength and Substance: The First Maryland Regiment and the Continental Army" (paper given at the Sixth Annual Conference of the Omohundro Institute of Early American History and Culture, Toronto, June 9–11, 2000).
23. John Banister to Theodorick Bland, June 19, 1778, in *The Bland Papers: Being a Selection from the Manuscripts of Colonel Theodorick Bland, Jr.*, ed. Charles Campbell, 2 vols. (Petersburg, Va.: Ruffin, 1840–43), 1:86–87; John Banister to Theodorick Bland, [1781?], in Campbell, *Bland Papers*, 2:67; David Jameson to James Madison, August 10, 15, 1781, in Hutchinson and Rachal, *Papers of James Madison*, 3:215–216, 227–28; "Address to Congress," [March 1781?], Rives Family Papers, Alderman Library, University of Virginia; Pendleton to Madison, March 26, 1781, in *The Letters and Papers of Edmund Pendleton, 1734–1803*, ed. David John Mays, 2 vols. (Charlottesville: University Press of Virginia, 1967), 1:346.
24. Pendleton to Madison, May 28, 1781, in Mays, *Letters and Papers*, 1:359; Lafayette quoted in John E. Selby, *The Revolution in Virginia, 1775–1783* (Williamsburg, Va.: Colonial Williamsburg Foundation, 1988), 297–98.
25. Garrett van Meter to Jefferson, April 11, 1781; April 14, 1781; and April 20, 1781, in *The Papers of Thomas Jefferson*, vol. 5, ed. Julian P. Boyd (Princeton: Princeton University Press, 1950), 409–10, 455, 513–14; Lafayette to Greene, June 3, 1781, in *Lafayette in the Age of the American Revolution: Selected Letters and Papers, 1776–1790*, ed. Stanley J. Idzerda, 5 vols. (Ithaca, N.Y.: Cornell University Press, 1977), 5:162–65.
26. Quoted in McDonnell, *Politics of War*, 460.
27. Richard Buel Jr., *Dear Liberty: Connecticut's Mobilization for the Revolutionary War* (Middletown, Conn.: Wesleyan University Press, 1980), 253–54.
28. Ibid., 231–32; Robert A. Gross, *The Minutemen and Their World* (New York: Hill & Wang, 1976), 150.
29. Buel, *Dear Liberty*, 203, 256–57.

30. Edmund Pendleton to James Madison, December 4, 1780, and December 11, 1780, in Mays, *Letters and Papers*, 1:325, 326. Citizens of Franklin County, North Carolina, directed their anger at Continental officers too, when they complained about the "careless and barbarous usage" to "horses and carriages impressed in the service." They were tired, they said, of "ill treatment" from imperious officers. Ronald Hoffman and Michael A. McDonnell, "The Ideology of Disaffection in the American Revolution" (paper presented to the Brunel/Cambridge Conference on Early American History, Middlesex University, London, June 1999), 18, 19.
31. Charles Royster, *A Revolutionary People at War: The Continental Army and American Character, 1775–1783* (Chapel Hill: University of North Carolina Press, 1979), chap. 5; Martin and Lender, *Respectable Army*, 195, Plumb Martin quoted on 196–97.
32. For a summary of loyalist refugees, see Maya Jasanoff, *Liberty's Exiles: American Loyalists in the Revolutionary World* (New York: Knopf, 2011). The effect of such an exodus on politics and social relations in the new republic will likely remain unmeasurable, but numbers such as these alone give the lie to anodyne accounts of the Revolution that stress consensus over conflict.
33. Quoted in Kammen, "The American Revolution as a *Crise de Conscience*," 172.
34. Proceedings of a General Court Martial, June 18–19, 1781, quoted in McDonnell, *Politics of War*, 449–50.
35. Sung Bok Kim estimates that even after intense efforts to mobilize people in Cortlandt Manor, no more than about 20 percent of the adult male population of the manor ever committed themselves to one side *or* the other, even by the middle of 1776. "Limits of Politicization," 875. That left up to 80 percent of the population in the middle, trying to steer a neutral course. Though that figure is on the high side of estimates of the number of neutrals among the general population, it is not exceptional; in nearby Queens County, more than 60 percent of the population preferred neutrality, while only 12 percent became active patriots, and 27 percent supported the Crown. Joseph S. Tiedemann, "A Revolution Foiled: Queens County, New York, 1775–1776," *Journal of American History* 75, no. 2 (September 1988), 419.
36. For the political, social, and cultural implications of this long, violent, and divided Revolutionary War and its effects on nation building in the early republic, see especially Kulikoff, "Revolutionary Violence"; Kulikoff, "War in the Countryside"; McDonnell, *Politics of War*, epilogue; and Gary B. Nash, *The Unknown American Revolution: The Unruly Birth of Democracy and the Struggle to Create America* (New York: Penguin Books, 2005).
37. Kim, "Limits of Politicization," 887.
38. Pittsylvania County Petition, November 5, 1787, Virginia Legislative Petitions, Library of Virginia, Richmond. That these wartime divisions and conflicts continued in the postwar period is well established. For two classic overviews, see Merrill Jensen, *The New Nation: A History of the United States during the Confederation, 1781–1789* (New York: Knopf, 1950); and Richard B. Morris, *The Forging of the Union, 1781–1789* (New York: Harper & Row, 1987). Cf. Terry Bouton, "A Road Closed: Rural Insurgency in Post-independence Pennsylvania," *Journal of American History* 87, no. 3 (December 2000): 855–87; Bouton, *Taming*

Democracy: "The People," the Founders, and the Troubled Ending of the American Revolution (New York: Oxford University Press, 2009); McDonnell, *Politics of War*, epilogue; and Woody Holton, *Unruly Americans and the Origins of the Constitution* (New York: Hill & Wang, 2008).

39. Kim, "Limits of Politicization," 888–89. Cf. McDonnell, *Politics of War*, 345–54, for similar midwar sentiments. "Abuses" were "enormous and almost without number," William Gordon wrote to John Adams in 1777, and "instead of having our affairs conducted with economy, the Continent hath been plundered, and business carried on at the most expensive rate, that Jack, Tom and Harry might make a fortune & live like gentlemen." Lester H. Cohen, "Creating a Usable Future: The Revolutionary Historians and the National Past," in *The American Revolution: Its Character and Limits*, ed. Jack P. Greene (New York: New York University Press, 1987), 314. Gordon's worries were echoed by literate commentators and politicians alike, from David Ramsay and Mercy Otis Warren, to George Washington and Thomas Jefferson. For the worries of other early historians, see Cohen, "Creating a Usable Future," 314–17.

40. Belknap quoted in Cohen, "Creating a Usable Future," 328. Jefferson feared that from the conclusion of the war onward, men were likely to forget the struggle for liberty and equality and "forget themselves but in the sole faculty of making money." Quoted in Mark Kann, *A Republic of Men: The American Founders, Gendered Language, and Patriarchal Politics* (New York: New York University Press, 1998), 41–42.

41. Murrin, "Roof without Walls," 345. Murrin's metaphor of the Constitution as a "roof without walls" is particularly apt. His insightful essay is one of the few that deals with the lack of a widespread national identity at the time of the founding. For another essay that tries to distinguish elite versus popular national sentiment, see Elise Marienstras, "Nationality and Citizenship," in *Companion to the American Revolution*, ed. J. R. Pole and Jack P. Greene (Oxford: Blackwell, 2000), 682.

42. This story has been well told, but for one now-classic account, see Stanley Elkins and Eric McKittrick, *The Founding Fathers: Young Men of the Revolution* (Washington, D.C.: American Historical Association, 1961). Bouton, in "Road Closed," also redraws attention to the economic motivations of more nationalist-minded elites in that state.

43. Murrin, "Roof without Walls," 345. The disingenuousness of the Founding Fathers is well documented, and many historians now recognize that the passage of the Constitution was achieved only through a number of clever subterfuges. For one convincing argument that those in favor of the Constitution were in the minority, see Lee Soltow, *Distribution of Wealth and Income in the United States in 1798* (Pittsburgh: University of Pittsburgh Press, 1989), esp. chap. 10.

44. As Joyce Appleby, Lynn Hunt, and Margaret Jacob have argued, "the Constitution provided new institutions for national governance, but its very success in removing power from local majorities worked against the forming of a popular patriotic culture." *Telling the Truth about History* (New York: Norton, 1994), 95–96. Saul Cornell, in *The Other Founders: Anti-Federalism and the Dissenting Tradition in America, 1788–1828* (Chapel Hill: University of North Carolina Press, 1999), shows that there were multiple layers of anti-Federalist thought beyond

that espoused by its leading elite and articulate proponents and that both anti-Federalism and its legacy were much stronger than previously thought.

45. Benjamin Rush, "Address to the People of the United States," January 1787, in *Friends of the Constitution: Writings of the "Other" Federalists, 1787–1788*, ed. Colleen A. Sheehan and Gary L. McDowell (Indianapolis: Liberty Fund, 1998), prologue. Cf. Cohen, "Creating a Usable Future."
46. François Furstenberg, *In the Name of the Father: Washington's Legacy, Slavery, and the Making of a Nation* (New York: Penguin, 2007).
47. David Ramsey, for example, one of the first historians of the Revolution, was one of the earliest to re-remember the war as the key to forging national unity: "A sense of common danger," he wrote, "extinguished selfish passions [and] local attachments were sacrificed on the altar of patriotism." Quoted in Kann, *Republic of Men*, 41. But Ramsey's nationalism has been placed into context by studies that emphasize the later need and desire of politicians and ordinary citizens to elevate the War for Independence in the individual and collective memory as a nation-building war. The tendency was particularly pronounced during what some have called the second war for American independence, the War of 1812. See, for example, Charles Royster, "Founding a Nation in Blood: Military Conflict and American Nationality," in *Arms and Independence: The Military Character of the American Revolution*, ed. Ronald Hoffman and Peter J. Albert (Charlottesville: University Press of Virginia, 1984), 25–49; and John Resch, *Suffering Soldiers: Revolutionary War Veterans, Moral Sentiment, and Political Culture in the Early Republic* (Amherst: University of Massachusetts Press, 1999).
48. Ernst Renan, *Qu'est-ce qu'une nation? Conférence faite en Sorbonne, le 22 mars 1882*, 2nd ed. (Paris: Calman-Lévy, 1882), 7–8.

"A Natural & Unalienable Right"

New England Revolutionary Petitions and African American Identity

Daniel R. Mandell

On January 13, 1777, Prince Hall and seven other black men submitted a petition to the Massachusetts General Court, which consisted of the Massachusetts Revolutionary Council and the House of Representatives. The men sought freedom for "a great number of Negroes who are detained in a state of slavery in the Bowels of a free & Christian Country" and insisted on "a natural & unalienable right" to freedom, "which they have never forfeited by any compact or agreement."[1] Such a petition was not unique—it was the fifth plea to end slavery sent to Massachusetts authorities since 1772—but what made it distinctive was the way it called on the Revolutionary principles of liberty and rights set forth less than a year before in the Declaration of Independence. Some subsequent petitions elsewhere in the region demanded emancipation in similar terms; one even claimed a right to "perfect equality with other men."[2]

Historians typically use these appeals to highlight the obvious contradictions between racial slavery and the American Revolution, but they also constitute some of the earliest written expressions of African American identity.[3] Examining them can thus allow consideration of the genesis and nature of this identity in Revolutionary-era America. Literary scholars have searched for this identity in expressive poetry, sermons, and fiction, with some following Paul Gilroy in viewing this writing as evidence of a "black Atlantic" that challenged contemporary conceptions of nation, reason, and individual freedom (a "counter-culture of modernity"), and others agreeing with Philip Gould that early black writing was linked in complex ways to Enlightenment liberalism and sentimentalism.[4] In fact, these petitions reveal a people who identified as both Africans *and* Americans; a people who held strong transatlantic connections *and* at the outset of the war embraced Enlightenment ideals, sentimentalism, and Protestant notions of virtue. They were the first wave in a series of antislavery appeals launched on both sides of the Atlantic, paralleled by other protests such as Lemuel Haynes's unpublished "Liberty Further Extended" (ca. 1776), written in petition form though never submitted to an official body, and Olaudah Equiano's renowned *Interesting Narrative* (1789), which contained petitions to Parliament and Queen Charlotte.[5]

Petitions of this kind played a critical role in ending slavery above the Mason-Dixon Line by bringing the system under governmental scrutiny. They also overlapped with similar efforts by blacks to gain access to civic benefits such as pensions and past wages.[6] But nearly as important was the role these Revolutionary efforts played in forming a cosmopolitan African American identity. The signatories claimed to represent the pleas of Africans stolen from their Edenic homeland—pleas based on a memory, developed in America and England, of Africa as an unspoiled natural paradise—and in some cases asked the legislature to pay for their return.[7] But the petitioners also grounded claims for freedom on the transatlantic ideals and concerns that motivated their Anglo-American neighbors: Enlightenment concepts of natural rights; the developing culture of sentimentalism; and the older, more deeply rooted Protestant language of Christian virtue and biblical commandments, including Puritan patriarchal norms and strictures against "man stealing." As a result, among blacks in New England—and perhaps more generally throughout the North—the ideals of the Revolution emerged alongside and even intertwined with elements of an invented African identity.

This nascent African American identity gained strength during the war but even at the end of the century remained fragile. Although the cosmopolitan aspect of that identity seems a noticeable exception to the idea that localism was a systemic problem during the Revolution—indeed, those aspects could be seen as a transcendent challenge to the petty prejudices and local assumptions that supported slavery—for a half century or longer it was limited to the North, where slavery was challenged during the war and phased out afterward. African American institutions founded after the war were small, local, and limited to larger cities where most blacks moved when freed, although prominent black leaders such as Prince Hall and Philadelphia AME preacher Richard Allen worked to create wider networks. During the first half of the nineteenth century that identity and those networks would broaden and become more national—though not without tensions and conflicts—as southern slaves escaped to northern cities and brought with them different memories and customs.

The number of Africans and their descendants in southern New England rose from about one thousand in 1700 to roughly eleven thousand by 1750. Their social, economic, and legal circumstances played a significant role in shaping their Revolutionary efforts and memories. Most lived in port towns and a sizable minority were free. Blacks, like indentured whites, were subject to special laws designed to control potentially dangerous adult dependents. Like white servants and apprentices, blacks lived as dependents in the homes of their masters as part of an extended household, and newcomers were expected to adapt quickly to the dominant culture and community by, for example, learning to read so that they could understand the Bible. Slaves worked alongside free and indentured laborers and often caroused with them in pubs after work. In the 1740s some took part in Boston's violent resistance to efforts by the British Navy to impress sailors.[8]

Although servitude and racism were facts of life in eighteenth-century New England, the region's culture also provided African slaves with unique legal, social, and cultural opportunities. Those in Massachusetts had recognized civil rights, including trial by jury, the right to make contracts, and the right to sue if abused.[9] Throughout the region enslaved and free African Americans gathered in annual "Negro elections" to celebrate—at their masters' expense—and elect a "king" as representative to Anglo-American leaders.[10] The Puritan tradition also nurtured a nascent opposition to the slave trade, rooted in the biblical view that "man stealing" was illegal. In 1700 Massachusetts chief justice Samuel Sewall published *The Selling of Joseph: A Memorial*, which began, "It is most certain that all Men, as they are the Sons of *Adam*, are Coheirs; and have equal Right unto Liberty."[11] At midcentury, as the imperial crisis spawned calls for liberties, such misgivings about slavery became clearer. In 1764 Boston attorney James Otis, in his famed pamphlet *The Rights of British Colonies*, wrote, "The Colonists are by the law of nature free born, as indeed all men are, white or black. . . . Does it follow that 'tis right to enslave a man because he is black?"[12] A few years later some slaves, with the support of sympathetic whites, filed a series of lawsuits challenging their status, and in 1767 the Massachusetts legislature debated a bill to end slavery in the province. Three decades later John Adams remarked that he "never knew a Jury, by a Verdict to determine a Negro to be a slave—They always found them free."[13]

The eruption of petitions for *collective* freedom, along with the construction of an African American people, was clearly linked in time and space to the protests of Massachusetts colonists.[14] On January 6, 1773, as Boston radicals organized committees of correspondence to coordinate opposition to Parliament's measures, "Felix" submitted a plea on behalf of "many slaves" to the General Court, which wielded judicial as well as legislative powers.[15] He began with a transatlantic appeal to Christianity and the Somerset decision in England, invoking God, who "hath lately put it into the Hearts of Multitudes on both Sides of the Water, to bear our Burthens, some of whom are Men of great Note and Influence; who have pleaded our Cause."[16] Felix also grounded his plea for relief—but *not* freedom explicitly—in Anglo-America's patriarchal culture, observing that male slaves were deprived of everything considered proper for men, including control over their wives and children, as well as the right to own property. In submitting this petition, Felix was exercising a common law right of "every individual"; he was not claiming or seeking full citizenship.[17]

Three and a half months later came a very different petition from four men, calling explicitly for freedom. Addressed to individual delegates in the House of Representatives, it was printed so that it could be distributed widely—evidence of the support the appeal enjoyed from white men in Boston with money and influence. The petition began by noting with considerable irony that the House's efforts "to free themselves from slavery"—that is, the colony's opposition to the Sugar Act, Stamp Act, and Townshend Duties—"gave us, who are in that deplorable state, a high degree of satisfaction." It then continued, "We expect great things from men who have made such a noble stand against the designs of their *fellow-men* to enslave them." The petitioners regarded freedom as their "natural right" and offered to submit themselves to whatever laws and regulations were imposed until they could earn enough money to sail to the coast of Africa—a goal not mentioned in the petition of January 1773.[18]

Approximately one year later, on May 25 and again in June 1774, two more petitions were produced, submitted to British governor general Thomas Gage and the government that had just been imposed on Massachusetts as part of the Coercive (Intolerable) Acts. The first of these petitions alluded to the Somerset decision, asserting that "the laws of the Land . . . doth not justify but condemns Slavery" and that those held in bondage had a "natural right" to freedom. But the overwhelming emphasis was on how slavery destroyed the natural order, including proper masculine authority, and the petitioners questioned, "How can a husband leave master and work and Cleave to his wife[,] how can the wife submit themselves to their Husbands [*sic*] in all things?" The petitioners concluded with requests to be "liberated and made free men" and to be given land for farms. The second petition also pointed to the Somerset decision and noted that no laws or contracts had made blacks slaves, but it put more emphasis on religion and even hinted at a connection between the forced servitude of African Americans and that of the Israelites in Egypt. It asked for recognition of the "Natural rights or freedoms" of slaves and for their children to be freed at age twenty-one but made no request for land and made no mention of Africa.These petitions may have been responsible for generating the rumor in Boston that "a conspiracy of the negroes" had offered Gage their service if he freed and armed them, as reported by Abigail Adams to her husband John on September 22.[19]

While African Americans initially sought freedom in any form, as the conflict escalated into war they demonstrated in various ways that they were part of the New England community and that they were as deserving of liberty as their neighbors. On February 10, 1774, the radical Whig newspaper the *Massachusetts Spy* published, alongside various condemnations of the Tea Act, a letter from "An African" condemning slavery as "contrary to the Laws of God, and the Laws of Great-Britain" and asking the (mostly Anglo-American) readers, "Are not your hearts also hard, when you hold them in slavery who are intitled [*sic*] to liberty, by the law of nature, equal as yourselves?"[20] In late March 1775 some in Bristol and

Worcester Counties asked the Revolutionary committees of correspondence to help them gain freedom. On April 19 came the outbreak of war at Lexington and Concord; in both places free and enslaved African Americans fought as members of town militias. They were also among the provincial forces at Charlestown that besieged Boston and tried to hold the line on June 17 at the Battle of Bunker Hill. And after George Washington took command of those forces in the name of the Continental Congress, the militia officers (along with British efforts to enlist blacks) compelled the slaveholding Virginian to allow blacks to join up. Most African American soldiers served in integrated units—an experience not to be repeated until the Korean War—and New England companies contained very high percentages of blacks.[21]

Six months after Congress declared independence, the Prince Hall petition, submitted January 13, 1777, appealed to the Massachusetts General Court on behalf of "a great number of Negroes" asking for freedom.[22] After issuing the Enlightenment clarion call that blacks had "a natural & unalienable right" to freedom, the petition appealed to moral sensibility, believed by British and American intellectuals to be tied to higher reasoning. It charged that the "cruel hand" of the slave traders who had "unjustly dragged" blacks "from the embraces of their tender Parents" violated the "Laws of Nature & of Nation" and "all the tender feelings of humanity." The petitioners also explicitly connected those "tender feelings" to an idyllic African past, noting how they had been stolen from a "populous, pleasant and plentiful Country"—a description that went against the usual depiction of the African continent as dark and savage. They also linked their demand for black emancipation to the Revolution's already powerful ideals, praising New Englanders for resisting "the unjust endeavors of others to reduce them to a State of Bondage & Subjection," and voicing their bewilderment at how, "in imitation of the laudable example" of colonial protests, they had without avail submitted "petition after petition" to the legislature. In addition, they expressed "their astonishment" that their fellow Americans had not yet conceded that the principles on which the Revolution was grounded pleaded "stronger than a thousand arguments" in support of their freedom from slavery.

The petition called on the state to pass a gradual emancipation measure, under which the children of those still enslaved would serve until they reached the age of twenty-one, and did not suggest relocating to

Africa. The legislature responded, drafting a bill that would have not only outlawed slavery as "unjustifiable" but also given freedmen full civil and political "rights, privileges and immunities."[23] In the end the measure did not pass. Nevertheless, the 1777 petition and the earlier efforts may have had some influence on the wording of the Massachusetts Constitution and the outcome of two pivotal legal cases that were critical in ending slavery in the state. Several towns rejected the first proposed state constitution partly because it contained no explicit condemnation of slavery, and although the final version, accepted in 1780, also lacked a ban on slavery, its first article did declare that "all men are born free and equal." One year later Elizabeth Freeman successfully cited this article in her lawsuit for freedom, and that same year Chief Justice William Cushing told the jury judging Quock Walker's suit for freedom that the first article had banned slavery in the state.[24]

During the war African Americans in Connecticut and New Hampshire submitted petitions that similarly drew on the transatlantic Enlightenment and on sentimental ideals and that connected emancipation to the Revolution's goals. In May 1779 several Connecticut men approached the state legislature, asking for freedom. They bemoaned how they had been "unjustly torn, torn from the Bosom of their dear Parents, and Friends," saluted the state's leaders "nobly contenting, in the Cause of Liberty," and insisted that "Reason & Revelation" showed that they were created equal with their masters and had the right "by the Laws of Nature and by the whole Tenor of the Christian Religion . . . to be Free."[25] Five months later twenty New Hampshire "natives of Africa" told state officials that "the God of Nature gave them life and freedom, upon terms of the most perfect equality with other men; that freedom is an inherit right of the human species, not to be surrendered, but by consent." In even more strident language, the petitioners noted that neither Christianity, nor "reason and justice," nor the "volumes of Nature" justified those "who claim us as their property." The particularly radical language of this petition reflected the experiences of the Revolution, including the increased confidence of veterans: one of its signatories was Prince Whipple, who served in the Continental Army and helped row Washington across the Delaware River.[26]

The petitions demonstrate that enslaved and free people in different parts of New England claimed an African identity during the American Revolution. The initial January 1773 appeal did not mention Africa, and while petitioners of the next one, issued in April, made no explicit claim to African origins, they did conclude with the proposal that after gaining freedom they would pool their savings and "transport ourselves to some part of the coast of *Africa,* where we propose a settlement." In the course of the following year something happened to make that African connection more powerful, meaningful, and, perhaps, useful, because all the subsequent petitioners would reflect, as the May 1774 petition did, on how they had been stolen from their friends and "the bosoms of our tender Parents" and forced to leave a "Populous Pleasant and plentiful country" to "be made slaves for Life in a Christian land." Historians of northern blacks generally identify this consciousness as appearing at the turn of the century, with "African" churches and societies and the efforts to go to Africa. But these petitions clearly show that identity emerging earlier, during the Revolutionary crisis. While we can retrieve only scant information about those who signed these New England petitions, we do know that although many blacks were brought directly from Africa, a large percentage was born in the Americas or perhaps even in Europe. As one might expect from people who came from different cultures and continents, the petitions contained language that was quite cosmopolitan, referring to the important Somerset decision in England, transatlantic Enlightenment concepts of natural rights, and their origins in Africa and their terror during the slave trade.[27]

Somehow newcomers and creoles together created this African American identity, even though the former were more deeply connected to particular villages or clans and the latter had no personal memory of the African continent. These circumstances show how the very idea of being *African,* like other modern ethnic identities, was not indigenous to that continent but rather crafted by individuals originally from different continents, kingdoms, or villages. These individuals, raised in America and in England, often wrote for motivations as political as these petitions. James Sidbury points to Phillis Wheatley in America and Sancho in England as the first self-identified "Africans." In the early 1770s both Wheatley and Sancho published descriptions of their continental homeland in Edenic terms and their people as wounded outsiders. Similarly, Sidbury identifies the post-Revolutionary autobiographies by Afro-Englishmen Quobna Ottobah Cugoano (1787) and Olaudah Equiano (1789) as the clearest sources of an African identity.[28]

It might seem contradictory that the American Revolution became the stage for the emergence of an African "memory" among this transatlantic people. But the rich intellectual and cultural stew of the Revolutionary crisis—radical Whiggism, Enlightenment thought, common law, suspicion of power and corruption—developed in similar ways among Anglo-Americans. In particular, New Englanders drew contemporary lessons in politics from memories of Puritan resistance to arbitrary authority, from King Charles I to Sir Edmund Andros. Just as these provincials reached back to an often-imagined past to justify a radical break with the present, so too did black petitioners. Ironically, the American Revolution thereby helped to create contradictory memories: not just of freedom-loving colonists uniting to throw off unjust authority but of Africans joining together to overcome enslavement.[29]

The timing and shared language highlight the critical role played by Wheatley. Born in West Africa (possibly the Senegambian region), she was enslaved as a child, taken to different American markets, sold in Boston to a family in which she was taught to read and write—something that was far more common in New England than in the South. She began writing poetry, gaining the approval of her mistress and a circle of elites in the town. In September 1773 her *Poems on Various Subjects, Religious and Moral* was published in England. A short while later, copies of it were sold in Boston, and the volume was celebrated on both sides of the Atlantic. One of her poems began by celebrating the liberty for New England that came with the repeal of the Townshend Duties and then informed her readers that her "love of Freedom" came because:

> I, young in life, by seeming cruel fate
> Was snatch'd from *Afric's* fancy'd happy seat:
> What pangs excruciating must molest,
> What sorrows labor in my parents' breast?[30]

Wheatley's sentimental reference to Africa may have drawn inspiration or authority from Anthony Benezet's *Some Historical Account of Guinea* (1771), one of the first antislavery works to depict Africa as Eden.[31] While the sources of Wheatley's own inspiration are open to debate, what is known for certain is that her work was very influential among African Americans in New England. Jupiter Hammond, a slave in Hartford, for instance, wrote a poem in 1778 celebrating her life and talent.[32] Wheatley's personally reflective imagery is therefore a logical origin for the language used in subsequent petitions, which describe Africa as a "Pleasant and plentiful country" and condemn how the slave trade had ripped them from friends and families—although their *immediate* use of this sympathetic depiction of Africa shows that this "invented" memory was already important for free and enslaved blacks in the region. African Americans would have also been encouraged to add these ideas to their petitions for freedom because so many prominent Anglo-American intellectuals and elites applauded Wheatley's poetry.[33]

Like the work of Wheatley, the petitions reflected ideas and assumptions that had developed in the Atlantic world during the eighteenth century, including those concerning the superiority of Christian virtues (when practiced), Enlightenment notions of inherent human rights, and essentialist characteristics of a people—social, moral, intellectual—that approached racialist concepts. Their descriptions of bereft families and of "the tender feelings of humanity" also appealed to an emerging culture of sentimentalism: the idea that virtuous and benevolent *feelings* formed critical social and political bonds uniting civilized people, particularly those in a republic.

As the Revolution developed, the petitioners grew in confidence and expressed ideas that went far beyond those articulated by Wheatley. In January 1773 Felix bowed to prejudice by noting that "some of the Negroes are vicious," although he tempered this observation by adding that more were "discreet, sober." Subsequent petitioners dropped such a contrite tone and instead laid claim to their natural right to freedom, with the last one in 1779 insisting on their "perfect equality with other men." They connected emancipation with the Revolution's ideologies and passionate politics—the Prince Hall petition of January 1777 is a milestone—creating muscular philosophical and historical arguments that enjoyed far more immediate resonance than did appeals to Christian charity. In addition, the prominent involvement of black men in the fight first to protect New England towns from British regulars and then to win American independence brought their interests and concerns into close step with those of their white neighbors.

After the Revolution this intertwining of African and American identities with threads of Revolutionary ideals was brittle and sometimes contested. By 1782 Prince Hall was the head of an all-black Masonic lodge in Boston. The lodge had no charter, but Hall called it "African Lodge No. 1." In late November 1786 he offered the services of seven hundred men to the

Massachusetts governor to help put down Shays's Rebellion, partly as a mark of appreciation for the way "we have been protected for many years" by the state constitution.[34] Angered by the governor's rebuff, two months later Hall submitted a very different petition to the legislature, signed by about sixty-five "African blacks"—representing about 35 percent of black men in the city—asking for help to "return to Africa" in order to leave their "very disagreeable and disadvantageous circumstances" for "our native country, which warm climate is much more natural and agreeable to us; and for which the God of nature has formed us; and where we shall live among our equals."[35] In 1792 Hall delivered an address to the African Lodge that celebrated great figures from that continent's past, including the Queen of Sheba, who, he said, brought Masonry's deepest secrets directly from Solomon.[36]

Such ambivalence and tension were not unique: ideological, geographic, and class conflicts existed in the larger sphere of culture and politics, as illustrated by the Shays, Fries, and Whiskey Rebellions and by the nasty quarrels between Jeffersonians and Federalists. During the early republic, blacks organized "African" self-help societies and churches and in the face of intensifying hostility some made efforts to leave for Africa, but they also embraced the emerging American values of education and enterprise, joined in the larger public sphere despite increasingly violent racism, and cherished, as noted in 1808 by an anonymous member of the Boston African Society, the "liberty to enjoy [their] own opinions in matters civil and religious." After 1810 "Negro elections" gave way to parades to celebrate the abolition of the slave trade and on July 5 American independence, ending in banquets and orations that celebrated local emancipation, republican virtues, and the future worldwide abolition of slavery. Organizations became "Colored American" instead of "African," and in 1837 Hosea Easton told readers that "the colored people who are born in this country, are Americans in every sense of the word—Americans by birth, genius, Habits, language, &c." Yet Colored Americans still valued their African heritage: in July 1831 a correspondent in the *Liberator* suggested "Afric-American" or "Africamerican" as their most appropriate appellation, and in the 1850s black leaders such as Martin Delany and Henry Highland Garnet again called for emigration to West Africa.[37]

Regardless of whether blacks identified as "African" or "Colored" Americans, for them the Revolution retained a strong connection to ideals of freedom and the power of petition. In October 1787 Hall brought another petition to the state legislature, this time decrying the refusal of Boston schools to enroll black children. The state did nothing, but just four months later, after three Boston blacks were kidnapped and taken to the West Indies to be sold into slavery, Hall again gathered black Masons to sign a petition to the legislature asking for help to get the three back. This time he received a very different reaction: a law was passed that penalized such kidnapping and offered help to victims' families, and the governor worked successfully to get the three returned home. These ideals and methods were not limited to New England: at the end of 1799 seventy leading black Philadelphians petitioned Congress for gradual emancipation and the recognition of their "Liberties and unalienable Rights," particularly against fugitive slave laws.[38]

Even as the concerns of northern blacks shifted to fighting slavery in the South and prejudice in the North, black intellectuals occasionally reached back to the memory and ideals of the Revolution. In Rutland, Vermont, on July 4, 1801, black Congregationalist minister Lemuel Haynes preached (and later published) a sermon that emphasized how liberty and rights were irretrievably connected to independence and the Constitution. In 1829, at the end of his *Appeal,* David Walker threw the Declaration of Independence in his readers' faces, pointing to the clause that states, "when a long train of abuses and usurpation, pursuing invariably the same object, evinces a design to reduce them under absolute despotism, it is their *right,* it is their *duty,* to throw off such government." In 1851, after Americans generally began celebrating the memory of the Revolution, a committee of leading Boston African Americans staked their connection to that increasingly sacred event, petitioning (in the end, unsuccessfully) the Massachusetts legislature to erect a statue to Crispus Attucks as its first martyr. Four years later the head of that committee, William Cooper Nell, published the first African American historical study: *Colored Patriots of the American Revolution.*[39]

New England blacks between 1773 and 1779 rested their case for freedom on an idealized African past, Atlantic cosmopolitanism, Anglo-American sentimentalism, and Enlightenment ideology. These petitions formed, or at least represented, what quickly became the dualistic nature of African American identity, drawing on both their quasi-racial origins and their participation in the American Revolution. Depending on the immediate needs and circumstances, African Americans would draw on one, the other, or both. The language, pleas, and targets of the petitions also pointed to the emotional and political connections that free blacks formed with Anglo-American elites, who had the power to end slavery and, after freedom was achieved, to offer some protection from popular prejudice. These documents not only indicate that an African American identity emerged during the Revolution, they also highlight the essential links between their embrace of the Revolution and rapid adoption of an African identity. African American petitioners used the upheaval, rich language, and political and intellectual opportunities of the Revolution to develop, claim, and promote an idealized vision of their past, and to join that memory to Enlightenment concepts of natural rights and human equality. In this fashion, Revolutionary rhetoric and memories—African and American—became vital aspects of black identity.

NOTES

Many thanks to John Saillant and the editors of this volume for their careful reading and substantive suggestions to help me improve this work.

1. "From a Great Number of Negroes" to "the Honorable Council and House of Representatives for the State of Massachusetts," petition, January 13, 1777, SC1/series 45X, Massachusetts Archives Collection, Boston, 212:130–31.
2. Nero Brewster "and others," Portsmouth, New Hampshire, to New Hampshire Assembly, November 12, 1779, *New Hampshire Gazette,* July 15, 1780, quoted in Sidney Kaplan and Emma Nogrady Kaplan, *The Black Presence in the Era of the American Revolution,* rev. ed. (Amherst: University of Massachusetts Press, 1989), 30.
3. James Oliver Horton and Lois E. Horton, *In Hope of Liberty: Culture, Community, and Protest among Northern Free Blacks, 1700–1860* (New York: Oxford University Press, 1997) 55–56; Gary Nash, *Race and Revolution* (Madison, Wis.: Madison House, 1990), 174–75; Woody Holton, ed., *Black Americans in the Revolutionary Era: A Brief History with Documents* (Boston: Bedford/St. Martin's, 2009), 16, 42–43; Herbert Apthetker, ed., *Documentary History of the Negro People in the United States,* vol. 1 (New York: International, 1951), 5–12. Thomas J. Davis noted how the April 1773 petitioners "expressed a further sense of self identity by referring to themselves as *Africans,* and by coupling emancipation with emigration." But otherwise Davis discusses the petitions in terms of their Revolutionary rhetoric and does not analyze them as expressions of African American values and identity. "Emancipation Rhetoric, Natural Rights, and Revolutionary New England: A Note on Four Black Petitions in Massachusetts, 1773–1777," *New England Quarterly* 62, no. 2 (June 1989): 257, 248–63. For an overview of this literature, see Richard S. Newman and Roy E. Finkenbine, "Black Founders in the New Republic: Introduction," *William and Mary Quarterly* 64, no. 1 (January 2007): 83–94.

4. Paul Gilroy, *The Black Atlantic: Modernity and Double Consciousness* (Cambridge: Harvard University Press, 1993); Joanna Brooks, *American Lazarus: Religion and the Rise of African-American and Native American Literatures* (New York: Oxford University Press, 2003), 15–16, 198n20; Philip Gould, "Early Black Atlantic Writing and the Cultures of Enlightenment," in *Beyond Douglass: New Perspectives on Early African American Literature*, ed. Michael J. Drexler and Ed White (Lewisburg, Pa.: Bucknell University Press, 2008), 107–22.
5. Richard Newman, ed., *Black Preacher to White America: The Collected Writings of Lemuel Haynes, 1774–1833* (Brooklyn: Carlson, 1990), 28–30; John Saillant, *Black Puritan, Black Republican: The Life and Thought of Lemuel Haynes, 1753–1833* (New York: Oxford University Press, 2003), 15–23, 42–46, 101–2; Saillant, "'Profitable Reading': Literacy, Christianity, and Constitutionalism in Olaudah Equiano's *Interesting Narrative*" (public lecture, Mayaguez Campus, University of Puerto Rico, April 22, 2009).
6. See, for example, Roy Finkenbine, "Belinda's Petition: Reparations for Slavery in Revolutionary Massachusetts," *William and Mary Quarterly* 64, no. 1 (January 2007): 95–104.
7. Ian Frederick Finseth, *Shades of Green: Visions of Nature in the Literature of American Slavery, 1770–1860* (Athens: University of Georgia Press, 2009), 54–73.
8. Ira Berlin, "Time, Space, and the Evolution of Afro-American Society on British Mainland North America," *American Historical Review* 85, no. 1 (February 1980): 51–54; William D. Piersen, *Black Yankees: The Development of an Afro-American Subculture in Eighteenth-Century New England* (Amherst: University of Massachusetts Press, 1988), 1–19, 59–61, 165; Robert J. Cottrol, *The Afro-Yankees: Providence's Black Community in the Antebellum Era* (Westport, Conn.: Greenwood, 1982), 17–29; Lorenzo J. Greene, *The Negro in Colonial New England* (New York: Columbia University Press, 1942), 72–99, 134–42. The most spectacular anti-impressment effort in the British Atlantic colonies came in 1747 when British Commodore Knowles ordered his crew into Boston to search for sailors. Fearful and angry laborers, sailors, and others burned a navy longboat, took three officers hostage, kept the navy at bay for three days, and forced provincial officials to seek refuge at Castle William in the harbor. See Denver Alexander Brunsman, "The Knowles Atlantic Impressment Riots of the 1740s," *Early American Studies* 5 (2007): 324–66.
9. Piersen, *Black Yankees*, 14–16, 165. In the late eighteenth century, some Englishmen suggested that slaves might be considered subjects of the king rather than property, with some of the civil rights of other subjects. Christopher L. Brown, *Moral Capital: Foundations of British Abolitionism* (Chapel Hill: University of North Carolina Press, 2006), 221–28.
10. Shane White, "'It Was a Proud Day': African Americans, Festivals, and Parades in the North, 1741–1834," *Journal of American History* 81, no. 1 (June 1994): 13–34; Joseph P. Reidy, "'Negro Election Day' and Black Community Life in New England, 1750–1860," *Marxist Perspectives* 1 (Fall 1978): 102–14.
11. Samuel Sewall, *The Selling of Joseph: A Memorial* (Boston: Green & Allen, 1700), 1.
12. James Otis, *The Rights of British Colonies Asserted and Proved* (Boston: Edes & Gill, 1764), 29.

13. Nash, *Race and Revolution* 8–9; John Adams to Jeremy Belknap, March 21, 1795, in "Letters and Documents relating to Slavery in Massachusetts: Queries relating to Slavery in Massachusetts," Massachusetts Historical Society, *Collections*, 5th ser., 3 (1877): 401–2; William Nell, *Colored Patriots of the American Revolution* (Boston: Walcott, 1855), 42–45.
14. The grounding of these petitions in New England's Revolutionary culture is emphasized by Dickson D. Bruce, *The Origins of African American Literature, 1680–1860* (Charlottesville: University of Virginia Press, 2001), 53–58. Bruce does not, however, explore whether or how these petitions, along with Phillis Wheatley's writings, shaped African American identity.
15. *The Appendix; or, Some Observations on the Expediency of the Petition of the Africans, Living in Boston, &c.* (Boston: Russell, 1773), 9–11, 13–15.
16. Brown, *Moral Capital*, 290. In the Somerset case, the chief justice of the King's Bench had issued a ruling in June 1772 that seemed to many to say that slavery could not exist in England or its colonies unless explicitly established by written law (97–101); Edlie L. Wong, *Neither Fugitive nor Free: Atlantic Slavery, Freedom Suits, and the Legal Culture of Travel* (New York: New York University Press, 2009), 29–31.
17. William Blackstone, *Commentaries on the Law of England*, 4 vols. (Oxford: Clarendon, 1765–1769), 1:138–39.
18. Peter Bestes et al., *Boston, April 20th, 1773: Sir, the Efforts Made by the Legislative [sic] of This Province in Their Last Sessions to Free Themselves from Slavery* (broadside; Boston: s.n., 1773). In *Colored Patriots of the American Revolution* William Nell wrote that this petition was submitted to the General Court on June 23, 1773, and that in January 1774 a bill was passed by both houses but that on March 8, when a committee of blacks sought Hutchinson's consent, "he told them that his instructions forbade [it]. His successor, General Gage, gave them the same answer, when they waited on him" (41–42). Nell's description seems to conflate the 1773 and 1774 petitions. Kaplan and Kaplan identify the April 1773 petition as the one in which the committee sought the governor's help but says that the House had tabled the petition. *Black Presence*, 12.
19. "Petition for Freedom to Massachusetts Governor Thomas Gage, His Majesty's Council, and the House of Representatives, 25 May 1774," *African Americans and the End of Slavery*, Massachusetts Historical Society, www.masshist.org/database/onview_full.cfm?queryID=589; "Petition for Freedom to Massachusetts Governor Thomas Gage, His Majesty's Council, and the House of Representatives, June 1774," *African Americans*, www.masshist.org/database/onview_full.cfm?queryID=590; Abigail Adams to John Adams, September 22, 1774, *Adams Family Correspondence*, ed. L. H. Butterfield, 10 vols. (Cambridge: Harvard University Press, 1963), 1:162.
20. A Son of Africa, "For the Massachusetts Spy," *Massachusetts Spy*, February 10, 1774.
21. Kaplan and Kaplan, *Black Presence*, 203–5, 15–24, 34–73.
22. "From a Great Number," petition, SC1/series 45X, Massachusetts Archives Collection.
23. Draft legislation, 1777, SC1/series 45X, Massachusetts Archives, 212:130–31; Nell, *Colored Patriots*, 45–47.

24. Kaplan and Kaplan, *Black Presence*, 245; Horton and Horton, *In Hope of Liberty*, 71.
25. Prime and Prince, Fairfield, Conn., to the Connecticut Assembly, May 4, 1779, transcript in Nash, *Race and Revolution*, 174–75.
26. Kaplan and Kaplan, *Black Presence*, 29, 30, 49–50.
27. Horton and Horton, *In Hope of Liberty*, 177–79; Patrick Rael, *Black Identity and Black Protest in the Antebellum North* (Chapel Hill: University of North Carolina Press, 2002), 84–90.
28. James Sidbury, *Becoming African in America: Race and Nation in the Early Black Atlantic* (New York: Oxford University Press, 2007), 17–65. On the formation and nature of identity and memory, see Fredrik Barth, introduction to *Ethnic Groups and Boundaries: The Social Organization of Cultural Difference* (Boston: Little, Brown, 1969), 9–38.
29. Bernard Bailyn, *The Ideological Origins of the American Revolution* (Cambridge: Harvard University Press, 1967).
30. Wheatley, "To the Right and Honorable William, Earl of Dartmouth," in *Poems on Various Subjects, Religious and Moral* (Philadelphia: Crukshank, 1786), 50–51. In *Origins of African American Literature*, Bruce notes that Wheatley used the term "African nation" in her writings primarily to stress their "common humanity" with other peoples but also to indicate "the distinctive position of their own 'nation' in relation to that of Anglo-America" (78). Bruce does not, however, link those nascent ideas about ethnic identity to the Revolution.
31. Anthony Benezet, *Some Historical Account of Guinea* (Philadelphia: Joseph Crukshank, 1771); Finseth, *Shades of Green*, 53–55.
32. Kaplan and Kaplan, *Black Presence*, 193–95.
33. Bruce connects this romantic praise for Africa to the "tendencies toward a gold-enage primitivism informing the thinking of at least some Revolutionary figures," because it offered "a world in which the corrupting force of greed and materialism appeared to be absent." *Origins of African American Literature*, 59.
34. Kaplan and Kaplan, *Black Presence*, 205–6. Shays's Rebellion was an uprising in western Massachusetts that broke out in the fall of 1786, after the state legislature increased taxes and required payment in specie in order to redeem its war debt—nearly all of which had been obtained by wealthy merchants in Boston and Salem. Not only did the farmers lack the money, but they were outraged at the prospect of losing their property and falling into debt in order to pay a small group of already wealthy men. The "regulators" closed county courts, preventing farm foreclosures, and marched on the state armory in Springfield. The uprising was put down by a force raised by Boston merchants—which is the point at which Prince Hall offered help—but not before alarming many of state and national leaders.
35. "A Number of African Blacks" to the Massachusetts House, January 4, 1787, documents relating to Unpassed House Legislation, no. 2358, Massachusetts Archives. The 1790 census shows 761 free blacks living in Boston, 4.4 percent of the city's total; I assume that about a fourth of those (190) were adult men.
36. Prince Hall, *A Charge Delivered to the Brethren of the African Lodge on the 25th of June, 1792* (Boston: Fleet, 1792); Bruce, *Origins of African American Literature*, 82–83.

37. Horton and Horton, *In Hope of Liberty*, 125–202, 258–61; *The Sons of Africans: An Essay on Freedom, with Observations on the Origin of Slavery, by a Member of the African Society in Boston* (Boston: Members of the Society, 1808); David Waldstreicher, *In the Midst of Perpetual Fetes: The Making of American Nationalism, 1776–1820* (Chapel Hill: University of North Carolina Press, 1997), 327–47; Hosea Easton, *A Treatise on the Intellectual Character, and Civil and Political Condition of the Colored People of the United States; and the Prejudice Exercised towards Them* (Boston: I. Knapp, 1837), 21–22; "Subscriber," *Liberator*, July 16, 1831, no. 29, 114–15.
38. Kaplan and Kaplan, *Black Presence*, 209–10, 272–76.
39. Haynes 1801 sermon in Newman, *Black Preacher to White America*, 82–87; Saillant, *Black Puritan, Black Republican*, 125; David Walker, *An Appeal in Four Articles, Together with a Preamble, to the Coloured Citizens of the World* (1829; repr., Boston: David Walker, 1830); Nell, *Colored Patriots*, 13–15.

Forgotten Founder

Revolutionary Memory and John Dickinson's Reputation

Peter Bastian

If any politically aware colonist in mid-1774 were to name the best-known patriot in North America, it would not have been anyone we now think of as being among the Founding Fathers. Instead, the most likely answer would have been John Dickinson, the "Pennsylvania Farmer." Dickinson had been a delegate to the Stamp Act Congress, where he provided the draft for most of its resolutions. Opposing British attempts to tax the colonies, he penned *Letters from a Pennsylvania Farmer*, making a clever distinction between Parliament's right to regulate trade and the power to tax directly.[1] After this publication he was denounced by the British government but celebrated in popular parades and toasts from New England to the South, with crowds singing the "Freedom Song" he composed.[2] Many delegates arriving in Philadelphia to attend the First Continental Congress were eager to meet this famous figure, with at least a dozen of them already among his friends or correspondents. Samuel Adams described Dickinson at the time "as a true Bostonian"—his ultimate compliment.[3]

Yet Dickinson is no longer remembered as a preeminent Revolutionary.[4] This change in fortune had much to do with his opposition to the timing of American independence, a position that left some of his contemporaries livid. That Dickinson's hesitancy at that particular time could have cast such a long-lasting pall over his reputation also suggests just how important that founding moment has been in national mythology. When George Bancroft came to write his monumental nineteenth-century history of the United States, he repeated the view of Dickinson's critics that he was essentially a flawed patriot who "wanted boldness of will."[5] Although Moses Coit Tyler and Charles J. Stillé, writing toward the end of that century, pointed to Dickinson's considerable contributions to the American cause, their efforts were never enough to restore him to the pantheon of Revolutionary patriots.[6] Since then, only a handful of works on Dickinson have been published, the last appearing more than twenty-five years ago. These have been dwarfed by the abundant studies focusing on those seen as the heavyweights of the Revolution—Adams, Franklin, Hamilton, Jefferson, Madison, and Washington.[7] Dickinson, meanwhile, remains a forgotten patriot.

Dickinson's current obscurity raises some key issues in relation to Revolutionary memory. Of the many people involved in furthering the Revolutionary cause, which of them were remembered and why?[8] How do we account for Dickinson's insignificance in Revolutionary memory? His position over independence was certainly not unique. Moreover, he subsequently remained faithful to the Revolution and served the patriot movement in various capacities. He and his wife, Mary, went on to become good republican citizens, supporting many worthwhile causes along with the 1787 Constitution. Yet despite this, in the contested arena of memory and history making, Dickinson was still left out. Part of the reason lies in the expectations surrounding him as a result of his previous fame and the importance of independence to national mythmaking. His hesitation at that fateful moment, seemingly undercutting his assumed patriotism, was difficult to forgive.

Dickinson's fall from grace also highlights the ongoing contentiousness of memory and history making after independence. Numerous studies have shown how other figures vigorously promoted their Revolutionary roles in the decades after 1776 to secure their historical reputations.[9] Dickinson certainly lived long enough to restore his Revolutionary credentials. Yet, apart from some early efforts, he was unwilling to engage in the type of self-promotion needed to cement his legacy, meaning that his repute ultimately failed to endure. That subsequent generations and contemporary historians have not rehabilitated Dickinson's reputation speaks volumes about the enduring power of a seamless and consensual founding narrative.[10]

The younger Dickinson might have been surprised by his subsequent fall from fame, since his parents had encouraged him from an early age to be successful. Born in 1732 and largely raised in Kent County, Delaware, John was the first son from Samuel Dickinson's second marriage to Mary Cadwalader. Samuel was a wealthy farmer who served as a local assemblyman and justice of the peace. Although both parents came from Quaker backgrounds, Samuel was involved in an earlier falling out with the Friends and no longer attended their meetings.[11] Despite their standing in Delaware, his parents expected young John to seek success in the much larger world of nearby Philadelphia.[12] Dickinson commenced his law studies in that city, but his parents agreed that he should study instead at Middle Temple in London. Although he found the years 1754–56 in the English capital emotionally trying, Dickinson valued its cultural and social influences and the way it furthered his legal qualifications. After returning to the family estate at Poplar Hall, Dickinson soon moved back to Philadelphia, where he quickly established a successful legal practice. He also pursued several commercial ventures and began acquiring large tracts of western land for farming and timber. His public writings in the 1760s show just how much Dickinson was at home in the commercial economy of Philadelphia, conversant with issues such as the circulation of paper currency and the development of local trading practices.[13] Yet, as his subsequent *Letters from a Pennsylvania Farmer* also reveal, there was an unresolved tension in Dickinson's outlook between the obvious attractions of social advancement in Philadelphia and the simpler values of his parents' agrarian world.[14]

One way in which Dickinson resolved these tensions was by endowing all his Philadelphian activities with public-spirited objectives. The law became the noblest profession, he wrote in a letter to his mother, because it undertook "the defence of innocence, the support of justice and the preservation of peace and harmony amongst men."[15] When first elected to the Pennsylvania Assembly in 1762, Dickinson informed supporters that he was there to serve the public good.[16] Yet he had a personality that remained extraordinarily sensitive to any questioning of his motives. When his political rival, Joseph Galloway, claimed in 1764 that Dickinson harbored "a thirst after promotion," he challenged him to a duel. This characteristic inability to accept criticism eventually became his undoing.

John's domestic life provided him with another form of success. His wife, Mary, was the eldest daughter of Isaac Norris, former Speaker of the Pennsylvania Assembly and one of the wealthiest men in the colony. Mary was a Quaker—one of the few religious groups that gave women equal roles in the church—and her life revolved around the meeting house, where she enjoyed considerable status. Despite the family wealth, Mary lived a simple lifestyle, in which companionship with her younger sister, Sally, and her widowed aunt were her most important relationships. When Norris died in 1766, it was Dickinson who provided the sisters with business and legal advice. Sally died suddenly of smallpox in June 1768, and John then monopolized a devastated Mary's time before she eventually agreed to marry him in a civil ceremony in July 1770. Immediately following the marriage John moved into his wife's home at Fairhill, some six miles outside the city limits. He remodeled the old-fashioned and simply furnished Jacobean house, transforming it into a Georgian-style mansion. With a four horse-drawn carriage and a retinue of servants, the couple's lifestyle was as close to an aristocratic one as could be achieved in the old Quaker colony. John Adams recorded his admiration for Fairhill on his first visit in 1774.[17] Dickinson's social advancement seemed complete, and Mary accepted these changes willingly enough at first. Yet there was an underlying uneasiness on her part over this sudden pursuit of such a lavish lifestyle.

By 1774 Dickinson's success in many fields concealed his one major failure—his aborted political career within Pennsylvania. His personality made him unsuited to the rough-and-tumble of politics in a colonial assembly riven with factions. While his reputation meant that in the right circumstances supporters drifted to him, they tended to fall away when times changed.[18] This pattern would be repeated during his tenure in the Continental Congress. Typically, he saw himself as refusing to bow to factions and pretended to have retired from colonial politics for health reasons. The reality, however, was somewhat different. After initial electoral successes in the early to mid-1760s, he had lost out badly to his main rival, Galloway. Changing circumstances saw Dickinson reemerge into active political life during 1774. This was partly due to the long-term decline of the pro-British Galloway's influence within the colony, subsequently hastened by the meeting in Philadelphia of the First Continental Congress, where Galloway was clearly out of step with most delegates.

Dickinson was reelected to the Assembly on October 1, 1774, and appointed as a congressional delegate in mid-October. He was responsible for substantially revising several important congressional documents during the last ten days of its sittings. By the time this body had completed its proceedings, Dickinson still enjoyed a position of high prestige in the eyes of most delegates.[19] But from the meeting of the Second Continental Congress in May 1775 until the Declaration of Independence some fourteen months later, Dickinson's reputation as a leading American patriot would be badly eroded.

Dickinson vacillated over the movement toward American independence as the answer to the dispute with Britain, and he upset many delegates at the Second Congress by proposing another petition to the king, even though the first had been ignored. His clashes with John Adams on the floor of the Congress led to an angry confrontation between the two men outside the building, followed by a rash letter by Adams that described Dickinson as "a certain great fortune and piddling genius."[20] Unfortunately, the correspondence was captured and printed by the British, thus further alienating the two former allies, with Adams furiously adding to his diary any stories that cast Dickinson's character in a bad light.[21] As the two men were no longer on speaking terms, Dickinson was subsequently shut off from those delegates who sought independence and who later represented themselves as constituting the true core of Revolutionary patriots, which proved to be an important and enduring bond between these men. During the 1790s John Adams, for example, remained close to Samuel Adams, Elbridge Gerry, and Benjamin Rush, even though all three men had become supporters of his rival Thomas Jefferson. Their friendships continued because the worth of these men had been proven to Adams by their earlier support of the Revolutionary cause. In contrast, Dickinson, by his actions, had failed this crucial test of character.

Dickinson also saw his newfound political influence within Pennsylvania begin to wane, as more radical proindependence factions began to create new political structures to control the colony. It would be in their interests to subsequently disparage Dickinson's patriotism because he remained their political rival. Such character assassination had been an accepted part of the political culture of colonial Pennsylvania, continuing into the Revolutionary period. The task of his opponents was made easier by the fact that when the final debates over independence took place in June and July 1776, Dickinson spoke on the floor of the Congress against the timing of this pronouncement.[22] He deliberately absented himself on July 2 when independence was voted on, even though it was inevitable that his actions would be seen as controversial.[23]

John Adams later claimed that Dickinson's policies were influenced by the pacifism of both his mother and his wife and by their fears for his safety and the fate of their estates.[24] Mary certainly worried over the prospect of war, and while it is possible that she reinforced her husband's attempt to try for compromise, it is likely that political factors played a more prominent role in her husband's considerations. Whereas historian Jane Calvert suggests that John Dickinson inherited a Quaker framework of civil disobedience, which served him well during the colonial protest movements but was no longer suited to the circumstances of 1776, the fact is that he was never a pacifist and always believed in the principle of defensive wars.[25] He admired the use of citizen forces over standing armies and served in the militias of Pennsylvania and Delaware; he also supported the creation of the Continental Army and the appointment of Washington to command it.[26] Only a fine, but nevertheless important, line separated Dickinson from Adams in 1776.

Adams thought that independence was necessary to show other powers, especially the French, that the colonists were serious in seeking an alliance. Such a declaration would also be necessary to convince the colonists to enter into a formal confederation, although Adams hoped this might be done simultaneously with a Declaration of Independence. Whether it was realistic or not, Dickinson wanted to obtain foreign assistance before declaring independence, because he thought the colonists would not be able to defeat Britain by themselves. A formal and strong confederation was also needed first, to prevent the future states from turning on one another. While he was more hopeful than Adams that the British cabinet might come to its senses, Dickinson's speeches in the first half of 1776 suggested that he thought such an outcome unlikely.[27] He was not alone in holding these cautious views. Delegates such as James Duane, John Jay,

Thomas Johnson, Edward Rutledge, and Robert Morris, to name a few, shared his concerns. Like Dickinson, their moderation served to ensure that they would never receive the same historical status as those who argued for the break from Britain early and clearly. But Dickinson's persistent belief that he was right in his views on the timing of independence not only harmed continental unity but also led to highly critical evaluations of his display of character at such a defining moment in the Revolution.

By 1776 many of these revolutionaries were conscious of living through significant events and, as historian Douglass Adair notes, they were "fantastically concerned with posterity's judgment of their behavior."[28] John Adams had already purchased a folio book to preserve copies of his letters to record "the great events which are passed and those greater which are rapidly advancing" and had previously urged his wife, Abigail, to keep all his letters to her.[29] Dickinson was certainly aware of the judgment of others, admitting to delegates that his opposition to the timing of independence would give the "finishing blow" to his "once great popularity."[30] He was correct in his estimation, for the diminution of his reputation began almost immediately. His friend Charles Thomson claimed that he had deserted the people in their hour of need. Samuel Adams, no longer an admirer, believed Dickinson had poisoned the minds of the people with his policies.[31] John Adams reported him to be in total disgrace in early 1777 and, in a reply to the French in 1779 as to why such a well-known figure had disappeared from public life, put it down to Dickinson's "timidity and avarice."[32] Joseph Reed claimed to remember that Dickinson's nerves were so weak in June 1774 that he could only reluctantly address a public meeting after being plied with alcohol and that his large fortune made him "cautious and timid" in opposing British measures.[33]Jefferson described him in 1786 as a lawyer of "more ingenuity than sound judgment and still more timid than ingenious."[34]

Of all the views expressed about Dickinson's character, it is those of John Adams that have probably been the most damaging. In the 1780s Dickinson agreed to serve as a delegate to the Annapolis Convention and ended up chairing it, as well as attending the 1787 Constitutional Convention in Philadelphia. But the latter convention proved fraught with difficulties. In moments of stress Dickinson's health began to fail; he fought with James Wilson and James Madison on various issues, and although his presence was symbolically important, he was no longer the leading figure he had been in earlier congresses.[35] Although he never again held political office, Dickinson, writing as "Fabius," supported the new Constitution in a series of newspaper articles. If it had not been for his earlier controversy over independence, Dickinson might have secured a greater reputation as one of the Founding Fathers in another moment of national mythology. Earlier patriots such as Samuel Adams and Richard Henry Lee, who had been consistent advocates of independence, now suffered in terms of their subsequent fame because they refused to support the new Constitution.

During the 1790s Dickinson also approved of the French Revolution because he had lost confidence in the British and, like Jefferson, increasingly hoped that Republican France would become the natural ally of his nation.[36] In 1797 Thomas McKean arranged for the publication of the Fabius articles into one edition, and Dickinson agreed to write additional material in support of Jefferson's pro-French policies against those of Adams, who was then serving as president.[37] These efforts reconciled Jefferson to Dickinson and the two men wrote regularly to each other thereafter. But believing the president was ignorantly undermining the new Constitution, Dickinson devoted much of Letter 13 of the new Fabius material to proving this point by ridiculing Adams's attempts at constitution writing in his 1776 pamphlet *Thoughts on Government.* Adams had always been proud of these efforts in providing what he believed was a model for various state constitutions, but Dickinson denounced the pamphlet as an "indefensible scheme."[38]

After his defeat by Jefferson in 1800 the embittered Adams determined to restore his reputation by writing his memoirs and emphasizing his crucial role in the quest for American independence.[39] This act in itself suggests the importance that participants attached to the memory of these events. Among other intentions, Adams hoped to minimize Jefferson's achievements as author of the Declaration of Independence. Since Jefferson had always been firm in his support for independence, however, the best that Adams could do was paint his former friend as a minor player in these crucial years.

Instead, Adams turned his ire on Dickinson. After first linking him as a supporter of Jefferson in 1800, Adams went on to depict Dickinson as the most influential member of the early congresses opposed to the movement toward independence. Attributing Dickinson's timidity to the Quaker influence of his wife and mother, Adams then contrasted the wavering attitudes emanating from Fairhill with the staunch patriotism of his own household. Forgetting the large degree of consensus among congressional delegates over most crucial issues, Adams instead claimed to remember a period where policies were carried by only one or two votes and he—the "Atlas of Independence"—had battled against Dickinson's misguided views.[40] Given Adams's trenchant condemnation and Dickinson's relative silence, there was no way the latter's reputation could survive such an attack. Even down to the present day, Adams's voluminous writings have managed to obscure other points of view. The 2008 HBO series *John Adams*, for instance, obviously drew from his autobiography to depict its subject as the leading light in the movement toward independence, with Dickinson as his main opponent. Following Adams's claim, the series put Dickinson's opposition down to an overly cautious nature and the influence of Quakerism.[41]

Adams, also a successful lawyer in his early career, wrote his autobiography at his farm, reminiscing about a more innocent time in the America of his youth. The outlooks of Adams and Dickinson in their old age were, in reality, far closer than either man could share with Jefferson, who lived out his remaining days on a debt-laden hilltop estate, surrounded by black slaves. But despite the falling out between Adams and Jefferson, they remained linked by their earlier Revolutionary experiences. By contrast, Adams believed that Dickinson did not deserve to be included in the pantheon of Revolutionary patriots and went out of his way to ensure his exclusion.

Despite living well into his seventies, Dickinson made no sustained efforts to redeem his reputation. At first glance this failure is surprising, because during the colonial period he had been quite successful, even clever, at self-promotion: his famous Farmer persona, the best example. Aside from hesitating over independence, Dickinson's behavior immediately after July 1776 was to prove an extra handicap to his rehabilitation. Most of the Revolutionary elite took pride in their service in some form or another during the Revolutionary War years. Dickinson began well in this regard when, in August 1776, he led his militia company to New Jersey, claiming rather melodramatically that he would gladly embrace death on the battlefield to prove his patriotism. But he subsequently resigned his commission in September when his political opponents appointed their allies to more senior positions of command.[42] He was elected to the new Pennsylvania Assembly in November but found his supporters in a minority and so returned to Delaware. Here, in a letter he unwisely advised his brother Philemon not to accept continental currency. This correspondence was intercepted and opened by the Committee of Safety in Philadelphia, leading to accusations that Dickinson had deserted the American cause.[43] He returned to Philadelphia in early 1777 to counter these charges but could not get any satisfaction and so went back to his Delaware estate for the next two years, making no real contribution to the war effort at a crucial time.

In 1779 Dickinson finally returned to public life as a delegate for Delaware to the Continental Congress before being chosen as president of that state in late 1781.[44] In November of the following year he was elected to the Executive Council in Pennsylvania, and his supporters had him selected as state president. Holding public office in this fractured political culture, Dickinson immediately aroused controversy, because it was in his opponent's interest to belittle his character and achievements. The Philadelphia newspapers in late 1782 contained a series of partisan attacks about him, especially those by "Valerius," which questioned Dickinson's character and commitment by pointing to his lack of support for independence in 1776; his supposed "deserting" of his militia command; his opposition to the new Pennsylvania Constitution; and his controversial advice to Philemon.[45] The attacks could not be ignored, and for the first time Dickinson publicly wrote to defend himself. His arguments, however, tended to be lengthy, convoluted, and written in the style of a legal brief, a weakness evident even in his earlier and most popular writings. By late 1782, with the War for Independence effectively won with the help of the French, Dickinson had to publicly concede that the Congress had been right in declaring independence when it did and therefore, by implication, that his reasons for opposing this move had been wrong. The weakness of his newspaper arguments, which were poorly received by the public, appeared to have made him wary of engaging in any subsequent historical revisionism.

Important changes in Dickinson's domestic situation from 1785 also added to this lack of interest in promoting his public image. When his three terms as president were complete, Dickinson and his wife were glad to leave Philadelphia and move to Wilmington. Mary was attracted to it partly because the meeting house contained welcoming relatives but also because the Quaker-founded village reminded her of her childhood days in Philadelphia.[46] Their new house, although small, was comfortable and it made the raising of their two daughters, Sally and Maria, more intimate and personal. Mary's new life seemed to conform to changing concepts of the republican mother and wife in the wake of the Revolution. She was still confined to domestic roles, but relations with her husband became more equal and informal than they had been in the colonial period, and letters between them reflected a growing degree of intimacy.[47] Although never completely reconciled to Quakerism, John bowed to domestic influences by accompanying his devout female family members to the meeting house. Mary reported to friends that she enjoyed her small garden and had "learnt a Lesson that Happiness is not confined to the Grandness of Life—perhaps seldom found there."[48] During the war invading British troops had partially burned Fairhill, and she now looked back on this act as punishment for her earlier extravagances and her husband's social pretensions.

This reappraisal of their domestic lives meant that Mary's influence over John was greater than in his days as an ambitious lawyer and politician. Mary had always opposed slavery and, in theory, so had her husband, even though he had been the largest slave owner in Philadelphia before the Revolution. In 1781 Dickinson freed his remaining slaves and urged his brother to do the same. Education was another common interest, and in 1783 Dickinson College was established by charter and endowed with two farms by Dickinson as well as the library of Isaac Norris. The couple gave money for various other educational projects for poor and orphaned children run by the Society of Friends, supported prison reform, and offered charitable aid to less affluent relatives. Mary spent hours assisting her husband sifting through the various cases and remained active in these pursuits until ill health in her final years lessened her interests. She died, lamented by her grieving husband, in July 1803.[49]

Although he retained some business investments in Philadelphia, John no longer directly managed them. Instead he focused on his estate in Delaware and every year spent varying periods there. Like his wife he enjoyed mulling over childhood memories. "Here I am, on the lands of my ancestors for several generations," he noted to his family.[50] The older rural values had now triumphed for Dickinson, and he celebrated this life free of the stresses of Philadelphia that, like Mary, he associated with his discarded social ambitions, a commercial economy, and the painful memories of the

Revolutionary period. Like his father in retirement, John now spent hours alone in his library. Here he could actually act out the literary image he had created in the 1760s—the detached citizen writing public tracts and letters in his spare time. In 1804 when his parents' comfortable but aging house accidentally burned down, Dickinson insisted it be rebuilt to its original design.

The Revolution, painful though it had been, seemed liberating for Dickinson because it freed him to think about returning to a better age. There was a period that he believed existed in the rural America of his youth and contained values that had been in danger of being lost. The Revolution—American separation from the British Empire—allowed the restoration of such a value system that seemed to fit perfectly the needs of a new republican society. But this outlook, while allowing Dickinson to partially excise the more painful memories of the Revolutionary years, also contributed to his loss of public recognition. Most of the leading participants may have had different memories of the Revolution and have often been divided over what they thought had happened, but they nonetheless shared the view that they had been participants in momentous events. As they grew older, most became increasingly conscious of fostering their public persona and their place in the Revolutionary story. As Joseph J. Ellis points out, "All of the vanguard members of the Revolutionary generation developed a keen sense of their historical significance even while they were still making the history on which their reputations would rest."[51]

This quest for self-promotion by the elite took different forms. After relinquishing his command, Washington had a group of young ex-army officers edit and cull his wartime correspondence with one eye on its future value as a historical record of his achievements. By the 1780s Mount Vernon was already a growing place of pilgrimage, and Washington and his supporters were kept busy fine-tuning his reputation as a national icon. They would perpetuate his fame well beyond anything Dickinson had once enjoyed.[52] Although well respected in Delaware, Dickinson did not have the advantage of being identified with a large and important state to push his cause for inclusion in the pantheon of heroes. Some twenty thousand residents turned out for Benjamin Franklin's funeral in Philadelphia in 1790, and despite character attacks by John and Samuel Adams and the Lee family, Franklin's adopted city helped propagate his fame thereafter.[53] Dickinson also failed to hold any political office in the 1790s, a decade that Ellis has argued was crucial in consolidating the importance of the leading

Revolutionary figures in the public mind. Dickinson did not attempt to write his memoirs, and he always refused requests to be painted on canvas as a hero of 1776.[54] Although he corresponded with Jefferson from the 1790s on, he largely dealt with contemporary issues such as the abolition of the slave trade rather than try to promote his role in the Revolution. It would be Adams and Rush and, more famously, Adams and Jefferson, who in their old age quite consciously corresponded on the great themes of the Revolution through their selected memories of these events. These men were acutely conscious that their correspondence served as much to secure their reputations for posterity as to renew their old friendship.[55]

Dickinson was unusual in that, unlike most of the Founding Fathers, he had once enjoyed enormous fame, and so it was harder for him to retain this popularity, let alone promote his subsequent Revolutionary efforts. Only on a few occasions did he ever set out to revisit the past, and in one surviving record he agreed to answer Mercy Otis Warren's by now inevitable questions as to why he had taken the course of action that he did during 1775–76. He still pointed to the exigencies of Pennsylvanian politics and his hope that the British ministry would eventually change its policies as the motives for his stance. But Dickinson usually preferred to spend his energies writing on religious and moral topics as well as on contemporary events, leaving historical revisionism and national mythmaking to others.[56]

When Dickinson died in 1808, five years after his wife, Jefferson described him as a "true patriot" and predicted that his name would "be consecrated in history as one of the great worthies of the Revolution."[57] Jefferson was wrong. Dickinson would not be remembered in this way, nor would he ever regain the immense fame that he had enjoyed in the colonial period. His story reveals the selectiveness of Revolutionary memories, where, whatever his contributions, his actions in 1776 marked him off from those who would come to be regarded as the real founding heroes. It also suggests that a Revolutionary reputation and a place in the nation's historical memory could be ensured only by a degree of self-promotion. Although not lacking such skills during the colonial period, after 1776 Dickinson found it too difficult to secure this reputation and so abandoned the field to others with their own agendas while he pursued other interests. Clearly, among some of his contemporaries it was desirable that Dickinson be deliberately excluded as a founding father. As a result he became an almost forgotten patriot, with most historians coming to accept the assessment of Dickinson's opponents regarding his character and behavior. He would be remembered for his apparent failings as a Revolutionary patriot, even though he subsequently lived quite happily as a good republican in an independent America.

NOTES

1. While the Farmer's Letters first appeared in newspapers, various compilations were later published; see John Dickinson, *Letters from a Pennsylvania Farmer to the Inhabitants of the British Colonies* (Philadelphia: Hall & Sellers, 1768).
2. *A New Song to the Tune of Heart of Oaks* (Philadelphia: Hall & Sellers, 1768), broadsheet.
3. Samuel Adams to James Warren, September 23, 1774, in *Letters of Delegates of the Continental Congress*, ed. Paul H. Smith et al., 26 vols. (Washington, D.C.: Library of Congress, 1976–), 1:100 (hereafter cited as *Letters of Delegates*).
4. John Adams, *Diary and Autobiography of John Adams*, ed. L. H. Butterfield, Leonard C. Faber, and Wendell D. Garrett, 4 vols. (Cambridge: Harvard University Press, 1961), 3:316.
5. George Bancroft, *History of the United States*, 6 vols. (New York: Appleton, 1888), esp. 4:11–12 and 4:32–33.
6. Moses Coit Tyler, *A Literary History of the American Revolution, 1765–1783* (New York: Putnam's Sons, 1897); Charles J. Stillé, *The Life and Times of John Dickinson* (Philadelphia: Lippincott, 1891).
7. These works include Robert Richards, *The Life and Character of John Dickinson* (Wilmington: Historical Society of Delaware, 1901); David L. Jacobson, *John Dickinson and the Revolution in Pennsylvania, 1764–1776* (Berkeley: University of California Press, 1965); and Milton E. Flower, *John Dickinson: Conservative Revolutionary* (Charlottesville: University of Virginia Press, 1983).
8. Historians have tended to emphasize those radical individuals and currents of the Revolution that failed to make their way into postwar memorial ceremonies, histories, or public celebrations. Yet Dickinson was forgotten not because he was too radical but because he was not radical enough. Gary B. Nash, *The Unknown American Revolution: The Unruly Birth of Democracy and the Struggle to Make America* (New York: Penguin Books, 2005); Alfred F. Young, *The Shoemaker and the Tea Party: Memory and the American Revolution* (Boston: Beacon, 1999).
9. So successful were these leading patriots that it was not until they began to pass away that memories of the Revolution became more democratic, and ordinary soldiers' efforts came to be more widely recognized and celebrated. On the Revolutionary elite and their efforts at making sense of the events of the Revolution, see Michael Kammen, *Season of Youth: The American Revolution and the Historical Imagination* (New York: Knopf, 1978); and, in particular, the works of Joseph J. Ellis, *Passionate Sage: The Character and Legacy of John Adams* (New York: Norton, 1993); Ellis, *American Sphinx: The Character of Thomas Jefferson* (New York: Norton, 1997); Ellis, *Founding Brothers: The Revolutionary Generation* (New York: Knopf, 2000); and Ellis, *His Excellency*

George Washington (New York: Knopf, 2004). On the later appreciation of common soldiers, see Caroline Cox's chapter, "Public Memories, Private Lives: The First Greatest Generation Remembers the Revolutionary War," in this volume.

10. Alon Confino, "Collective Memory and Cultural History: Problems of Method," *American Historical Review* 102 (1997): esp. 1399–1400.
11. Stillé, *Life and Times,* 14–38.
12. John Dickinson to Samuel Dickinson, January 18 and September 6, 1754, in "A Pennsylvania Farmer at the Court of King George: John Dickinson's London Letters, 1754–1756," ed. H. Trevor Colbourn and Richard Peters, *Pennsylvania Magazine of History and Biography* 86 (1962): 252, 283.
13. See, especially, [John Dickinson], *The Late Regulations respecting the British Colonies* (Philadelphia: Bradford, 1765), 3–4, 9–12, 14–18, 31–33.
14. Stanley K. Johannesen, "John Dickinson and the American Revolution," *Historical Reflections* 2 (1975): esp. 40–41.
15. John Dickinson to Mary Dickinson, August 15, 1754, in Colbourn and Peters, "Pennsylvania Farmer," 280.
16. "Reply to a Speech of Joseph Galloway," in *The Writings of John Dickinson,* ed. Paul Leicester Ford (Washington, D.C.: Government Printing Office, 1905), 109.
17. Adams, diary entry, September 12, 1774, in Adams, *Diary and Autobiography,* 2:133.
18. Jane E. Calvert, *Quaker Constitutionalism and the Political Thought of John Dickinson* (New York: Cambridge University Press, 2009).
19. David Ammerman, *In a Common Cause: American Responses to the Coercive Act of 1774* (Charlottesville: University of Virginia Press, 1974); Jack N. Rakove, *The Beginnings of National Politics* (New York: Knopf, 1979).
20. John Adams to James Warren, July 24, 1775, in *The Warren-Adams Letters,* ed. W. C. Ford, 2 vols. (Massachusetts Historical Society Collections 72–73), 1:88.
21. Adams, diary entries, September 16 and 24, 1775, in Adams, *Diary and Autobiography,* 2:73–174, 184; 3:318–19.
22. "John Dickinson's Notes for a Speech in Congress, May 23–25, 1775," *Letters of Delegates,* 2:371; "John Dickinson's Notes for a Speech in Congress, January 24, 1776," *Letters of Delegates,* 3:132–39; [John Dickinson], *Remarks on a Late Pamphlet Entitled Plain Truth by Rusticus* (Philadelphia: Hall, 1776); "John Dickinson's Notes for a Speech in Congress, July 1, 1776," *Letters of Delegates,* 4:351–57.
23. It appears, however, that Dickinson was present on July 4; he must have voted to adopt the Declaration of Independence because the delegates carried it unanimously on the day.
24. Adams, *Diary and Autobiography,* 3:316. Few historians have ever questioned this account, yet Dickinson's mother left Philadelphia in early 1775 to live in New Jersey with her other son, Philemon, and died the following year. It is unlikely that she could have directly influenced John in the way Adams claimed.
25. Calvert, *Quaker Constitutionalism,* 222–34.
26. John Dickinson to Tench Coxe, January 24, 1807, Coxe Family Papers, 2049, Historical Society of Pennsylvania, Philadelphia; John Adams to Abigail Adams, February 13, 1776, *Letters of Delegates,* 3:241.
27. [Dickinson], *Remarks on a Late Pamphlet,* esp. 15–17, 22, and 31.

28. Douglass Adair, "Fame and the Founding Fathers," in *Fame and the Founding Fathers: Essays by Douglass Adair*, ed. Trevor Colbourn (New York: Norton, 1974), 7.
29. John Adams to Abigail Adams, June 2, 1776, in *Adams Family Correspondence*, ed. LH. Butterfield, 10 vols. (Cambridge: Harvard University Press, 1963), 2:3.
30. "John Dickinson's Notes for a Speech in Congress, July 1, 1776," *Letters of Delegates*, 4:351
31. Charles Thomson to John Dickinson, August 16, 1776, *Letters of Delegates*, 4:562; Samuel Adams to James Warren, December 12, 1776, *Letters of Delegates*, 5:600–601.
32. Adams, diary entry, June 20, 1779, Adams, *Diary and Autobiography*, 2:385–86.
33. "Narrative of Joseph Reed," New York Historical Society, *Collections* 11 (1878): 269–73.
34. Thomas Jefferson to James Madison, May 25, 1784, and Thomas Jefferson to Soule's Inquiries, September 13–18, 1786, in *Papers of Thomas Jefferson*, ed. Julian P. Boyd et al., 39 vols. (Princeton: Princeton University Press, 1953), 7:289, 378–79.
35. Both Calvert and Flower claim Dickinson played an active role at the Philadelphia Convention, but James H. Hutson puts his contributions into a more balanced perspective. Calvert, *Quaker Constitutionalism*, 279; Flower, *John Dickinson*, 241–43; James H. Hutson, "John Dickinson at the Federal Constitutional Convention," *William and Mary Quarterly* 40 (1983): 256–82.
36. *The Letters of Fabius in 1788 on the Federal Constitution, and in 1797 on the Present Situation of Public Affairs* (Wilmington: Smyth, 1797); John Dickinson, *A Caution: Reflections on the Present Contest between France and Great Britain* (Philadelphia: Franklin Bache, 1798).
37. G. S. Rowe, *Thomas McKean* (Boulder: Colorado Associated University Press, 1978), 291–92.
38. *Letters of Fabius in 1788*, esp. 13:149.
39. A number of commentators on the Adams autobiography have argued that Adams's real motive in writing his memoirs was to deal with Alexander Hamilton and events of the 1790s. But the time spent on Hamilton was far less than the sustained attack on Dickinson partly because Adams wrote his account in chronological order and left his narrative unfinished by the time he began to deal with the events of his presidency. The fact that he spent so much time on the events of 1775–76 suggests their obvious importance to him.
40. Adams, *Diary and Autobiography*, 3:316–19, 321, 324–25, 327, 330, 335, 370, 396–97.
41. The TV series at least gave Dickinson some sympathy. At the end of the second episode, he was seen dressed in his military uniform and leading his men off to defend the newly proclaimed Declaration of Independence.
42. John Dickinson to Charles Thomson, August 6, 1776, *Letters of Delegates*, 5:102.
43. Elbridge Gerry to James Warren, December 23, 1776, *Letters of Delegates*, 5:689.
44. John H. Powell, "John Dickinson, President of the Delaware State, 1781–1782," *Delaware History* 1 (1946): 1–54, 110–34.
45. Stillé argued that it was these articles that influenced Bancroft's later unfavorable evaluations of Dickinson's character. See *Life and Times*, 238, regarding

Stillé's comments on Bancroft; and Bancroft, *History of the United States*, 4:12.

46. Mary Dickinson to Deborah Logan, February 3, 1786, Logan Family Papers, 2023, Historical Society of Pennsylvania.
47. John Dickinson to Mary Dickinson, August 30, 1787, Loudoun Papers, LCP107, Historical Society of Pennsylvania.
48. Mary Dickinson to Margaret Moore, December 4, 1785, Howland Collection, Haverford College, quoted in Flower, *John Dickinson*, 236.
49. Flower, *John Dickinson*, 264–66.
50. John Dickinson to Mary Dickinson, April 4, 1801, Loudoun Papers.
51. Ellis, *Founding Brothers*, 18.
52. For aspects of Washington mythmaking, see Barry Schwartz, *George Washington: The Making of an American Symbol* (New York: Free Press, 1987); Ellis, *His Excellency George Washington*, chap. 5; and Seth C. Bruggeman's chapter, "'More Than Ordinary Patriotism': Living History in the Memory Work of George Washington Parke Custis," in this volume.
53. Gordon S. Wood, *The Americanization of Benjamin Franklin* (New York: Penguin, 2004); and my review "'Let's Do Lunch': Benjamin Franklin and the American Character," *Australasian Journal of American Studies* 24, no. 1 (July 2005): 83–89.
54. Flower, *John Dickinson*, 256
55. Ellis, *Founding Brothers*, chap. 6.
56. Dickinson was pleased in 1805 with Mercy Otis Warren's history, describing it as a balanced account of the Revolutionary period. In contrast, John Adams was upset by what he saw as his lack of prominence in the events and its pro-Jeffersonian outlook.
57. Thomas Jefferson to Joseph Bringhurst, February 24, 1808, Papers of Thomas Jefferson, University of Virginia Library, Charlottesville, quoted in Stillé, *Life and Times*, 336.

The Graveyard Aesthetics of Revolutionary Elegiac Verse

Remembering the Revolution as a Sacred Cause

Evert Jan van Leeuwen

In his essay on the role poetry plays in constructing a collective memory of American origins, Robert Pinsky defines Henry Wadsworth Longfellow's "Paul Revere's Ride" (1861) as a "conscious effort" to construct a long-lasting myth of the Revolution. Pinsky highlights the poem's success by pointing out that "many Americans, including [the late] Senator Edward Kennedy, have much of the poem by heart."[1] In his folk ballad, Longfellow overtly casts the Revolution in a heroic and adventurous light—as the victory of a small group of men that "ended with the overthrow of a tyrannical monarchy and its replacement with a republican government," to use Michael A. McDonnell's words.[2] By centering the action around the "North Church tower" overshadowing the graves of American patriots and by giving the church tower the symbolic function of a "signal light" (line 9) to the Revolution, Longfellow managed to fuse two popular historical Revolutionary narratives: the republican and the millennial.[3]

Longfellow's poem literally created a moment in history. The current traditions surrounding the legend of Paul Revere's ride were born only after his poem's publication in 1860. But the ideological nature of this work—its unifying of republican and millennial discourse—was anything but original. In fact, the poem's success was probably due to the fact that Longfellow followed an already well-established tradition of Revolutionary War poetry that sought to appeal to readers' emotions rather than to their reason. Indeed, as historian Michael Kammen has suggested, Longfellow had numerous precursors who made a significant contribution to the way their contemporaries experienced and remembered the Revolution—among them Joel Barlow (1754–1812), David Humphreys (1752–1818), and Philip Freneau (1752–1832).[4] Whereas other scholars have focused on the epic poems of these three major Revolutionary-era poets, this chapter instead analyzes their more emotive work. It illustrates that they utilized the conventions of an emotive poetic genre—much as Longfellow would do at a later date—to memorialize personal experiences that they felt to be iconic to the Revolutionary moment and through which they could unify republican and millennial Revolutionary narratives.

In structuring his poem around the North Church tower in Concord, Boston, Longfellow can be said to have followed Emma Willard's "physicalist" theory of memory, as explored in Keith Beutler's chapter in this volume. Beutler illustrates how, according to Willard, "geographic locations" and "objects of sight" played a crucial role in constructing a collective memory of the Revolution. He discusses various cases, including one narrative in which a physical relic functioned as a teaching aid and a classroom textbook contained a first-person plural narrative about visiting General Washington's house and tomb. Beutler highlights the latter case as "most inspiring as a locus of memory." It is here that the narrative voice, through the association of ideas, is led toward a "rapid communion with the past, and with the spirits of the past," and thenceforth to intimations "of their immortality and our own!" What happens here is that while the historical events themselves remain locked in an irretrievable past, the young antebellum reader is putatively able to experience the same sublime feelings as Washington himself.[5]

In the 1820s Willard's "physicalism" constituted a new way of doing history, so to speak. Yet an understanding of how the human mind's associative powers were constantly constructing mental bridges between concrete physical objects, the feelings they impressed on the mind, and the memories they evoked had been a structural aspect within the literature of sensibility since the mid-eighteenth century.[6] Sensibility was understood as a physiological as much as a mental phenomenon. The human nervous system and human feelings were seen to be inherently intertwined.[7] The literature of sensibility centered on the expression of feeling and the cultivation of sympathy in direct relation to sense impressions received from external realities. The sorrowful plight of individuals often formed the basis for pathetic tableaux to which the reader could respond in sympathy and, through the natural association of ideas, be led toward acts of benevolence and charity.[8]

Unsurprisingly, the idea of visiting a tombstone or a graveyard to experience such fine, often transcendent, feelings became a specific literary convention within the broader literature of sensibility. Tombstones and graveyards were associated in the mind with human mortality and death, but within a Christian context they also suggested spiritual immortality and heavenly eternity. The publication of Edward Young's *Night Thoughts* (1742–46), followed shortly later by Robert Blair's *The Grave* (1743) and Thomas Gray's *Elegy Written in a Country Churchyard* (1751), established a popular genre of elegiac poetry, centered around visits to memorial sites, but characterized by a more general meditative exploration of earthly human suffering, pain, and woe rather than being concentrated on a specific, individual loss.[9] These poems were also marked by expressions of fear and desire for death, often culminating in a sublime vision of death as a personal revolution that will transform the suffering soul into a celestial spirit. As a consequence, the tone of much popular elegiac verse or graveyard poetry is celebratory, even if its imagery is funereal.[10] The wide range of contrasting emotions that can be expressed by juxtaposing graveyard imagery with millennial themes—fear and hope, sorrow and joy, pain and release—also explains why the genre was so popular during an age marked by a cult of sensibility, an evangelical revival, and political upheaval in Europe and America.

Joel Barlow was studying aesthetic and moral philosophy at Yale at the time that the literature of sensibility experienced a boom in popularity. He undoubtedly read Lord Kames's *Elements of Criticism* (1762)—an influential text in the development of the culture of sensibility.[11] In this work,

Norman Grabo has argued, Kames taught America's young intellectuals that "the fine arts were more than entertainment or recreative diversions, that they were significant expressions of human nature, especially of human passions," and as such no state could "wisely ignore the role of the fine arts in furthering political order."[12] Barlow clearly followed Kames when he took his passion for poetry with him into the political arena. During the Revolution he served as chaplain to the Continental Army. Later, while in Paris on a political mission, he helped publish Thomas Paine's *Age of Reason*. In 1796 he became the American consul at Algiers, before taking up the post of minister plenipotentiary in France in 1811. Throughout his political career Barlow wrote numerous public poems on the state of the nation, which gave him a "literary reputation [that] was uncritically high throughout the army," according to one scholar.[13] His most famous and overly political poem was *The Vision of Columbus* (1787), an "epic portrayal of the new American republic as the shining symbol of progressive history."[14]

Much of Barlow's Revolutionary verse drew on a popular neoclassic style, focused around an "Augustan warfare against corruption and social decline" and grounded in "a real sense that individuals and societies are constituted in an essential way by systems of ideas or perceptions, and that literature may intervene in this process in a decisive way."[15] In his *Elegy on the Late Honorable Titus Hosmer, Esq.* (1780), however, Barlow turned to elegiac and graveyard conventions to transform his private emotion of despair at the death of Titus Hosmer—a delegate to the Continental Congress, signer of the Articles of Confederation, and later a Connecticut senator, as well as Barlow's personal friend—into a public expression of hope: memorializing the millennial spirit he believed had been instrumental to the Revolutionary cause, while lamenting the death of one of its guiding republican lights.

As was customary in most graveyard poems, Barlow's speaker seeks out the graveyard as a landscape complementary to his state of mind and therefore best suited to set in motion the train of thought he desires to pursue in his melancholy mood. Just as antebellum schoolchildren could later visit Washington's tomb by reading elegies in their textbooks, Barlow visits the grave of Hosmer in his poem. Following graveyard conventions Barlow's speaker invokes the dead spirit of his friend and asks it to:

> Come on the gale that listening midnight heaves,
> When glare ey'd phantoms, bending with a bier,

Stalk thro' the mist, ascend the sounding graves,
And wake wild wonders in the startled ear.
(lines 21–24)[16]

Here, Barlow constructs a sublime scene in which phantoms are raised in the middle of a stormy night. Initially, the "dread scene" (25) painted is analogous to the dark state of mind of the speaker, who desires his soul "to mingle and to soar with thine" (28), suggestive of a death wish. Following a traditional elegiac pattern, the speaker's grief leads him to sympathize with the sorrow of Hosmer's wife and children. Yet an analysis of the imagery in stanza 16 shows that Barlow's rhetorical strategy yoked Hosmer's life and death to that of the nation as a whole, turning Hosmer into a metonym for the United States:

But thou alas! no more on earth wilt tread,
Nor one short hour thy blest employments leave,
Tho' the sad knell, that hail'd thee to the dead,
Had doom'd thy helpless country to her grave.
(61–64)

In these lines Barlow places the conventional funereal imagery of the tolling bell, which most often functions to make public the death of an individual, in a pivotal position within the stanza. In addressing Hosmer directly, the first two lines stress the speaker's private grief. By contemplating the public sounds of the tolling bell, the speaker effectively transforms Hosmer's death into an emblem of the demise of the colonies, for which he, as a key representative, fought so many political battles.

The personification used in the opening lines of stanza 17 consolidates this shift from private grief to public concern:

Thy country, whose still supplicating moan,
Implores thy counsels with an infant cry.
(65–66)

By personifying the United States as a suffering child, and thereby identifying all patriots with Hosmer's bereaved children, Barlow grants his mentor mythic proportions, venerating him as father of the nation. For readers unfamiliar with Hosmer the person, this conflation enables a shared memory of a Revolutionary hero.

Barlow goes so far as to memorialize Hosmer as a prophet of a Christian utopia, an American Moses whose vision had persuaded the Senate of "their sure salvation" (108). By casting Hosmer as a biblical prophet of the new Eden, a guiding light for the United States, Barlow overcomes any personal emotions of grief and produces a vision of the American people united by feelings of heroic patriotism and a shared political goal:

> Let thy own wisdom's ever beaming light
> Illume their well-known dignity of soul,
> Let thy benevolence their hearts unite,
> and every voice, and every wish control.
>
> (113–16)

The release of Hosmer's soul from a corrupt physical body into the divine celestial sphere functions in this poem as a symbolic representation of the United States' transformation from oppressed colony to a new Promised Land. Even after death Hosmer's role remains that of a father-figure prophet, as the speaker asks for "blest approvance [sic]" (97) for the deeds of "our laurel'd heroes striving for the day" (94) among "the confus'd uproar" (89) in the "towns curl'd in smoaky columns mounting high" (90), destroyed in the name of the earlier disowned father figure: King George.

As a divine prophet who guided Americans with "his unseen hand . . . thro' the dark paths" (219–20) and could "make the person as the place divine" (160), the spirit of Hosmer, as God's right-hand man, has the power to:

> Unfold to their keen penetrating view,
> What to the infant empire should be known,
> That worlds' and ages' happiness or woe,
> Hang on th' important issue of their own.
>
> (121–24)

In this stanza Barlow's elegy for Hosmer reveals itself to be in fact a highly emotionally charged appeal to the reader: to remember the Revolution as a seminal event in a larger millennial movement, the success or failure of which would determine the establishment of a worldwide Christian utopia. The elegy is rhetorically powerful, not in its expression of private grief for the death of a respected mentor but in how it constructs an image of Hosmer as a prophet of the Promised Land, who will counsel future generations of Americans from his seat in heaven so that they will establish the new Eden.

In 1793 Elihu Hubbard Smith included Barlow's elegy in the first major anthology of American poetry: *American Poetry: Selected and Original.* This anthology also featured David Humphrey's *Elegy on Lieutenant De Hart,* analyzed later in this chapter. The inclusion of both poems in this volume ensured them a wide readership in the early republic, allowing them to perform the cultural work of memorializing the Revolution as a millennial event and casting its republican heroes as martyrs in a sacred cause.[17]

Like Barlow, David Humphreys was a Yale graduate and had served in the Revolutionary Army. Humphreys became a colonel and later aide-de-camp to George Washington. Also like Barlow, Humphreys became a diplomat after the Revolution. He was ambassador to Portugal and Spain. His first major poem, Addressed to the Armies of the United States of America (1780), like Barlow's The Prospect of Peace, was distributed throughout the army and "enthusiastically read by many officers and soldiers."[18] Multiple editions of his georgic poem *On the Happiness of America* were published on both sides of the Atlantic. One reviewer of this pastoral idyll called it a production of "American genius," highlighting the author's "truly patriotic soul" and the "genuine poetic fire" of his mind.[19] Such praise shows that apart from being a military and political figure and an ideological poet during the Revolution, Humphreys was also thought to be a man of feeling.

Humphreys followed Barlow in adapting the elegiac mode and graveyard aesthetics to transform a singular Revolutionary event into a collective memory of a moment of patriotic martyrdom. In a classic study of the early Connecticut poets, Leon Howard acknowledged Humphreys's "genuine patriotism" and his services to the Revolutionary War effort but criticized the poet for the gloomy imagery and tone of his "Elegy on Lieutenant De Hart" (1788). According to Howard, the poet "was so solemn about his patriotism and the subject seemed to him so grave that he felt it entirely appropriate to call up 'visionary shapes,' 'red in their wounds,' before his readers in order to arouse their emotions—and it did not occur to him that the emotions aroused would not be proper ones."[20]

For contemporary readers of Humphreys's poem, this combination of melancholy and euphoria would have been a recognizable feature of some of the most frequently read graveyard poems of the time, as well as the often-reprinted work of prose *Meditations among the Tombs* (1746) by James Hervey.[21] The setting that Humphreys constructs,

When autumn all humid and drear,
With darkness and storms in his train,
Announc[es] the death of the year,
(lines 1–3)

would have been immediately recognizable as a typical graveyard setting, because it is congenial to the development of the melancholy, yet sublime theme explored: the martyrdom of a true American patriot.[22]

As such, it is no surprise that the decaying state of nature during autumn observed by the speaker would set in motion a train of thought on the theme of death. The associative qualities of a cold, wet, and dreary autumn day make the speaker stop and linger at the sight of a young woman mourning the loss of her brother. Rather than evoking negative emotions, the speaker claims that the scene arouses a "horror congenial" (5)—an affective oxymoron typical of graveyard poems. Readers in the 1780s and 1790s, familiar with the use of this stylistic convention in much of the fashionable poetry of the day, would not have considered "horror congenial" a paradox, because it expressed spontaneous feelings produced by the coming together of opposites through the natural association of ideas in the mind.

Once the graveyard scene and mood have been set, the speaker in the poem transforms into a spectator and listener: the lens through which the reader will observe and listen to De Hart's sister's lament. As in conventional elegies, the initial contemplation of the dead body of her brother, with its "visage . . . ghastly in death" (17), leads the young woman to praise De Hart's human qualities. These feelings of personal loss prompt the sister, through the natural association of ideas, to transform the event of his untimely demise from a tragic personal loss into a universal public symbol of the possible fate of all patriots.

In 1780, before the end of the Revolutionary War, Barlow had used graveyard conventions to cast Hosmer as the American Moses leading his people to freedom; in the process he worked through his own grief for the loss of his mentor. In 1788, after the establishment of the republic, Humphreys went one step further in sacralizing the Revolution by casting the relatively unknown Lieutenant De Hart as the American Christ. The sister dwells on the wound in his breast, which was "transpierced . . . with a ball" (13) and recollects the "red fountain . . . gushing in waves still and small [that] Distain'd his white bosom and side" (14–16). His sister recalls

His hair, that so lavishly curl'd,
I saw, as he lay on the heath,
In blood, and with dew-drops impearl'd.
(18–20)

By drawing together the image of a bloodstained corpse with that of morning dew—a traditional Christian image representing God's blessing, and as such a source of comfort—Humphreys reinforces the idea that De Hart's death is also a symbolic death in the broader context of the Revolution. The dew of heaven on his body will not only cleanse the bloody corpse but is a divine sign acknowledging that De Hart has sacrificed himself for a sacred cause. As such he becomes implicitly an emblem of the act of filicide for which King George is responsible.

As a Yale graduate Humphreys would have been familiar with the distinction that philosophers made at the time between the concepts of emotion and passion. In *Elements of Criticism,* for instance, Kames defined emotions as experiences in the mind that passed away without arousing desire. Passions, by contrast, were emotions that engendered a desire in the feeling subject. Kames called desire "that internal impulse which makes us proceed to action."[23] In his poem Humphreys follows this distinction between emotion and passion. At the very moment when the sister seems at her most melancholy, contemplating her brother as a wilted blossom, the tone of despair changes into one of defiance, not against death—which was common in more conventional elegies—but rather against the forces that have killed De Hart: the British Army. By musing on her brother's ruined prospects, the sister is led to remember the "rapture" with which he had looked on nature and the passion he had felt for his own country, which had been the reason behind his taking up arms in the first place. De Hart's passion for his country, which had arisen out of a love for its natural beauty, is described as literally running through his veins in the seventh stanza. De Hart's passion has made him one with the land, arousing in him a natural patriotism, a desire to defend his own body and the soil to which it is bound.

By constructing De Hart's death as an act of martyrdom, and his grave as a symbolic site of the king's act of filicide, Humphreys transforms the sister's personal emotions of despair into positive passions. Rather than expressing resignation—often a feature of conventional elegies—she calls on her brother's fellow "heroes" (63) to "come weep o'er this sorrowful urn" (58), not to mourn his death but to "ease the full heart with a tear"

(59) and to let themselves be impassioned to "defend the same cause" (63) and "avenge, with your country, his death" (64).

In the closing stanza, the speaker, who had initially introduced and then observed the scene, once again speaks in his own voice and makes it explicit that viewing, listening to, and sympathizing with De Hart's sister has ignited his own patriotic zeal. Because this speaker also represents the eyes and ears of the reader, his perspective and interpretation of the scene determines to a large extent the reader's emotional response. Humphreys must have hoped that, along with his fictional speaker, the patriotism of his readers would also be fired up and their passion moved to lead them into action against "the guards of the foe" (70).

Poems such as "The Rising Glory of America," "American Liberty," and "America Independent" turned Philip Freneau (1752–1832) into the poet of the Revolution.[24] But Philip Freneau's biographers have struggled to present him as a patriot.[25] In the years leading up to the Revolution, Freneau studied theology and law and had expressed hopes for accommodation rather than a desire for independence. He had planned a trip to England to take Orders, but when the Revolution broke out, he chose instead to sail to the West Indies, leaving behind his family, friends, and Washington's troops to face the guards of the foe without him. As a youth Freneau, like Barlow and Humphreys, admired Horace and the neoclassic poetry of Alexander Pope. His early poem "The Rising Glory of America" fits into the same category as Barlow's and Humphreys's Augustan poems expounding republican ideology. Importantly, after his return from the West Indies and after experiencing the war directly, Freneau's style became much more emotionally charged and his scenes at times graphically disturbing, especially when it came to depicting America's greatest foe, George III.

Freneau's most harrowing Revolutionary experience was his imprisonment on the prison ship *The Scorpion*, which left him lying seriously ill on the decks of the dilapidated hospital ship *The Hunter*. A close reading of the poems that chronicle this traumatic Revolutionary experience demonstrates that, like Barlow and Humphreys, Freneau also turned to the conventions of graveyard poetry to express his personal feelings of fear, pain, and suffering at the hands of the British; feelings he believed many of his fellow Americans had similarly endured during the Revolution. As with Barlow and Humphreys, Freneau found a way of working through his traumatic experience by defining the Revolution as a sacred cause, a rhetorical strategy that simultaneously justified the often aggressive and violent imagery he used to describe the Revolution.

In *Sensibility and the American Revolution,* Sarah Knott shows that motifs from the popular literature of sensibility played a significant role during the Revolutionary era as a discourse through which American patriots could eventually justify violent actions taken against the British. Sentimental narratives were almost always domestic narratives concerned with familial harmony. Their plots often revolved around the overcoming of injustices perpetrated by unfeeling or unreasonable patriarchs. Knott discusses various instances during the Revolution in which sentimental motifs such as virtue in distress (America as the land of liberty and justice), the virtuous man of sensibility (the republican patriot), the patriarchal tyrant (King George III), as well as the benevolent father (George Washington) were important rhetorical concepts through which patriots, sometimes individually and at other times collectively, differentiated themselves from the British, who were in turn cast in the role of villain. Knott argues that both republican ideology as well as sentimental culture advocated a harmony between feeling and reason that kept violent passions in check, which presented a problem with respect to the obvious violent resistance that Americans had put up against British rule since the mid-1770s. Knott explains, however, that "the insistent patriot claim to sensibility worked to deflect from the violence of the war throughout its course." As long as patriots cast themselves in the role of men and women of sensibility, who sympathized with the sorrowful plight of all those who suffered during the Revolution, they were "not accomplices . . . not inhumane." In this way, according to Knott, "sensibility might compensate for the most violent figuration of war: patricide or regicide."[26]

In the 1786 version of his graveyard poem "The House of Night," Freneau utilized the concept of sympathy, as it was understood within the culture of sensibility, to transform America's symbolic act of regicide into an act of benevolence, by casting King George III in the role of Death, a horseman of the apocalypse, and a representative American republican as his deathbed confessor. To transform what had hitherto been a popular genre of religious meditative poetry into a political allegory, Freneau set out to literalize much of the metaphoric imagery of traditional graveyard poems.

Part of the pleasure experienced during melancholy graveyard musings at midnight, graveyard poets implied, was the fact that when the optic nerves are at rest in darkness, the mind's eye can see all the more clearly into the human soul, which can thus reveal the mysteries of God's creation.

By contrast, in "The House of Night" the speaker's first words are "Trembling I write my dream" (1). Rather than stressing a metaphysical theme, Freneau foregrounds the physical state of the speaker. Just as he had stressed at the outset of canto 2 of "The British Prison-Ship" that he would not let his own physical and mental frailties stop him from shooting his "best arrows" at the English "hell-hounds" (8), so too do the opening stanzas of "The House of Night" ring with a tone of defiance, as the trembling speaker recollects a "fearful vision" (2) of a "malignant power" (4).[27] The emotive adjectives highlight Freneau's interest in exploring the relationship between arbitrary authority and individual suffering, rather than peace in the grave and ecstasy in heaven.

"Fancy" (16), a soothing force to most speakers in graveyard poetry, which leads them along the path of pleasurable melancholy, plays a "wild delusive part" (18) in Freneau's poem and introduces only a living nightmare to the speaker's eyes. During his prison-ship experience Freneau had suffered from a raging fever that "revel'd through [his] veins" (2.186), while he lay on deck among the sick, the dying, and the dead. Freneau confessed how a vision of his keepers still haunted his sight long afterward. In Freneau's vision the Hessians and Scots are slaves to the English generals, who in turn are portrayed as demons: Satan's henchmen. Freneau's prison-ship poem is one of the many texts documenting traumatic personal experiences of the Revolution that James Paxton and William Huntting Howell also explore in their chapters in this volume.[28] Such texts are often repressed by the grand narratives of history, and it is not surprising therefore that of all of Freneau's Revolutionary poetry it is his most private and emotional responses that are least studied today.

One of the reasons why "The British Prison-Ship" is today less well known than "The Rising Glory of America" is that it was primarily conceived to expose the cruelty of the British toward the colonists and as such is overly subjective. On top of this, it is filled with phantasmagoric descriptions of hellish soldiers inhabiting a surreal environment, which highlights the extent to which the delirious Freneau had trouble distinguishing sober reality from mental delusion during his imprisonment. This lack of objectivity does not make the experience any less real, however, as the nightmarish style of "The British Prison-Ship" informed much of Freneau's later poetry on the Revolution, especially the poems he revised in light of this experience, such as "The House of Night" and "George the Third's Soliloquy."

In the 1786 version of "The House of Night," Freneau expanded his description of the graveyard setting, adding four new quatrains. Most striking in these new stanzas is the use of negative terminology: flowers "ceas'd to rise" (50), "withdrew" (51) their bloom, or "quench'd" (52) their many vibrant colors. The sound effects in the phrase "weeping willows grew" (58) are rhetorically powerful, as they suggest that this domain is a place where only negative emotions bloom. Freneau also personifies the tombstones, now marked by "strains of woe" and "lamented for the dead that slept below" (66–68). While in conventional graveyard poems such a midnight scene is portrayed as facilitating the speaker's turn inward toward the soul and upward toward heaven, the negative diction used in Freneau's description highlights the graveyard as a site of physical decay only. It literally becomes a gateway toward the house of Death.

Significantly, Death, with his "fleshless limbs" (100), is accompanied by all sorts of personifications of suffering:

> Around his bed, by the dull flambeaux' glare,
> I saw pale phantoms—Rage to madness vext,
> Wan, wasting grief, and ever musing care,
> Distressful pain, and poverty perplexed.
>
> (105–8)

What is striking about this otherwise generic personification of Death is that the human passions and distresses on which Death traditionally feeds have become distressed themselves because of their master's imminent demise. Such a melodramatic rendering of Death foregrounds the sense of chaos that characterized Freneau's Revolutionary experience.

In the earlier prison-ship poem Freneau had identified the British specifically as the harbingers of chaos, comparing them to a pack of "famish'd wolves" (2.17) preying on their own kind. His description of the soldiers as "these sons of death" (2.51) implies that Freneau had come to envision George III as the earthly embodiment of the grim reaper. Important here is how Freneau used the aesthetics of graveyard poetry to work through his own traumatic experience of having suffered physical and mental pain on board of a British prison and hospital ship, with the ultimate aim of exacting poetic justice on the monarch he believed responsible for his and his country's suffering.

Within the narrative patterns of the conventional graveyard poems, speakers can take their "pensive way . . . down to the gloom" (3.23) of Death's realm in safety, because Death will always be defeated at the Second Coming of Christ. Earthly suffering is merely a trial to be endured before temporary incarceration in the grave will lead to the new life in heaven. In "The House of Night," Death is cast as an invader, however, who has used force to intrude into the "sequestered dome" (135) in which Cleon, the original occupant, had "sweetly slept" (134). Cleon now weeps because his home has been usurped by a tyrant but also because he simultaneously feels sympathy for Death, who reveals that he is dying. Like a good Christian and man of feeling, Cleon approaches his enemy as a "brother" (138) whom he " 'tended faithful round his gloomy bed" (139). Freneau's characterization of Cleon as the sympathetic sufferer illustrates Knott's contention that the identity of the American Revolutionaries was suffused with sensibility. It is important that Cleon stand morally above Death, who desires only to kill and has gone mad at the idea of his own mortality. Even though Death is his greatest enemy, it is Cleon's Christian duty that he do the best he can to alleviate the suffering of his adversary.

In a lengthy speech Cleon reveals to Death that he has already taken from him his beloved Aspasia, who is described in the same way that Lucian had described his Aspasia: as an intelligent, beautiful, and, above all, influential woman. If Cleon's lover embodies the virtues of the classical Aspasia, then the youth himself is Freneau's version of Pericles, the famous Athenian statesman and general who fostered democracy, literature, and the arts: a true embodiment of classical republicanism and a model for the American patriot.

In "The British Prison-Ship" Freneau had used classical allusions to make direct political statements. For instance, he described *The Scorpion* as Pandora's box (2.101). The allusion to Aspasia and thus implicitly to Pericles, her lover, foregrounds the latent political allegory running under the graveyard narrative. Death confesses to Cleon that he "came . . . to conquer—not to die" (220). Contemporary readers of Freneau's poetry would have been familiar with his description of the English as a legion of devils in the "The British Prison-Ship," who

> pant to stain the world with gore,
> And millions murder'd, still would murder more;

They are a "selfish race" who "perpetual discord spread throughout mankind" and who "aim to extend their empire o'er the ball" and to "subject, destroy, absorb and conquer all" (3.201–7). Reading "The House of Night," these same readers would have understood this poem's imagery and would not have been surprised to find George III cast as heir to Death's throne.

Allen Andrews has pointed out that in the period leading up to the Revolution, "it was King George III who was always pushing his ministers to re-establish full authority over America." Through his political battles with John Wilkes and Samuel Adams, George III developed "an obsessional personal vendetta against Wilkes" as well as against the colonists, to the extent that it was reported that " 'the King hates most cordially every American because he thinks they have an attachment to their Liberty,' " and he demands "unconditional subjection of the American people." Freneau's allegorical portraits of the English and their king as the heirs to Death and his demons are clearly in line with this popular prejudice of the period.[29]

As if fearing that his readers might mistake "The House of Night" as merely another fashionable poem on death and the afterlife, Freneau explicitly reveals the political allegory when the fast-withering Death passes on his command to "George my deputy" (348). The six stanzas that follow George's promotion to rider of the pale horse are crucial to understanding Freneau's emotional response to his traumatic prison ship experience. Freneau constructs a melodramatic scene in which Death first has his coffin measured while he reminisces about his friendship with Satan. Significantly, he then asks for the coffin to be made strong enough to withstand any attempt by the Devil to open it and retrieve his remains. This turn of events suggests that Cleon's speech has reformed Death on his deathbed. The once all-powerful destroyer of humans now laments his past actions. If Death realizes that "hell is my inheritance" (369), then the power that George III has just inherited is a curse.

In the 1786 edition of "George the Third's Soliloquy," Freneau again uses the metaphor of the king as Death to memorialize the Revolution as a sacred war between the followers of God and those of Satan. The poem opens with George III asking himself,

> What mean these dreams, and hideous forms that rise
> Night after night, tormenting to my eyes—
> No real foes these horrid shapes can be,
> But thrice as much they vex and torture me.[30]

Freneau portrayed George III as suffering from mental illness even though the king's symptoms had not yet been officially revealed. Freneau's portrayal of George III as overwhelmed with guilt and mentally unstable is entirely in line with Knott's contention that within the late eighteenth-century culture of sensibility, violence was linked to unreason and barbarity. Most important, in both the 1786 editions of "George the Third's Soliloquy" and "The House of Night," Death as the king, or the king as Death, are portrayed as guilt-stricken sufferers, whose thirst for dominion has driven them to despair. King George laments with Death:

> How cursed is he—how doubly cursed am I—
> Who lives in pain, and yet who dares not die.
>
> (5–6)

The King of England, as Death personified, now knows what Freneau himself had suffered on *The Scorpion*, their positions as tormentor and sufferer are reversed.

The public neoclassic-style poems of the Revolutionary period remain useful documents for studying the political discourses that vied for dominance in the early republic. When it came to memorializing the Revolution, however, overtly emotional poetic genres aimed at a wider, popular reading audience also conducted important cultural work. By turning toward the conventions of popular religious verse forms defined by their emotional rhetoric, these poets were able not only to express their own personal feelings of loss, pain, suffering, and rage but also to cast the political and military struggle into a form that highlighted their personal belief that the historical event was in fact a sacred one.

NOTES

1. Robert Pinsky, "Poetry and American Memory," *Atlantic Monthly*, October 1999, 60–61.
2. See Michael A. McDonnell's chapter, "War and Nationhood: Founding Myths and Historical Realities," in this volume.
3. Henry Wadsworth Longfellow, "Paul Revere's Ride," in *The Poetical Works of Henry Wadsworth Longfellow* (London: Collins, n.d.), 257–61.
4. Michael Kammen, *A Season of Youth: The American Revolution and the Historical Imagination* (New York: Knopf, 1978), chap. 4.
5. Keith Beutler, "Emma Willard's 'True Mnemonic of History,'" in this volume.

6. See Martin Kallich, *The Association of Ideas and Critical Theory in Eighteenth-Century England* (The Hague: Mouton, 1970), chap. 1.
7. See George S. Rousseau, *Nervous Acts: Essays on Literature, Culture and Sensibility* (Basingstoke: Palgrave, 2004), 32–68.
8. For an analysis of the literature of sensibility, see G. J. Barker-Benfield, *The Culture of Sensibility* (Chicago: University of Chicago Press, 1992). The best study of graveyard poetry as a genre is Eric Parisot, "The Paths of Glory: Authority, Agency and Aesthetics in Mid-Eighteenth-Century Graveyard Poetry" (PhD diss., University of Melbourne, 2008), forthcoming as a monograph published by Ashgate.
9. See Stephen Cornford, ed., *Edward Young's Night Thoughts* (Cambridge: Cambridge University Press, 1989); James A. Means, ed., *Robert Blair's The Grave* (Los Angeles: Augustan Reprint Society, 1973) and Thomas Gray, *Elegy Written in a Country Churchyard* (New York: Heritage Press, 1951). On top of the countless British editions of *Night Thoughts, The Grave*, and Gray's *Elegy*, the Library Company lists twelve Philadelphia, eight New York, seven Hartford, and various others editions of *Night Thoughts* published in America between 1777 and 1847. The first American edition of *The Grave* was published in New York in 1753; seven more editions appeared in Philadelphia, Newbury Port, and Elizabeth Town. Gray's *Elegy* went through five official editions in Britain during the first year of its publication alone and was frequently printed alongside *The Grave* throughout the eighteenth century. In America, editions of *The Grave* that included Gray's *Elegy* appeared in Boston in 1772 and in Philadelphia in 1773 and 1786. The poem was also reprinted in American periodicals such as *The Gentlemen and Ladies' Town and Country Magazine* (September 1789) and the third issue of *the Literary Miscellany* (1795).
10. See Evert Jan van Leeuwen, "Funeral Sermons and Graveyard Poetry: The Ecstasy of Death and Bodily Resurrection," *Journal for Eighteenth-Century Studies* 32, no. 3 (2009): 353–72.
11. Norman S. Grabo, "The Cultural Effects of the Revolution," in *The Blackwell Encyclopedia of the American Revolution*, ed. Jack P. Greene and J. R. Pole (Oxford: Blackwell, 1994), 580; Lord Kames, *Elements of Criticism*, 3 vols. (New York: Johnston, 1967). Leon Howard points out that cheap editions of Kames's *Elements of Criticism* were advertised in 1770; see *The Connecticut Wits* (Chicago: University of Chicago Press, 1943), 26. Terence Martin underscores the widespread popularity of this text in intellectual circles in *The Instructed Vision: Scottish Common Sense Philosophy and the Origins of American Fiction* (Bloomington: Indiana University Press, 1961), 19.
12. Grabo, "Cultural Effects of the Revolution," 580–81.
13. Howard, *Connecticut Wits*, 143.
14. Joel Barlow, *The Vision of Columbus* (Hartford, Conn.: Hudson & Goodwin, 1787); William C. Dowling, *Poetry and Ideology in Revolutionary Connecticut* (Athens: University of Georgia Press, 1990), 1. George Washington sponsored the publication of *The Vision of Columbus* by ordering twenty copies in advance; other "sponsors" were Lafayette, Benjamin Franklin, Alexander Hamilton, Thomas Paine, and Aaron Burr. In 1807 it was expanded and retitled *The Columbiad*. Barlow's significance as an early American political writer is supported by the inclusion of

several of his pieces in the anthology *American Political Writing during the Founding Era*, ed. Charles S. Hyneman and Donald S. Lutz (Indianapolis: Liberty Press, 1983) and of a lemma in *Blackwell Encyclopedia*.

15. Dowling, *Poetry and Ideology*, xv. For other accounts of early American poetry as primarily neoclassic in style and public in nature, see Jay Parini, ed., *The Columbia History of American Poetry* (New York: Columbia University Press, 1993); and Michael T. Gilmore, "Poetry," in *The Cambridge History of American Literature*, ed. Sacvan Bercovich, vol. 1 (Cambridge: Cambridge University Press, 1994), 591–619.
16. Joel Barlow, *Elegy on the Late Honorable Titus Hosmer Esq.* (Hartford, Conn.: Hudson & Goodwin, 1780).
17. Elihu Hubbard Smith, ed., *American Poems, Selected and Original* (Litchfield, Conn.: Collier & Buel, 1793).
18. Joel Barlow, *The Prospect of Peace* (New Haven, Conn.: Thomas & Samuel Green, 1778). Frank Landon Humphreys, *Life and Times of David Humphreys*, 2 vols. (New York: Putnam, 1917), 1:148. After the success of the first edition of this poem, Humphreys revised and published it—with his name on the title page—as *A Poem Addressed to the Armies of the United States of America* (London: Kearsley, 1785). This edition and a French translation, published in 1786, received positive reviews. The final version of the poem was published in the *American Museum*, March 1787. See Humphreys, *Life and Times*, 2:314–17.
19. Anonymous Reviewer, "Remarks on 'The Happiness of America,'" *Columbian Magazine* 1, no. 2 (October 1786): 67–69.
20. Howard, *Connecticut Wits*, 117.
21. James Hervey, *Meditations among the Tombs* (London: J. & J. Rivington, 1746).
22. David Humphreys, "An Elegy, on Lieutenant De Hart," *American Museum* 3, no. 3 (March 1788): 273–74.
23. Kames, *Elements of Criticism*, 1:55.
24. Philip Freneau, "The Rising Glory of America" (1772), "American Liberty" (1775), and "America Independent" (1809), in *The Poems of Philip Freneau*, ed. Fred Lewis Pattee, 3 vols. (Princeton: The University Library, 1902–7), 1:49–83, 1:142–51, 1:271–83. The anthologies *Poems on American Affairs* (New York: Longworth, 1815) and the posthumous *Poems relating to the American Revolution* (New York: Widdleton, 1865) helped to establish this reputation.
25. See, for instance, Mary Weatherspoon Bowden, *Philip Freneau* (Boston: Twayne, 1976).
26. Sarah Knott, *Sensibility and the American Revolution* (Chapel Hill: University of North Carolina Press, 2009), 191–92.
27. Philip Freneau, "The House of Night" (1786), in *Poems of Philip Freneau*, 1:212–39. Freneau, "The Prison-Ship," ibid., 2:18–38.
28. James Paxton, "Remembering and Forgetting: War, Memory, and Identity in the Post-Revolutionary Mohawk Valley," and William Huntting Howell, "'Starving Memory': Antinarrating the American Revolution," both in this volume.
29. Allen Andrews, *The King Who Lost America: George III and Independence* (London: Jupiter, 1976), 130, 157, 160.
30. Freneau, "George the Third's Soliloquy" (1786), in *Poems of Philip Freneau*, 2:3–6.

"Starving Memory"

Antinarrating the American Revolution

William Huntting Howell

Like so many wars of the distant past, the American Revolution narrates beautifully in the popular imagination. There is a beginning: April 1775—what Ralph Waldo Emerson calls "the shot heard round the world"—in which a once-reluctant and economically diverse populace beats its ploughshares into swords.[1] There is a set of progressive middles, unfolding against now-hallowed spaces: independence is declared in Philadelphia, epic battles are fought at Bunker Hill, at Saratoga, at Trenton, at Cowpens, at Yorktown. There are colorful heroes—George Washington, Ethan Allen, the Marquis de Lafayette, Tadeusz Kosciuszko, Casimir Pulaski—who rise to their various occasions; there are villains—King George, Lord Cornwallis, Lord North, Benedict Arnold, Banastre Tarleton—who fall victim to their various fates. Running through it all are thematic leitmotifs: taxation without representation is tyranny; death is preferable to political slavery; the colonies constitute, and of right ought to be, a free and independent nation. And then, finally, there is the sense of an ending: Cornwallis surrenders at Yorktown in October 1781; two years later the Peace of Paris puts a formal end to the war and establishes the United States of America. There are many ways to tell the story—different personnel, different motive forces, different perspectives on the ultimate outcomes—but the essential plot (and plottedness) remains the same. The Revolution fits narrative patterns that we recognize—the flows of conflict and resolution, of call and response, of change over time.

As devoted to such narrative patterns as we are—they allow us to make sense of the past, to forge *history* from the unfathomable welter of time gone by—we must also recognize their essential artificiality; they are products of historiography, not intrinsic features of the events themselves. And these narrative patterns are anything but neutral or disinterested: different frames for events lead to different senses of the whole.[2] To borrow from Hayden White, these forms have a content; narrative constructions create the difference between "Revolution" and "Rebellion," between "freedom fighting" and "terrorism."[3] As such stark oppositions suggest, historical stories and their forms claim an enormous amount of cultural power. In the United States the narrative elegance of the Revolution has for quite some time slotted neatly into (or emerged out of) persistent fantasies of American exceptionalism: the deep telic structure of the journey from colonial discontent through gallant war fighting to a new, legally constituted United States—not to mention the spontaneous popular rejection of monarchical rule in favor of representative democracy—confirms the essential unity of the "American" people and the unique importance of the U.S. project. Pace some important dissenting voices (from S. G. Fisher to Howard Zinn), for the most part it has been a short, bright line from conventional histories of the Revolution to a largely triumphalist foreign and domestic policy: varieties of American exceptionalist storytelling have provided philosophical cover for everything from the continuation of racial slavery, Indian removal, and anti-immigrant riots to the prosecution of the Cold War and the Bush Doctrine.[4]

But not every version of the Revolution story serves such heroic-nationalist ends. Joseph Plumb Martin's *Narrative of Some of the Adventures, Dangers, and Sufferings of a Revolutionary Soldier*, first published in Hallowell, Maine, in 1830, offers both a counter-record of the facts of the war and a countermethod for relating them—a bimodal alternative to the exceptionalist paradigm.[5] Born in western Massachusetts in the fall of 1760 and raised largely by his grandparents in Connecticut, Martin enlisted as a private in the Continental Army at the age of fifteen. He was present for many of what we now think of as the Revolution's significant events. He saw action in the Battle of Brooklyn, the Battle of White Plains, the Battle of Kip's Bay; he encamped at Valley Forge during the winter of 1777. Promoted to sergeant in a sappers and miners regiment near the end of the war, he helped lay siege to Yorktown. When the army was dissolved in 1783, Martin settled on a farm in Downeast Maine. He did not prosper especially, but he married, served as a selectman and clerk for the town of Stockton (now Stockton Springs), and lived long enough to apply for a government pension of ninety-six dollars a year.[6] He wrote his memoir in the late 1820s—perhaps in response to the Jacksonian moment's resurgent interest in the aging Revolutionary generation or as a reply to the triumphalist fantasias of Lafayette's Grand Tour of 1824–25 or as a belated plea to enforce the Pension Act of 1818.[7] He published it anonymously, relatively locally (Hallowell lies about sixty miles west-southwest of Stockton), and with limited contemporary success; although we do not have evidence of the text's print run or its circulation, it seems to have existed only in that single edition during Martin's lifetime. Martin died, relatively poor and relatively obscure, in the spring of 1850.

If this version of Martin's biography suggests a familiar story arc of American heroism—the everyman who nobly sacrifices his youth for the sake of his country, who takes up arms and then retires to obscurity and rural quiet—his autobiography follows a rather less familiar one. As Martin says in his preface, the *Narrative* will

> give a succinct account of some of my adventures, dangers and sufferings during my several campaigns in the revolutionary army. My readers, (who, by the by, will, I hope, none of them be beyond the pale of my own neighbourhood,) must not expect any great transactions to be exhibited to their notice, "No alpine wonders thunder through my tale," but they are here, once for all, requested to bear it in mind, that they are not the achievements of an officer of high grade which they are perusing, but the common transactions of one of the lowest in station in an army, a private soldier. (1)

As a corrective to the endlessly circulating stories of soldiering that center on the merits of the elite (as in Mason Locke Weems's hagiography of George Washington) or that offer novel-ready derring-do (as in James

Fenimore Cooper's *The Spy*, published in 1821), Martin's *Narrative* recalls the everyday drudgery of an enlisted man.[8] Setting aside "alpine wonders" in favor of what Catherine Kaplan characterizes as the "picaresque," Martin finds heroism in the endurance of poverty, cold, hunger, boredom, confusion, and mismanagement; he shifts the terms and the burdens of American virtue from the gentry to the commoner, from the purposeful hero to the undistinguished wanderer.[9]

But Martin's memoir does not merely question the grand narratives of the Revolution by speaking only to his "own neighbourhood" or by recalling in plain language the lives and times of persons without political or economic capital—elements continually obscured by the cult of celebrity around generals and statesmen, by republican ideas of the ennoblement of the citizen-soldier, and by Whiggish ideologies of American progress. More than simply offering different plots with different perspectives, Martin's counterstories work against the forms and rules of a totalizing *story* itself. For Martin, it seems that making narrative sense of the war is a privilege accorded only to the higher-ups and to the historians: to tell a clear, sequential tale about the confusing, recursive, and often-unspeakable hardships of actual fighting would be to mischaracterize entirely the actual soldier's experience. Put another way: for the sake of candor and for the sake of representing the powerless, Martin abandons not only conventional history but also the narrative conventions of historical writing.[10]

Such resistance is most visible in Martin's discussions of privation and plenty; his account, like Napoleon's army, marches (or fails to march) on the private soldier's stomach. In contrast to the breathless flows of other people's relations of the war (in eighteenth- and nineteenth-century histories such as Mercy Otis Warren's, David Ramsay's, or George Bancroft's), Martin is forever breaking from narrating linear sequences of events to recount shambling anecdotes and to record vivid (and static) sense-memories, especially those arising from being hungry. Hardly a paragraph goes by without a long and wistful digression on the acquisition of a particular chicken, a reverie about a jug of wine, or a rueful meditation on what it means to starve to death in the service of a nation that does not yet exist. In leaving behind the sweep of chronological organization and linear cause-and-effect to focus intently and repeatedly on timeless and cyclical matters of the belly, Martin urges his readers to think of war as a state absolutely incommensurable with coherent storytelling.

Martin begins his recollections of the Revolution with his own entrance into it. Intrigued by tales of adventure and heroism that far outstrip life on his grandfather's farm in Connecticut, the teenaged Martin enlists in the Continental Army.[11] His regiment departs for New York City, where it is to meet up with several others for the purpose of defending the city from the gathering British armies. It takes only a few weeks as a soldier for the adventure stories in Martin's fancy to be proven false: Martin's first taste of the conflict is not long in coming, but it takes a somewhat surprising form.

> The [Continental] soldiers at New-York had an idea that the enemy, when they took possession of the town, would make a general seizure of all property that could be of use to them as military or commissary stores, hence they imagined that it was no injury to supply themselves when they thought they could do so with impunity, which was the case of my having any hand in the transaction I am going to relate. . . . I was stationed in Stone-street, near the southwest angle of the city; directly opposite to my quarters was a wine cellar, there were in the cellar at this time, several pipes of Madeira wine. By some means the soldiers had "smelt it out." Some of them had, at mid-day, taken the iron grating from a window in the back yard, and one had entered the cellar, and by means of a powder-horn divested of its bottom, had supplied himself, with wine, and was helping his comrades, through the window, with a "delicious draught." (19–20)

There is more here than just the deep cynicism of ordinary soldiers imagining a battle already lost and acting accordingly. As the big story of the British invasion gives way to the immediate problem of satisfying the desires of the belly, the scene distills the narratively difficult relationship between personal appetite and political violence that runs through Martin's book. The Continental soldier's fear of armed occupation, as Martin has it, translates into a fear of starvation; the advent of the British Army promises not only military or ideological confrontation, but a grave threat to the distribution and enjoyment of rations. Martin and his colleagues resist this worry the only way they can—by immediately and immoderately consuming whatever stores they come across. That such actions traduce notions of the sanctity of private property and liberal consent so often held up as central to the story of the American cause is evidently a matter of no importance whatsoever to the soldiers themselves: they have a thirst for wine, they smell it out, and they turn housebreakers. Indeed, in what amounts to a complete reversal of the swords-to-ploughshares trope of the American soldier so dear to the generals and the historians, the men even convert their tools for fighting into utensils for gluttony; in a pinch, a decommissioned powder horn makes a fine goblet or wine funnel.[12]

As Martin's anecdote shambles on, the significance of this crowd action becomes clear: this war he finds himself a part of is, quite literally, out of control—its chaos cannot be managed in or through the settled rules and narratives of the marketplace or the military hierarchy. When the cellar's owner catches on, he decides to make a virtue of the depredation; he opens the cellar doors and sells the wine to all comers at a dollar per gallon. The soldiers are far from impressed.

> While the owner was drawing for his purchasers on one side of the cellar, behind him on the other side, another set of purchasers were drawing for themselves, filling . . . flasks. As it appeared to have a brisk sale, especially in the latter case, I concluded I would take a flask amongst the rest, which, I accordingly did, and conveyed it in safety to my room, and went back into the street to see the end. The owner of the wine soon found out what was going forward on his premises, and began remonstrating, but he preached to the wind; finding that he could effect nothing, with them, he went to Gen. [Israel] Putnam's quarters . . . ; the general immediately repaired in person to the field of action; the soldiers getting wind of his approach hurried out into the street, when he, mounting himself upon the door-steps of my quarters, began "harangueing [sic] the multitude," threatening to hang every mother's son of them. (20)

Denying the relevance of the owner's claims about his right to sell his commodities, Martin and his friends take what they want without regard for long-held economic conventions. They act as "purchasers" while pointedly resisting the symbolic necessities of purchase (the consensual disbursement of money or letters of credit) and the stories (about the value of currency or reputation, about the alienability of property) that those symbols structure. The same sort of antinarrative energy reveals itself in Martin's characterization of the ransacked wine cellar as a "field of action," both for himself and his general. Applying the formal language of military theory and history to drunken riot, Martin sets new terms for success in battle—maximum wine, minimum payment—that no commanding officer could accept. His ironic report (just like his reported action) upsets the platitudes of the historical record: heroism may be as simple as getting ripping drunk without getting in trouble; military leadership may consist in threatening into temporary submission the rogues under one's command.[13]

Indeed, Martin's reaction to his general officer's diatribe mixes awe, contempt, and a strong sense of the utter inconsequentiality—the ahistoricity—of it all:

> Whether he was to be the hangman or not, he did not say; but I took every word he said for gospel, and expected nothing else but to be hanged before the morrow night. I sincerely wished him hanged and out of the way, for fixing himself upon the steps of our door; but he soon ended his discourse, and came down from his rostrum, and the soldiers dispersed, no doubt much edified. I got home as soon as the general had left the coast clear, took a draught of the wine, and then flung the flask and the remainder of the wine out of my window, from the third story, into the water cistern in the back yard, where it remains to this day for aught I know. However, I might have kept it, if I had not been in too much haste to free myself from being hanged by General Putnam, or by his order. I never heard anything further about the wine or being hanged about it; he doubtless forgot it. (20–21)

Instead of the hero-exhorter of Bunker Hill (as he was popularly characterized, both during the war and in its wake), Putnam becomes a loudmouth buffoon—complete with ironically edified troops. The private worries enough about the possibility of a kernel of truth in the general's hangman bluster that he gets rid of his stolen wine, but not before he has taken a healthy swig. As Martin's abasement of Putnam begins to suggest, the meaninglessness of this breakdown in order—no one is actually hanged, the general forgets the incident entirely, and the private moves immediately on to the next formless adventure—is itself richly meaningful. The false, enduring pieties of official heroism and military glory will not be allowed to stand in Martin's text; the tightly structured moral and ideological fable of the great and just war must give way to the evanescence, raggedness, and literal amorality of sensual remembrance.

When Martin turns to recounting more well-known scrimmages of the war, his antinarrative priorities remain consistent. Consider his account of what he calls "the famous Kipp's Bay affair, which has been criticised so much by the Historians of the Revolution." Against totalizing history, he offers particular witness: "I was there," he tells his readers, "and will give a true statement of all that *I* saw during that day" (30). Like his somewhat shapeless wine-battle anecdote, Martin's version of the "affair" is both food-centered and skeptical about lucid plotting; as the text focuses on the trials of the stomach, it resists assimilation into historiographically stable narrative claims about the valor of the Americans.

> In retreating we had to cross a level clear spot of ground, forty or fifty rods wide, exposed to the whole of the enemy's fire; and they gave it to us in prime order; the grape shot and language flew merrily, which served to quicken our motions. When I had gotten a little out of reach of their combustibles, I found myself in company with one who was a neighbour of mine when at home, and one other man belonging to our regiment; where the rest of them were I knew not. We went into a house by the highway, in which were two women and some small children, all crying most bitterly; we asked the women if they had any spirits in the house; they placed a case bottle of rum upon the table, and bid us help ourselves. We each of us drank a glass, and bidding them good bye, betook ourselves to the highway again. (31–32)

This brand of nonchalance—bullets rarely fly "merrily" in the genres of the military history or the war memoir—is not, it seems, merely a consequence of Martin's battlefield cynicism. It is, rather, further evidence of the psychological and ideological priorities of the enlisted man—priorities in conflict with the overarching themes of Revolutionary historiography. Martin emphasizes fellowship constituted through proximity and happenstance instead of through military designation—he does not seem particularly upset about losing his regiment, so long as his neighbor and another never-named comrade are still around. More than this, he manifests little concern for the civilians that he finds: the women and children may be "crying most bitterly," but their sorrows pale in comparison with Martin's need for drink. It may be that the sympathy for countrymen that constitutes national feeling lies at the root of the women's gift of spirits (instead of, say, self-preservation in the face of three armed and uninvited guests), but an appeal to a narrative of American solidarity is nowhere in evidence in Martin's request. Putting his friendships and personal appetites and a kind of compulsory hospitality—not his patriotism or his courage or his devotion to the American cause—at the center of the story of his first battle, Martin works to unwrite the myth of Revolution as a product of incipient nationalism: social affiliation travels not under the sign of an Americanizing ideology but rather under the sign of bare life.

Soon after, Martin arrives at the site of a much-larger battle. "When I came to the spot where the militia were fired upon, the ground was literally covered with arms, knapsacks, staves, coats, hats and old oil flasks, perhaps some of those from the Madeira wine cellar, in New-York; all I picked up of the plunder, was a blocktin syringe, which afterwards helped to procure me a thanksgiving dinner" (32). What for other tellers might be a particularly poignant scene of battlefield desolation—of the material sacrifices demanded by a love of liberty, perhaps—represents for Martin a means for promoting another meal. Just as before, intimate needs and the modes (perhaps inglorious, perhaps merely incompatible with strict notions of glory) by which they may be met take precedence over symbolic grandiosity or historical synthesis.

The first in-depth account of Martin's own fighting follows hard on his depictions of the Battle of Kip's Bay. It begins with the sort of narrative description of an engagement typical of nineteenth-century war biography:

> In the forenoon, the enemy, as we expected, followed us "hard up," and were advancing through a level field; our rangers and some few other light troops, under the command of Colonel Knowlton, of Connecticut, and Major Leitch of (I believe) Virginia, were in waiting for them. Seeing them advancing, the rangers, &c. concealed themselves in a deep gully overgrown with bushes; upon the western verge of this defile was a post and rail fence, and over that the forementioned [sic] field. Our people let the enemy advance until they arrived at the fence, when they arose and poured in a volley upon them. How many of the enemy were killed and wounded could not be known, as the British were always as careful as Indians to conceal their losses. There were, doubtless, some killed, as I myself counted nineteen ball-holes through a single rail of the fence at which the enemy were standing when the action began. The British gave back and our people advanced into the field. The action soon became warm. Colonel Knowlton, a brave man, and commander of the detachment, fell in the early part of the engagement. It was said, by those who saw it, that he lost his valuable life by unadvisedly exposing himself singly to the enemy. (37–38)

Although his noncommissioned perspective is unusual, Martin otherwise performs perfectly here the duty of the conventional historical witness: he lays out a coherent story in which he records terrain, identifies important officers, acknowledges individual and collective bravery, aligns the enemy with inscrutable Otherness (in his remark about the British gathering their casualties like Indians), and recognizes patriotic sacrifice. As he continues, however, Martin's relish for such conventionality begins to fade.

> The men were very much fatigued and faint, having had nothing to eat for forty-eight hours,—at least the greater part were in this condition, and I among the rest. While standing on the field, after the action had ceased, one of the men near the Lieut. Colonel, complained of being hungry; the Colonel, putting his hand into his coat pocket, took out a piece of an ear of Indian corn, burnt as black as a coal, "Here," said he to the man complaining, "eat this and learn to be a soldier." (38)

Again diverting his descriptive energies from the larger narratives of combat—of ideals shared, territory contested, and lives lost—Martin lingers on the sensory experience of starving in the field. It is hunger that brings the "greater part" of these men together—and Martin "among the rest"—rather than ideological or political congruence. With his burned corn, the colonel reinforces the point: "eat this and learn to be a soldier." To be a Continental is not necessarily to believe in the sovereign right of a people to govern themselves, nor to stand up for American freedom, nor to engage the enemy, nor to make sense of the events of the war (or even, it seems, to pay them much mind) but rather to starve or eat terrible food without complaint.[14]

The recollection of this burned corn episode spurs Martin further still from the story of his formative skirmish: after returning to camp, he finds the "invalids" of his company to be "broiling . . . beef on small sticks, in Indian stile, round blazing fires, made of dry chestnut rails. The meat, when cooked, was as black as a coal on the outside, and as raw on the inside as if it had not been near the fire. 'I asked no questions, for conscience's sake,' but fell to and helped myself to a feast of this raw beef, without bread or salt." Martin's prior descriptions of military engagement pale in comparison with his descriptions of the beef, its preparation, and its consumption; measured in terms of detail, the emotional (and extranarrative, digressive) weight of the dinner far exceeds the emotional (and narrative) weight of the fighting. Only as an afterthought does he add the following: "We had eight or ten of our regiment killed in the action, and a number wounded, but none of them belonged to our company" (38–39).

Moments like this one proliferate: whenever the text threatens to fall neatly into a standard military story, Martin's appetite drags it back out. One of his most piquant memories (the one that gets the "starving memory" appellation from which this chapter takes its title) is of the "rice and vinegar thanksgiving" of 1777 (218). In Philadelphia, participating in the defense and eventual retaking of that city from the British, Martin watches the army and its livestock waste away to nothing. Then, at long last, the new national government intervenes—in a manner of speaking.

> While we lay here there was a Continental thanksgiving ordered by Congress; and as the army had all the cause in the world to be particularly thankful, if not for being well off, at least, that it was no worse, we were ordered to participate in it. We had nothing to eat for two or three days previous, except what the trees of the fields and forests afforded us. But we must now have what Congress said—a sumptuous thanksgiving to close the year of high living, we had now nearly seen brought to a close. Well—to add something extraordinary to our present stock of provisions, our country, ever mindful of the suffering army, opened her sympathizing heart so wide, upon this occasion, as to give us something to make the world stare. And what do you think it was, reader?—Guess.—You cannot guess, be you as much of a Yankee as you will. I will tell you: it gave each and every man half a gill of rice, and a table spoon full of vinegar!! After we had made sure of this extraordinary superabundant donation, we were ordered out to attend a meeting, and hear a sermon delivered upon the happy occasion. (87)

As in Martin's preface, we see the dissonance between the general officer's sense of the story of the war and that of the enlisted man: the wicked irony of the small amount of rice and vinegar as an "extraordinary superabundant donation"—and as evidence of the "sympathizing heart" of the "country"—makes the case clearly enough. Kaplan, quite rightly, casts this as a moment in which the higher-ups both mask "the economics of the soldier's bond" and make a case that "a compliant soldiery accept not only ill treatment but also the mystification of that ill treatment by the rhetoric of duty and benevolence."[15] Again, though, the structure of Martin's complaint is as important as its content: where Congress orders and declares, he defers and delays. His dashes and his rhetorical questions multiply out of narrative control. He pauses repeatedly, interrupting his story to embroider his ironies, to insert surplus phrases ("I will tell you"; "upon this occasion"), and to feign audience participation. In so doing, not only does he heighten the impact of the rice-and-vinegar denouement and suggest that congressional policy is better suited to shaggy-dog jokes than to linear histories, he also recreates in miniature the experience of privation. The reader, just as Martin himself, must wait and wait for closure—the tale recapitulates in its halting narrative form the problems of fighting in the Revolution: expectations are made to be frustrated, promises and rewards always just around the corner. As the grumbling stomach makes itself heard, the conventional narrative claims of a Revolutionary American nationalism are indefinitely suspended; the exigencies of hunger on the ground disrupt political theory and received historiographic convention.

Martin's account of the Campaign of 1782 rehearses a new variant in the galaxy of deprivation and narrative false starts. Lacking much else to do, Martin is sent with a couple of other men to track down a deserter in the New Jersey countryside. Martin prefaces his account of this adventure with a promise of its exceptionality: "And now, my dear reader, excuse me for being so minute in detailing this little excursion, for it yet seems to my fancy, among the privations of that war, like one of those little verdant plats of ground, amid the burning sands of Arabia, so often described by travellers" (214). This sense of an oasis of story in the desert of smooth descriptions of undifferentiated daily horror rapidly dissipates: the intriguing (and progressive) processes of tracking a man and returning him "to his duty" are forgotten immediately. By way of beginning this "little excursion" Martin recalls,

> One of our Captains and another of our men being about going that way on furlough [i.e., into New Jersey], I and my two men sat [sic] off with them. We received, that day, two or three rations of fresh pork and hard bread. We had no cause to call this pork "carrion" or "hogmeat," for, on the contrary, it was so fat, and being entirely fresh, we could not eat it at all. The first night of our expedition, we boiled our meat; and I asked the landlady for a little sauce, she told me to go to the garden and take as much cabbage as I pleased, and that, boiled with the meat, was all we could eat. (214–15)

The "setting off" is immediately postponed to discuss the state of the provisions received and the problems of cooking them; whatever narrative promise the "expedition" holds is subordinated to complex and static relations of appetite and to the niceties of eating and drinking. A day later and only a few miles down the road, Martin finds the same thing:

> In the morning, when we were about to proceed on our journey, the man of the house came into the room and put some bread to the fire to toast; he next produced some cider, as good and rich as wine, then giving each of us a large slice of his toasted bread, he told us to eat it and drink the cider,—observing that he had done so for a number of years and found it the best stimulater imaginable. (215–16)

Although there is a certain narrative progression—the bread turns into toast, the toast is distributed among the men, the toast is eaten and digested (with cider as a "stimulater" for the latter)—the larger story of the journey is deferred; the men are always "about to proceed," never actually proceeding.

Martin then supplies a series of punch lines:

> We again prepared to go on, having given up the idea of finding the deserter. Our landlord then told us that we must not leave his house till we had taken breakfast with him; we thought we were very well dealt by already, but concluded not to refuse a good offer. We therefore staid and had a genuine New-Jersey breakfast, consisting of buckwheat slapjacks, flowing with butter and honey, and a capital dish of chockolate [sic]. We then went on, determined not to hurry ourselves, so long as the thanksgiving lasted." (216)

Martin moves on to describe another breakfast the next day and a subsequent "hearty dinner" (217). In these reports of hospitality, the thread of the "excursion" peters out: as Martin's recollections continue, the project of finding the deserter—of recalling the wayward man to the requirements of "national" service—is now and forever absolutely abandoned. Instead, there are meals, recalled some fifty years after the fact with an enviable delight. The point here is clear: faced with choosing the potentially unnarratable joy of pancakes or the narrative pursuit of the overt ideological interests of his country, Martin opts for the pancakes.

For the past fifty years—ever since Little, Brown brought out George Scheer's edition of Martin's *Narrative* as *Private Yankee Doodle*—the text has been a staple of Revolutionary reading lists in schools. There are now multiple versions of Martin's life in print, including several intended for younger audiences (Jim Murphy's *A Young Patriot;* Peter and Connie Roop's *The Diary of Joseph Plumb Martin*). And Martin's afterlife is not just on the page: he shows up several times (played by Philip Seymour Hoffman) in the 1997 PBS miniseries *Liberty! The Story of the American Revolution;* he appears in PBS's animated *Liberty's Kids* (2002), voiced by quondam pop-star Aaron Carter. In all of these cases, Martin is a useful representative for the common soldier: his experience as a Continental adds visceral interest to what might otherwise be abstract political or military accounts; for middle-schoolers and war buffs alike, Martin's life humanizes the story of the American Revolution.[16] As I have hoped to show, though, there are ways in which Martin's text allows us to see how that story itself betrays complex depictions of on-the-ground humanity.

To frame some of the larger questions that Martin's antinarrative narrative can help us to ask—both about his historical moment and about our own—it may help to return to an apparently throwaway moment in the first lines of Martin's memoir, in which the potentially distorting and dehumanizing nature of stories is fully on display. "The heroes of all Histories, Narratives, Adventures, Novels and Romances, have, or are supposed to have ancestors, or some root from which they sprang. I conclude, then, that it is not altogether inconsistent to suppose that I had parents too" (5). Savvy enough to know that the memoirist is a literary character like other literary characters and that the tale he would tell is subject to the rules established by other (potentially fictional) narratives, Martin cultivates an ironic distance from his subject and underscores the artifice of his work. But there is more here than a straightforward acknowledgment of authorial conventionality: Martin imagines a reader who may suppose that a memoirist has parents only *because* narrative convention has always insisted on it. Parentage becomes a matter of literary form rather than biology; only because other writers' "heroes" had ancestors can Martin be said to have them himself.

In conjuring an audience for which the rules of fictional narrative are more immediately recognizable and count as surer argumentative proof than the empirical facts of the everyday, Martin neatly distills some of the stickiest problems of his past and our present. How do received plot structures, which reinforce our expectations of narrative coherence, distort or displace what we might think of (or wish for) as historical reality? Are stories—especially the ones that comprise historiography—in and of themselves tools of entrenched and essentially conservative power? The links between nation building, nationalism, and traditional narration have been made clear enough over the years; might we fashion other modes of community or associative feeling in and through antinarrative?[17] Can we mobilize counterstories like Martin's to undo the work of providential tales of American exceptionality—which have served, after all, as elaborate rationalizations for imperialism abroad and dizzying socioeconomic inequality at home? Can we use them to reimagine the political character of the United States?

For Martin himself, answers seem to be forthcoming: with his emphasis on speaking to his "neighborhood" and on finding patriotism and commonality in lack, in hunger, in improvisation, and in comparative (if necessarily incomplete) expressions of personal feeling, he writes a life in which the conventional expectations of nationalist myth fall away. For our lives during wartime, though—as the days past "Mission Accomplished" in the Middle East march on, as casualty figures on all sides edge up and up, as the U.S. commander in chief participates in a photo op with an inedible turkey for a new "rice and vinegar thanksgiving" (as George W. Bush did in Baghdad in the fall of 2003)—such questions remain both uncomfortably open and increasingly urgent.[18]

NOTES

1. Ralph Waldo Emerson, "Hymn: Sung at the Completion of the Concord Monument, April 19, 1836," *Essays and Poems* (New York: Library of America, 1996), 1175.
2. Indeed, as Eileen Ka-May Cheng has shown, even historiographical fantasies of "objectivity" or "disinterest" have often been made to serve American exceptionalist and nationalist ends. See *The Plain and Noble Garb of Truth: Nationalism and Impartiality in American Historiography, 1784–1860* (Athens: University of Georgia Press, 2008), esp. chap. 4.
3. See Hayden White, *The Content of the Form: Narrative Discourse and Historical Representation* (Baltimore: Johns Hopkins University Press, 1987). T. H. Breen's work on the beginnings of the Revolution, casting popular colonial resistance to British policy as an "insurgency," is a case in point; see his *American Insurgents, American Patriots* (New York: Hill & Wang, 2010).

4. On the history and consequences of American exceptionalist ideology, see Donald E. Pease, *The New American Exceptionalism* (Minneapolis: University of Minnesota Press, 2009); and Geoffrey Hodgson, *The Myth of American Exceptionalism* (New Haven, Conn.: Yale University Press, 2009).
5. Joseph Plumb Martin's text is available in an inexpensive trade edition, *A Narrative of a Revolutionary Soldier* (New York: Signet Classics, 2001), and in a much more scholarly (though expurgated) form in *Ordinary Courage: The Revolutionary War Adventures of Joseph Plumb Martin*, ed. James Kirby Martin (Oxford: Wiley-Blackwell, 2008). The Signet Classics edition has become quite a popular classroom text. For that reason, and because some of the material that I use in this chapter has been removed from the Wiley-Blackwell edition, all quotations from Martin are taken from the Signet Classics version.
6. Martin, *Ordinary Courage*, xii, n7.
7. For detailed and utterly convincing accounts of the nationalist mythologizing of the Revolutionary generation in the Jacksonian period, see Sarah J. Purcell, *Sealed with Blood: War, Sacrifice, and Memory* (Philadelphia: University of Pennsylvania Press, 2010); Alfred F. Young, *The Shoemaker and the Tea Party* (Boston: Beacon, 1999); and Michael Kammen, *A Season of Youth* (Ithaca, N.Y.: Cornell University Press, 1978); as well as Caroline Cox's contribution to the present volume. The speculation that Martin's *Narrative of a Revolutionary Soldier* emerges from the insufficiency of the Pension Act of 1818 is Catherine Kaplan's; see her "Theft and Counter-Theft: Joseph Plumb Martin's Revolutionary War," *Early American Literature* 41, no. 3 (2006): 515–34.
8. The trope of the suffering Continental soldier, enduring privation for the good of the army and the people that it stood for, became more and more common in the culture as veterans applied for pensions in the early nineteenth century. See John Resch, *Suffering Soldiers: Revolutionary War Veterans, Moral Sentiment, and Political Culture in the Early Republic* (Amherst: University of Massachusetts Press, 1999).
9. Kaplan, "Theft and Counter-Theft," 517. In generally declining to frame his story in terms of heroism or nationalist ideology, Martin also fits in rather well with the Continental veterans' narratives that Cox surveys: the project of gaining a pension (predicated on the demonstration of continued hardship) seems to have rewarded detailed accounts of suffering—along with specific recollections of particular deployments—more readily than patriotic bluster.
10. At the moment of the composition of Martin's *Narrative of a Revolutionary Soldier*, as Cheng reminds us, the conventions of historiography were themselves not especially settled: the idea of the historian as impartial moralizer of evidence and the idea of the historian as Rankean curator of objective facts came into direct conflict in the antebellum period. Under both sets of conditions, though, the production of coherent stories about the past remains a categorical imperative. See Cheng, *Plain and Noble Garb*, esp. chap. 1.
11. Beyond the romantic stories he has heard, Martin's motivations for enlisting are necessarily somewhat obscure. Certainly economic factors would have been important—as one of seven children in an unmoneyed family, Martin's financial prospects were mixed at best—though Martin does not seem especially concerned with his long-term future at the opening of his text. Yet he does not seem to

fall comfortably into what Charles Royster has characterized as a "revolutionary character." His interest in ideologies of American independence is attenuated by more local (and less articulate) concerns. For more on the conflicting motivations of Continental soldiers, see Royster, *A Revolutionary People at War: The Continental Army and the American Character, 1775–1783* (Chapel Hill: Omohundro Institute of Early American History and Culture, 1979). Royster's appendix details economic arguments for enlisting, while the rest of the text explores ideological arguments. See also Charles Neimeyer, *America Goes to War: A Social History of the Continental Army* (New York: New York University Press, 1996).

12. Kaplan, too, lingers on this moment (and on several of the other moments of food-related high jinks that I look at in this chapter), rightly finding in them examples of "counter-theft"—in which soldiers robbed of their provisions and their dignity strike back at the forces oppressing them and take what should (by dint of legal *and* social contracts) be properly theirs. See "Theft and Counter-Theft."
13. In Kaplan's analysis this moment reveals that the "war . . . is indeed almost as much between men and their officers as it is between Americans and British." "Theft and Counter-Theft," 521.
14. Compare Timothy Dwight Sprague's account of the same incident: The British were "marching to intercept Putnam's retreat, and the enemy thus closing in upon him on each side. Putnam urged his men with all the vehemence of his natural ardor, increased by the perilous situation in which he found himself. Riding backwards and forwards in his impatience, he encouraged the soldiers, who were, in many instances, fainting from fatigue and thirst. A portion of the British army was already seen descending upon the right, and the rear of Putman's [*sic*] division was fired upon. But his exertions saved them, and they slipped through just before the enemy's lines were extended from river to river." "General Israel Putnam," *American Literary Magazine* 2, no. 2 (February 1848): 77–78. For Sprague, as for most nineteenth-century historians of the Revolution, thirst, starvation, and desperate fatigue in the ranks are quickly overcome by the "natural ardor" and the heroic efforts of a commissioned officer; Putnam's singular "exertions" and exhortations restore order and unit coherence long enough for the Continentals to make their retreat. As is customary, the distribution of gallantry is minimal: one man on horseback "encourages"—that is, lends courage and form to—the ragged masses; no matter how many other actors are present, the story belongs to him alone.
15. Kaplan, "Theft and Counter-Theft," 530.
16. For more on the enduring popularity and populism of these sorts of anecdotal forms, as well as their role in consolidating collective memory, see Emily Lewis Butterfield's contribution to the present volume.
17. See, for instance, Benedict Anderson, *Imagined Communities*, rev. ed. (New York: Verso, 1991); and Homi K. Bhabha, *The Location of Culture* (New York: Routledge, 1994), esp. 139–70.
18. Mike Allen, "The Bird Was Perfect, but Not for Dinner," *Washington Post*, December 4, 2003.

Public Memories, Private Lives

The First Greatest Generation Remembers the Revolutionary War

Caroline Cox

On July 4, 1837, a large crowd gathered in Newburyport, Massachusetts, to hear John Quincy Adams, Congressman and former president, give a speech at the town's Independence Day festivities. He encouraged those in the audience to reflect on evil British "usurpations" before the war and celebrated "the good name, the sufferings, and the services of that [Revolutionary] age." Then Adams invited those gathered to "look . . . forward" and consider the political problems of their own time as the Revolutionary generation passed away.[1]

By the time Adams delivered his speech in Newburyport, orations by prominent figures on the Fourth of July and on the anniversaries of battles or other significant events were regular features of the national calendar. Crowds gathered to watch parades and listen to orators in towns great and small. Such days created a national memory of the Revolutionary era. They celebrated the collective sacrifice, emphasized shared political ideals, and were a central component of an emerging American national identity. These festive occasions also took on a crucial unifying role as people argued about the kind of society they hoped to create from the bloodshed and upheaval of that critical time.[2]

The formula for these celebrations changed over the years. Immediately after the war, orators honored only the great figures of the era: the commander in chief George Washington and such men as General Richard Montgomery and Joseph Warren, two famous patriots killed in action early in the conflict. But as the Revolutionary generation aged and died, ordinary soldiers—men rarely respected at the time of their service or in the intervening years—became celebrated heroes and were toasted at public gatherings and invited to lead the parades. As in the political structures of the society at large, the events and public memory of the Revolution became more democratic.[3]

Despite this change, other parts of the festivities followed a familiar pattern. Orators reminded audiences of prewar grievances and Revolutionary heroism and then introduced present-day concerns. In 1790, in Carlisle, Pennsylvania, Robert Duncan had recalled "tyrannical [British] laws and legislation"; paid tribute to the living, "the heroes and patriots who have nobly distinguished themselves"; acknowledged the fallen, "who devoted their lives to the salvation of their country"; and tackled problems of the present, speaking of commerce and education. In 1808, in his Fourth of July speech, Nathaniel Cogswell similarly honored the past, then defended President Thomas Jefferson's trade embargo. But such opinions never interfered with the mission of the day: honoring the "heroes and patriots" of the Revolutionary generation. Such reverence befitted men who had participated in what Edwin Forrest, speaking in New York in 1838, called "the most august event . . . in the political annals of mankind." The participants in the events may have changed, but the celebratory public rhetoric remained the same.[4]

But ordinary veterans, the now-celebrated heroes and patriots of the Revolutionary era, used very different language to tell their stories when they recalled those years. Many of their personal accounts were devoid of rhetorical flourishes. They did not share the circumstances or purpose of public orators. Writing at kitchen tables, recording their experiences for the benefit of family members, friends, and neighbors, they reflected in a language more measured and personal. If applying to a court for a veterans' pension, they also had reason to speak or write plainly. Neither of these occasions had cheering audiences, parades, or picnics to inspire stylistic embellishment.

Contrasting the recollections that veterans set down in pension applications and memoirs with the public oratory of the Fourth of July and related occasions reveals the differences between public and personal memories of the Revolution. Public speeches, with their rhetorical flourishes, created what J. H. Plumb called a "purposeful past," in which key wartime events led directly and inevitably to greatness. Veterans may have enjoyed listening to these. Those present when the printer and founder of the *Vermont Gazette*, Anthony Haswell, gave the oration at the 1799 anniversary of the patriot victory at the Battle of Bennington probably cheered lustily when he paraphrased Julius Caesar and exclaimed of the militia, "They came, they saw, they conquered." When, years later, Haswell's son-in-law, Darius Clark, who had taken over the newspaper, continued the tradition of delivering a stirring anniversary speech, they probably still applauded loudly. But in their private reflections, the grizzled veterans told a different story of the Revolution, one more haphazard and uncertain. Veterans recollected friendship and family, toil and travail, anchored by the chronology of Revolutionary events rather than shaped by them. Veterans' stories, then, highlight the ways in which public and private memories converged and diverged.[5]

Scholars have used veterans' recollections to examine the role these old soldiers played in shaping a national memory of the Revolution. But these previous studies have focused on their actions, particularly their participation in anniversary events, and the political uses that others made of them. Here, they tell their own stories of their Revolutionary experiences, incorporating the great events of the war years into a larger tapestry of life experience. In stark contrast to the "purposeful past" of celebratory rhetoric, we find individuals, sometimes flawed, often uncertain, at the center of Revolutionary change.[6]

In autobiographies and pension applications, veterans recorded their memories of the nation's founding events. The pension records especially provide a particularly rich and underused source. Although Congress did not pass legislation awarding pensions to the majority of Revolutionary War veterans until decades after the war, not every veteran waited so long. Servicemen who had been permanently disabled and the widows of men killed in the struggle received pensions shortly thereafter. But in 1818

Congress also granted pensions to Continental Army veterans who could demonstrate pressing financial hardship, following up this legislation in 1832 by awarding pensions based on merit alone to any man who had served in any branch of the service for any length of time (and, later, to any veteran's widow). Over the decades roughly eighty-eight thousand people applied.[7]

These records, put on microfilm in the early 1970s and now digitized, provide historians with information about veterans' youthful experiences and some details of their lives in the intervening years. With little paper evidence to show proof of service (few saw the point of keeping a discharge certificate, even if they had been given one) and with muster rolls notoriously incomplete, veterans' memories of service became critically important. The pension office was vigilant about fraud and applicants had to make their claim by being deposed in court and getting depositions from fellow veterans, former officers, family members, or neighbors who could remember their service or testify to their character as men of "truth and veracity." Some of the materials in the files are in the form of handwritten letters or statements subsequently notarized by the clerk of the court. Most, though, are transcriptions of statements made in open court. Thus, the Revolutionary War pension-application files are a wonderful collection of personal memories of the era and one of the great oral history projects of all time.[8]

Because individual memories are known to be unreliable, historians have given considerable thought to the ways in which recollections of events recorded decades afterward might be approached. They suggest that while many people struggle to remember details or an exact chronology, memory does not decline uniformly for all life occurrences. Rather, experiencing an intense emotion around an occasion makes the subsequent memory of it more vivid. Many other and sometimes contradictory factors can also shape the way events are remembered. Values and beliefs acquired later in life may be a prism through which people view more youthful experience. Also, even though the elderly may be inclined to celebrate, and perhaps even aggrandize, the accomplishments of their youth, both the passage of time and physical distance from the tumult of emotions surrounding an event can allow for greater objectivity. Additionally, the distance of time may allow people to feel less inhibited and less concerned about revealing emotions or actions that do not conform to social expectations. Even their temperament may shape the ways in which they view earlier life events. As historian Alfred F. Young suggested, all these factors, "values, attitude, and temperament," alter the ways in which people remember events. Despite these problems, veterans' recollections remain a vital historical source and, importantly, represent the only kind produced by men of all social ranks. Thus, the problems of human memory notwithstanding, we can nevertheless make use of the pension applications to study veterans' experiences and the ways in which they remembered them.[9]

But there is another important ingredient that shapes what people remember and the way they do so: the social context. Memories are, as W. Fitzhugh Brundage has observed, "innately elusive and ephemeral." It is hard to retain clear images of particular events and the personal, emotional, and practical responses to them. Individual memories and collective social memories can never be truly separated. Thus, veterans' recollections were shaped not only by their own individual life experiences but also by the political events that had transpired since the Revolution, by the major conflict of the War of 1812, and by what they had since learned about wartime events in the intervening years. For example, in his application New York veteran John Yerks recounted details of the night when he and others captured the British officer Major John André, who was dressed in civilian clothes and who had an assignation with the American general Benedict Arnold. When Arnold's treachery later became known and André was subsequently executed as a spy, the whole episode became legendary. Not only did Yerks describe many details of the occasion few others would know, but he also included information he probably discovered years later. On the night in question, he may not have been clear about what was happening and certainly could not have completely grasped its full implications.[10]

That famous night and other memorable occasions that public orators marked bring the difference between personal and public memory into sharp relief. That veterans homed in on such events is, in itself, a testament to the ways in which certain incidents of the war had become focal, celebrated, or notorious. But in contrast to the orators who remembered these events as leading inevitably to the creation of a glorious republic, former soldiers told very different stories about them. For these men, writing about an important victory, surrender, or another key occurrence often became simply a way to locate themselves in a specific place and time. It was events and experiences often tangential to the larger historical moment that captured their attention or that they particularly recalled because of a connection with incidents that occurred later in their lives. Their own trials or successes colored not only their perceptions of earlier events and influenced the kind of language they used to recall the memorable days of their youth but also what they actually remembered. In their recollections pivotal wartime events became incidental to the narrative of their own lives.[11]

To complicate the matter of memory, pension applicants wanted to receive that state benefit and to present themselves as worthy of it. To limit a veteran's temptation to self-aggrandize and to keep applicants focused, the pension office laid out the information it required. It wanted to know the place and approximate date of the veteran's enlistment, the names of the officers under whom the applicant served, and any battles in which he might have been engaged—all information that would generally locate him in space and time. Additionally, the pension office requested details on how long the applicant had lived in the place in which he was making his application. Thus, like the speech makers on anniversary occasions, the pension applicants followed the three-part formula of their immediate prewar circumstances, wartime occurrences, and postwar lives.

War memoirs also followed the same narrative arc. Whether published or written for the restricted audience of his community, the writer usually began with a scant family history that took him up to the moment of his enlistment. This was usually done very efficiently, though there are some exceptions. For instance, in Joseph Plumb Martin's book-length memoir, the subject of William Huntting Howell's chapter in this volume, the author devoted several pages to illuminating his own character and prewar circumstances. Another memoir writer, Ebenezer Fox, did the same. But most authors got to the war much more quickly: John Blatchford, who published his account shortly after the war, and Ebenezer Fletcher, who wrote decades later, got themselves into the service by the second line. And for all writers, information on their postwar lives was given short shrift. Like public orators and pension applicants, they knew what their audience wanted.[12]

Despite this formulaic structure that kept veterans focused on the war itself and the desire to receive a benefit or the praise of one's neighbors or family, pension applications and memoirs were remarkably free of the kind of glorious language that characterized the public speeches marking important anniversaries. Their statements were plain and matter-of-fact. Indeed, considering they were recounting momentous events, the vast majority make tedious reading. Perhaps this quality was the result of modesty or disingenuousness. A more likely explanation is that while a particular battle may have been a landmark event for the nation, it may not have been of critical importance in individual men's lives. Whatever the cause, it was a popular trope used by thousands.

Just as public orators generally reminded listeners of the British policies and actions that drove the colonists to revolt, so too did veterans occasionally note what motivated them to fight. A few introduced their service with the simple phrase, "I enlisted in the cause of my country," implying that the desire for political liberty was what had inspired them. Although this was a set phrase, perhaps it was no less deeply felt for that. But most veterans did not provide any reason for their actions. If, as young men, they had been outraged over political matters, they gave little vent to such feelings in old age. Whether they were from property-owning families with a material stake in the political arguments of the war or poorer men with none, few offered any explanation of what prompted them to act.

It was often only if the pension office or other interviewer questioned veterans' truthfulness that they offered clarification on their reasons for enlisting. A few explicitly cited the cause, occasionally inspired by their families' politics. Bishop Tyler, for instance, when questioned why he had enlisted at the age of thirteen when "no law required" his participation, replied that he had been prompted to enlist by his father's staunch patriotism and by the rousing sermons of his minister. And Jehu Grant, a slave in Rhode Island who had run away from his loyalist master and joined the Massachusetts Continentals, specified that he had been motivated by the "songs of liberty that saluted my ear, [and] thrilled through my heart." Like Tyler, Grant was under no legal obligation to serve—being a slave exempted him from duty; so both veterans had to come up with explanations for their voluntary enlistment. Only when thus pressed did their language turn to a more florid style. Both were indignant at having to defend their decision to enlist. Tyler, buoyed with the confidence brought by his prominent position in the community and with a term as a state legislator behind him, was ultimately persuasive and his pension was granted. Grant, in a less secure position, resorted to irony, resting his case "upon the well-known liberality of government." In the end, the pension commissioner was persuaded that Grant had indeed served but denied him a pension because the service of runaway slaves was not specifically covered under the pension act.[13]

Given the institutional and reader interest in their journeys toward service, it would have been easy for applicants or memoir writers to aggrandize their motivations for enlistment or at least to couch them in the same terms that public orators did, by expressing outrage at British tyranny. But, in fact, many petitioners cited more pedestrian reasons. For Thomas Painter, it was a desire for adventure and a chance to escape his planned future as a shoemaker that had stimulated him to join. Eli Jacobs, meanwhile, enlisted for a short term at the beginning of the war, inspired by the political cause, but served again four years later only after a quarrel with his stepmother provided him with a reason to want to leave home. Difficulties with his new stepmother similarly induced Cyprian Parrish to seek to enlist. Because he was young, his father made him wait a while. But the very day he turned sixteen, Parrish enlisted in the New York Continentals and served for a year. Others were motivated by financial considerations: John Chaney of South Carolina, for instance, was enticed by the money and land bounties offered by service. It may be that political outrage was simply too obvious an impetus to warrant a mention, but the reasons presented were generally more personal and prosaic.[14]

Despite wanting a pension or public recognition and enjoying an invitation to lead Independence Day parades, some veterans were not inclined to conform to the image of noble warriors. Rather, they wanted a public forum to reveal long-held grudges. Joseph Plumb Martin, who wrote one of the longest and most engaging memoirs of the war, provided grisly details of the hardships of his service: days spent "pinched with hunger" and "enduring hardships sufficient to kill half a dozen horses." William Walton expressed bitterness about the unacknowledged hard labor he had supplied, hauling grain to the troops in the Virginia backcountry. He recalled that in "this most disagreeable service I was compelled to continue twelve months, finding my own horse & fixtures, thinly clad in homespun furnished by my Mother, in one of the coldest Winters almost ever known." And in his pension application Walton was prepared to admit that he had not done this duty willingly. Rather, a Continental officer had "impressed" him—something he bitterly resented. And even Yerks, in an interview with a local historian in the 1840s in which he related his heroic arrest of Major André, admitted that he and his comrades were out that night, with their officers' permission, not to fight the British but to steal from loyalist refugees making their way into New York.[15]

When it came to discussing the fighting of the war itself, veterans shared a convention with orators and yet also departed from it. Although they did note great military events that everyone would have heard of, they often did so only in passing—after all, such events were rare. A short period of service may simply have consisted of the tedium of standing guard, foraging for food, or chopping firewood. Even during longer service, a veteran may have seen little action. Martin, one of a small cohort of soldiers who served for seven long years, rarely saw the enemy and never fired his weapon in battle. Commanders in eighteenth-century armies tried to avoid fighting, which might be costly in men and war materiel. Instead, they focused on interfering with one another's supply lines and on limited engagements that targeted small strategic posts. Thus, while the larger national story of the war involved a sequence of critical military engagements that led to ultimate victory, many veterans, like civilians, had often only heard about these events secondhand. If they had participated in a major engagement, it was just one day among hundreds of others that each presented their own peculiar challenges. But such routine days did not inspire exalted language.

Consider the rhetoric surrounding the Battle of Bennington. Fought on August 16, 1777, it would figure largely in the public memories of the Revolution for the communities residing in the areas that surrounded the site. It marked a stunning patriot victory over the British and their Hessian, loyalist, and Indian allies. The conflict involved about one thousand enemy troops who had left the protection of a large contingent of British forces led by General John Burgoyne, making its way south from Quebec. On going out to search the countryside for horses and other supplies, they found instead patriot militia. In the ensuing battle the militia killed two hundred enemy soldiers, took another seven hundred prisoner, and chased the rest away in disarray. The militia, in contrast, were left with only thirty dead and forty more wounded. Officers John Stark and Seth Warner were the heroes of the hour and the ordinary militiamen basked in the glow of their accomplishments.[16]

Within days broadsheets and newspapers all along the eastern seaboard celebrated the victory and the militia's "spirit and fortitude." A month later, when Burgoyne's whole army was defeated by a large American force at Saratoga, New York, the people of the region were sure that the Battle of Bennington had been instrumental in bringing about the victory. A few years later, after it was clear that the defeat of Burgoyne's army had been a pivotal event, prompting France and other European nations to enter the war as patriot allies, orators regularly celebrated that fateful August day. They honored the militia's virtue, "valour and wisdom" and remembered when the battlefield "was wet with the best blood" of the community.[17]

Three American soldiers who fought that day, however, remembered it with very different language. One of them was William Gilmore. By the time of the battle, he was already a seasoned veteran, approximately twenty-six years old. He initially served a short term in the Continental Army in a regiment from his home state of Massachusetts, but in July, 1777, he migrated to Vermont to begin a new life. His timing was spectacularly bad: he arrived just as the British Army began its campaign into the region, and within a month he was called out with the local militia to face the advancing enemy. Years later, when applying for a veteran's pension, all he had to say about the confluence of events was that he had gone to the place where "the Bennington Battle so called was fought and in which he was ingaged [*sic*] through the day." He had then "helped the next day to bury the dead"—a fact that stayed in his mind for a particular reason. For, apart from the gruesomeness of the task, it was the day he met Austin Wells, a man who would become his neighbor and lifelong friend.[18]

Only eighteen years old at the time of this meeting, Wells shared with his new friend the status of both veteran and recent migrant. His family had moved to the area only a couple of months before from Connecticut, where Wells had already done a year of military service in the Continental Army. He also was called out for militia duty that August, now serving as a sergeant, and fought in the battle "from the commencement to the close thereof." This was his only reference to the conflict. At that point Wells and Gilmore did not know each other, but they met the following day, August 17, when together they buried the dead. While they did so, they recalled and compared notes about their experiences the previous day but neither man thought to explicitly state what those were. The two did not meet again for some weeks, as Wells was put in charge of a group of men guarding the "Cattle Horses & other property" taken from the enemy in the battle. But they met several times afterward over the course of the war when they went out on militia service. It was an unusual beginning to their lifelong association. At age ninety-one Gilmore reflected that the two men had known each other "upwards of sixty-four years." Although the battle attained a status of great importance in the nation's memory of the Revolution, it was the chance personal encounter that produced their lifelong friendship that stayed with Wells and Gilmore.[19]

They were not alone in subordinating the national to the personal. Fellow militiaman, Samuel Younglove, had his baptism of fire at Bennington. He had arrived in the region with his family when he was about nine years old. In August 1777, at the tender age of fourteen, Younglove went with the militia for the first time when it was called out to challenge the enemy. Because he experienced battle at such a young age, we might expect the excitement and horror of the day to have been deeply imprinted on his mind and to figure largely in his memory. But in both his pension application and a very short memoir—only a few pages in length and written solely for the benefit of family members—Younglove simply noted that he "took a very active part in the battle." He observed that he was busy the next day taking care of the wounded, but he had nothing else to say about the engagement. He recounted many other details of the comings and goings of his military service but, writing in old age, it was not wartime events but rather the emotional upheaval that immediately followed the war that he remembered. At that time his beloved mother had died and his father quickly remarried—an event that he recalled "drove me almost to distraction." He "chose solitude," he noted, and found himself "caught in a great vortex of dissipation." The long journey back from that state overshadowed his memories of wartime activities. Thus, while in public, patriot orators focused on heroic exploits, in private, veterans remembered events that connected them to other times in their lives.

Even soldiers who had endured more sustained combat experience were not inclined to say anything about it. Isaac Artis is a case in point. Serving for three years in a Virginia regiment of the Continental Army, Artis had fought "at the battles of Brandywine, Germantown and Monmouth and the siege of Stoney Point," experiencing two American defeats, a draw, a victory, and many other skirmishes. But he offered no other information about those events, even in a second deposition. When interviewing Artis to verify his identity, former army captain Uriah Springer was impressed not by the veteran's recollections of the battles but rather by the "many little occurrences of minor importance" that Artis remembered. One of these, from the winter of 1778, Artis recalled in immense detail: it was a "great quarrel" between the Virginia and Pennsylvania troops "in consequence of throwing snow balls at each other." Such were the events that rooted themselves firmly in the veterans' memories and that they chose to record decades later.[20]

Not only did the veterans usually eschew heroic statements, they also occasionally admitted to less than valiant conduct. Take the case of Garret Watts of North Carolina, for instance. Having already completed several terms of militia service, in the summer of 1780 he found himself on the field of battle that became known as Camden—a significant British victory. While standing in court remembering the day, Watts included information about the makeup of the British Army and the disposition of troops on the field that he probably only discovered later. But when it came to recounting his own actions, he was quite clear about them. He was sure that his was "the first gun fired" on the morning of the battle. But he also recalled that when the militia line broke in panic as the British advanced, "I confess I was amongst the first that fled. The cause of that I cannot tell, except that everyone I saw was about to do the same." This confession—quite unnecessary to the pension process—seemed to constitute a burden that Watts had carried with him for years that he now wanted to lay down.[21]

There were also veterans who had changed sides at different times in the war. James Hollis had deserted from the British Army and subsequently served for a year and a half on the patriot side. Josiah Brandon had switched sides also. Serving multiple terms in the North Carolina patriot militia—contrary to the wishes of his loyalist father—on one occasion Brandon acceded to his father's demands and fought at the 1780 Battle of King's Mountain on the loyalist side. His father was killed in the battle, and Brandon returned to the patriot militia a few weeks later. Neither Brandon nor Hollis made any secret of their unusual life journeys when they successfully applied for pensions, but their stories reveal the complications of life from which orators at public festivals steered well clear.[22]

Not only do private memories, then, reveal personal pieces of information and quirky or unusual recollections, they also gave veterans an opportunity to step off the pedestal onto which the public had placed them. But it is their recollections of famous events that reveal the intersection, convergence, and divergence of public and private memory. Orators such as Nathaniel Cogswell publicly celebrated the Revolutionary soldiers going to war, supported "by the principles of eternal justice . . . fondly anticipating the glory, freedom, and happiness of your country." In contrast, veterans' personal recollections—whether recounted in court for a pension claim or written in letters read by pension office clerks or in memoirs read by friends, family, and neighbors—brought readers and listeners back to earth. While veterans may have shared the orators' sentiments, their private reflections remind us that life is more complicated. Human frailty, deeply personal experiences, and the unusual all jogged in uncertain and unpredictable tandem with larger national stories of the war years. Considered together, public and private memories provide a more nuanced understanding of what the Revolutionary War meant to those who fought it.[23]

NOTES

1. John Quincy Adams, *An Oration Delivered before the Inhabitants of the Town of Newburyport . . . July 4th, 1837* (Newburyport, Mass.: Whipple, 1837), 13, 21, 15.
2. Sarah Purcell, *Sealed with Blood: War, Sacrifice, and Memory in Revolutionary America* (Philadelphia: University of Pennsylvania Press, 2002), 1–3.
3. François Furstenberg, *In the Name of the Father: Washington's Legacy, Slavery, and the Making of a Nation* (New York: Penguin, 2006), 20–21; Purcell, *Sealed with Blood,* 188; John Resch, *Suffering Soldiers: Revolutionary War Veterans, Moral Sentiment, and Political Culture in the Early Republic* (Amherst: University of Massachusetts Press, 1999), 3–5. For public toasts see, for example, Anon., *Baltimore Patriot,* July 8, 1826, 2.
4. Robert Duncan, "Oration Delivered by Mr. Robert Duncan," *Carlisle Gazette and the Western Repository of Knowledge,* July 14, 1790, 2; Nathaniel Cogswell, *An Oration Delivered before the Republican Citizens of Newburyport . . . on the 4th of July, 1808* (Newburyport: Gilman, 1808), 4; Edwin Forrest, *Oration Delivered by Edwin Forrest, New York, 1838* (Philadelphia: Ferral, 1838), 3.
5. J. H. Plumb, *The Death of the Past* (New York: Houghton Mifflin, 1970), 17; Purcell, *Sealed with Blood,* 188; Anthony Haswell, *An Oration Delivered at Bennington, Vermont, August 16, 1799: In Commemoration of the Battle of Bennington* (Bennington: Haswell, 1799), 24.
6. Purcell, *Sealed with Blood,* 188; Haswell, *Oration Delivered at Bennington, Vermont,* 24; Plumb, *Death of the Past,* 17.
7. Resch, *Suffering Soldiers,* 203; Constance M. Schulz, "The Revolutionary War Pension Applications: A Neglected Source for Social and Family History," *Prologue* 15 (Summer 1983): 104–11.
8. Schulz, "Revolutionary War Pension Applications," 104–11.
9. Alfred F. Young, *The Shoemaker and the Tea Party: Memory and the American Revolution* (Boston: Beacon, 1999), xii–xiii, 12; W. Fitzhugh Brundage, "No Deed but Memory," in *Where These Memories Grow: History, Memory, and Southern*

Identity, ed. W. Fitzhugh Brundage (Chapel Hill: University of North Carolina Press, 2000), 3–4.

10. Brundage, "No Deed but Memory," 3–4; John Yerks, S23502, Revolutionary War Pension Application (hereafter RWPA), RG 15, National Archives, Washington, D.C.
11. Yerks, S23502, RWPA.
12. William Huntting Howell, "'Starving Memory': Antinarrating the American Revolution," in this volume; Ebenezer Fox, "The Adventures of Ebenezer Fox," in *Narratives of the American Revolution*, ed. Hugh Rankin (Chicago: Donnelley & Sons, 1976); John Blatchford, *The Narrative of John Blatchford*, ed. Charles Bushnell (New York: privately printed, 1865); Ebenezer Fletcher, *Narrative of the Captivity and Suffering of Ebenezer Fletcher of New Ipswich* (New Ipswich, N.H.: Wilder, 1827).
13. Bishop Tyler, S17192, and Jehu Grant, R4197, RWPA. Extracts of Jehu Grant's application are in John Dann, ed., *The Revolution Remembered: Eyewitness Accounts of the War for Independence* (Chicago: University of Chicago Press, 1980), 26–28.
14. Bishop Tyler, S17192, and William Hutchinson, S5570, RWPA; Thomas Painter, *Autobiography of Thomas Painter relating His Experiences during the War of the Revolution* ([Washington, D.C.]: privately printed, 1910), 9; Eli Jacobs, W1193, Cyprian Parrish, S29363, and John Chaney, S32177, RWPA. Extracts from the applications of Hutchinson, Jacobs, and Chaney appear in Dann, *Revolution Remembered*, 145–55, 59–62, 228–33.
15. Joseph Plumb Martin, *Ordinary Courage: The Revolutionary War Adventures of Joseph Plumb Martin*, ed. James Kirby Martin (New York: Brandywine, 1993), 47, 53; William Walton Jr., S17184, RWPA; John Yerks, in John McDonald Interviews, 1845–49, New York Historical Society, New York, 1:278. Originals are in the Westchester County Historical Society, Elmsford, N.Y.
16. Craig L. Symonds, *A Battlefield Atlas of the American Revolution* (Baltimore: Nautical & Aviation, 1986), 45; Harold Selesky, ed., *Encyclopedia of the American Revolution*, 2nd ed. (New York: Scribner's Sons, 2006), s.v. "Battle of Bennington."
17. Anthony Haswell, *Moral Songs Composed to Be Sung August 16, 1788, at the Celebration of the Eleventh Anniversary of the Battle of Bennington* (Bennington, Vt.: Haswell & Russell, 1788); Samuel B. Young, *An Oration, Pronounced at Bennington, August 16, 1819: In Commemoration of the Battle of Bennington, Fought August 16, 1777* (Bennington, Vt.: Clarke, 1819), 1.
18. William Gilmore, S8571, RWPA.
19. Austin Wells, S32054, RWPA. Gilmore's account of their relationship is in Wells's file.
20. Isaac Artis, S39943, RWPA.
21. Garret Watts, R11213, RWPA. Extracts of Watts's application is in Dann, *Revolution Remembered*, 193–96. Dann also speculates that Watts's feelings of guilt prompted his confession.
22. James Hollis, S21290, and Josiah Brandon, W335, RWPA.
23. Cogswell, *Oration Delivered*, 4.

Part II

Transmitting Memories

"More Than Ordinary Patriotism"

Living History in the Memory Work of George Washington Parke Custis

Seth C. Bruggeman

Americans love revival. Renaissance fairs, battle reenactments, and time-traveling television shows have all become enduring fixtures in the cultural landscape. At historic sites and museums where playacting passes for pedagogy, the phrase "living history" distinguishes studied reenactment from amateur histrionics. Plimoth Plantation, Conner's Prairie, and Greenfield Village are just a few examples of living-history museums where education and research commingle with high-order simulation. Virginia's Colonial Williamsburg is probably the most famous, but it too is only one of many whose intellectual roots historians usually associate with either the historic-house museum movement born at Mount Vernon during the 1850s or Artur Hazelius's open-air Skansen museum, which set out during the 1890s to protect Nordic folkways from the onslaught of industrial modernity. In both instances, we are told, a combination of politics and nostalgia motivated men and women to dress like their ancestors and play the part for the sake of posterity. Although this kind of fanciful remembering has earned its share of detractors, living history still ranks among the most popular ways to learn about history in the United States today.[1]

That it does should not surprise us. Living history's theatrical immediacy, its claims to authenticity, and the patriotism it implies through shared experience speak loudly to Americans who have grown distrustful of discursive pasts conjured in stuffy classrooms and tired textbooks.[2] They want a *real* story about the past, and they want it to captivate them. It makes perfect sense that their late nineteenth-century counterparts turned to memory in the midst of whirlwind technological, political, and social change. It makes *such* perfect sense, in fact, that historians may have overlooked an even earlier precedent for the present preoccupation with the performance of public memory.

During the nation's first two decades, before Americans had even decided how to remember the Revolution and its heroes, George Washington Parke Custis staged the kind of mnemonic spectacles that keep places like Colonial Williamsburg in business today. Custis was George Washington's adopted grandson, the first of the nation's First Children. As an adult he built the iconic white house that now looms over Arlington National Cemetery. There Custis publicly reenacted his memories of Washington in performances so grand that one observer considered them evidence of "more than just ordinary patriotism."[3] Revisiting Custis's memory work gives us a new benchmark by which to measure the significance of mimesis in the American historical imagination. It shows us that performative pasts have ensured Washington's place at the forefront of American national memory since nearly the beginning.

We would be wrong, though, to mistake Custis's patriotism for just that. Sifting through what little we know about his life and work suggests that living history, no matter how powerful its promise of impartiality, has always been complicit in the politics of nation making. Indeed, if Custis's patriotism was more than ordinary, what made it so was the mingling of personal and political motives underlying his hope that Americans would always remember Washington at the center of the Revolution. Bringing those motives into view sheds light on the earliest stirrings of Revolutionary memory, while reminding us that, even today, authenticity is not always what it seems.

A Man Born to Remember

With very few exceptions, historians have either overlooked Custis or treated him incidentally in connection with his more famous relatives. One history of Arlington National Cemetery, for instance, devotes far fewer pages to Custis than to his eminently more famous son-in-law, Robert E. Lee.[4] Custis's obscurity in the historical record is consistent with his own biography, which itself is a study in mnemonic rupture. From the beginning Custis struggled with familial continuity, albeit amid the staggering fortunes of Virginia's plantocracy. His father died only months after Custis's birth in 1781, leaving behind a wife, Eleanor Calvert, and Custis's three older sisters. John Parke Custis, who was Martha Washington's son by her first marriage, had succumbed to "camp fever" (probably typhus) shortly after the victory at Yorktown, where he served as a civilian aide-de-camp to General Washington. Martha, who had lost both of her children and had none with George, persuaded her daughter-in-law that the Washingtons should raise Custis and his sister, Eleanor, as their own. With that, "Wash" and "Nelly" began life anew at Mount Vernon, where, in the shadow of the First Couple, they became the nation's first celebrity children.[5]

Custis made a career of remembering his childhood for patriotic Americans. But precisely because his published *and* private letters are so carefully crafted, making sense of Custis's childhood experiences and their imprint on his later life requires some speculation if we are to parse the man from the memory. It is not too great of a leap to infer that the American Revolution profoundly affected Custis's early life in at least two ways. First, without him even knowing it at the time, the war had extracted one set of parents and sutured another into their place. We know that the disjuncture haunted Nelly Custis throughout her life. Nelly resented, for instance, Martha's insistence that she spend time with her mother's new family at its remote Virginia plantation, where scads of unfamiliar stepsiblings clamored against her preference for Mount Vernon's prestige and comforts. Historian Patricia Brady points out that Nelly's "adult obsession with mother love" suggests that she never quite resolved these early traumas.[6] If Nelly struggled with maternal disequilibrium, one can only imagine Custis's paternal dilemmas. One father died at war. Another, his stepfather, had lured Custis's mother to a distant plantation. The third, whose obligations to Custis were even more tenuous, he shared with an entire nation. Whatever advantages Custis enjoyed, his path to manhood was complicated by impossible role models.

And yet, at the same time, the remarkable stature of Custis's prosthetic family extended him unprecedented contact with the people, places, and ideas that had made the Revolution possible. The war's legacy pervaded every aspect of Custis's life from his earliest days. Although most Americans' love affair with monuments and memorials did not blossom until the 1820s, Mount Vernon already bustled during the first months of Custis's life with protocommemorative commotion. Washington's assistants quietly organized and carefully edited the wartime papers that continue to shape the official memory of the conflict. His admirers assured him that "in every possible way, your country wishes to erect public monuments to you."[7] In those first years after the war, Washington could already anticipate a time when a document like his resigned commission as commander of the Continental Army might become, as biographer Joseph Ellis puts it, "a religious relic worshipped by his descendants." Publicly, George and Martha received waves of "distinguished guests who thronged that hospitable mansion" and lavished young Custis with "caresses and attention." Jean Lee recognizes within these visits the "beginnings of the process whereby Mount Vernon was incorporated into the remembered Revolution." Custis's peculiar circumstances thus entwined him with a particularly potent and very public memory of the American Revolution.[8]

The parade of guests and celebrities only intensified when Washington became president and moved the family briefly to New York and then to Philadelphia in 1790. Custis, nearly ten by this time, came of age among the highest ranks of one of the most cosmopolitan cities in the Atlantic World. Nelly cherished her family's Philadelphia associations and particularly enjoyed mingling with foreign dignitaries. As Custis matured during those years, so must have his awareness of his guardian's place in American memory. How could it not? By 1790 Washington's birthday had become a national holiday. His name and visage graced everything from commemorative medals to teapots.[9] And in 1793 Custis watched as Washington presided over the laying of the Capitol building's cornerstone in the new city that bore his name. Custis's early life with Washington unfolded in a chain of spectacular moments. The president's presence sanctified every place they visited and carried with it the weight of war. For Custis, then,

Custis observes George Washington set the capital cornerstone, as portrayed in a mural painted by Allyn Cox. Copyright by the George Washington Masonic Memorial, all rights reserved. Photograph by Arthur W. Pierson, Falls Church, Va.

each and every day involved at least some small act of mnemonic obeisance to his guardian and to the war that shaped his fate.

That being the case, it is not surprising that Custis acted out from time to time. History tells us that, despite his great advantages, Martha's unfettered indulgence of young Custis supposedly so spoiled him that George's stern parenting could not stem the tide. Custis instead squandered his education, shirked honest labor, passed up a military career, and even flaunted the law, as in 1798, when he failed to appear in court on charges of stealing two silver spoons from John Gadsby's tavern in Arlington, Virginia. "The term *dilettante,*" wrote one chronicler, "describes his character exactly." In hindsight, however, one might wonder if Custis, shorn of a father and distanced from his mother and sisters, was not rather confounded by the world's constant awareness of his certain inability to emulate Washington's impeccable manhood. His life had become so public, after all, that word of Custis's hunting exploits even appeared in distant newspapers. Having lived life as a prop in the country's most popular pageant, Custis certainly must have struggled to recognize in himself something other than vestiges of Washington. Whatever demons haunted him, and despite having "started in life under the most favorable influences," history has frequently recalled Custis as a young man bereft of "force and ambition" who "accomplished very little."[10]

Like all good American mythology, however, history has also woven into the Custis saga a tale of redemption. As Roger Kennedy puts it, Washington's death in 1799 "freed Custis from the Presence, while putting him in servitude to his guilty memories of rebellion and the ways he had disappointed the departed." The news came at a time of particular uncertainty in Custis's life. Only a year earlier Washington had helped him secure a commission in the U.S. Army so that Custis might test his mettle in what seemed like certain war with France. But the Quasi War (1798–1800) quickly exhausted itself at sea, and once again Custis confronted the impossibility of walking in any of his fathers' footsteps. When Washington died Custis was away visiting a portion of the massive land inheritance that would accompany his approaching majority. Looking *forward* to something, anything, must have intoxicated a nineteen-year-old so accustomed to retrospect. When he returned, however, Custis surely learned that the general had asked for him from his deathbed.[11] Once again, Custis had disappointed.

Kennedy and others may be correct in assuming that guilt motivated Custis's immediate response to Washington's death. In the following months mourners across the new nation commemorated Washington in hundreds of ceremonies that themselves constituted a significant moment in the history of American public memory.[12] Consequently, Custis encountered representations of Washington's greatness at every turn, and his actions during the next two years certainly suggest a young man bent on filling a father's shoes. He remained ensconced at Mount Vernon, attending to Martha and managing George's will. In the meantime, and perhaps emboldened by his new responsibilities at Mount Vernon, Custis tried his hand at politics. In April 1802, and in the wake of Thomas Jefferson's Republican revolution, Custis cast himself as an "old-line" Federalist in a contest against Republican opponents for a seat in the Virginia General Assembly. Like Washington,

Custis feigned disinterest in political appointment, and yet he campaigned for it by railing against universal suffrage and the easing of property qualifications for voters. Unlike Washington, Custis lost his bid, leaving him eager for the day that his opponents might "plunge into the foaming Tiber of trouble."[13] Custis had, once again, failed to emulate the man with whose memory his own life had become so entwined.

And then two events, each in rapid succession, set Custis on a new path. The first, coming only three weeks after Custis's failed bid for office, was the sudden death of Martha Washington. Second, Martha's death meant that Washington's nephew and heir, Bushrod Washington, would inherit Mount Vernon. Despite Custis's entreaties, Bushrod refused to sell. Although Custis had inherited his own treasures—including three plantations spanning nearly ten thousand acres and a corps of slaves—Martha's death and Bushrod's ascendancy suddenly separated him from the home that gave his life meaning. Custis responded by buying up as much Washingtonia as he could get his hands on. Kennedy describes him "recklessly bidding at the auctions" that proceeded from Martha's death, assuming great debt only to acquire assorted farm contrivances, Washington's battle tents, some old furniture, and a stash of worn flags.[14] Custis, as if hoping to preserve something of the world he had just lost, ferried his loot across the Potomac and set to building his own manorial estate on an eleven hundred–acre tract inherited from his biological father.

Although perhaps paved with guilt, as the story goes, Custis's new path suggests also that the celebrated "child of Mount Vernon" was growing up and developing a sense of himself distinct from, even if tied to, Washington's memory. He married Mary "Molly" Lee Fitzhugh in 1804 after a playful courtship during which Custis decorated his love letters with kisses and bragged about reading Edward Gibbon's *Decline and Fall of the Roman Empire*, which Custis—notorious for his unwillingness to read—judged "an excellent work." When the time came, the couple notably exchanged their vows in Alexandria, not at Mount Vernon. And, perhaps most telling, although Custis initially named his new Alexandria estate "Mount Washington," he changed his mind and, in honor of the Custis family's ancestral seat, renamed the property "Arlington."[15] Whether by necessity, choice, or both, Custis had begun to establish himself as his own man, even though his political values and ideological commitments would always remain indelibly bound to Washington.

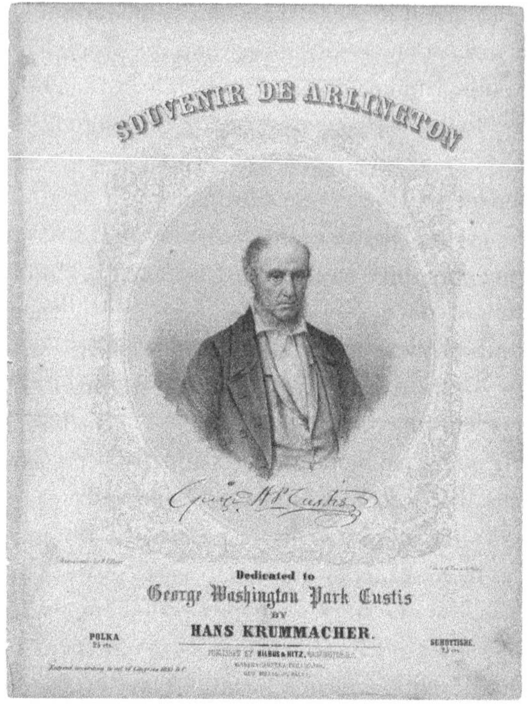

Custis rendered on the cover of the sheet music for Hans Krummacher's "Arlington Polka," a tribute by one of his many admirers. Courtesy of the Virginia Historical Society, Richmond.

New Memories for a New Nation

Alongside these signs of Custis's developing individuality and his interest in written history, his aggressive collecting of Washington's things reveals the early stirrings of a historical enterprise. Custis would have recognized objects and memory as natural partners from his years in Philadelphia. He knew Charles Willson Peale, for instance, who painted Washington on several occasions. Custis would have known Peale's museum, the first of its kind in North America, which dazzled visitors with lifelike nature tableaux, rows of Revolutionary portraits, and assorted historical curiosities. Peale's exhibits, intentionally didactic and decidedly public, anticipated modern museums. Custis also developed an early friendship with John Trumbull, whose *George Washington before the Battle of Trenton* (1792) marks, in Simon During's estimation, a pivotal moment in the development of protohistorical reenactment. From his Philadelphia studio Trumbull illustrated Washington's memory of the battle so that the viewer witnesses "the elder Washington *becoming* the younger Washington, reenacting his earlier military self." Custis was so impressed by Trumbull's painting that, as William Buckner McGroarty pointed out long ago, it inspired his own *Washington at Yorktown.*[16]

These are just two examples of Custis's contact with a marked cultural shift in historical consciousness that scholars associate, in part, with the aftermath of the American and French Revolutions. The change was particularly evident in history writing. Sir Walter Scott's historical novels exemplified the trend with their invocation of romantic medieval pasts draped in bygone landscapes and dreamy antiquities. Scott's suggestion that ordinary life was much different then to how it is now was indicative of what During calls the "historicization of everyday life," a growing awareness born of the Revolutionary era that historical change is constant and transformative. During notes that this shift accompanied a coincidental penchant in the literary and visual arts for historical verisimilitude that often "involved a disposition to live among mementos, images and traces of the past." And, at the same time, Scott's rendering of a Gothic past sought to build national allegiances among Britons and Scots at a time when Britain's boundaries declined sharply with American independence. In time, as Americans struggled to devise their own sense of shared nationalism, the example inspired a rising generation of American writers, including William Gilmore Simms, who mimicked Scott's literary nationalism in its own imagined pasts. Scott's example seems to have inspired Custis as well, who sometime before 1815 named his private schooner after Scott's poem, *Lady of the Lake* (1810).[17]

To whatever extent he was aware of it, then, Custis had grown up conversant in an emerging vernacular of memory and objects, a commemorative lingua franca worked out amid the celebratory hubbub of Mount Vernon and Washington's presidency. And it was Custis's mastery of this language that eventually enabled him to become more than just a character in the story that he so adored. Between Martha's death in 1803 and his own in 1857, Custis made it his life's work to preserve and perform George Washington's memory. Americans mostly eschewed commemoration prior to the 1820s for fear of enshrining precisely the sort of corrosive traditionalism they had fought to escape. What few obelisks and columns they did erect echoed European memorials in form and stood silent guard over the sites of important battles.[18] Custis, however, remembered differently. In 1815, for instance, he traveled to Virginia's Northern Neck Peninsula and erected a small freestone marker atop the supposed site of Washington's birth. Birthplace commemoration was novel at the time, and Custis's was likely the first on American soil. The diminutive monument implied, in juxtaposition with the sprawling fields that surrounded it, that the place itself was somehow special. This was not a place sanctified by the deeds of men, but rather one that endowed a particular man with the qualities necessary for greatness.[19]

More so than at Washington's birthplace, however, Custis's memory work at Arlington earned him considerable notice. No sooner had he begun to collect Washington's belongings than Custis engaged Capitol architect George Hadfield to devise a Greek Revival mansion with two wings flanking a central domed portico overlooking Washington, D.C. Though perpetually strapped for cash, Custis completed the wings in 1804 and moved in with his new wife and his collection of Washington artifacts. The portico, built on the cheap with hollow columns painted to resemble marble, took another decade to complete. Once done, however, Arlington House was much more than a home. Rather, Custis created there an elaborate memory theater. Inside, "precious relics of the great Patriot" recalled life at Mount Vernon.[20] Arrangements of china sets, serving bowls, assorted porcelain, and various furniture all scavenged from Custis's childhood home anticipated the period rooms typical of late-century house museums. Displayed beneath portraits of the Washington, Parke, Custis, Lewis, and Lee families, including noted works by Peale, these artifacts conspired alongside remnants of the family's clothing, its papers, and Washington's deathbed to conjure a sense of physical presence.

Arlington House evoked equal parts shrine and curiosity cabinet. Custis's curatorial intervention, however, prefigured the modern American history museum. His exhibitionary strategy followed that of Peale. Like Peale's museum, Arlington House ordered portraits, natural curiosities (Custis decorated his walls with hunting trophies), and historical objects in a vertical hierarchy befitting tall ceilings and Enlightenment taxonomy. And just as Peale animated his nature settings, so did Custis create a backdrop for Arlington's mix of objects and stories. Including the portrait of Washington at Yorktown inspired by Trumbull's, Custis painted several large murals of Washington in various battle scenes. "As works of art," his daughter recalled, "they have but little merit. Their chief value lies in their truthfulness to history in the delineation of events, incidents, and costumes." Custis would have agreed. His was not the work of an artist, but rather of the historian, curator, and dramaturge. Wandering through Arlington's rooms, visitors beheld portraits of bygone Washingtons surrounded by the objects they had possessed in life. Custis followed along all the while providing the narrative that bound it all together. For more than three decades, Custis serially published his recollections of Washington in newspapers, often on patriotic occasions. These preserve in content, at least, the broad strokes of his early interpretive script.[21]

And, in this regard Custis's museum practice, insomuch as it might be called that, was unabashedly theatrical. Whether at Mount Vernon or in Philadelphia, Custis had always been on stage, and the tendency persisted in adulthood. Even after his failed bid for office, Custis remained a tireless orator and never passed up an opportunity to invoke Washington's legacy on behalf of the Federalist cause or nationalist movements abroad. He enjoyed success during the 1830s as a playwright. Custis penned a number of nationalist plays that commemorated everything from American Indians to the coming of the railroad. Some of these, particularly his Indian plays, earned him acclaim for staged performances in Philadelphia. On learning of a successful showing in Baltimore, Custis assured his wife that "I should sooner get out of debt by the labour of my brains than of my ploughs." At Arlington, however, Custis was both playwright and actor. Although he had been compelled to perform the "child of Mount Vernon" during his early life, Arlington provided the stage on which Custis commanded the role. He even dressed the part. Tromping about the place in knee breeches, "ruffled wristbands and [a] rich old-fashioned vest," long after they had passed from fashion, Custis relished "the many visitors who . . . call here to see the Washington Treasury, old Pictures, and the Old Man, the most curious of all."[22]

Custis's awareness of himself as one of Arlington's curiosities or, as he put it, "the Last Relic of the domestic family of the beloved chief," distinguishes this mnemonic project as something distinctly modern by virtue of its reflexivity. Custis was well aware that he had become the centerpiece of his own collection. Correspondents who considered Custis "the only living person, whose memory . . . is able to recall the particulars of that far off time" assured him of it. Custis relished performing his own authenticity. Every April thirtieth—the twin anniversary of Washington's first inaugural and Custis's birth—from 1805 to 1812 Custis hosted a sheep-shearing festival in celebration of American agriculture. To accommodate the crowds Custis built a veritable visitor center at Arlington, including a public wharf, dining hall, and even a dancing saloon. The highlight of each festival was a shearing contest intended to promote American manufacturing and to encourage independence from foreign goods. But these events also provided Custis an opportunity to perform alongside his other relics. Surrounded by his murals and framed by Washington's battle tent, Custis closed each event with a grand oration that culled from his remarkable archive of possessions and stories a sweeping panoramic vision of the American past.[23] If Trumbull's portrait of Washington remembering himself flagged an early moment of figurative reenactment, then Custis's first-person portrayal of himself as one of Arlington's many relics achieved something akin to our modern notion of living history, and for a far broader public.

Custis's mastery of Arlington's stage set also permitted a degree of mnemonic erasure. No matter how compulsively he commemorated Washington, Custis could not ameliorate the shortcomings of a nation that never quite fulfilled its own Revolutionary aspirations. Those shortcomings were powerfully evident in Custis's life. Neighbors complained, for instance, about the atrocious conditions that slaves endured on his New Kent County plantation. And at home, among Arlington's many visitors, Custis could not disguise his obvious indiscretions. Custis brought several of the slaves he inherited from Martha Washington to toil at Arlington. That number included Airy Carter, with whom Custis fathered a daughter named Maria. Custis openly favored Maria with an education, land, and, informally at least, freedom. Perhaps Custis recognized that she, more than himself, ranked among the last of Mount Vernon's living relics.[24] If so, the realization did not move Custis to free his slaves. Despite his public support for the American Colonization Society and his wife's committed abolitionism, Custis refused to part ways with the institution that had bankrolled his memory projects. Although he freed his slaves in death, in life Custis was not above selling people to ease his own economic failures.

Living History's Lost Legacy

A fuller account of Custis's life, which is long overdue, would augment our growing awareness of the indelible link between race and memory in

American history. That project would also explore Custis's support of a failed attempt in 1832 to reinter Washington's body beneath the Capitol building and his prominent role in the triumphal return of Washington's *other* adoptive son, the Marquis de Lafayette, in 1824. Custis's love of relics—at Washington's tomb, he presented Lafayette with a ring containing a lock of the general's hair—deserves mention too because, by cutting out signatures from Washington's papers and sending them along with other heirlooms to well-wishers across the country, the great guardian of Washington's legacy partially destroyed one of its greatest collections.[25] What remained of that collection after Custis's death in 1857 suffered with the Civil War. Custis left Arlington to his only living *legitimate* child, Mary Anna Randolph Custis, whose marriage to Confederate general Robert E. Lee made the house a target for Union troops. By 1861 what remained of Arlington's treasures had been secreted away by family members, hauled off to the U.S. Patent Office, or looted by soldiers.

What is more, Lee's connection to Arlington House has since obscured our memory of Custis's role there even while ensuring its preservation. Because of its associations with Lee and the slave South, Arlington House shouldered the burdens of symbolic vindication during the war and after. Union troops occupied it in 1861 and a freedmen's village flourished on the property after emancipation. Most famously, of course, the national cemetery established at Arlington in 1864 figured the house as a temple of national mourning. And yet, memories of Lee have proved so alluring to Americans of all stripes that, during its administration by the War Department and, since 1933, by the National Park Service, Arlington House was restored to its prewar condition and designated a permanent national memorial to Robert E. Lee in 1955. Visitor brochures from the time figure Custis's role as part of the "early history" of a more significant story about Lee and disunion. Tourists still visit the historic building and its grounds. The National Park Service has even expanded its programming over the years to recall Custis and the lives of Arlington's slaves. But most Americans—certainly most of the millions who visit Arlington National Cemetery every year—regard Arlington House, which is managed separately, as a minor element in what has become the nation's most honored stage for the performance of patriotic memory.[26]

That they do is a fitting tribute to the man who more than any would have delighted in knowing that Arlington remains a place where memory, history, and patriotic nationalism coincide. He would also enjoy knowing that costumed interpreters revisit his life from time to time. But, like all monuments, Arlington's meanings are as carefully crafted today as they were two centuries ago. Custis's lifelong compulsion to honor Washington's principles and policies meant that Arlington always served a political agenda. Custis's performance of a decidedly Federalist memory was, in the context of early nineteenth-century politics, feverishly political, vehemently anti-Republican, and blatantly anti-Jefferson. Republican critics ridiculed the "little Arlington Ram" for "*butting* at the *whole* nation." Roger Kennedy argues that Custis even intended Arlington House's boxy Greek Revivalism to mock Jefferson's love of Roman domes.[27] The obvious dissonance between Custis's "treasures" at Arlington House and Jefferson's natural and scientific curiosities at Monticello suggests that culture wars are nothing new in American display spaces. It also suggests that Custis was anything but a hapless dilettante. From high atop his perch overlooking the nation's capitol, this fiery political ideologue waged a war to shape the country's future. Forgetting to remember Custis clouds our awareness that the public performance of patriotic memory, even in a space as sacred as Arlington, is never free of motive. Rather, Custis's memory work suggests that living history has, from its beginnings, been bound up in the politics of national memory.

NOTES

This chapter benefited tremendously from conversations with Sara Bearss, Hilary Iris Lowe, Jill Ogline Titus, and David Waldstreicher. I am indebted also to the Virginia Historical Society and its staff for supporting my work with an Andrew W. Mellon Research Fellowship.

1. For an overview of living-history scholarship, see Scott Magelssen, *Living History Museums: Undoing History through Performance* (Lanham, Md.: Scarecrow, 2007), xiv–xix, chap. 1. Mark B. Sandberg discusses Skansen in *Living Pictures, Missing Persons: Mannequins, Museums, and Modernity* (Princeton: Princeton University Press, 2003), chap. 9.
2. Roy Rosenzweig and David Thelen, *The Presence of the Past: Popular Uses of History in American Life* (New York: Columbia University Press, 1998), 27–28, 109–14, 168–69.
3. David Bailie Warden to George Washington Parke Custis, May 23, 1811, sec. 3, Mary Custis Lee Papers, 1694–1917, Virginia Historical Society, Richmond.
4. Robert M. Poole, *On Hallowed Ground: The Story of Arlington National*

Cemetery (New York: Walker, 2009). The earliest notable account of Custis is in Murray H. Nelligan, "Old Arlington: The Story of the Lee Mansion National Memorial" (PhD diss., Columbia University, 1954). Sara B. Bearss, whose essays are cited throughout this chapter, has written most effectively on Custis. See also Elizabeth Brown Pryor, *Reading the Man: A Portrait of Robert E. Lee* (New York: Viking, 2007), and Karal Ann Marling, *George Washington Slept Here: Colonial Revivals and American Culture, 1876–1986* (Cambridge: Harvard University Press, 1988), 25–26.

5. Sara B. Bearss, "Custis, George Washington Parke," *Dictionary of Virginia Biography*, ed. Sara B. Bearss et al., 3 vols. (Richmond: Library of Virginia, 2006), 3:630; Patricia Brady, ed., *George Washington's Beautiful Nelly: The Letters of Eleanor Parke Custis Lewis to Elizabeth Bordley Gibson, 1794–1851* (Columbia: University of South Carolina Press, 2006), 1–3; Frank Grizzard, *George Washington: A Biographical Companion* (Santa Barbara: ABC-CLIO, 2002), 64; William M. S. Rasmussen and Robert S. Tilton, *Lee and Grant* (London: Giles, 2007), 89.
6. Brady, *George Washington's Beautiful Nelly*, 3.
7. George Washington Parke Custis, Mary Lee Custis, and Benson J. Lossing, *Recollections and Private Memoirs of Washington, by His Adopted Son* (1860; repr., Bridgewater, Va.: American Foundation Publications, 1999), 373–74; William Smith to George Washington, August 18, 1782, reproduced in William Smith, *An Account of Washington College, in the State of Maryland* (Philadelphia: Crukshank, 1784), 24.
8. Joseph J. Ellis, *His Excellency: George Washington* (New York: Vintage, 2005), 148; Custis, Custis, and Lossing, *Recollections and Private Memoirs*, 38; Jean B. Lee, "Historical Memory, Sectional Strife, and the American Mecca," *Virginia Magazine of History and Biography* 109 (2001): 257, 260.
9. Brady, *George Washington's Beautiful Nelly*, 3; William Ayres, "At Home with George: Commercialization of the Washington Image, 1776–1876," in *George Washington, American Symbol*, ed. Barbary J. Mitnick (New York: Hudson Hills, 1999).
10. "Dilettante" appears in Karl Decker and Angus McSween, *Historic Arlington: A History of the National Cemetery . . . with Descriptions of Life in Virginia during the Early Part of the Century* (Washington, D.C.: Decker & McSween, 1892), 23. Grizzard, *George Washington*, 64–66; "George Washington Custis, Martha Washington's Grandson, Charged with Suspicion of a Felony at Gadsby's Tavern," *Fireside Sentinel* (Alexandria Library, Lloyd House Newsletter), September 1987; Sara B. Bearss, "The Federalist Career of George Washington Parke Custis," *Northern Virginia Heritage* 8 (February 1986): 16; "Custis, George Washington Parke," in *The South in the Building of the Nation*, ed. Walter Lynwood Fleming (Richmond, Va.: Southern Historical Publication Society, 1909), 11:246; Decker, *Historic Arlington*, 15; Edward G. Lengel, *Inventing George Washington: America's Founder, in Myth and Memory* (New York: Harper Collins, 2011), 33–36.
11. Roger Kennedy, "Arlington House, a Mansion That Was a Monument," *Smithsonian* 16 (October 1985): 158; Bearss, "Custis, George Washington Parke," 630; Grizzard, *George Washington*, 66–67.
12. Gerald Edward Kahler, "Washington in Glory, America in Tears: The Nation

Mourns the Death of George Washington, 1799–1800" (PhD diss., College of William and Mary, 2003).

13. Bearss, "Federalist Career," 16; Bearss, "Custis, George Washington Parke," 630.
14. Kennedy, "Arlington House," 158.
15. Custis to Mary Lee Fitzhugh, 1803, sec. 3, Mary Custis Lee Papers; Bearss, "Custis, George Washington Parke," 630.
16. Gary Kulik, "Designing the Past: History-Museum Exhibitions from Peale to the Present," and Thomas Schlereth, "History Museums and Material Culture," both in *History Museums in the United States: A Critical Assessment*, ed. Warren Leon and Roy Rosenzweig (Urbana: University of Illinois Press, 1989); Simon During, "Mimic Toil: Eighteenth-Century Preconditions for the Modern Historical Reenactment," *Rethinking History* 11 (September 2007): 328–30; William Buckner McGroarty, "A Letter and a Portrait from Arlington House," *William and Mary College Quarterly Historical Magazine* 22 (January 1942): 52–53; T. Michael Miller, "The Mystery Surrounding G. W. Custis' Painting of George Washington at Yorktown," *Alexandria Chronicle* 6 (Fall 1998): 1–11.
17. During, "Mimic Toil," 315–16; David Moltke-Hansen, "The Fictive Transformation of American Nationalism after Sir Walter Scott," *Historically Speaking: The Bulletin of the Historical Society* (June 2009): 24–27; Custis, Custis, and Lossing, *Recollections and Private Memoirs*, 127.
18. Michael Kammen, *Mystic Chords of Memory: The Transformation of Tradition in American Culture* (New York: Knopf, 1991), 19, 41–42; David Lowenthal, *The Past Is a Foreign Country* (Cambridge: Cambridge University Press, 1985), 117–21; Alfred F. Young, *The Shoemaker and the Tea Party: Memory and the American Revolution* (Boston: Beacon, 1999), particularly chap. 3.
19. On Custis and Washington's birthplace, see Seth C. Bruggeman, *Here, George Washington Was Born: Memory, Material Culture, and the Public History of a National Monument* (Athens: University of Georgia Press, 2008).
20. Benson J. Lossing, "Arlington House," *Harper's New Monthly Magazine* 7 (September 1853): 433–55.
21. Custis, Custis, and Lossing, *Recollections and Private Memoirs*, 68; David G. Lowe, "A Son's Tribute," *American Heritage* 17 (February 1966): 16–21, 85–87; Sara A. Reed, *A Romance of Arlington House* (Boston: Chapple, 1908), 37–41. Custis's daughter, Mary Custis Lee, published Custis's collected stories with Benson J. Lossing beginning in 1859 as *Recollections and Private Memoirs of Washington*.
22. Murray H. Nelligan, "American Nationalism on the Stage: The Plays of George Washington Parke Custis (1781–1857)," *Virginia Magazine of History and Biography* 58 (July 1950); Bearss, "Custis, George Washington Parke," 632; Bearss, "Federalist Career," 19; Kennedy, "Arlington House," 163–64; Custis to Mary Anna Randolph Custis, July 19, 1833, and to Lydia H. Sigourney, March 10, 1855, sec. 3, Mary Custis Lee Papers.
23. Custis to Lewis W. Washington, February 1857, and William Walcott to Custis, August 30, 1852, sec. 3, Mary Custis Lee Papers; Lossing, "Arlington House," 437; Bearss, "The Farmer of Arlington: George W. P. Custis and the Arlington Sheep Shearings," *Virginia Cavalcade* 38 (1989): 124–33.
24. See the account of Custis's plantation in William Meade to Mary Lee Custis,

May 29, 1821, sec. 10, Mary Custis Lee Papers. See also Bearss, "Custis, George Washington Parke," 630–31; Dana Priest, "Arlington Bequest a Footnote in Black History," *Washington Post*, February 27, 1990; Rasmussen and Tilton, *Lee and Grant*, 91–92; Pryor, *Reading the Man*, 138–39.

25. Bearss, "Custis, George Washington Parke," 632.
26. National Park Service, "Custis-Lee Mansion: The Robert E. Lee Memorial" (Washington, D.C.: Government Printing Office, 1956); James Oliver Horton, "Slavery in American History: An Uncomfortable National Dialogue," in *Slavery and Public History: The Tough Stuff of American Memory*, ed. James Oliver Horton and Lois E. Horton (Charlotte: University of North Carolina Press, 2009), 48–49.
27. Freeman Tilden, *Interpreting our Heritage* (Chapel Hill: University of North Carolina Press, 2007), 110–11; Bearss, "Federalist Career," 17; Kennedy, "Arlington House," 162–63.

Plagiarism in Pursuit of Historical Truth

George Chalmers and the Patriotic Legacy of Loyalist History

Eileen Ka-May Cheng

In 1844 George Bancroft indignantly dismissed charges that he had plagiarized from the loyalist George Chalmers for the fourth volume of his history. He characterized such charges as "a tissue of falsehoods from beginning to end," arguing, "who would suppose that I would break the unity and consistency of my own style and narrative by patching upon it the language and doctrines of an English tory respecting our American revolution? The suggestion is ridiculous."[1] Yet plagiarize from the "tory" Chalmers's *Political Annals* is just what Bancroft did in the first two volumes of his history, following the lead of other early nineteenth-century historians who also copied or paraphrased from Chalmers's work without attribution. While plagiarism was a widespread practice among American historians in this period, what is striking about these historians' use of Chalmers is their willingness to lift material from a loyalist known for his scathing condemnation of the patriot cause, even as their goal was to vindicate the Revolution and promote nationalism.[2]

The widely shared belief in the nationalist function of history resulted in an outpouring of writing about American history in the decades after the Revolution, as Americans actively struggled for ways to shore up the tenuous bonds that held the new nation together.[3] The political and intellectual elite led the way in using history to define and unify the nation. Wishing to defend a hierarchical social order based on deference to elite authority from the popular challenges unleashed by the Revolution, elite historians interpreted the Revolution in conservative terms, obscuring the often bitter social conflict that, as Michael A. McDonnell has described, characterized the Revolution in so many quarters.[4] Disseminating their conservative social message through formal histories as well as schoolbooks and Fourth of July orations, these historians laid the basis for the exceptionalist narrative of American origins that came to dominate public memory of the Revolution in their time and that continues to this day.[5] Although this narrative did not go uncontested, as the other chapters in this volume demonstrate, even challengers like Joseph Plumb Martin defined his "antinarrative" in opposition to it, revealing how influential elite historians were in setting the terms of the debate over the meaning of the Revolution.[6] While Bancroft was the most successful of these historians, his predecessors Hugh Williamson and John Marshall helped lay the groundwork for the exceptionalist view of the Revolution as an orderly and unified struggle to overthrow British tyranny and effect higher ideals that were deeply rooted in the colonial past. Among the leading casualties of this view were the loyalists. Unable to fit the vicious wartime struggles between loyalists and revolutionaries into their seamless narrative of order and consensus, historians of all stripes—from the local historians discussed by James Paxton in this volume to elite historians like Williamson, Marshall, and Bancroft—either vilified or erased the loyalists from their histories.[7]

Yet, paradoxically, the same concern with order that led the three elite historians to disown the loyalists as Americans also led them to incorporate loyalist historiography into their narratives by plagiarizing Chalmers's work. As fearful of popular unrest as his American nationalist opponents were, Chalmers made what he considered to be the dangerous rebellious tendencies of the colonists a central theme throughout his *Political Annals.* Rather than repudiating Chalmers's scathing portrait of colonial disorder, Williamson, Marshall, and Bancroft adapted it to serve their own nationalist purposes and reinforce their conservative social message.[8] Their plagiarism of Chalmers suggests, then, that they and other American nationalist historians had more in common with their loyalist counterparts than either they or modern scholars have acknowledged. If, as Paxton has shown, local historians in the Mohawk Valley obscured the affinities between revolutionaries and loyalists by vilifying the loyalists and excluding them from claims to American nationality, then Williamson, Marshall, and Bancroft achieved the same goal by co-opting Chalmers's message of social order and absorbing loyalist historiography into their vision of American nationhood.[9] The loyalist historians were thus not as marginal to American historical and national consciousness as the long-standing perception of them as the "losers" of the Revolution has assumed.[10]

Williamson, Marshall, and Bancroft were able to adapt Chalmers's analysis to reconcile their desire for order with their allegiance to the Revolution because plagiarism was not simply a matter of copying for them, but an interpretive choice. Yet they were not just propagandists manipulating Chalmers's account for their own ends at the expense of truth. Writing at a time before history had become a professionalized discipline, these three historians shared their modern counterparts' commitment to truth but differed in their standards and methods for achieving this goal.[11] Hence, rather than a sign of intellectual dishonesty or lax scholarship, their plagiarism of Chalmers actually reflected their concern with critical analysis and accuracy, providing them with a vehicle for reconciling their social purposes with their desire for truth. Their plagiarism of Chalmers therefore puts into question the distinction that J. H. Plumb once made between critical (or, for him, "true") history and the use of the past by the guardians of tradition to sanctify the established social order and give meaning to the present—or what, as Gordon Wood has noted, would now be deemed the preserve of memory. In its skeptical and dispassionate perspective and its concern with truth, critical history was, for Plumb, "by its very nature" opposed to the qualities that gave the past its social power.[12] While epitomizing the use of the past to sanctify the present that characterized the guardians of tradition, Williamson, Marshall, and Bancroft revealed that this imperative was not as opposed to critical history as Plumb had suggested.[13]

Even while their plagiarism seemed to be the antithesis of the critical methods that have come to define professional scholarship, their appropriations from Chalmers were the product of a critical analysis of their sources, and they used those appropriations for one of the same purposes that professional scholars use footnotes—to validate their claims to truth. Far from undermining the social function and meaning of the past for these historians, their critical approach and concern with truth actually furthered their social purposes and enhanced the stabilizing power of their historical narratives.[14] Bancroft differed from his predecessors, however, in his understanding of truth—hence the differences in the character of his plagiarism from Chalmers. These differences were in turn a function of the more self-confident nationalism that had emerged by Bancroft's time, which made him more willing than Williamson and Marshall to acknowledge both his use of and his differences from Chalmers. At once the most chauvinistic in his nationalism and the most committed to critical history, Bancroft exemplified the way in which critical history and the social power of the past could reinforce, rather than oppose, each other.

Early national historians could draw on Chalmers not only because they shared his conservative fear of popular disorder but also because his faith in commercial progress and his commitment to scholarship made his work more than just a reactionary diatribe against the Revolution. Best known to American historians for his works on American history, the *Political Annals* (1780) and *An Introduction to the History of the Revolt of the Colonies* (1782), Chalmers had emigrated to Maryland from Scotland in 1763, but had to leave the colony in 1775 because of his loyalist activities.[15] Although the first volume of his *Political Annals* covered colonial history only up to 1688, Chalmers used his account of this period to critique and explain the Revolution, structuring the text around the contrast between the loyalty and respect for tradition that characterized Virginia and Maryland and the spirit of independence and innovation that he believed defined the New England colonies.[16] According to Chalmers, the Revolution came about through a combination of the New England colonists' fanatical opposition to British authority, and the weakness and vacillation of British policymakers, which allowed the rebellious tendencies of the New England colonists to infect the rest of the colonies, culminating with the revolutionaries' outright repudiation of British authority.[17]

While conservative in his regard for tradition, Chalmers at the same time embraced a dynamic vision of commercial progress that had its roots in Scottish Enlightenment thought.[18] The result was a duality in his portrayal of the New England colonists, which pointed to the tensions created by his twin commitment to order and liberty. As much as he condemned the fractiousness of New England colonists, he also spoke admiringly of their rapid economic growth and prosperity, which he attributed to the energizing effects of the liberty they enjoyed.[19] But he found it impossible to dissociate such liberty from the turbulence it created, concluding that "no man has been found who can unravel the intricate knot, by making the advantages of union and the interests of freedom coalesce."[20]

Reflecting Chalmers's commitment to factual accuracy, the *Political Annals* was also a work of serious scholarship based on extensive research in both published primary sources and unpublished government documents. Chalmers verified that research by appending to the end of each chapter a detailed list of citations that identified the sources he had used, as well as giving lengthy extracts from his primary sources.[21] Early national historians widely recognized and used Chalmers's *Annals* for its value as a source of factual information and primary source material. Among those who drew from or plagiarized Chalmers were such leading historians as David Ramsay, Abiel Holmes, Jedidiah Morse, and John Palfrey. Jared Sparks in 1844 pointed to Chalmers's influence on early national historians and the value that they placed on his factual accuracy when he noted that "although he [Chalmers] wrote under prejudices, yet no one has disputed his facts, and his Annals have always been quoted as high authority by our best writers."[22]

Yet early national historians turned to Chalmers for more than the facts he provided, for they shared some of his "prejudices." Plagiarism enabled Hugh Williamson, for instance, to appropriate Chalmers's conservative social message without acknowledging its loyalist origins. A prominent supporter of the Constitution, Williamson served as one of North Carolina's delegates to the Constitutional Convention, and his plagiarism of Chalmers for his *History of North Carolina* (1812) revealed the concern with order and stability that made him such an active champion of the Constitution.[23] Although Williamson did not directly copy from Chalmers's work, he paraphrased passages from the *Annals* without acknowledgement, mentioning the first volume of the *Annals* in his preface only to dismiss it as a "ministerial work."[24] While unabashed in his plagiarism, Williamson was highly selective in what he took from Chalmers, suggesting that his plagiarism was a conscious ideological choice. Rather than lifting passages from Chalmers wholesale, he modified them to suit his own purposes, as in his analysis of Culpeper's Rebellion.[25] Chalmers depicted this rebellion—in which North Carolinians rose up in 1677 to overthrow an acting governor they considered unjust—as the result of "deliberate contrivance" by unprincipled individuals concerned only with their own profit. The ability of such schemers to manipulate the people into rebelling against the government revealed for Chalmers how "the people are made the constant bubbles of their own credulity and of others [*sic*] crimes: We may deplore their miseries, though it seems to little purpose to lament what cannot possibly be in future prevented!" What made Culpeper's Rebellion so deplorable in Chalmers's eyes was the harmful precedent it set for the revolutionaries' challenge to British authority, and he concluded ominously by speaking of those who "foretold" that the colony would later "regret the evil of bad example, which must necessarily result from successful insurrection."[26]

Williamson, on the other hand, denied any such connection between Culpeper's Rebellion and the Revolution, at the same time that he lifted the rest of Chalmers's explanation for the rebellion. Williamson even echoed Chalmers's wording when he proclaimed, "We lament the credulity of our fellow citizens, when we observe instances of this kind, in which harmless undesigning men are made the tools of faction, and are persuaded to risk their lives in supporting the private and personal views of some idle, worthless adventurer." By plagiarizing from Chalmers's condemnation of Culpeper's Rebellion as an example of how easily people could be manipulated by unscrupulous demagogues into dangerous unrest, Williamson expressed his own distrust of the people and his own fear of social disorder. But whereas Chalmers condemned the Revolution as the culmination of such unrest, Williamson dissociated the Revolution from this kind of disorder by omitting Chalmers's concluding comment about the dangerous precedent set by Culpeper's Rebellion. Instead, directly contrary to Chalmers, he emphasized the orderly character of the Revolution in the second volume of his history.[27]

Yet Williamson provided little explanation for how the social disorder that characterized North Carolina in his first volume transformed into the respect for law and order that characterized the revolutionaries of the second volume, revealing the tensions created by his simultaneous desire to vindicate the Revolution and discourage popular upheaval. Williamson's inability to explain this transformation demonstrated how tenuous and unclear the basis was for revolutionary order in his own mind. Writing at a time when the Revolution was a living memory and its outcome was still in doubt, and feeling uncertain about whether the Revolution had established a secure basis for social order, Williamson could not acknowledge his debt to Chalmers for his condemnation of popular disorder, since to do so would be to give credence to the lurking fear that the loyalists may have been right in their warnings about the centrifugal effects of the Revolution.[28] Thus the same anxieties about social cohesion and national unity that contributed to Williamson's reliance on Chalmers also prevented him from acknowledging that dependence.

The nature of John Marshall's plagiarism from Chalmers was more complex than that of Williamson, as Marshall responded to these shared anxieties not by disguising his reliance on Chalmers but by selectively divulging it and using it to demonstrate his commitment to truth. The result was that Marshall was more successful in reconciling his desire for social order with his allegiance to the Revolution, as he both plagiarized Chalmers more extensively than did Williamson and challenged Chalmers's portrayal of the colonists more profoundly in the first volume of his *Life of George Washington* (1804). Although better known in his capacity as chief justice of the Supreme Court, Marshall was also a well-regarded historian in his own time. Marshall's five-volume biography of Washington was successful enough for him to publish revised editions of the first volume in 1824 and the other four in 1832, followed by a single-volume school edition in 1838. Marshall's first volume offered a general history of the American colonies, plagiarized from many different histories besides Chalmers's.[29] Marshall openly admitted to what today would be considered plagiarism in the preface to the 1804 edition, declaring that he had "sometimes" used the language of his sources "without distinguishing the passages" by quotation marks. Yet he also displayed a recognition of plagiarism as an offense, emphasizing that he had cited such sources "in the margin" and expressing his hope that this would absolve him "of wishing, by a concealed plagiarism" to present the work of others as his own.[30] Clearly more ambivalent than Williamson about intellectual theft, Marshall made a limited effort to cite his sources at the end of each chapter in the 1804 edition of the first volume of his history. In later editions published in 1805 and 1828, he provided even more extensive and precise citations, although he continued to use the language of his sources without quotation marks and was inconsistent about acknowledging the sources from which he copied or paraphrased.[31]

When he declared that his citations would attest to the truthfulness of his claims by providing authority "for the establishment of their verity," Marshall revealed a concern with truth that also accounted for his decision to plagiarize from Chalmers. Since Marshall believed that truth was a matter of collecting and synthesizing facts, what was important for him were the facts his sources had provided, not how they were presented, making it unnecessary to indicate that he was using their language through quotation marks. When he spoke of how his sources "are quoted for all those facts which are detailed in part on their authority," he suggested that copying their language would actually enhance the truthfulness of his own account by ensuring the most accurate rendering of the material they presented.[32] Hence in plagiarizing so heavily from Chalmers's history, which he singled out as a "very valuable work" that "has furnished almost all the facts" necessary to write a history of the United States for the period up to 1688, Marshall grounded his claim to present the truth on the basis of his fidelity to Chalmers's supposedly comprehensive and accurate account of the facts of American colonial history.[33]

Believing that truth required the historian to provide an impartial and unbiased account of the facts, Marshall related the events he discussed in a dispassionate tone, without expressing his own opinions, to such a degree that his work has been criticized as little more than a colorless pastiche of extracts and paraphrases taken from other sources without an interpretive viewpoint to unify them.[34] Yet Marshall's work was more coherent and skillfully crafted than his critics recognized. It wove together extracts from sources as different as Chalmers's *Annals* and Jeremy Belknap's *History of New-Hampshire* (1784–1792) and incorporated his own paraphrases and modifications to form a seamless and fluid narrative. His apparent colorlessness was itself an interpretive choice that both reflected a critical analysis of his sources and served his social purposes, enabling him to mediate between his fear of popular disorder and his allegiance to the Revolution.[35] Because Chalmers was so scathing in his condemnation of the colonists, Marshall was able to achieve this dispassionate tone only by leaving out Chalmers's harshest criticisms of the colonists or softening the language of those comments when he plagiarized from Chalmers.

The result of such changes was to make colonists appear less unruly and rebellious than they had in Chalmers's account, without denying such dissension altogether. For example, following Chalmers closely in wording and structure as he condensed his predecessor's account of Culpeper's Rebellion, Marshall gave this summary: "Having thus taken possession of the government, they established courts of justice, appointed officers, called a parliament, and for several years exercised the powers of an independent state; yet they never formally disclaimed the authority of the proprietors."[36] But where Chalmers unequivocally denounced the rebellion as an example of the "credulity" of the people, Marshall omitted this statement as well as all of Chalmers's other critical comments about the rebellion, leaving ambiguous his own judgment of its rightfulness. Yet this very ambiguity served an ideological purpose for Marshall. As a leading Federalist, he did not wish to sanction popular disorder by defending Culpeper's Rebellion. At the same time, however, to vindicate the Revolution and dissociate it from such disorder, he also had to challenge Chalmers's portrayal of the rebellion as part of a pattern of dangerous upheaval that culminated with the Revolution.[37] Unlike Williamson, who reconciled these imperatives by leaving out Chalmers's statement linking the two events, Marshall mediated between them through the noncommittal language that he used to describe the rebellion, which enabled him to soften Chalmers's attack on the insurgents without sanctioning the rebellion itself. Selectively paraphrasing from Chalmers in his statement that the rebels never "formally disclaimed the authority of the proprietors," Marshall further mitigated their actions by implying the limits of their challenge to established authority. Thus, the words that Marshall used to paraphrase Chalmers exculpated the colonists from Chalmers's characterization of them as incorrigibly fractious without overtly disputing Chalmers or praising the colonists, further legitimizing his vindication of them as the expression of impartial truth.

Marshall brought together his regard for truth with his desire for unity and order not just in the content of his appropriations from Chalmers but also in the means he used to validate those borrowings. Throughout his analysis Marshall would often cite Chalmers for sections that mixed material drawn from Chalmers with his own conclusions or with material taken from other historians, without making clear what precisely came from Chalmers and what did not. For example, sharing his faith in the benefits of commerce, Marshall drew directly from Chalmers to comment on the "unexampled state of prosperity" the New England colonists enjoyed until the Restoration, attributing this condition to their "free and unrestrained commerce." Yet contrary to Chalmers's portrayal of the tensions between commercial prosperity and social order, Marshall's account highlighted the compatibility between these imperatives by describing the New England colonists as "sober industrious people" in the next paragraph.[38] Instead of openly disputing Chalmers's interpretation, Marshall's footnote cited both Chalmers and Thomas Hutchinson, even though this paragraph was based on material taken from Hutchinson's *History of Massachusetts-Bay* only, and the terms "sober" and "industrious" were his addition.[39] The effect of Marshall's citations to Chalmers and his failure to distinguish his own authorial interventions was to create a greater sense of coherence and unity to American history than was actually the case, by denying the existence of conflict over interpretations of the nation's past. By merging together material from these sources and citing different ones for different sections without acknowledging any disagreement between them, Marshall made it seem as though he was simply putting together pieces of a puzzle that formed a harmonious whole; his role as historian was simply to select the right pieces and show how they fit together.

This strategy revealed Marshall's ambivalence about relying on Chalmers. Unwilling to deny that reliance as Williamson had, Marshall could claim Chalmers's reputation for factual accuracy for his own work by aligning himself with Chalmers and obscuring his departures from the *Political Annals* through both his citations and his use of Chalmers's language. Furthermore, Chalmers's identity as a loyalist could actually have enhanced his value in validating Marshall's claims to truth, for if even the research of a loyalist hostile to the Revolution confirmed Marshall's findings, then that provided all the more proof that they were true. Fearing the heated party conflicts of the 1790s and the ascendancy of the Jeffersonian Republicans in the election of 1800 as threats to social order, however, Marshall was still too insecure, about whether the Revolution had established a stable basis for national unity to note Chalmers's identity as a loyalist. To bring Chalmers's opposition to the Revolution out into the open would have highlighted the very divisions Marshall wished to cover up.[40] Marshall's ambiguity about both the nature of his appropriations from Chalmers and the political sympathies of his predecessor thus allowed him to have it both ways, enabling him to obscure such divisions while benefiting from the validation that Chalmers could confer on his work for those familiar with the *Political Annals.*

Seemingly the polar opposite of Marshall in his democratic political sympathies and his Romantic writing style, Bancroft also differed from Marshall in his understanding of truth. Moreover, he expressed a more self-confident nationalism than either Marshall or Williamson. The result of these differences was that Bancroft was more willing to acknowledge both his use of and disagreement with Chalmers through his footnotes. An ardent Jacksonian who used history to legitimize his democratic principles, Bancroft was instrumental in promoting the more chauvinistic nationalism that took hold after the War of 1812. While new sources of anxiety and conflict also arose in this period, the nation's ability to survive another test of war made the success of the Revolution seem more assured to Americans.[41] As members of what George B. Forgie has termed the post-heroic generation, Bancroft and his contemporaries viewed the Revolution as more a legacy to be preserved than an ongoing event whose outcome had yet to be determined.[42] Interpreting the Revolution as the realization of providential destiny for human history, Bancroft crystallized the basic assumptions of American exceptionalist ideology in his *History of the United States,* the first volume of which was published in 1834 to wide popular and critical acclaim, followed by nine more volumes, the last one published in 1874.[43]

Known for its celebratory nationalism, Bancroft's *History of the United States* was also a work of serious scholarship based on extensive research in primary and secondary sources. While he generally cited his sources, providing regular footnotes throughout most of the first six volumes, he often lifted words and language from Chalmers and other secondary sources without providing quotation marks or replicated their structure so closely that today it would be considered plagiarism.[44] Yet overall, Bancroft was both more scrupulous about acknowledging his debt to Chalmers and more critical of Chalmers than Marshall had been. Thus he provided more precise and detailed footnotes than Marshall did, often commenting on Chalmers's reliability as a source and comparing him to the other sources he had examined. But in doing so, Bancroft simultaneously distanced himself from Chalmers, for he repeatedly criticized Chalmers in his footnotes on both interpretive and factual grounds. And when Bancroft paraphrased from Chalmers, he rephrased the passages more fully into his own words and made more substantial changes than Marshall had, repeatedly reinterpreting Chalmers's material to come to completely opposite conclusions.[45]

For example, although Bancroft, like Marshall, to some extent followed Chalmers in the structure and language of his account of Culpeper's revolt, he went even further than Marshall in repudiating Chalmers's portrayal of the rebellion. Like Marshall, Bancroft eliminated Chalmers's disparaging reference to how easily the people were turned into "the constant bubbles of their own credulity and of others [*sic*] crimes." But whereas Marshall only indirectly challenged Chalmers's interpretation of the revolt as an expression of popular anarchy by softening Chalmers's condemnation of it, Bancroft added phrases of his own that explicitly vindicated the rebellion as "a deliberate rising of the people," in which the people soon "recovered from anarchy, tranquilly organized a government, and established courts of justice." Bancroft's direct challenge to Chalmers's attack on the rebellion reflected his Jacksonian sympathies, which gave him greater faith in popular authority and the "common man" than Marshall had possessed. Yet Bancroft shared Marshall's and Chalmers's hostility to social chaos, as his use of such phrases as "tranquilly" and "deliberate" to emphasize the people's respect for order demonstrated. Where Bancroft differed, however, was in his greater confidence in the people's capacity for maintaining order. Therefore, Bancroft, unlike Marshall and Williamson, agreed with Chalmers in interpreting the rebellion as a precursor to the Revolution, speaking of how the rebels "formed conclusions as just as those which a century later pervaded the country." Bancroft simply reversed Chalmers's conclusions and used this linkage to demonstrate the orderly character of both events when he suggested that the rebels displayed the same devotion to order and liberty that would characterize the revolutionaries.[46]

Consequently, Bancroft avoided the tensions created by Williamson's desire to simultaneously condemn the rebellion as an expression of popular disorder and vindicate the Revolution. Bancroft himself pointed to the disjunction that these dual imperatives created for Williamson's narrative and suggested that he was reacting specifically to this problem in his reinterpretation of Chalmers when he spoke of how "Williamson has allowed himself to be confused by the judgments of royalists," in calling "the fathers of North Carolina a set of 'rioters and robbers.'" In contrast, for Bancroft, as wrongheaded as Chalmers was in his condemnation of the Revolution, he at least demonstrated the merit of "great consistency" when he "condemned Culpeper, just as he condemned Bacon and Jefferson, Hancock and John Adams."[47] Not only did Bancroft go further than Marshall and Williamson in reinterpreting Chalmers; he was also far more willing to acknowledge in his footnotes the interpretive differences behind the changes that he made. He directly attacked Chalmers in another footnote, questioning his factual accuracy, when he warned that Chalmers's account "must be received with great hesitancy. The coloring is always wrong; the facts usually perverted. He writes like a lawyer and a disappointed politician; not like a calm inquirer."[48]

Through such assessments, Bancroft adhered to the critical methods of scholarship that his studies at Göttingen had trained him to consider a requisite for impartial truth.[49] Thus, where Marshall sought to demonstrate his impartiality by blurring the differences between himself and his sources and by muting his own disagreements with them, Bancroft sought to achieve the same goal by acknowledging the interpretive disagreements between his sources and openly expressing his own opinions about them. And by condemning Chalmers specifically for his lack of impartiality and defining himself in opposition to Chalmers's loyalist bias, Bancroft enhanced his own claims to that ideal. Bancroft's more impassioned style therefore did not mean that he was any less committed to impartial truth than Marshall was. But whereas Marshall sought to live up to this ideal by incorporating Chalmers's loyalist perspective into his analysis, Bancroft did so by defining himself against that perspective.

While, like Marshall, Bancroft's concern with truth and his desire for national unity reinforced each other, they did so in different ways because Bancroft placed both these ideals on a different basis. His belief that truth required a critical analysis of sources served his nationalist purposes by allowing him to appropriate from Chalmers what he found useful for his text, while giving him a vehicle to differentiate himself and defend the Revolution from Chalmers's attacks through his commentary in the footnotes. At the same time, Bancroft's chauvinistic nationalism contributed to his adoption of the methods of critical scholarship in the first place by enabling him to acknowledge such interpretive differences without fearing, as Marshall had, that it would endanger national unity. On the contrary, Bancroft's faith in the underlying unity to American history allowed him to view such conflicts as transient and superficial or as necessary evils that in the long run would actually help Americans realize the unity that had been destined to them by providence.[50] Bancroft's ability to adapt the material he took from Chalmers to his own purposes would simply have been all the more proof to him of how apparent conflicts would all eventually coalesce into a larger whole.

If William Huntting Howell has shown the complex strategies by which Joseph Plumb Martin destabilized nationalist narratives of the Revolution, Williamson, Marshall, and Bancroft revealed the equally complex strategies that gave those narratives their stabilizing power. Their reliance on a loyalist for this purpose demonstrated how precarious the foundations were for their orderly vision of American history, subject as it was to continual challenges from Americans wishing to subvert that vision, whether in the form of antinarratives like Martin's or anecdotes about such legends as Molly Pitcher.[51] That very precariousness made truth all the more important for these historians, not only as a means of validating their conservative social message but also as itself a source of stability and order. Thus, rather than denying their reliance on Chalmers as Williamson had, Marshall and Bancroft turned that reliance to their advantage by using it in different ways to enhance their claims to truth, plagiarizing from Chalmers not just despite but because of his loyalist identity. Where Marshall used his commitment to truth to promote stability, Bancroft showed how a greater sense of national stability in turn contributed to a redefinition of historical truth to encompass the critical methods that have come to define professional history.

NOTES

1. George Bancroft to Joseph Buckingham, December 4, 1844, George Bancroft Papers, Massachusetts Historical Society, Boston.
2. George Chalmers, *Political Annals of the Present United Colonies, from Their Settlement to the Peace of 1763* (1780; repr., New York: Franklin, 1968). On the prevalence of plagiarism among American historians in this period, see Orin G. Libby, "Some Pseudo-Historians of the American Revolution," *Transactions of the Wisconsin Academy of Sciences, Arts, and Letters* 13 (1900): 419–25; and Sydney G. Fisher, "The Legendary and Myth-Making Process in Histories of the American Revolution," *Proceedings of the American Philosophical Society* 51 (April–June 1912): 56.

3. Lester Cohen, *The Revolutionary Histories: Contemporary Narratives of the American Revolution* (Ithaca, N.Y.: Cornell University Press, 1980); David D. Van Tassel, *Recording America's Past: An Interpretation of the Development of Historical Studies in America, 1607–1884* (Chicago: University of Chicago Press, 1960); William Raymond Smith, *History as Argument: Three Patriot Historians of the American Revolution* (The Hague: Mouton, 1966); George Callcott, *History in the United States, 1800–1860: Its Practice and Purpose* (Baltimore: Johns Hopkins Press, 1970); Peter Messer, *Stories of Independence: Identity, Ideology, and Independence in Eighteenth-Century America* (DeKalb: Northern Illinois University Press, 2005); Eileen Cheng, *The Plain and Noble Garb of Truth: Nationalism and Impartiality in American Historical Writing, 1784–1860* (Athens: University of Georgia Press, 2008); Arthur Shaffer, *The Politics of History: Writing the History of the American Revolution, 1783–1815* (Chicago: Precedent, 1975).
4. Michael A. McDonnell, "War and Nationhood: Founding Myths and Historical Realities," in this volume; Shaffer, *Politics of History*, 120–31; Michael Kammen, *A Season of Youth: The American Revolution and the Historical Imagination* (New York: Knopf, 1978), 3–75; Harlow W. Sheidley, *Sectional Nationalism: Massachusetts Conservative Leaders and the Transformation of America, 1815–1836* (Boston: Northeastern University Press, 1998), 118–34; Alfred F. Young, *The Shoemaker and the Tea Party: Memory and the American Revolution* (Boston: Beacon, 2000), 108–27.
5. Kammen, *Season of Youth*, 3–75; Sheidley, *Sectional Nationalism*, 134–47; Young, *Shoemaker and the Tea Party*, 108–27, 135–36.
6. William Huntting Howell, "'Starving Memory': Antinarrating the American Revolution," in this volume.
7. James Paxton, "Remembering and Forgetting: War, Memory, and Identity in the Post-Revolutionary Mohawk Valley," in this volume; Shaffer, *Politics of History*, 120–23.
8. For a different view of how early national historians appropriated Chalmers for conservative purposes, see Wesley Frank Craven, *The Legend of the Founding Fathers* (New York: New York University Press, 1956), 54–55.
9. Paxton, "Remembering and Forgetting."
10. On this marginalization, see Bernard Bailyn, "The Losers: Notes on the Historiography of Loyalism," in *The Ordeal of Thomas Hutchinson* (Cambridge: Harvard University Press, 1974), 383–408; Wallace Brown, "The View at Two Hundred Years: The Loyalists of the American Revolution," *American Antiquarian Society Proceedings* 80 (1970): 25–47; and George A. Billias, "The First Un-Americans: The Loyalists in American Historiography," in *Perspectives on Early American History: Essays in Honor of Richard B. Morris*, ed. George A. Billias and Alden T. Vaughan (New York: Harper & Row, 1973), 282–324. For challenges to this marginalization, see Edward Larkin, "What Is a Loyalist? The American Revolution as Civil War," *Common-Place* 8, no. 1 (2007),www.common-place.org/vol-08/no-01/larkin; Larkin, "The Cosmopolitan Revolution: Loyalism and the Fiction of an American Nation," *Novel: A Forum on Fiction* 40, no. 1 (Fall 2006): 54–61; Keith Mason, "The American Loyalist Diaspora," in *Empire and Nation: The American Revolution in the Atlantic World*, ed. Eliga

Gould and Peter Onuf (Baltimore: Johns Hopkins University Press, 2005), 239–59; and Maya Jasanoff, *Liberty's Exiles: American Loyalists in the Revolutionary World* (New York: Random House, 2011).

11. Shaffer, *Politics of History*, 32–35; Cohen, *Revolutionary Histories*, 161–67, 181–88, 212–19; Cheng, *Plain and Noble Garb.*
12. Gordon S. Wood, "No Thanks for the Memories," *New York Review of Books* 58, no. 13 (January 2011): 41–42; J. H. Plumb, *The Death of the Past* (Middlesex: Penguin Books, 1973), 11–16.
13. For a different view of Bancroft and his contemporaries, see Plumb, *Death of the Past*, 72–74.
14. On plagiarism as the antithesis of scientific history, see Libby, "Some Pseudo-Historians," 419–25; and Fisher, "Legendary and Myth-Making Process," 56. For a different view of the nationalist function of plagiarism, see Peter Hoffer, *Past Imperfect: Facts, Fictions, Fraud—American History from Bancroft and Parkman to Ambrose, Bellesiles, Ellis, and Goodwin* (New York: Public Affairs, 2004), 13–31. For a more complex perspective on plagiarism, see Anthony Grafton, *The Footnote* (Cambridge: Harvard University Press, 1997); and Giovanna Ceserani, "Narrative, Interpretation, and Plagiarism in Mr. Robertson's 1778 'History of Ancient Greece,'" *Journal of the History of Ideas* 66, no. 3 (2005): 413–36.
15. Grace Amelia Cockroft, *The Public Life of George Chalmers* (New York: Columbia University Press, 1933); Lawrence Henry Gipson, "George Chalmers and the *Political Annals*," in *The Colonial Legacy: Loyalist Historians*, ed. Lawrence H. Leder (New York: Harper Torchbooks, 1971), 13–14; John Schutz, "George Chalmers and *An Introduction to the History of the Revolt*," in Leder, *Colonial Legacy*, 50–51.
16. Chalmers, *Political Annals*, 1:256.
17. Cockroft, *Public Life of George Chalmers*, 59; Schutz, "George Chalmers," 58; Peter Hoffer, "Fettered Loyalism: A Re-evaluation of Robert Proud's and George Chalmers' Unfinished Colonial Histories," *Maryland Historical Magazine* 68 (1973): 166–72; Craven, *Legend of the Founding Fathers*, 51–53.
18. Schutz, "George Chalmers," 55, 57; Cockroft, *Public Life of George Chalmers*, 27. For a different view that emphasizes Chalmers's misgivings about commerce, see Messer, *Stories of Independence*, 55–56.
19. Chalmers, *Political Annals*, 1:99; Craven, *Legend of the Founding Fathers*, 52.
20. Chalmers, *Political Annals*, 2:162.
21. Cockroft, *Public Life of George Chalmers*, 60–61; Gipson, "George Chalmers," 32–33.
22. Jared Sparks to Obadiah Rich, August 15, 1844, Jared Sparks Papers, MS Sparks 147h, Houghton Library, Harvard University, Cambridge, Mass.; Craven, *Legend of the Founding Fathers*, 50–55; Cockroft, *Public Life of George Chalmers*, 61–62; Gipson, "George Chalmers," 13–14; Schutz, "George Chalmers," 50–51; Harvey Wish, *The American Historian: A Social-Intellectual History of the Writing of the American Past* (New York: Oxford University Press, 1960), 38.
23. Shaffer, *Politics of History*, 24–27, 105.
24. Hugh Williamson, *The History of North Carolina*, 2 vols. (Philadelphia: Thomas Dobson, 1812), 1:x.

25. For a different view of Williamson's plagiarism, see Richard C. Vitzthum, *The American Compromise: Theme and Method in the Histories of Bancroft, Parkman, and Adams* (Norman: University of Oklahoma Press, 1974), 62–63.
26. Chalmers, *Political Annals*, 1:535–36. Culpeper's Rebellion was provoked by acting governor Thomas Miller's arbitrary treatment of his opponents and his efforts to enforce the customs duties imposed by the Navigation Acts. After overthrowing Miller the rebels established their own assembly and council, which ran the colony until the restoration of a legal government in 1679. See Noreen McIlvenna, *A Very Mutinous People: The Struggle for North Carolina, 1660–1713* (Chapel Hill: University of North Carolina Press, 2009), 46–70.
27. Williamson, *History of North Carolina*, 1:132, 2:161; Shaffer, *Politics of History*, 123–31.
28. Cohen, *Revolutionary Histories*, 185–211; Shaffer, *Politics of History*, 23–28, 123–31.
29. William Foran, "John Marshall as a Historian," *American Historical Review* 43 (October 1937): 51–64; Jean Edward Smith, *John Marshall: Definer of a Nation* (New York: Holt, 1996), 330–31; Daniel Gilbert, "John Marshall and the Development of National History," in *Historians of Nature and Man's Nature: Early Nationalist Historians*, ed. Lawrence H. Leder (New York: Harper & Row, 1973), 196.
30. John Marshall, *The Life of George Washington*, 5 vols. (London: Phillips, 1804), 1:xix; Cheng, *Plain and Noble Garb*, 109–11.
31. Foran, "John Marshall as a Historian," 51–64.
32. Marshall, *Life of George Washington* (1804), 1:xviii–xix; Cheng, *Plain and Noble Garb*, 110–11. On the role of citation in legitimizing the historian's claims, see Grafton, *Footnote*, 7–8. On how a view of truth as the accumulation of fact could sanction plagiarism, see Hoffer, *Past Imperfect*, 20.
33. Marshall, *Life of George Washington* (1804), 1:xxii
34. On this understanding of truth, see Cheng, *Plain and Noble Garb*, 53–64, 106–15. For assessments of Marshall's history, see Foran, "John Marshall as a Historian," 51–64; Albert Beveridge, *The Life of John Marshall* (Boston: Houghton Mifflin, 1916), 239–73; Smith, *John Marshall*, 331–32; R. Kent Newmyer, *John Marshall and the Heroic Age of the Supreme Court* (Baton Rouge: Louisiana State University Press, 2001), 20; Gilbert, "John Marshall," 177–99; Shaffer, *Politics of History*, 151–57.
35. On the interpretive character of this editorial conception of authorship, see Jay Fliegelman, *Declaring Independence: Jefferson, Natural Language, and the Culture of Performance* (Stanford, Calif.: Stanford University Press, 1993), 170–81.
36. Chalmers, *Political Annals*, 1:535; John Marshall, *The Life of George Washington*, 5 vols. (Philadelphia: Wayne, 1805), 1:185. References hereafter to Marshall's work are to this edition.
37. Gilbert, "John Marshall," 185–87, 198–99; Newmyer, *John Marshall*, 124–28.
38. Marshall, *Life of George Washington* (1805), 1:149–50; Chalmers, *Political Annals*, 1:192; Gilbert, "John Marshall," 192–94; Newmyer, *John Marshall*, 210–65; Messer, *Stories of Independence*, 105–10.

39. Thomas Hutchinson, *The History of Massachusetts, from the First Settlement Thereof in 1628, until the Year 1750* (Boston: Thomas & Andrews, 1795), 1:89.
40. Newmyer, *John Marshall,* 69–72, 102–209.
41. Roger Brown, *Republic in Peril* (New York: Columbia University Press, 1964); George Dangerfield, *The Awakening of American Nationalism, 1815–1828* (New York: Harper Torchbooks, 1965); Fred Somkin, *Unquiet Eagle: Memory and Desire in the Idea of American Freedom* (Ithaca, N.Y.: Cornell University Press, 1967); Paul C. Nagel, *This Sacred Trust: American Nationality, 1798–1898* (New York: Oxford University Press, 1971); Kammen, *Season of Youth,* 26–27, 41–52.
42. George B. Forgie, *Patricide in the House Divided: A Psychological Interpretation of Lincoln and His Age* (New York: Norton, 1979), 3–12, 55–87.
43. Lilian Handlin, *George Bancroft: The Intellectual as Democrat* (New York: Harper & Row, 1984), 115–33; Russel Nye, *George Bancroft: Brahmin Rebel* (New York: Knopf, 1944), 94–105; Dorothy Ross, "Historical Consciousness in Nineteenth-Century America," *American Historical Review* 89 (October 1984): 909–28; Sacvan Bercovitch, *The Rites of Assent* (New York: Routledge, 1993), 173–89; David Noble, *Historians against History: The Frontier Thesis and the National Covenant in American Historical Writing since 1830* (Minneapolis: University of Minnesota Press, 1965), 18–36.
44. Vitzthum, *American Compromise,* 42–76; Hoffer, *Past Imperfect,* 22.
45. Vitzthum, *American Compromise,* 51–53, 62–65.
46. George Bancroft, *A History of the United States, from the Discovery of the American Continent to the Present Time,* vol. 2 (Boston: Charles Bowen, 1837), 159–60; Chalmers, *Political Annals,* 1:535–36; Vitzthum, *American Compromise,* 32–33, 62–65; Bercovitch, *Rites of Assent,* 169–82; Handlin, *George Bancroft,* 146–53; Noble, *Historians against History,* 22–24.
47. Bancroft, *History of the United States,* 2:161n2.
48. Bancroft, *History of the United States,* 2:162n6; Vitzthum, *American Compromise,* 63.
49. Cheng, *Plain and Noble Garb,* 143–52; Handlin, *George Bancroft,* 65–66, 126–27, 341–42; Nye, *George Bancroft,* 94–98; John W. Rathbun, "George Bancroft on Man and History," *Transactions of the Wisconsin Academy of Sciences, Arts and Letters* 43 (1954): 51–56, 62–66.
50. Vitzthum, *American Compromise,* 15–41, 74–75; Bercovitch, *Rites of Assent,* 177–89.
51. See Howell, "Starving Memory," and Emily Lewis Butterfield, "'Lie There My Darling, While I Avenge Ye': Anecdotes, Collective Memory, and the Legend of Molly Pitcher," both in this volume.

Emma Willard's "True Mnemonic of History"

America's First Textbooks, Proto-Feminism, and the Memory of the Revolution

Keith Beutler

On Thursday, May 1, 1828, in Troy, New York, schoolmistress Emma Willard, author of the soon-to-be best-selling *History of the United States*, dedicated the work in verse to her mother, Lydia Hinsdale Hart:

> Accept this offering of a daughter's love . . .
> Mother, few are left,
> Like thee, who felt the fire of freedom's holy time
> Pervade and purify the patriot breast.
> Thou wert within thy country's shattered bark,
> When, trusting Heaven, she rode the raging seas,
> And braved with dauntless death-defying front
> The storm of war. With me retrace the scene,
> Then view her peace, her wealth, her liberty and fame.[1]

Willard thus reflected her generation's fear that losing their parents, the last aged eyewitnesses of the Revolution, might complicate continued transmission of the memory of that epoch to future generations. Emma Willard believed that the nation's natal memories would be effectively conveyed only in accord with what she labeled "the true mnemonic of history."[2] Willard, and many Americans of her era, advocated a memory strategy that did justice to an increasingly popular, self-consciously scientific understanding of the faculty of memory itself, one that privileged material supports of memory. Members of Willard's mother's generation had been, in their very persons, physical props of patriotic memory, embodied relics of the Revolutionary era. Going forward, America's children would have mothers who, not having lived through the Revolution, would not themselves be material icons of the Revolutionary period. They would need to be taught the history of the Revolution before they could communicate its memory to their children.

In 1819, consistent with that encroaching challenge, Emma Willard composed a petition to New York's legislature, reasoning from the then fashionable materialist view of memory to a state responsibility to support liberal education for girls: today's girls will be tomorrow's mothers. As mothers they will be in physical proximity to their children, literally in the best position "to soften their minds and fit them to receive impressions."[3] Ergo, New York's legislature ought to make girls' education a policy priority. Situating Willard's logic in the context of her and other contemporary pedagogues' preoccupation with preserving and promoting remembrance of the Revolution, suggests a larger lesson to be drawn: to understand the memory of the American Revolution historically, we must historicize memory itself, considering how Americans' changing beliefs about the faculty of "memory" may have shaped contemporaneous performances of patriotic memory and their reception.[4]

Willard's Physicalist View of Memory

In 1890 women in Troy, New York initiated a campaign to erect "a statue of [the late] Mrs. [Emma] Willard," founding schoolmistress of a local women's academy. Documenting a legacy that they believed justified a material, public depiction of her, the monument committee solicited testimonials, including one from the children of a certain Cornelia Keeler. The siblings remembered listening awestruck as their mother recited "verbatim paragraph after paragraph . . . which she had not seen since her school-days." When they asked her "how it was possible to remember so perfectly," she enthused, "I learned to study at Mrs. Willard's."[5]

Willard would have been pleased. She regarded monuments as

efficacious, tangible supports of memory. The founder and principal of Troy Female Seminary in New York and author of popular U.S. history textbooks in the 1820s and 1830s, Willard claimed to have independently—albeit contemporaneously with others—empirically inferred the "true mnemonic of history" education, an avowedly sensate assay of memory. With coauthor, William Channing Woodbridge, Willard published a geography text that prominently pictured a monument in Baltimore to George Washington, reflecting their contention that able teaching relies "upon the principle of making the eye the medium of instruction." The book's preface, written by Willard, explained that they would "admit little" pedagogically "which may not be traced to one of these two laws of intellect—first, that the objects of sight more readily become the subjects of conception and memory than those of the other senses; and secondly that the best of all methods to . . . enable the memory . . . is to class particulars under general heads." Thus, Willard promoted a version of what contemporaries could recognize as the "local memory" tradition.[6]

Conveyed in the early republic's newspapers, magazines, and books, including popular textbooks, local memory theory traditionally prescribed that those who wished to remember should imagine rooms, loci, in their minds wherein they were to mentally place evocative images. To recollect information thus encoded, they would mentally visit the relevant space and be prompted into recall by associations suggested by its "contents." As shown by the scholarship of William H. Burnham in the late nineteenth century, of Frances A. Yates in the mid-twentieth century, and of Dowe Draaisma at that century's end, the local memory tradition had oscillated for centuries since its beginnings in ancient Greece between less and more physicalist ontologies—between a Platonist rendition that treated prescribed places of memory—or loci—as abstractions and a competing moderately physicalist Aristotelian rendition that inspired the materially real "memory palaces" of the Renaissance. In the early American republic, local memory theory was tacking in a sharply physicalist, bodily direction. Received classical theories about local memory were being biologically reified, as in the case of the phrenology fad, champions of which claimed that an "organ of locality" in the human brain was physically responsible for local memory. The broader medical community, too, increasingly described memory in reductively material terms until such descriptions became axiomatic. As Isaac Taylor asserted in his

1836 *Physical Theory of Another Life,* even "abstract conceptions" are necessarily "*remembered* . . . only as" they are "conjoined with" material "circumstances of place or company, or with physical sensations. The memory leans upon the material world."[7]

Willard and Woodbridge endorsed a concretized version of local memory theory of the sort then gaining currency. In her textbook *History of the United States,* Emma Willard argued directly that time-honored local memory techniques, or "mnemonics," though valuable "so far as they aid the recollection of facts" were in need of adjustment.[8] While in received classical theory, places or loci of memory might be abstract, Willard, given her emphasis on the role of physical "objects of sight" in encouraging lasting memories, stressed that she taught her students to associate happenings and personages in American history with concrete, real-world geographic locations. Making the learning sensate—and, thus, as Willard's physicalist view of memory would have it, pupils' memories of lessons enduring—the principal of Troy Female Seminary prescribed that "localities of history" mentioned in her book should be constantly pointed out to students on maps physically reproduced from memory by the children themselves, presumably based on the atlas that she published and marketed as a companion volume to the textbook.[9]

Each classroom, explained Willard, would be "furnished with a black board, about two feet in length, and nearly the same in breadth." As a pupil studied her assigned history lessons, she was required "to draw with chalk as large as her board will admit, a sketch of that part of the country which is the seat of the portion of history which the lesson contains; marking slightly the track of navigators and march of armies." For purposes of examination, the "pupil brings her black board to her classroom, and her recitation, in part, consists of the explanation, which, agreeably to the accounts derived from the book, she gives of her sketched map." Such sensory-based, geographically centered historical instruction, Willard promised, would cause "the present generation of our youth" to experience the nation's natural vistas as props evocative of nationalistic memory. They would "learn to connect the mental sublime of the story of our fathers with the natural grandeur of our scenery."[10] The territory of the new nation would be their memory palace.

The Physicalist Turn in American Pedagogy

Willard's advocacy of sensory-driven mnemonics in education exemplified a general bodily turn in contemporaneous pedagogy. Bernard Wishy has noted that from the mid-eighteenth-century Enlightenment well into the next century, educators began emphasizing "concrete and observable" bodily "responses of the young . . . to the gradual derogation of . . . abstract" instruction.[11] The new physicalist imperative was literally apparent in the 1820s and 1830s in textbooks. Now as a matter of principle, conveniently abetted by new technologies of printing, books drew more heavily on illustrations to convey lessons. Proponents boasted that the "Picture System" was more effective than prior pedagogies at working to "store the memory" of each pupil with crucial lessons.[12] Critics, meanwhile, complained that pictures were spoiling children. Young scholars were allegedly becoming as dependent on the external stimulus of pictures as drunkards on booze.[13] Dueling appraisals notwithstanding, the Picture System, observers agreed, was emblematic of a new era in which childhood education had become more sensate.[14] The dawn of the transformation, one discussant allowed, came in the 1820s with Willard and Woodbridge's popular geography, "one of the most highly-pictured school-books" in the United States, a work that, in its preface by Willard, persuasively enunciated fundamental philosophical and pedagogical reasons to teach with pictures.[15]

Textbook Memory Culture

Not only did early American textbooks champion physicalist philosophies of memory in prefaces aimed at teachers.[16] In main-body sections, the texts taught physicalist understandings of memory to students. Thus, an 1828 reader edited by George Merriam featured a passage asserting that bodily and mental developments are necessarily coeval: "As the body passes through infancy and childhood, so does the mind. Feeble at first, it 'grows with the growth and strengthens with the strength' of the corporeal system." The same book printed another selection that made the complementary assertions that "it has been found that all mental susceptibilities are strengthened by exercise, much the same as our bodily powers; and the faculty of memory certainly not less than others," with "conceptions of *sight*" being very vivid and more easily recalled to remembrance than others." In an apparent allusion to the local memory tradition, the excerpt continued, "our remembrances are assisted by the law of contiguity in place, which is known to be one of the most efficient aids" of memory.[17]

An 1830 government textbook by William Sullivan indicated that it is when "the senses have conveyed to the mind a knowledge of things without us, that we have the power of retaining that knowledge, and can recall the impressions made, and think of them."[18] An 1831 anthology for young women included a passage on the human "faculty of associating remembrance of characters and events, which have most interested our passions, with the [physical] spot whereon the former have lived and the latter have occurred." It explained that "the potency of local associations is not limited to the sphere of our personal experience" but also makes "sacred or fabulous history" more memorable, creating in the mind of the person who remembers trains of perception which either rush unbidden on his mind, or are courted by voluntary efforts." Most efficacious of "all the objects of mental association" in evoking historical memory, the essay explained, are such relics as "ancient extant buildings and ruins."[19] Similarly, an 1832 reader put together by J. L. Blake stressed that "human nature" demands physical "objects, whether animate or inanimate" to facilitate recollections of "persons whose memory we love and admire."[20]

Textbooks regularly acquainted students with performances of patriotic American memory that smacked of self-conscious physicalism. Passages of this kind were often in the first person, allowing reciting students to vicariously experience the recollections they represented. Thus, an anonymous piece in Moses Severance's 1835 reader, *The American Manual,* on "The Grave of Jefferson" described how "I ascended the winding road which leads from Charlottesville to Monticello, up the miniature mountain" to the "spot"—a word charged with significance in local memory theory—at which is the "grave of Jefferson," where "the visitor sees . . . a low unmortared stone wall, which he enters by a neat wooden gate" to find the humble "resting place of the patriot and philosopher."[21]

James Hall's 1834 *Western Reader* had its intended audience—western youth residing in regions physically distant from where the Revolution had occurred—effectively take on the persona of someone living at the time of George Washington's death in an area charged with memories of the Revolution: "And when the news arrived (I was then a little lad at school,) that the great Washington was dead we all wept" in a "scene of spontaneous sorrow," the "impression" of which will never "be effaced while memory endures." Using language strikingly congruent with sensate, locality-oriented memory theory, the reminiscence continued with a caveat about how the memory of George Washington had been transmitted to the young scholars: to be sure, "None of us—I mean the children at school—had ever seen him—but our fathers and mothers had seen him, and they told us about him—and we were in the vicinity of many of his disasters and of many of his brightest achievements."[22]

Similarly, an 1833 *Rhetorical Reader* by Ebenezer Porter had students practice public-speaking skills by recounting in the first-person plural voice a visit to Washington's house and tomb at Mount Vernon: "We drove to the entrance of the old gateway, and alighted in the midst of what appeared to be a little village, so numerous and scattered were the buildings. About those which we came upon, there was an air of dilapidation and neglect that was rather unpromising." Yet one of them, Washington's former mansion, proved to be an evocative memory palace filled with "rooms made interesting by the hallowed associations that came fast upon us as we traversed them," gawking at the relics with which they were adorned. Most inspiring as a locus of memory was the general's tomb: "It was a happy moment to visit the spot. . . . Who can analyze his feelings as he stands before that sepulcher! Who can tell the story of his associations. . . . Strange power of human mind! What intimation does this rapid communion with the past, and with the spirits of the past, give at once of their immortality and our own! . . . It was with reluctance I turned away, after gathering a relic or two."[23] In such schoolbook passages the classical tradition of local memory theory was concretized.

Reflecting the jointly physicalist and physiognomic turn in patriotic American memory culture, textbooks evidenced clear interest in bodies of the Revolutionary generation as reminders of, and clues about, the nation's founding epochs and leaders. An 1810 reader divulged, "in the last six years" of the Revolution "upwards of eleven thousand persons died on board the [British] prison ship New Jersey . . . stationed in the East River near New York. On many of these, the rights of sepulcher were never, or were but very imperfectly, conferred. For some time after the war was ended, their bones lay whitening in the sun, on the shores of Long Island." The same volume offered a reverent description of Washington's physiognomy: "General Washington was in his person about six feet in height, his eyes were gray, but full of animation; his visage was serene." His "limbs were well proportioned and muscular, and his deportment carried an air of solemnity in it, that was altogether awful to folly."[24]

An 1836 reader compiled by John Hall urged students to "Mourn Washington's death, when ye think of his birth" and bemoaned that "the dust of his body is all that is left" to "hallow his funeral pile."[25] Likewise, an 1840 textbook life of Washington described him as someone with "whose countenance it was impossible to connect any other qualities than those of wisdom, benevolence, and magnanimity" and, just before ending with an engraving of Washington's tomb, quoted an apologia for interest in Washington's body: "It is natural to view with keen attention the countenance of an illustrious man with a secret hope of discovering in his features some peculiar" physiognomic traces "of excellence," and such "expectations are realized in . . . viewing the person of Washington."[26] An 1805 collection of exemplary lives, after going into great detail about Washington's death and burial, lingered over his "shrouded corpse—the countenance still composed and serene . . . so that it seemed to express the dignity of that spirit which so lately actuated the lifeless form."[27] Emblematic of how not only Washington's body, but those of Revolutionary War veterans generally, were hallowed for inspiring memories of the Revolution, A. M. Blake's 1830 *Historical Reader* featured a poem that celebrated men in America who, having fought in the Revolution in their youth, could "strip their sleeves" to "show their [battle] scars."[28] In these general references to those who served we may detect some faint beginnings of the democratization of American memory.

Prominent in the pantheon of Revolutionary veterans being pointed out to children as relics of nationalistic memory was General Lafayette. When "Peter Parley," in Samuel G. Goodrich's *First Book of History*, exclaimed of the Frenchman: "I suppose many of my little readers saw him," he was being literal.[29] During Lafayette's ranging 1824–25 memory tour of the United States, children were often given pride of place in welcoming him, as the man himself was treated as a material relic. In 1824, reporting Lafayette's triumphal visit to Philadelphia, Sybilla Simmons observed that "on Tuesday morning he received all the schools in the state house yard." It "was absolutely crammed full," as were "all the streets round." Some "of the schools spoke addresses and sang songs of welcome."

Everywhere "he went," Simmons observed, "everybody wanted to shake hands with him."[30]

Visiting Bunker Hill in 1824, Lafayette expressed a "wish to subscribe" in support of the monument to him that was to be erected on the site. Utilizing the hero's cachet with the rising generation, the Monument Association placed Lafayette "at the head of the list" of pledged donors but asked that he not "place any sum against his name." Eventually, the association promised, a sum would "be placed against the name of Lafayette" equal to "the whole amount of all the sums, which the little children throughout the state . . . subscribe, or give to the erection of the Monument." Thus the "little ones" would show "gratitude to this . . . noble benefactor" and their efforts at physically commemorating the Battle of Bunker Hill would identify them with Lafayette.[31]

Whether they ever personally glimpsed Lafayette during his tour or subscribed to the Bunker Hill monument in his name, schoolchildren could easily meet him vicariously in textbooks that, after 1824, commonly drew attention to the general's storied visit, often while simultaneously implicating him in physicalist practices of patriotic American memory. Thus in *History of the United States,* for instance, Willard stressed that Lafayette "arrived in season to participate in the ceremony of laying the corner stone of a monument which was to commemorate the battle of Bunker's Hill" and noted that, during a visit to Washington's tomb at Mount Vernon, Lafayette was presented by "Mr. Custis, the adopted child of Washington" with "a ring containing a portion of the locks from that venerated head, which for so many toilsome days, and unpillowed nights, had devoted all its energies to that cause for which La Fayette had toiled and bled with kindred devotion." This occurred in an era when, as an essay in the popular magazine the *Polyanthos* had exemplified in 1807, a lock of hair could be understood as an efficacious prop on the mnemonic principle of loci, or local memory. It was, to say the least, not without reason that President John Quincy Adams, as cited in an 1833 textbook, promised Lafayette, "our [American] children in life and after death shall claim you for our own."[32]

Mnemonics and "Mary, the Mother of Washington"

In the opinion of Emma Willard and other influential pedagogues of the era, if the rising generation did effectively claim their nation's natal memories, women would deserve a lion's share of the credit. The preeminently physical nature of memory itself, coupled with the fact that women, especially as mothers, were dominant physical presences in children's lives, suggested that they play a privileged role in the formation of every generation's foundational memories. In the 1830s one iconic figure popularly invoked to illustrate such reasoning was "Mary, the Mother of Washington."[33] Only a few years before, George Washington's late mother was "little known" to Americans.[34] Then, beginning in the late 1820s, popular essays drawing primarily on writings of Mary Washington's great-grandson, George Washington Parke Custis, began to introduce her posthumously to the American public.[35] Among the articles was one published in 1831 in a leading women's magazine. It reported that when George Washington visited his chronically ailing mother for what the general anticipated would be the last time, he wept as "memory, retracing scenes long past, carried him back to the paternal mansion, and the days of his youth, and there, the center of attraction was his mother; whose care . . . prepared him to reach the topmost height of laudable ambition."[36]

The language, emphasizing Washington's memory of a locale (his boyhood home) and of an embodied object (his mother, its "center of attraction"), was the very sort then affiliated with physicalist memory theory. It may well have been meant to suggest anachronistically that Mary Ball Washington presciently influenced young George to remember what was important, including his mother, in ways prescribed by physicalist adaptations of classical local memory theory more current in 1831 than in Mary Washington's lifetime.

In any case, it became a commonplace that Mary Washington had used her physical proximity to her son, as his maternal caregiver, to memorably impress on him foundational lessons that underwrote his history-making exploits. In Lydia H. Sigourney's judgment, cited in an 1831 school reader, Mary Washington thus evidenced the "immense force of first impressions" that is "on the side of the mother. An engine of uncomputed power is committed to her hand. If she fix her lever judiciously, though she may not, like Archimedes, aspire to move the earth, she may hope to raise one of the inhabitants of earth to heaven."[37] In 1833 the *Christian Watchman* similarly used physicalist language to explain that the lesson to be taken from Mary Washington's life was that mothers shape their children's formative memories: "Impressions made in infancy, if not indelible, are effaced with difficulty and renewed with facility; and upon the mother therefore, must frequently, if not generally, depend the fate of the son."[38]

Complementing popular invocations of Mary Washington as an exemplar of the effectiveness of a physicalist pedagogy if practiced by children's nearest physical companions—their mothers—were contemporaneous efforts to make her tomb a physical locus of attraction. In 1831 locals in Fredericksburg, Virginia, seeking to build a monument at the "locality" of her burial place, explained that it would give a "local habitation" to her "memory."[39] Advocates of the monument argued too that, as a physical tribute, it would work on the educative principle that "sight is the liveliest of impressions," and by its locality it would draw attention not merely to Mary Washington but also to her pedagogy. Mary Washington, they reported, was buried at a "favorite spot" of hers, a "beautiful" unspoiled location to which she often repaired with "her only daughter and grandchildren. It was *here* that she impressed upon their infant minds the wonderful works of the great Creator of all things."[40]

For Emma Willard there was a profound public policy lesson to be drawn from such scientific, physicalist perspectives on memory and motherhood. In her 1819 petition to New York's legislature, Willard observed that "the ductile mind of the child is" chiefly "intrusted to the mother; and she ought to have . . . knowledge of this noble material, on which it is her business to operate, that she may best understand how to mould it to its most excellent form." Women, she maintained, should be prepared to reason pedagogically not only as mothers but also as teachers in "common schools." The feminization of the American teaching profession that was at the time manifestly underway would, Willard claimed, be a special benefit to the rising generation of the United States. Women, she argued, have been given by "nature . . . in a greater degree than men, the gentle arts of insinuation to soften" children's "minds and fit them to receive impressions."[41] In 1836, reasoning from the criticality of "first impressions" in forming the memories of children, Willard insisted that American women ought to be taught well academically and especially should learn "the science of the mind." Such knowledge would prepare and motivate them to effectively convey "correct impressions" to their young charges, whose minds would thus be "indelibly stamped" with foundational knowledge well before they came "under the care of learned male instructors."[42] So it was that schoolmistress Willard argued shrewdly on numerous fronts:

from expressing ideas on culturally prevalent physicalist beliefs about the nature of memory itself, to issuing an apologia for women as mothers and educators, and thence to advocating a change to public policy that would encourage the liberal education of girls.[43]

Conclusion

The popular physicalist assumptions about the nature of memory that underwrote Willard's pedagogy and politics can readily be seen as survivals from a cluster of materialist epistemological ideas that, Gordon Wood has argued, contributed to the coming of the Revolution by suggesting an essential equality among human beings as alike-embodied sentient knowers. Emma Willard's case illustrates that "sensationalism," to use Wood's label, having helped to precipitate the Revolution by making democracy thinkable, remained influential after the war and had a democratizing influence on both the content and politics of remembrance of the Revolution. Realizing this, much of the self-consciously physical, hands-on, democratizing quality of post-Revolutionary patriotic memory culture suddenly becomes legible: the well-known contemporaneous surge of attention paid to average Revolutionary War survivors as "living relics" in the 1820s and 1830s; the mass compulsion to see and touch the Marquis de Lafayette during his wide-ranging 1824–25 memory tour of the United States; public lamentation in 1838 by twenty-eight-year-old Abraham Lincoln, himself a grandson of a Revolutionary War veteran, that the "artillery of time" was shooting down the "living history" of the Revolution, its last remaining eyewitnesses "in every family."[44]

Willard's work reflects not only an emotional urgency but also a presence of mind and intellectual sophistication—exemplified in the attention to then prevalent physicalist memory theory—that many in her generation brought to the pressing task of preserving sacred the memory of the young nation's fast-dying parental generation. They could not act too soon. On Tuesday, January 18, 1831—two years, nine months, two weeks, and three days after Willard dedicated her *History of the United States* to her mother—the "artillery of time" claimed Revolutionary War eyewitness Lydia Hinsdale Hart as its latest casualty.[45]

NOTES

Memory across generations being a subject of this chapter, I am honored to dedicate it to the precious memory of my beloved father, Tony Beutler. I wish to thank Melissa Goin Beutler for her continuous encouragement and love. I am also grateful to Missouri Baptist University for a sabbatical leave during the Fall 2009 academic semester, giving me time to write, and to the following organizations for awarding the research fellowships that funded the investigatory work on which this work is based: the Virginia Historical Society, Gilder Lehrman Institute of American History, New-York Historical Society, Massachusetts Historical Society, Pennsylvania Historical Society, Library Company of Philadelphia, American Philosophical Society, International Center for Jefferson Studies at Monticello, College of Physicians of Philadelphia, David Library of the American Revolution, and Washington University in St. Louis. Special thanks are due too to staff at the Monroe C. Gutman Library at Harvard University who gave me permission to roam freely for three weeks in 2003 amid the stacks of their priceless Historical Textbooks Collection; without that extraordinary, timely access, I would never have begun to comprehend prevalent patterns in textbook culture during Emma Willard's era that must be understood to interpret her work in its historical context.

1. Emma Willard, *History of the United States, or Republic of America: Exhibited in Connexion with Its Chronology and Progressive Geography; By Means of a Series of Maps* (New York: White, Gallaher & White, 1828); cf. Nina Baym, "Women and the Republic: Emma Willard's Rhetoric of History," *American Quarterly* 43 (March 1991): 11.
2. Emma Willard, preface to *A System of Universal Geography, on the Principles of Comparison and Classification*, ed. William Channing Woodbridge, 8th ed. (Hartford, Conn.: Beach, 1838), xi.
3. Emma Willard, as excerpted in "Mrs. Willard on Female Education," *American Ladies' Magazine* 7, no. 4 (April 1834): 177.
4. See Alon Confino, "Collective Memory and Cultural History: Problems of Method," *American Historical Review* 102 (December 1997): 1403, which made a like point; and a classic work that denied that such might usefully be done for early nineteenth-century America: Michael Kammen, *Mystic Chords of Memory: The Transformation of Tradition in American Culture* (New York: Knopf, 1991), 95. Two published works that have begun the necessary work are Susan M. Stabile, *Memory's Daughters: The Material Culture of Remembrance in Eighteenth-Century America* (Ithaca, N.Y.: Cornell University Press, 2004); and Seth C. Bruggeman, *Here George Washington Was Born: Memory, Material Culture and the Public History of a National Monument* (Athens: University of Georgia Press, 2008), esp. 44. For the present writer's detailed efforts, see "The Memory Revolution in America and the Memory of the American Revolution, 1790–1840" (PhD diss., Washington University, 2005); and his forthcoming book under contract to University of Virginia Press, provisionally titled *George Washington's Hair: How Early Americans Remembered the Founders.*
5. A.W. Fairbanks, ed., *Emma Willard and Her Pupils, or Fifty Years of Troy Female Seminary, 1822–1872* (New York: Mrs. Russell Sage, 1898), 73.

6. Willard, preface to Woodbridge, *System of Universal Geography*, xi. For the engraved picture of a monument, see the book's unpaginated front matter.
7. Amos Dean, *Lectures on Phrenology: Delivered before the Young Men's Association for Mutual Improvement, of the City of Albany* (Boston: Marsh, Capen & Lyon, 1835), 201; Isaac Taylor, *Physical Theory of Another Life* (New York: Appleton, 1836), 69–70; William H. Burnham, "Memory, Historically and Experimentally Considered: An Historical Sketch of the Older Conceptions of Memory," pt. 1, *American Journal of Psychology* 2, no. 1 (November 1888): 39–90, esp. 88; Frances A. Yates, *The Art of Memory* (Chicago: University of Chicago Press, 1966); Dowe Draaisma, *The Metaphors of Memory: A History of Ideas about the Mind*, trans. Paul Vincent (New York: Cambridge University Press, 2000). Douglas J. Herrmann and Roger Chaffin have ably anthologized in chronological order seminal passages in Western literature from antiquity to the late nineteenth century that bore on memory. Comparing their primary source excerpts, one can see sample evidences of the pendulum of Western thought about memory swinging over time, however irregularly, between views of memory influenced by Plato's idealism and alternative theories of memory informed by Aristotle's moderate ontological realism. *Memory in Historical Perspective: The Literature before Ebbinghaus* (New York: Springer-Verlag, 1988), 21, 28, 38, 61, 73, 78, 80–81, 99, 106, 122–23, 126–27, 168, 177, 190, 192–93, 233. For exemplifying physicalist reductionism in medicine, see Everard Home, "Observations on the Function of the Brain," *New-England Journal of Medicine and Surgery and Collateral Branches of Science* 4 (October 1815): 350; "Craniology. Extract of a Letter from an American Gentleman in Paris to Samuel Russell, Esq. of this City," *Medical Repository of Original Essays and Intelligence, Relative to Physic, Surgery, Chemistry, and Natural History* (February–April 1808): 438–39.
8. Willard, preface to Woodbridge, *System of Universal Geography*, xi; Willard, *History of the United States*, vi, x.
9. Willard, *History of the United States*, x.
10. Ibid., ix, xv.
11. Bernard Wishy, *The Child and the Republic: The Dawn of Modern American Child Nurture* (Philadelphia: University of Pennsylvania Press, 1968), vii; cf. "The Teacher, or Moral Influence Employed in the Education of the Young," *North American Review* 49, no. 104 (July 1839): 246. For an excellent summary of the history of beliefs about mind and body in early America with a concentration on how changes in such beliefs influenced pedagogues in the 1820s and 1830s, see John R. Betts, "Mind and Body in Early American Thought," *Journal of American History* 54, no. 4 (March 1968): 787–805.
12. Y., "The Origin and Value of 'the Picture System,'" *American Annals of Education* 10, no. 4 (October 1834): 475.
13. See, for example, "Machinery of Education," *Mechanics' Magazine and Journal of the Mechanics' Institute* 2, no. 2 (August 1833): 93.
14. See "Machinery of Education," 93; X., "Influence of the 'Picture System' of Education," *American Annals of Education* 4, no. 5 (May 1834): 206; Y., "Origin and Value," 474; Edward Mansfield, *Lecture on the Qualifications of Teachers* (Cincinnati: Johnson, 1837), 13.
15. Y., "On the Use of Pictures in School Books," *American Annals of Education* 4, no.

11 (November 1834): 513; cf. Willard, preface to Woodbridge, *System of Universal Geography*, xi. Woodbridge, in the context of addressing controversy over the Picture System, explained that he had planned publication of the pictures that made it into his geography even before his affiliation with Willard, but that she articulated similar "principles and methods." [William Channing Woodbridge], "The Rudiments of Geography and the Picture System," *American Annals of Education* 4, no. 12 (December 1834): 581.

16. Besides references in the prefaces of Willard's and Goodrich's textbooks as already cited, see, for example, John Frost, *A History of the United States for the Use of Schools and Academies*, rev. ed. (Philadelphia: Biddle, 1837), 6.
17. George Merriam, *The American Reader: Containing Extracts Suited to Excite a Love of Science and Literature, to Refine the Taste, and to Improve the Moral Character* (Boston: Pierce & Williams, 1828), 9, 138. For another textbook allusion to the intellectual principle of "contiguity" as it relates to the association of ideas, see Jacob Abbott and Charles Edward Abbott, *The Mount Vernon Reader: A Course of Reading Lectures Designed for Senior Classes* (Boston: Crosby, 1840), 258.
18. William Sullivan, *The Poetical Class Book: Intended to Instruct the Higher Classes in Schools in the Origin, Nature, and Use of Political Power* (Boston: Lord & Hollbrook, 1830), 15.
19. H. G. Otis, as excerpted in Ebenezer Bailey, *The Young Ladies' Class Book* (Boston: Lincoln & Edmands, 1831), 160–61. For a poetic excerpt on the relation of memory to place see [Samuel] Rodgers, as excerpted in Anna Barbauld, *The Female Speaker; or, Miscellaneous Pieces in Prose and Verse* (Boston: Weels & Lilly, 1824), 80.
20. J. L. Blake, *The School Reader: Designed for a First-Class Book* (Boston: Hyde, 1832), 91–92.
21. Moses Severance, *The American Manual* (Cazenovia, N.Y.: Henry, 1835), 69.
22. James Hall, *The Western Reader* (Cincinnati: Copley & Fairbank, 1834), 32.
23. Ebenezer Porter, *The Rhetorical Reader*, 6th ed. (Andover, Mass.: Flagg, Gould & Newman, 1833), 159.
24. Joseph Richardson, *The American Reader* (Boston: Lincoln & Edmunds, 1810), 203, 116.
25. John Hall, *The Reader's Guide* (Hartford, Conn.: Canfield & Robins, 1836), 305.
26. "Dr. Thacher," quoted in [S. G. Goodrich], *The Life of George Washington* (Philadelphia: Thomas, Cowperthwait, 1840), 171; cf. 174. Though Samuel Goodrich disclaimed authorship of this volume, the copyright names "S. G. Goodrich" as author; see the note in the online catalog of the Walker Collection, Indiana State University, http://pumbaa.indstate.edu/record=b1659351~S1*eng.
27. [James Jones Wilmer], *The American Nepos* (Baltimore: Douglas, 1805), 368–71. Notice, too, on pages 377–81, how Wilmer's textbook devotes space to tracing George Washington's connection to a box of relic wood, to which there is evidence that he was actually indifferent, passed on to him by an admiring member of the British aristocracy.
28. A. M. Blake, *The Historical Reader* (Concord, Mass.: Hill, 1830), 300.
29. [Samuel G. Goodrich], *The First Book of History* (Boston: Richardson, Lord & Holbrook, 1831), 121.

30. Sybilla M[iriam Peale] Simmons to Elizabeth [De Peaster Peale] Patterson, October 6, 1824, Peale-Sellars Papers, American Philosophical Society, Philadelphia.
31. "Address by the Bunker Hill Monument Association to the Selectmen of the Several Towns in Massachusetts, Boston, October 1, 1824," transcription, 1823–44, Solomon Willard Papers, Massachusetts Historical Society, Boston.
32. Willard, *History of the United States*, 417; "Association," *Polyanthos* 4 (January 1, 1807): 88–89; cf. T[homas] Cogan, *A Philosophical Treatise on the Passions* (Boston: Wells & Lilly, 1821), 243; President John Quincy Adams, as quoted in C. B. Taylor, *A Universal History of the United States of America* (Buffalo, N.Y.: Strong, 1833), 413.
33. "Mary, the Mother of Washington," *Christian Watchman* 6 (June 1833): 266–69.
34. "The Mother of Washington," *Ladies' Magazine and Literary Gazette* 4 (September 1831): 384.
35. See, for example, "The Mother of Washington," *Saturday Evening Post* 5, no. 33 (August 1826): 1–2.
36. George Washington Parke Custis, as cited in "Mother of Washington," *Ladies' Magazine and Literary Gazette*, 393.
37. [Lydia H.] Sigourney, as excerpted in Bailey, *Young Ladies' Class Book*, 160–61; cf. Sigourney, as excerpted in Samuel Worcester, *A Fourth Book of Lessons for Reading* (Boston: Carter, Hendee, 1835), 97–100.
38. "Mary, the Mother of Washington," 269. On Emma Willard's enlistment in the 1840s of the cult of Mary Washington, see Baym, "Women and the Republic," 12.
39. "Letter, Printed, Dated Fredericksburg, June 1, 1831: Proposing a Monument to the Memory of the Mother of George Washington," Virginia Historical Society, Richmond; cf. Lawrence Lewis to George Washington Bassett, May 5, 1831, sec. 1, George Washington Bassett Papers, Virginia Historical Society.
40. "Mother of Washington," *Workingman's Advocate* 2 (June 4, 1831): 1. For a personal recollection of Mary Washington visiting the spot, given as part of an argument for the propriety of building a monument on the site of her burial, see Lewis to Washington Bassett, May 15, 1831, George Washington Bassett Papers. See also Lydia H. Sigourney's hope that, in the wake of the monument's construction, American mothers would undertake pilgrimages to the site, which would impress them with their own power to "impress" the rising generation. "The Mother of Washington," *Southern Literary Messenger* 1, no. 1 (August 1834): 6.
41. Emma Willard, as excerpted in "Mrs. Willard on Female Education," 168, 172; cf. 173.
42. Emma Willard, "Principles Contained in Stewart's Philosophy of the Mind, Applied to Show the Importance of Cultivating the Female Mind," *American Ladies' Magazine* 9, no. 1 (January 1836): 43–44. On a physicalist, "mechanical" view of human memory, and reflecting the commonplace belief in the era that memories physically laid down in youth are the most enduring, see "On Memory," *Pastime: A Literary Paper* 1, no. 24 (December 1807): 185; cf. "On Memory," *Weekly Visitor*, May 12, 1810, 6. For an exhortation to mothers to teach with sensate pedagogy, "giving the united assistance of the eye and the ear to the memory," and to particularly instruct their children in history, see [Elizabeth

Maria Budden], "Maternal Instruction," *American Journal of Education* 3, no. 11 (November 1827): 653.

43. Willard was effectively offering a scientific gloss on a notion already popularly put forward that republican children need to be taught by learned republican mothers; on that earlier rhetoric, see, for example, Linda K. Kerber, *Women of the Republic: Intellect and Ideology in Revolutionary America* (Chapel Hill: University of North Carolina Press, 1980).

44. Gordon S. Wood, *The Radicalism of the American Revolution* (New York: Vintage Books, 1993), 190, 236; cf. 240; Wood, *The American Revolution: A History* (New York: Random House, 2002), 101–6. Wood points to Locke as an exemplar and source of such materialist, sensate epistemology. For Locke's view of memory in particular, see, for example, John Locke, *An Essay concerning Human Understanding*, 24th ed. (London: Longman, 1824), 133, incl. marginal notes. On the growing interest in average veterans as relics, see generally John Resch, *Suffering Soldiers: Revolutionary War Veterans, Moral Sentiment, and Political Culture in the Early Republic* (Amherst: University of Massachusetts Press, 1999); and, particularly, for recognition in the 1830s that Americans were treating average veterans "like precious relics" in the context of a culture of patriotic remembrance that was privileging "palpable emblems" as memory props, see Gustave de Beaumont to Eugénie Beaumont, July 14, 1831, printed in Alexis de Tocqueville, *Letters from America*, ed. and trans. Frederick Brown (New Haven, Conn.: Yale University Press, 2010), 114. Abraham Lincoln, "Address to the Young Men's Lyceum," January 27, 1838, quoted in *Abraham Lincoln, Speeches and Writings*, ed. Don E. Fehrenbacher, vol. 1, *1832–1858*, Library of America (New York: Literary Classics of the United States, 1989), 36.

45. For the date of Hart's death, see Anne Firor Scott, Lucy F. Townsend, and Barbara Wiley, eds., *A Guide to the Microfilm Edition of the Papers of Emma Hart Willard, 1787–1870* (Bethesda, Mass.: LexisNexis, 2005), http://cisupa.proquest.com/ksc_assets/catalog/100436.pdf; Willard, *History of the United States*, front matter.

Remembering and Forgetting

War, Memory, and Identity in the Post-Revolutionary Mohawk Valley

James Paxton

Emerging silently from the woods, a party of Haudenosaunee (Six Nations) warriors stole unnoticed across the farmyard and through the cabin door. The killing began almost before the inhabitants, a mother and her several children, had time to register the intrusion. Later, while warriors hunched over corpses, working their knives to obtain scalps, a group of loyalist soldiers entered the cabin to survey the scene. Across the room, overlooked in the confusion, a baby stirred in its cradle. A warrior raised his tomahawk, but on seeing the infant dropped the weapon and bent to pick up the child. Cursing the warrior for his timidity, a loyalist impaled the baby on the point of his bayonet and, holding the squirming infant aloft, cried "*this too is a rebel.*"[1]

Taken from William W. Campbell's *Annals of Tryon County* (1831), this graphic account represents just one of the countless horrifying scenes of the Revolutionary War in New York's Mohawk Valley that filled the pages of nineteenth-century local histories.[2] So pervasive were stories about the indiscriminate killing and mutilation of women and children that they formed a powerful leitmotif capable of crowding out alternative versions of the past. Indeed, that was their purpose. Historian Peter Silver contends that similar stories published during the Seven Years' War constituted a literary subgenre he calls the "anti-Indian sublime." Frontier inhabitants manipulated highly charged images of mangled bodies for political purposes precisely because they admitted no counterargument. In the process a discordant and heterogeneous population forged a community of suffering in which members increasingly identified themselves as white.[3] More often political than racial, eighteenth-century constructions of whiteness divided European Americans not just from Aboriginals but also from other groups of European ancestry, such as the pacifist Moravians and Quakers, whose interest in preserving good relations with neighboring Native groups clearly placed them outside of the emerging white nationhood. Two decades later, during the Revolution, Whigs readily expanded the genre to include their enemies, the loyalists, a people condemned as being "worse than Indians." Although skin color became an increasingly important marker of identity in the eighteenth century, behavior, not biology, remained the surest indication of whiteness.

Between 1823 and 1856 amateur historians wove the anti-Indian sublime into at least five histories of the Mohawk Valley. Renewed interest in the Revolution and Native people reflected the values and concerns of contemporary nineteenth-century America more than those of the Revolutionary era. Local histories served several purposes for valley residents whose world, it seemed, was being rapidly transformed by forces beyond their control. Mohawk Valley inhabitants living on the Erie Canal zone were at the epicenter of economic and social change. As the disorienting turbulence of the market revolution threatened republican simplicity and virtue, people sought reassuring continuities across time that explained and legitimized the new world taking shape around them. Emphasizing stories of Indian and loyalist savagery during the Revolution consigned enemies to a state of nature and allowed historians to depict the past confidently and unambiguously as the triumph of new American values over primitivism. The Revolution was not in danger of being lost; rather, it was the mechanism that set in motion the machinery of progress.

Only in hindsight, after the Haudenosaunee had been dispossessed and confined to reservations or banished to Canada with their loyalist allies, was it possible to discern these patterns in the past. Doing so required the privileging of some memories over others in a creative process of remembering and forgetting. What locals tried to forget was that the conflict was, in the most immediate sense, a civil war. The combatants, both Natives and colonists, had once been inextricably linked by a variety of complex social, economic, and familial bonds. Colonists lived intermixed with Mohawks, spoke one or more Iroquoian dialects, traded and socialized with their indigenous neighbors and could, when occasion demanded, participate in important Haudenosaunee rituals. A 1720 petition written by Germans living on the Schoharie River (a tributary of the Mohawk River) seeking the Mohawks' assistance in defending their farms against speculators is suggestive. The authors likened themselves to babies who had "long sukled [*sic*]" at their Mohawk mother's breast and pleaded with the Mohawks "not to wean them so soon and Cast them [off]."[4] In a fascinating instance of cultural appropriation, the Germans declared their dependency on the Mohawks using the familial metaphors that structured Iroquoian society. A Mohawk would have said that his people and the Germans lived together under the Great Tree of Peace, a great, ever-growing pine tree that represented perfectly the Haudenosaunee's expansive notion of peace. When properly joined together, diverse peoples could be a source of unity and strength.[5] Ironically, the surreal acts of cruelty committed in the Revolution became possible not because the combatants stood on opposite sides of the frontier, as Campbell and others would have it, but because Mohawks, loyalists, and Whigs understood one another so well.

To view the writing of local history as separate and distinct from national history would be misleading. While most studies of memory and the American Revolution seek to explain the construction of a national identity, the public celebrations and memorials that articulated a developing national identity occurred in specific places and reflected local contexts.[6] Yet comparatively few scholars have examined how community members turned broader discourses to local purposes to create or recreate new identities in the postwar era. But local discourses did not remain local. They rejoined and influenced national conversations about the related subjects of modernity, national unity, and Indian removal.

The poignant and nearly simultaneous deaths of Thomas Jefferson and John Adams in 1826 on the fiftieth anniversary of the Declaration of Independence forcefully reminded Americans that the Revolution was rapidly passing from memory to imagination. The "true" history of the nation's founding would soon be beyond reach. Beginning in the 1820s civically minded citizens tried to forestall such a calamity by launching countless salvage operations to "rescue from oblivion, and to record the deeds, of those individuals, however humble, who were the pioneers of our country."[7] Voluntary groups founded historical societies, commissioned monuments, and promoted the writing of memoirs, histories, and biographies.

More than antiquarian interest drove the renewed interest in the Revolution. The rising generation that stood poised to take the reins of power had no experience of their own to compare to the Revolutionary generation. Thus, their own values and commitment to republicanism remained untested. At the same time the dizzying pace of change and the growing wealth of the nation's citizens seemed set to open a chasm between the growing luxury and corruption of Jacksonian America and an austere and virtuous republican past. The future of the country required that young Americans emulate the Revolutionaries to guide the nation successfully into the future. Public ceremonies and histories, therefore, served didactic purposes, inculcating particular values—industry, simplicity, virtue, duty, and self-sacrifice for the common good—without which the republic could not endure. For this reason, Jeptha Simms dedicated his work "to the young men of the Schoharie and Mohawk Valleys," who by learning about their ancestors' struggles might "increase their love of country and hatred of tyranny."[8]

Mohawk Valley veterans embraced their role as keepers of Revolutionary ideals and participated enthusiastically in the construction of a historical memory. Graying soldiers figured prominently in public commemorations, turning out in force when Lafayette's farewell tour brought him to the western Mohawk Valley cities of Rome and Utica in June 1825. Surrounded by officials and throngs of people, Lafayette shook hands and talked with the old soldiers, who, cheeks wet with tears, recalled their service together. The *Oneida Observer* lingered sentimentally on the scene. "No wonder," the newspaper reported, "it was impossible . . . to repress the gush of generous sensibility, or control the swelling emotion." The connection to one of America's last Founding Fathers enhanced the standing of local veterans and reinforced the importance of their sacrifices. They became, as Sarah Purcell has argued, "national cultural symbols."[9]

Local historians searching for suitable materials turned to these same veterans as living links with the past. With the exception of longtime Schoharie resident John M. Brown, none of the region's historians had lived through the Revolution and all depended on veterans and their families for information. Much of William Campbell's knowledge of the war came from his grandfather, who had been a militia colonel, and his father, who as a boy of seven had been captured by a war party and carried as a prisoner to Canada. Simms's history is even more obviously a disjointed collection of anecdotes gleaned from local informants. As most local histories sought to preserve and transmit for posterity the Revolutionary generation's achievements, they bore little evidence of rigorous source analysis.[10]

If local historians and their informants saw themselves as conservators, they also viewed history as a linear progression that drew together past, present, and future. The Revolutionary generation's sacrifices ushered in a new and better world for their children and grandchildren, or so it seemed to young historians. In living memory the Mohawk Valley had developed from a peripheral frontier into a modern, increasingly urban, and commercial region. The population of Utica, for example, more than doubled from about 3,000 to 8,323 between 1820 and 1830, the decade the Erie Canal was completed.[11] The canal, hailed as the greatest engineering feat of the age, was the immediate catalyst for change, but local historians agreed that the Revolution set the necessary preconditions for progress.

Consequently, most local histories accorded the colonial era secondary importance. Even so, the earlier period provided important lessons about how a sturdy and industrious people could by dint of hard work wrest profitable farms from an unforgiving wilderness. While crediting the region's Mohawks with assisting the earliest settlers, most histories focused not on coexistence but on how the two peoples grew apart. Savagery would always retreat before civilization. Farm making was the most obvious sign of progress. Campbell described ax-wielding Scots-Irish settlers transforming Cherry Valley's forests into the "abode of civilized man." Despite their rude surroundings, families attended church faithfully and provided as best they could for the education of their sons (but not their daughters). Following in this vein, the history of the colonial period was recounted as a series of "firsts"—first families, first towns, first mills, first churches, and first wheat crops—each an increment on the yardstick of modernity.[12]

In an important study of local histories published in nineteenth-century New England, historian Jean M. O'Brien has argued that "firsting" constituted settlers' origin stories. Each new achievement literally displaced First Peoples from the land and "appropriate[d] the category 'indigenous' away from Indians and for themselves [New Englanders]." Assuming that Native peoples created no durable institutions, the arrival of settlers marked the beginning of authentic history and allowed locals "to participate in the production of . . . modernity."[13] Together with their Yankee cousins, Mohawk Valley authors contributed to a national narrative that viewed progress and extinction as opposite but intertwined processes.

In the hands of local authors, the Revolution was the instrument of civilization and the doom of Native peoples. The war broke the back of the Six Nations Confederacy, making settlement west of the Mohawk Valley possible for the first time. Lured by glowing wartime reports of vast cornfields, vegetable patches, and orchards, settlers flooded west in a seemingly endless wave that, according to Campbell in 1831, "has not yet ceased to flow. Who that looked upon central and western New York then, would have dreamed of its sudden growth and prosperity—that in fifty years it would teem with more than a million of inhabitants, rich in education, rich in morals, rich in enterprise, both civil and religious, in all that adorns the state." Wherever one went in the state of New York, Simms declared, one could see evidence of the positive changes wrought by the Revolution. Where once had stood "dense forests, unbroken for many miles, may now be seen waving fields of grain, and flocks and herds upon a thousand hills—may now be heard the complicated machinery of the mechanic arts—may now be felt the genial influence of unfettered science." Simms extolled advances in transportation, noting especially the construction of the Erie Canal and the concomitant growth of manufacturing and cities "where but little more than half a century ago might have been heard the dismal howl of the wolf; the frightful scream of the panther; or the terrific yell of the savage."[14] Clearly, local historians had found meaning in the horrific and arbitrary violence of the Revolution. The war that had destroyed so many lives and had wasted so much of the valley had also banished savagery from the land, opened the west to settlement, and unleashed the population's creative energies.

Not all aspects of the past squared so easily with evolutionary theories of progress, and local authors took pains to explain them. Subscribing to a consensus view of history, Mohawk Valley authors assumed their colonial ancestors had held values similar to their own, by which they meant a shared commitment to liberal capitalism. Yet early settlers exhibited a range of behaviors that confounded later observers. If Campbell's Scots-Irish were hardworking individualists, others, most notably the Schoharie Germans, lived contentedly as semisubsistence farmers, preferring to save labor rather than maximize profits. Schoharie families pooled their work, owned goods in common, and employed women in the fields. As someone who benefited directly from the new economy, first as a merchant and then as a canal employee, Simms disapproved of subsistence activities that retarded economic development. Rationalizing their behavior, he reassured readers that the Germans were not like the Shakers, "who make all their earnings as common stock." Rather, "each labored for his own benefit, and . . . lands were marked out and bounds placed, so that every one knew and cultivated his own parcel."[15] Only the newness of the settlements and the want of infrastructure delayed liberal capitalism's full expression.

Questions about the distinctiveness of colonial German settlers were, of course, tied to nineteenth-century Americans' concerns about the assimilability of immigrants. Although most of the German speakers, their parents, and grandparents had been born in the valley, they were painted in the same broad and unflattering strokes as new immigrants. An 1823 travel account described the Mohawk Valley's German and Dutch population as an "unenterprising," irreligious, uneducated, and immoral people who spoke imperfect German and no English. The local gendered division of labor left the visitor aghast. "I do not know, that I was ever more struck with the strangeness of any sight," he confessed when seeing German women working like men in the fields.[16] How could Mohawk Valley historians promote the progress of their region when so many of the inhabitants seemed so backward?

Rising nativist sentiment forced local authors either to ignore or to integrate the valley's heterogeneous populations into a progressive Anglo-American tradition of the Revolution. Campbell, who later sat in Congress as a member of the nativist American Party, devoted only a single paragraph to the region's large German population. The second edition of *The Annals of Tryon County*, which appeared in 1849, further reduced the cultural complexity of the valley's population by lumping everyone together as members of the "Anglo-Saxon race," which was destined "to carry our own native language and . . . literature . . . over all the North American continent."[17]

Other authors imposed quintessentially American values on their subjects, homogenized diverse European settlers, and attested to the assimilability of the Germans. Jeptha Simms and Nathaniel Benton, for example, believed that Schoharie Valley Germans were an industrious people who had largely conformed to the dominant society's language and culture. The Germans that emerge from the pages of their histories appear surprisingly like Puritans propelled across the Atlantic by "religion and the love of liberty." Such an instinctive desire for freedom prompted Germans in large numbers to join the Whigs during the Revolution and placed them within the mainstream of Anglo-American tradition. General Nicholas Herkimer personified the courage, patriotism, and self-sacrifice of other German settlers. The son of a Palatine immigrant, Herkimer had acquired wealth and prominence before receiving a mortal wound while leading the militia against an invasion of loyalists and warriors at Oriskany. Local historians insisted that German veterans who had defended liberty during the war also embraced the democratic process afterward. Significantly, they also supported Anglo-American views of race.[18] Stretching Anglo-American myths and half truths to cover one of the valley's most distinct ethnic groups, local historians achieved two ends: they fitted the Germans within some of the young nation's most cherished traditions, and they made the Revolution the natural outcome of colonial developments.

Paeans to progress and unity could not overcome fears that the social changes brought about by technological and economic improvements threatened a radical break with the Revolutionary past. The completion of the Erie Canal in 1825 placed the Mohawk Valley at the center of the market revolution and altered the economic, social, and emotional context in which Americans operated. Their rapidly changing world looked less and less like the one that their Revolutionary ancestors had inhabited. In terms of wealth, technology, and social amenities, people living in the middle decades of the nineteenth century enjoyed advantages their forebears could scarcely have imagined. Nevertheless, the transition to a more acquisitive, individualist, and commercial society came at a price. Republican values seemed in danger of disappearing before an emerging liberal capitalist order, and even the most sanguine proponents of the canal worried about the perils of progress.[19]

Nathaniel Benton, who was no critic of modernity, reminded readers that not everyone benefited equally in the emerging market economy. Honest, hardworking men suffered economically once the canal opened. Location was everything. Towns and businesses south of the canal prospered while those to the north withered. John Beardslee was a case in point. Born in 1759 Beardslee moved to the Mohawk Valley, where he built mills and bridges, structures that served the public good, and eventually founded a small but thriving settlement. When the Erie Canal bypassed his village, commerce ceased. Due to no fault of his own, Beardslee had lost a "handsome estate," the product of nearly thirty years' hard work. Some people feared that success was no longer a matter of individual merit when the government, influenced by speculators and businessmen, made far-reaching economic decisions.[20]

The current generation's moral failings manifested in physical decline. "Americans as a people," Simms declared, "had degenerated from their ancestors in point of stature, limitation of life, and ability to endure fatigue." Simms drew specific attention to the women of his generation; in terms of strength, fortitude, and initiative, they failed to measure up to their grandmothers. Indolence and luxury were to blame. The leaders of the new economy, who constituted the growing ranks of the commercial classes, lived sedentary lives. Echoing Jacksonian Democrats, Simms intoned, "man shall acquire a living, by the sweat of his brow." Without hard work to "invigorate the bodily powers," people and nations became soft and effeminate. Whereas early pioneers had labored for little material gain, newly wealthy nineteenth-century Americans spent freely to acquire the trappings of respectability. Middle-class families consumed enervating drinks like coffee and tea, ate prepared foods, dressed inappropriately, and heated their homes with iron stoves rather than fireplaces. These new products made available by the Erie Canal "sapped the vigor from the present generation."[21] Simms's view that luxury and power eroded virtue was not shared equally by other authors. Whigs and later Republicans such as William Leete Stone and Benton identified problems with modern society but did not believe that social change was inherently corrosive.

To help ease internal tensions, historians identified First Peoples as a major ideological obstacle to narratives of progress and modernity. Many Americans who believed in the rightness and justness of U.S. expansion also recognized that the continent's original inhabitants not only had a prior claim to the land but could also serve as models of republican simplicity. Reconciling these opinions required some mental gymnastics. Many observers who identified republican principles operating within indigenous cultures hastened to add that societies and individuals had deteriorated after prolonged contact with Europeans. Having reached the pinnacle of achievement in some unspecified past, they had since become idle, cruel, and much addicted to alcohol. No longer adhering to traditional ways, these "inauthentic" Indians seemed bound to disappear. They certainly should not be allowed to halt or delay progress. Nor should Americans scruple too much about taking Native lands. Ignoring the centrality of horticulture to Iroquoian subsistence strategies, Americans falsely charged the Haudenosaunee with living in a nomadic, hunter state. Since they did not cultivate the land, they had no legitimate claim to it. The message was clear: unable or unwilling to improve, the inferior culture ought to give way before the superior.[22]

The myth of the "vanishing Indian," epitomized in the literature of James Fenimore Cooper and deployed by Andrew Jackson during the Indian-removal debates, found expression in local histories.[23] Campbell followed the story line precisely. After extolling the oratorical and military accomplishments of these "unlettered children of the forest" in the introduction to *Annals of Tryon County*, Campbell allowed the Six Nations to vanish temporarily from the story only to reappear in time for the Revolution, transformed from orators into skulking, bloodthirsty savages. The narrative of declension was so universal that the sudden change required no explanation. By war's end the Haudenosaunee were "passing away from among us, without leaving . . . any mementoes of their greatness." The Six Nations were not dispossessed so much as mysteriously vanished from the landscape.[24]

Framed as a struggle between nature and primitivism on the one hand, and modernity and progress on the other, the American Revolution was made to speak to contemporary nineteenth-century assumptions about the inherent incompatibility of indigenous and American societies. Popular opinion, which held that as settlers moved west First Peoples must retreat or be destroyed, of course informed the national debate on Indian removal. "Humanity has often wept over the fate of the aborigines of this country," claimed Andrew Jackson, the leading proponent of removal. "But progress has never for a moment been arrested, and one by one have many powerful tribes disappeared from the earth." With the outcome foreordained, Jackson antiseptically transformed a policy of ethnic cleansing into one of removal whereby a "few savage hunters" would be peacefully and benevolently relocated to western lands, where they could "pursue happiness in their own way and under their own rude institutions."[25] Although primarily concerned with local affairs, Mohawk Valley historians nonetheless waded into a national discourse. In detailing the savage nature of warfare on the New York frontier and subsequent dispossession of the Haudenosaunee, local authors foretold and justified the removal of the Cherokee and other southeastern groups in their own time.

Among accounts by local historians, only Stone's biography of Joseph Brant, the Mohawk war leader who together with his loyalist allies destroyed much of the Mohawk Valley, threatened to disrupt the dominant narrative. Anticipating the cultural relativism of a later generation, Stone argued that Native peoples had no monopoly on savagery. While he did not place indigenous and Anglo-American cultures on an equal footing, scalping and the practice of adopting prisoners, he asserted, made sense within the logic of Haudenosaunee culture. As an outsider to the region—he was born and raised in New Paltz, New York—Stone could view the frontier war with a degree of detachment and objectivity most Mohawk Valley residents found either objectionable or impossible to achieve. Nevertheless, he, like most Americans, was ambivalent about his subject. Brant fascinated Stone precisely because he seemed to transcend the limitations of his culture. Although Brant did not decry Native modes of warfare, he personally did not scalp, kill needlessly, or adopt his enemies, and he encouraged others to follow his example. What appeared to set Brant apart was his unusual association with British Indian Superintendent Sir William Johnson. Under Johnson's patronage Brant acquired a Western education, embraced Christianity, and adopted the trappings of civility. Yet as Brant steadily changed his lot in life, the Mohawks appeared to degenerate. Seeing his people much in need of "moral and social improvement," Brant behaved like the nineteenth-century reformers Stone admired by promoting Christianity, Western education, temperance, and agriculture. If Brant represented a different way for the Mohawks, the path he blazed led ultimately to extinction by assimilation. In the end Stone subscribed to prevailing notions about the "vanishing Indian" that buttressed progress and expansion.[26]

Transforming indigenous peoples into the savage Other became a necessary stage in healing internal divisions and redrawing community boundaries after the Revolutionary War. The postwar communities looked very different from the old as the wartime departure of large numbers of loyalists and nearly all the Mohawks removed sizable segments of the population. The ethnic and racial plurality of earlier times was erased when the boundaries of postwar communities were redrawn rigidly along racial lines. Mohawks and other indigenous peoples, once encountered as complex, flesh-and-blood human beings, were reduced to stock stereotypes to justify their exclusion. This act of Othering also permitted local residents to infuse the fratricidal conflict with moral significance. However painful, the Revolution had excised dangerous elements from the community, much as a doctor cuts cancerous cells from a patient's body. With the malignancy removed, the region could complete its evolution from a savage to a civilized state.

Communities that depended on popular tropes about savagery and the vanishing Indian for their very existence developed a form of selective amnesia that blocked from popular memory the existence of older, stable, multicultural communities. Acknowledging the presence of an alternate past would have challenged the racial binary that sustained teleological narratives of progress and raised uncomfortable questions about the civility of parents and grandparents. Authors, therefore, dared not probe too deeply the reasons why Mohawks and loyalists had sided with Britain. Yet some explanation was necessary.

Local historians found Mohawk behavior more explicable than that of the loyalists. Native peoples, they suggested, simply acted out their nature. Ignoring the fact that the Six Nations adopted a variety of responses to the Revolution, ranging from neutrality to active participation on one side or the other, most local histories described the Native confederacy as pro-British either out of habit or for mercenary reasons. The British had always been their allies and they had more gifts to give than the impecunious Americans. It scarcely occurred to Americans that the Native peoples too were "fighting for their freedom" and that their decisions were guided by calculations of self-interest. Mohawks had already been the victims of the colonists' (many of them Mohawk Valley Whigs) desire for land and appreciated Britain's efforts to prevent further encroachments. But believing the Six Nations to have acted habitually, almost instinctually, local historians had difficulty explaining the behavior of Oneidas, who allied with the Americans. Even Benton, who lived in the western valley near the Oneida homeland, says little about their wartime activities. If warriors were only acting out their nature in opposing the revolutionaries, then the blame lay with British officials and Tories for unleashing their savage allies on the frontier.[27]

Loyalists came in for the harshest condemnations because they had voluntarily chosen savagery over civilization. The loyalist reality was of course more complex. Ideology motivated few Mohawk Valley Tories, and in many cases prewar animosities and family alliances determined one's position in the Revolution. The unfortunate truth for many was that they did not choose sides at all but were carried along by events beyond their control. Authors trying to avoid difficult questions about why some members of the community turned against others charged loyalists with abandoning self-control. Restraint set civilized people apart from savages, and because the loyalists voluntarily surrendered to their base passions, they were considered worse than Indians. The incident that introduces this chapter illustrates major themes that were repeated over and over in local histories. Recounting how a loyalist soldier coldly shot and killed his Whig brother, even as he pleaded for his life, Simms declared that "the most unfeeling and inhuman acts of cruelty . . . were committed by *tories.*" Campbell agreed, stating that "the Tories . . . were the most barbarous," sparing neither adults nor children. During a raid on Cherry Valley, a Tory named Newbury brutally tomahawked a wounded twelve-year-old girl.[28] Taken collectively, these anecdotes depict Tories as so consumed with rage as to be wholly devoid of human feeling.

This line of attack had two advantages. First, it deflected analysis away from complex processes and the overzealousness of Whigs—who may have driven moderates and neutrals into the British camp—in favor of reducing loyalist behavior to a moral defect. Second, the fact that some frontier inhabitants did embrace a "primitive" state was cause for alarm. Intermixing had a doleful effect on both peoples, as the violence of the Revolution demonstrated, and should be avoided at all cost. The inhuman acts of "painted tories" both justified and necessitated the destruction or dispossession of all Native peoples and their allies. In this way local historians retrospectively fused the Revolution and progress while obscuring the ambiguities of the conflict.

Despite efforts to manufacture social unity, countervailing memories and alternate versions of the past could and did subvert the collective memory expressed in local histories. While visiting Utica, Lafayette inadvertently challenged the dominant narrative. When the general did not see any of the Americans' Oneidas allies present at the ceremonies, he asked whether any still lived in the area and whether a meeting could be arranged. It had never occurred to the organizers that the Oneidas ought to have received an invitation. Nonplussed by this surprising request, they discovered some Oneidas hunting nearby and brought them to Lafayette. Locals did not know what to make of this unplanned reunion. In contrast to the lengthy sentimental treatment accorded veterans, the newspaper devoted just a single sentence to his encounter with the Oneidas, the only private meeting the war hero granted in Utica. The Oneidas simply had no place in the history.[29]

While outsiders could temporarily disturb the equilibrium, locals possessed the knowledge to seriously challenge the dominant narrative. A close reading of several texts reveals that Natives and Revolutionaries shared more in common than the authors intended to reveal. Jeptha Simms tells the story of the Vrooman family during an especially anxious period in the war, when war parties and loyalist soldiers seemed to strike everywhere at once. After receiving warning of an attack, Ephraim Vrooman left his work in the fields and raced home to his wife and two children. As the family scrambled into the cover of a nearby cornfield, Mrs. Vrooman lost track of her daughter. Whispering in Dutch, she asked her husband if he had the girl. This alerted a warrior named Seth's Henry, who immediately shot Mrs. Vrooman. The warrior then reportedly spoke to the woman's body in Dutch, saying, "Now say—*what these Indian dogs do here?*"[30] While typical of the sort of incidents that made up the anti-Indian sublime, the attack on the Vrooman family reveals that the combatants knew one another intimately. Not only did Seth's Henry speak the same language as his victims, but he also targeted the Vrooman family precisely because he had known them before the war.

Later in the war a Schoharie warrior captured the prominent Whig George Warner with the intention of marching him to distant Fort Niagara. Warner feared that he could not make the trip because his shoes were inappropriate to the season. If he was unable to keep up with the fast-moving war party, he would be killed. Knowing that if he survived the journey he would likely be adopted into his captor's family, Warner turned his understanding of Haudenosaunee culture to his advantage. Appealing to the Schoharie as kin, he pleaded, "I now look to you for protection as to a father, and will try to love you as such."[31] The appeal to kinship worked, and the Schoharie gave Warner a pair of moccasins. Now suitably shod, Warner was able to make good his escape.

Mutual understanding rather than incommensurability are evident in Judge John M. Brown's 1823 self-published pamphlet history, *Brief Sketch of the First Settlement of the County of Schoharie*. In recounting an encounter between Whig militiamen and warriors in the forest, Brown contends the two sides carried on a brief conversation as they advanced warily on each other. Coming within arm's reach, a warrior named Hansyerry grasped and twisted the musket of militiaman Joseph Borst, spilling the powder from his pan. Speaking in Mohawk, he said, "It's good if this begone [*sic*]." The disarmed militiaman then wrenched the musket from Hansyerry's hands and replied in Mohawk, "It is good that this is just so." Then the two men, "whooping like Indians," wrestled until Hansyerry broke free and retreated into the woods. This encounter in the Schoharie woods was anything but anonymous. Borst and Hansyerry possessed a shared understanding of manhood and warfare that permitted and even required displays of coolness and bravery through boasting and personal contact.[32] These men knew each other, if not personally, then culturally.

Although difficult to demonstrate, such cross-cultural exchanges may have left a deep mark on Mohawk Valley society. In the second edition of *Annals of Tryon County*, William Campbell observed that the Haudenosaunee had passed away without a trace. It is interesting to consider the way in which Campbell, after erasing the indigenous presence from the Mohawk Valley altogether, described ideas of liberty and freedom. He likened liberty to a newly planted, ever-growing tree, "whose beautiful foliage and wide-spreading branches have excited universal admiration, and a scion from which may yet be engrafted into all the nations of the east."[33] The comparison was hardly novel. Liberty trees occupied a venerable place in Anglo-American popular culture, tracing their origins to the ancient and symbolically powerful oaks and elms of medieval England.[34] Yet the tree Campbell described differed in important details from those that dominated Anglo-American culture.

Campbell's tree was not ancient. Rather, it was freshly planted by the revolutionaries who expected it to grow forever and to draw together other nations beneath its protective boughs. Campbell's liberty tree resembled nothing so much as the Great Tree of Peace planted by the esteemed Haudenosaunee cultural hero, the Peacemaker. Doubtless, the similarities between Campbell's tree and the Great Tree of Peace, if any existed at all, were subconscious, but it is tantalizing to think that Campbell presented the young republic's most deeply held values using language and symbols imbibed from the region's original inhabitants.

The cultural complexity that occasionally appeared in postwar histories would not have surprised or dismayed the warriors and loyalist soldiers who so vigorously prosecuted the war against the Mohawk Valley before being exiled to Canada. They had taken quite different lessons from the conflict and thus told quite different stories about the war. For them, the shared experience of combat, defeat, and dispossession strengthened rather than weakened cross-cultural bonds. After settling in what would become Upper Canada (present-day Ontario), Mohawks and loyalist preserved and maintained the boundaries of their multiethnic communities through a regular and lively round of social activities. Visits, reunions, parties, and militia musters became occasions to celebrate shared experiences and a common identity and to help explain and give meaning to the war. Like Campbell and Simms, Mohawks and loyalists self-consciously built new communities in opposition to the ones they had left behind.[35]

While local historians in the Mohawk Valley sought to transform stories of messy cultural diversity with ones of racial simplicity, sometimes it proved impossible to make Indians and whites perform their assigned roles. Glimpses of an alternate history, one in which Mohawks and colonists shared a past and constructed common meanings, are revealed even in stories of murder and bloodshed. Yet if the fluid reality of life in the late colonial and Revolutionary era periodically bubbled to the surface of veterans' accounts, these anecdotes posed no serious challenge to the region's historical memory. The magnitude and force of the anti-Indian sublime absorbed and overwhelmed counternarratives.

Nevertheless, the unity and cohesiveness represented by the Great Tree of Peace was what local historians sought to achieve at a time when rapid social and economic change threatened to divide communities. Not simply victims of anonymous forces, residents of the Mohawk Valley turned in part to history to give shape and meaning to the changes besetting them. The American Revolution had, they believed, established timeless truths that, if properly learned and applied, would steer the rising generation through uncertain times. To construct plausible continuities between the Jacksonian and Revolutionary eras, however, historians selected certain memories that emphasized cohesion and purpose over others bearing evidence of division and dissention. Adopting the anti-Indian sublime smoothed over divisions within the community and helped resolve the war's disturbing ambiguities. Erecting immutable barriers between savagery and civilization, nineteenth-century historians placed their own Revolutionary descendants and thus themselves safely and squarely within an emerging national narrative of progress and expansion. Yet by casting First Peoples as obstacles to the region's evolution, Mohawk Valley authors cleansed popular memory and helped make possible the national project of ethnic cleansing.

NOTES

1. William W. Campbell, *Annals of Tryon County; or, The Border Warfare of New York, during the Revolution* (New York: Harper, 1831), 141; emphasis in original.
2. In this chapter the Mohawk Valley refers to a region embracing the Mohawk River west of Schenectady, its tributary the Schoharie River, and Cherry Valley, a branch of the Susquehanna historically linked to the Mohawk.
3. Peter Silver, *Our Savage Neighbors: How Indian War Transformed America* (New York: Norton, 2008), 83–85.
4. "The Condition, Grievances and Oppressions of the Germans," in *Documentary History of the State of New York*, vol. 3, ed. E. B. O'Callaghan (Albany, N.Y.: Weed, Parson, 1850), quotation on 711–12; David L. Preston, *The Texture of Contact: European and Indian Settler Communities on the Frontiers of Iroquoia, 1667–1783* (Lincoln: University of Nebraska Press, 2009); James W. Paxton, "Kinship, Communities, and Covenant Chains: Mohawks and Palatines in New York and Upper Canada, 1712–1830" (PhD diss., Queen's University, 2006), esp. chap. 3.
5. Arthur C. Parker, "The Constitution of the Five Nations; or, The Iroquois Book of the Great Law," in *Parker on the Iroquois*, ed. William N. Fenton (Syracuse, N.Y.: Syracuse University Press, 1968), 30, 50–52.
6. David Thelen, "Memory and American History," *Journal of American History* 75 (1989): 1121, 1123–24; W. Fitzhugh Brundage, "No Deed but Memory," in *Where These Memories Grow: History, Memory, and Southern Identity*, ed. W. Fitzhugh Brundage (Chapel Hill: University of North Carolina Press, 2000); Michael Kammen, *A Season of Youth: The American Revolution and the Historical Imagination* (New York: Knopf, 1978); David Waldstreicher, *In the Midst of Perpetual*

Fetes: The Making of American Nationalism, 1776–1820 (Chapel Hill: University of North Carolina Press, 1997); Sarah J. Purcell, *Sealed with Blood: War, Sacrifice, and Memory in Revolutionary America* (Philadelphia: University of Pennsylvania Press, 2002); Lorett Treese, *Valley Forge: Making and Remaking a National Symbol* (University Park: Pennsylvania State University Press, 1995).

7. Kammen, *Season of Youth;* Campbell, *Annals of Tryon County*, 17.
8. Gordon S. Wood, *Creation of the Republic, 1776–1787* (Chapel Hill: University of North Carolina Press, 1969), 68–69; Kammen, *Season of Youth*, 49–51; Jeptha R. Simms, *History of Schoharie County and Border Wars of New York* (Albany, N.Y.: Munsell & Tanner, 1845), quotation on iii.
9. *Oneida Observer*, June 14, 1825, quoted in *A Pilgrimage of Liberty: A Contemporary Account of the Triumphal Tour of General Lafayette through the Southern and Western States in 1825, as Reported by Local Newspapers*, ed. Edgar Ewing Brandon (Athens, Ga.: Lawhead, 1944), 422; Purcell, *Sealed with Blood*, 189–91, quotation on 191.
10. R. B. M., "William W. Campbell," in *Dictionary of American Biography*, vol. 3, ed. Ellen Johnson (New York: Scribners, 1929), 467–68; Campbell, *Annals of Tryon County*, 6; William Leete Stone, *Life of Joseph Brant*, 2 vols. (Albany, N.Y.: J. Munsell, 1865), 1:xix; Simms, *History of Schoharie County*, v–vii.
11. *Census for 1820: Fourth Census* (Washington, D.C.: Gales & Seaton, 1821), 11; *Fifth Census; or, Enumeration of the Inhabitants of the United States* (Washington, D.C.: Green, 1832), 42–43.
12. Campbell, *Annals of Tryon County*, 21–24, quotation on 21; John M. Brown, *Brief Sketch of the First Settlement of the County of Schoharie* (Schoharie, N.Y.: Cuthbert, 1823); Simms, *History of Schoharie County*, 3–181.
13. Jean M. O'Brien, *First and Lasting: Writing Indians out of Existence in New England* (Minneapolis: University of Minnesota Press, 2010), 1–53, quotes on 2 and 6.
14. Campbell, *Annals of Tryon County*, 190; Simms, *History of Schoharie County*, 153–54.
15. Simms, *History of Schoharie County*, 52–54, quotation on 54.
16. Timothy Dwight, *Travels in New England and New York*, 4 vols. (Cambridge: Belknap Press of Harvard University Press, 1969), 3:160–62, 165, quotation on 192.
17. R. B. M. "William W. Campbell," 467–68; Campbell, *Annals of Tryon County*, 19; Campbell, *The Border Warfare of New York during the Revolution; or, The Annals of Tryon County*, 2nd ed. (New York: Baker & Scribner, 1849), 393.
18. Nathaniel S. Benton, *A History of Herkimer County* (Albany, N.Y.: Munsell, 1856), 8–9; Simms, *History of Schoharie County*, 36–37, 44, quotation on 37; Philip Otterness, *Becoming German: The 1709 Palatine Migration to New York* (Ithaca, N.Y.: Cornell University Press, 2004), 162–64.
19. On the ambiguities of progress, see Carol Sheriff, *The Artificial River: The Erie Canal and the Paradox of Progress, 1817–1862* (New York: Hill & Wang, 1996).
20. Benton, *History of Herkimer County*, 438–39.
21. Simms, *History of Schoharie County*, 53, 157, 166–67. Richard L. Bushman, *The Refinement of America: Persons, Houses, Cities* (New York: Knopf, 1992).
22. Stone, *Life of Brant*, 2:330; Robert F. Berkhofer Jr., *The White Man's Indian:*

Images of the American Indian from Columbus to the Present (New York: Knopf, 1978), 86–96; Daniel H. Usner Jr., "Iroquois Livelihood and Jeffersonian Agrarianism: Reaching behind the Models and Metaphors," in *Native Americans and the Early Republic*, ed. Frederick E. Hoxie, Ronald Hoffman, and Peter J. Albert (Charlottesville: University of Virginia Press, 1999), 210–25.

23. Many scholars have made the myth of the disappearing Indian central to their work. See, for example, Henry Nash Smith, *Virgin Land: The American West as Symbol and Myth* (Cambridge: Harvard University Press 1950); Berkhofer, *White Man's Indian;* Laurel Thatcher Ulrich, *The Age of Homespun: Objects and Stories in the Creation of an American Myth* (New York: Knopf, 2001), 340–73; and Richard Slotkin, *Regeneration through Violence: The Mythology of the American Frontier, 1600–1860* (Middletown, Conn.: Wesleyan University Press, 1974).
24. Campbell, *Annals of Tryon County*, 9–15, 190, quotation on 190.
25. Andrew Jackson, "Second Annual Message, December 6, 1830," in *A Compilation of the Messages and Papers of the Presidents*, ed. James D. Richardson, vol. 2 (New York: Bureau of National Literature, 1897), 1082–86; James Taylor Carson, "'The Obituary of Nations': Ethnic Cleansing, Memory, and the Origins of the Old South," *Southern Cultures* 14 (2008): 6–31.
26. Stone, *Life of Brant*, 2:330; Alden T. Vaughan, *Roots of American Racism: Essays on the Colonial Experience* (New York: Oxford University Press, 1995), 31–32.
27. Campbell, *Annals of Tryon County*, 52; Simms, *History of Schoharie County*, 101; Barbara Graymont, *The Iroquois in the Revolution* (Syracuse, N.Y.: Syracuse University Press, 1972); Colin G. Calloway, *The American Revolution in Indian Country: Crisis and Diversity in Native American Communities* (New York: Cambridge University Press, 1995), xiii.
28. Simms, *History of Schoharie County*, 281; Campbell, *Annals of Tryon County*, 171, 148.
29. *Oneida Observer*, June 14, 1825, 422; Joseph T. Glatthaar and James Kirby Martin, *Forgotten Allies: The Oneida Indians and the American Revolution* (New York: Hill & Wang, 2006), 3–5, 315–16.
30. Simms, *History of Schoharie County*, 378.
31. Ibid, 518–19.
32. Brown, *Brief Sketch*, 4–12, quotation on 7.
33. Campbell, *Annals of Tryon County*, 17.
34. David Hackett Fischer, *Liberty and Freedom: A Visual History of America's Founding Ideas* (Oxford: Oxford University Press, 2005), 19–36; Arthur M. Schlesinger, "The Liberty Tree: A Genealogy," *New England Quarterly* 25 (1952): 435–58.
35. James W. Paxton, "Merrymaking and Militia Musters: (Re)Constructing Community and Identity in Upper Canada," *Ontario History* 102 (Autumn 2010): 218–38.

"Lie There My Darling, While I Avenge Ye!"

Anecdotes, Collective Memory, and the Legend of Molly Pitcher

Emily Lewis Butterfield

In July 1830 newspapers around the country published this reprint of "A Tale of '76" with the subtitle "Captain Molly":

> Before the two armies, American and English, had begun the general action of Monmouth, two of the advanced batteries commenced a very severe fire against each other. As the warmth was excessive, the wife of a cannonier constantly ran to bring water for him from a neighboring spring. At the moment when she started from the spring to pass to the post of her husband, she saw him fall, and hastened to assist him; but he was dead. At the same moment she heard an officer order the cannon to be removed from its place, complaining he could not fill his post with as brave a man as had been killed. "No," said the intrepid Molly, fixing her eyes upon the officer: "the cannon shall not be removed for want of some one to serve it; since my brave husband is no more, I will use my utmost exertions to avenge his death." The activity and courage with which she performed the offices of cannonier, during the action, attracted the at-

> tention of all who witnessed it, finally of General Washington himself, who afterwards gave her the rank of Lieutenant, and granted her half pay during life. She wore an epaulette, and every body called her "Capt. Molly."[1]

While modern readers might greet this tale with skepticism, contemporary audiences located Captain Molly within a larger context of popular culture rife with similar stories. Anecdotes giving snippets of Revolutionary and frontier violence, European notables' lives, and stinging accounts of personal foibles filled history books and provided copy for newspaper and journal editors. These tales featured commoners and elites alike, with both male and female characters. Although warfare was seemingly an explicitly male endeavor, Americans could read myriad anecdotal accounts of female patriotism, ranging from ancient Spartan mothers sending sons into battle to Mrs. Bailey sacrificing her flannel petticoat for cartridge wrappings in 1814. As Alfred F. Young has described, popular nineteenth-century plays, novels, and chapbooks included dozens of variations on the themes of warrior women, and women dressed as men serving aboard ships or in the army.[2]

Unlike most anecdotes which circulated for only a short time, accounts of Captain Molly / Molly Pitcher multiplied and expanded over the course of several decades. Through constant reprintings, adaptations, and occasional exclusions of a variety of anecdotes, antebellum Americans forged a collective memory of a virtuous, heroic Molly Pitcher that proved resistant to deconstruction, even by contradictory reports from well-known historians. This chapter explores early representations of Molly, tracing the interactions of incongruous accounts and attempts to reshape an already popular story. In so doing, this study reveals some of the complexities of validation and narrative authority in transforming folk stories and individual memories into national history. Additionally, the patterns of reprinting and circulation of the Molly anecdotes document the role of newspaper editors, encyclopedists, and local historians in remembering, or forgetting, stories from the Revolution.

Despite the trappings of authenticity surrounding the legend, there was no identifiable person known as Captain Molly or Molly Pitcher, nor was there initially a standardized narrative of her actions. Unlike the "action against the tea" in Boston harbor, or Deborah Sampson's military service, the woman at Monmouth was not publicly forgotten and then recovered, nor was her growing fame the result of a personal quest for recognition.[3] Instead, Molly's story first emerged well after the war, then spread rapidly. Differing, often conflicting, renditions of the tale circulated for more than twenty-five years before coalescing into a consistent form.

Beginning in the 1830s encyclopedia and newspaper stories of Molly presented a courageous and virtuous patriot. These accounts gave no descriptive information about Molly's appearance, nationality, or age, nor did they attribute the source of the information to specific witnesses. A decade later, as popularized histories of the Revolution became increasingly widespread, some works included very different versions of the woman at Monmouth. The Captain Molly who emerged from memoirs and personal interviews in the 1840s was an unruly, immodest, stout young Irish woman with a penchant for men's clothing.

Most editors, encyclopedists, and historians, however, rejected the sensationalism of the seemingly authentic Molly stories. Instead, they selectively incorporated a few of the new details into existing anecdotes, leaving out lines about torn skirts and heavy brogues. Very few reprinted negative versions unchanged, regardless of the popularity of the author. By the late 1850s Americans had largely rejected the image of a tawdry Molly in favor of a virtuous, if often-abstracted, heroine.

As Michael Kammen has explained, early nineteenth-century readers largely accepted anecdotes, whether dramatic or humorous, as legitimate historical truths, despite the critiques and laments of the nations' aging founders.[4] Eileen Ka-May Cheng's work on plagiarisms of George Chalmers's *Political Annals* reveals the ways selective editing or reinterpretation of anecdotes allowed authors to redefine the character and political meanings of even well-known events.[5] In a period when histories relied on appropriation and derivation from existing works, the presence of anecdotes served to validate the authenticity of historians' overall narratives, as well as the accuracy of their interpretations. When Rebecca Clendenin applied for a war widow's pension in 1840, she was able to prove her deceased husband's service in part by recounting Molly's story, explaining that her husband told her he had seen the heroine at Monmouth.[6] As a story within a story, the anecdote form also created openings in elite-dominated narratives of the Revolution, making places for local folk heroes and moments of unsung heroism. Regardless of Washington's actual treatment of camp followers, his reputation for magnanimity made it easy for the story of his leadership at Monmouth to expand to include a moment of recognition for a widowed heroine.

With the aging of the Revolutionary generation, Americans' efforts to commemorate battles, erect monuments, and write histories aggregated individual experiences into acceptable communal memories. Reconciliation of different versions of particular events sometimes meant silencing contradictory voices but frequently came through incorporation—attributing several similar actions at different times and places to one individual or stretching accounts through embellishment until they were large enough to explain seeming inconsistencies within the story. This process of amalgamation is particularly visible in the literary genre of the anecdote. Characteristically brief, self-contained stories with a single protagonist, anecdotes give snapshots of particular moments; they are detached from one another and from the larger context surrounding the event. As Joel Fineman and other New Historicists note, this very separation from larger narratives is key to the way an anecdote "produces the effect of the real" by demonstrating "the occurrence of contingency," and authors from Thucydides forward have used them to bolster the authenticity of their accounts.[7] Like the fateful nail from the "for the want of a nail the shoe was lost" moral rhyme, made famous in Franklin's *Poor Richard's Almanack,* these brief histories imply tantalizing connections to the outcomes of larger events.[8] Drawn from oral histories and reminiscences and passed along generations by storytellers, historians, and editors, anecdotes provide a unique glimpse into the process by which diverse recollections can condense into collective memories.

An important aspect of the role that printed anecdotes played in forging memories of the war was the concurrent advance in American print culture. Newspapers that published "A Tale of '76" in 1830 and 1832 took the story directly from Freeman Hunt's 1830 book, *American Anecdotes: Original and Select,* or reprinted the copy from other papers.[9] Authors and editors borrowed freely from one another, sometimes making changes in the process, other times reproducing word for word. This method of transmission allowed numerous variations of a tale to circulate simultaneously and to interact, as writers added or deleted authenticating or embellishing details.

But by the late 1830s the widespread publication of unsourced anecdotes and tall tales from the war also produced skeptics and critics. In response, authors and historians began to append comments about the veracity of their authenticating anecdotes. Editors assured readers their stories were indeed founded on facts and eyewitness accounts. The story of Captain Molly followed this pattern of circulation and validation, changing over time as authors included new information, offered additional sources as proof, and gradually excluded problematic elements to form a stable popularized character.

Camp Followers, Heroines, and a Fortune Teller

From the earliest print versions, anecdotes of Molly consistently repeated specific descriptors in a set pattern. These introductory details reinforced the well-known context for the tale. On June 28, 1778, Washington's army attacked the main British force as they marched across New Jersey, retreating from Philadelphia to New York. Temperatures reached the upper nineties with high humidity, and the fighting persisted for seven hours. Although the heat increased soldiers' need for water, the cannons demanded most of the ready supply. Artillery crews had to swab the cannon barrels with wet daubs to extinguish burning gunpowder residue before they could reload. Although the official responsibilities of camp followers were in support roles—washing, cooking, and providing medical care—many voluntarily engaged in combat activities like making bullets and supplying water.[10]

According to her biographers, Molly was among those carrying water; when her husband collapsed she ran to his aid, then took his place in the battle, loading and firing the cannon until nightfall. Under the cover of darkness, the British continued their retreat and broke contact. Both sides claimed the engagement as a victory, and newspapers printed widely differing accounts of the battle. None made the slightest mention of Molly, nor any other camp follower.[11] For half a century the legend of Captain Molly, like many stories of the Revolution, likely existed in an oral culture of war stories and bragging rights, but it was not recorded in print. When it emerged around 1830, Molly's story drew on two distinct strands of early nineteenth-century storytelling: one based on the actions of women in battle and the other surrounding the name "Moll Pitcher."

Although the vast majority of camp followers received no compensation for their work after the war ended, at least three women eventually received pensions for their own service, rather than for that of their husbands. Deborah Sampson enlisted under the name of Robert Shurtliff and served until the army discovered her true sex in October 1783. Her story began appearing in newspapers in January 1784, eight years before she submitted her formal petition to the Massachusetts legislature in 1792. Sampson's 1797 autobiography, lecture tours in 1802–3, and ongoing pension appeals all kept her story in periodic circulation, as did notices of her death in 1827. Elizabeth Ellet, the first historian to produce a volume collecting women's contributions to the war effort, included a lengthy description of Sampson's life and service in her 1848 work, *The Women of the American Revolution.* In Ellet's narrative, Sampson's patriotism, although misdirected, was equally matched by her commitment to female virtue, leading her to marriage and a return to feminine norms after her discharge from the army.[12]

In contrast to Sampson's popularity, two other pensioners, Margaret Corbin and Mary Hays McCauley, left almost no records of their lives beyond their pension applications. Corbin took her husband's place at a cannon during the defense of Fort Washington in 1776 and received disabling wounds. She remained with the army, registered on the invalid rolls, and applied for a federal pension. Like Sampson, after Congress approved Corbin's pension in 1779, newspapers periodically reprinted excerpts of the resolution with the title "Female Heroism Rewarded."[13] Although the papers consistently used Corbin's full name in pension stories, the name Margaret was often popularly shortened to Mary or Molly, providing a first instance of a cannon-firing woman potentially associated with the name Molly. A second Molly emerged in 1822, when the Pennsylvania Assembly passed "An Act for the relief of Molly McKolly, for her services during the Revolutionary war." Pennsylvania records identified McKolly (Mary Hays McCauley) as a "revolutionary heroine," not specifically associated with any particular battle or action. In reprinting the version of her story first published in the New York *National Advocate,* however, a number of papers reported that she had served disguised as a man until being wounded at the Battle of Brandywine. The *Advocate* explained that "it was not an unusual circumstance to find women in the ranks disguised as men, such was their ardor for independence."[14] Whether the *Advocate*'s version of McCauley's life was more or less accurate than the original, it followed the standard pattern of altering anecdotes by adding authenticating details and its own concluding bon mot. No report of Sampson, Corbin, or McCauley referred to Monmouth or to carrying water (in a pitcher or any other way), but several described McCauley with a sword, and Corbin's work at the cannon was clearly established.

While elements of the three stories overlapped, each contained distinct identities, locations, and actions. This variety suggests the complex origins of the Molly Pitcher story, particularly with the inclusion of a fourth character: Moll Pitcher, the fortune-teller of Lynn, Massachusetts. Three decades before any printed account of Molly-with-a-Pitcher, Americans in the Northeast were quite familiar with the name Moll Pitcher. Called a fortune-teller and a witch, she followed a family tradition of divination, reading tea leaves and reporting on the fate of long-absent sailors. She also unwittingly provided fodder for several generations of politicians, advertisers, poets, and dramatists. In November 1811 the Massachusetts *Scourge* suggested that given Moll's reported power, President Madison might find it more effective to defend against British harassment by replacing gunboats with her magic and popguns.[15] Although Moll, also called Mary and Molly, died in 1813, she remained a popular subject throughout the century. Abolitionist John Greenleaf Whittier wrote two versions of a poem about Moll, the 1832 piece simply titled "Moll Pitcher" and the revised 1840 epic "Moll Pitcher and the Minstrel Girl." Casting Moll as a wretched hag and villain, Whittier was among the first to describe her appearance in detail. His work brought the name and an accompanying depiction into wider circulation just as the story of a heroine firing a cannon at the Battle of Monmouth was becoming popular.[16]

Stories versus Memories of Captain Molly

Freeman Hunt's 1830 story given at the beginning of this chapter depicted a Molly who was not yet a Pitcher, who was "intrepid" but not entirely confident of her abilities. While Molly's husband was twice described as "brave," she simply vowed to "use my utmost exertions." This was more of a promise to try, rather than a blood oath. She was first identified as the "wife of a cannonier" and carried water for him. When moved by the need to avenge his death, she courageously "performed the offices of cannonier, during the action." This language reinforced Molly's femininity; she did not actually become a soldier, only fulfilled the duties of one in the absence of her husband. Following the publication of Hunt's

American Anecdotes, papers reprinted the entry on Captain Molly for several years, most often lifting the text word for word.

In 1835 Francis Alexander Durivage released the first edition of his *Popular Cyclopedia of History*, with a new version of the Molly story. Perhaps the first Monmouth woman to be called "Molly Pitcher," Durivage's heroine carried water not just to her husband but to his entire battery. Unlike the "Tale of '76" version, his Molly was not "the wife of"; instead, he cast the male figure in the story as a possessive object—"her husband." Durivage removed the words Hunt attributed to Molly, and in so doing, her claim to revenge. Upon hearing the command to withdraw the cannon, his Molly "offered her services," presumably for the Revolutionary cause. Rather than fulfilling an office, Molly Pitcher "fought well," and although Durivage left her unnoticed by General Washington, she retained the name "Captain Molly, ever after." These changes produced a character that acted as a patriot rather than as a wife.[17]

Two years later a third, even bolder, Molly appeared. Not simply bringing water as a kindness, Molly had been "contributing her aid" since the beginning of the battle. When she heard the order to remove the cannon after her husband fell, she was "indignant" and "she promptly opposed it—demanded the post of her slain husband" and "flew to the gun." Most of the printings of this version claimed that for her "sterling demonstration of patriot spirit," Molly received a commission, sword, and half pay for life from Washington, although the *New-Jersey State Gazette* and *Baltimore Sun* replaced "patriot spirit" with the politically useful "genuine Whig spirit." The *State Gazette* also added an introductory comment, noting that the story was for "the benefit of that class of full grown children and embryo patriots, who talk much more of New Jersey chivalry about election times than they ever learned, or [are] likely to learn from history, it may be proper here to add—what every New Jersey boy should know."[18] From the first sentence Molly's role as a model of active patriotism was clear. Not segregated as an example only for girls, the *State Gazette* insisted Molly's story was one that New Jersey *boys* should know.

As the 1830s versions of Molly's story continued to circulate, new information gave editors an increasingly wide array of descriptions to choose from when publishing an anecdote. While the earliest accounts of Molly at Monmouth labeled her "Captain Molly," printings of the 1837 version all used "Molly Pitcher" as their titles, suggesting that "Pitcher" was a surname unassociated with her actions and "Captain Molly" her postbattle honorific. Throughout the 1830s the Moll of Lynn and Molly of Monmouth existed independently in print, but the shift to "Molly Pitcher" in titles likely helped the stories begin to merge in the early 1840s. When Moll's daughter, Rebecca Short, died in 1841, the *Portsmouth Journal of Literature and Politics* noted in her obituary that she was "the daughter of the celebrated Moll Pitcher."[19] A reader promptly wrote to the paper, asking who Moll Pitcher was. Despite Moll of Lynn's fame, the *Journal* replied that Moll Pitcher was the heroine of Monmouth and gave an anecdote of the battle, and regional papers reprinted the explanation.[20]

Despite her "celebrated" status, not everyone depicted Molly Pitcher in such positive light, particularly those who claimed to have seen or known her. While many soldiers published memoirs in the 1820s and 1830s, none referred directly to Molly Pitcher, and only one described a woman at Monmouth. But the stream of interview-based histories of the war published in the 1840s and 1850s included several different accounts of Captain, or Sergeant, Molly. These more documented versions posed a number of challenges to the existing tales of Molly Pitcher's exemplary patriotism.

The first personal memory of a Molly-like character came from Joseph Plumb Martin, who served at the Battle of Monmouth with the Eighth Connecticut Regiment. Martin published his war memoirs in 1830, but reprints of the text were not widely available until the early 1850s. As William Huntting Howell describes, Martin's counternarrative was intentionally fractured, emphasizing the ridiculous or mundane over the noble or patriotic.[21] In addition to wrenching scenes of privation, survival-by-theft, and callous leadership, Martin included anecdotes and quips about a variety of unusual events. In one he wrote of an unidentified woman he saw at Monmouth:

> While in the act of reaching a cartridge and having one of her feet as far before the other as she could step, a cannon shot from the enemy passed directly between her legs without doing any damage other than carrying away all the lower part of her petticoat. Looking at it with apparent unconcern, she observed that it was lucky it did not pass a little higher, for in that case it might have carried away something else, and continued in her occupation.[22]

This story, with its bawdy innuendo, was not directly excerpted or republished anywhere other than in reprints of Martin's book, but it reinforced other personal accounts that described Molly having torn or damaged clothing.

George Washington Parke Custis, stepgrandson and adopted son of George Washington, wrote of Captain Molly at Monmouth and at Washington's camp in his anecdote column, "Recollections and Private Memoir of Washington," published serially beginning in 1840 and collected into a book in 1860.[23] As Seth C. Bruggeman describes, Custis situated himself as the primary mediator and guardian of Washington's legacy.[24] Writing with the authority of this position, he added a number of details to the existing Molly narrative, as if from Washington's memories or his own. Custis's Molly was a coarse and bossy camp follower with a heavy Irish brogue. In his 1840 piece, "The Battle of Monmouth," he explained that "Captain Molly" was "a *nom de guerre* given to the wife of a matross in Proctor's Artillery," who was stationed at an "unlucky gun," where six men fell before him. When her husband collapsed, the "heroine threw down the pail of water, and crying to her dead consort, 'Lie there my darling, while I avenge ye,' grasped the ramrod the lifeless hand of the poor fellow had just relinquished, sent home the charge, and called to the matrosses to prime the gun and fire." Not only did this Molly take her husband's place, she effectively took command of the cannon. Custis described Molly as an "Amazonian fair one," but not a lady, a woman whose just reward from Washington was a piece of gold, not official commendation, and who later went about "levying contributions upon both civil and military, whenever she recounted the tale."[25]

Perhaps from an appreciation for the dramatic flair Molly added to the story, or to provide cohesiveness with his published account, Custis also included Molly at a cannon as a background detail in his painting *The Battle of Monmouth.* Completed sometime before 1850, Custis's image of Molly depicted only a female figure working at a cannon, with none of the detail he provided in an 1843 column.[26] In his piece "The Headquarters" Custis returned to Captain Molly, describing her post-Monmouth life as a camp follower at Washington's headquarters. Working as a washerwoman, Molly "always wore an artilleryman's coat, with the cocked hat and feather, the distinguishing costume of Proctor's artillery." When Washington jokingly asked her if she found camp life dull after battle,

Molly expressed her desire to "have another clap at them red-coats." Washington commented on the likely damage to her clothing, to which she replied, "'Sure, and it is only in the artillery your Excellency knows that I would serve, and a divil a fear but the smoke of the cannon will hide my petticoats.'"[27] By these additions to the Molly legend, Custis further emphasized Molly's low social position; far from a respectable widow, she was an immodest Irish servant with a husband who was also "her consort." Washington's concern for Molly's torn skirts clearly drew on Martin's "cannonball through the petticoats" tale, while her unusual clothing and exaggerated brogue made her a caricature more than a patriot. Hardly an example for children, Custis's Captain Molly was rather an object of mockery, even to Washington.

Lacking the authority of participants, or Custis's authorial clout, John W. Barber and Henry Howe's 1844 book, *Historical Collections of the State of New Jersey*, reflected historians' growing need to argue for the validity of their information. Their account opened with the assertion, "The story of a woman who rendered essential service to the Americans in battle is founded on fact. She was a female of masculine mold, and dressed in a mongrel suit, with the petticoats of her own sex and an artilleryman's coat, cocked hat and feathers."[28] They repeated Custis's description of Molly's odd clothing and explicitly masculinized the result, labeling it a "mongrel suit" and even hinting that such was her prebattle garb.

Following Barber and Howe's method of collecting state history, Benson Lossing produced popular histories by gathering stories and information from interviews with surviving members of the Revolutionary generation, as well as descendants of deceased soldiers. His 1851 *Pictorial Fieldbook of the Revolution* expanded on Custis's and Barber and Howe's descriptions of Molly and added two entirely new aspects to the story. Citing information from interviews with eighty-year-old Rebecca Rose, eighty-seven-year-old Beverly Garrison, and the ninety-two-year-old widow of Alexander Hamilton, Elizabeth Schuyler Hamilton, Lossing combined the stories of Molly at Monmouth with accounts of Margaret Corbin and added a third combat location. Basing his account on Garrison's, Lossing told of Molly's presence at Fort Clinton in 1777: "She was in Fort Clinton, with her husband, when it was attacked. When the Americans retreated from the fort, as the enemy scaled the ramparts, her husband dropped his match and fled. Molly caught it up, touched off the piece, and then scampered off. It was the last gun fired by the Americans in the fort."[29] Remembering a woman she met in Washington's camp several years after Monmouth, Hamilton described Captain Molly as "the wife of a cannoneer—a stout, red-haired, freckle-faced young Irish woman named Mary." Lossing also included Rose's morbid conclusion to the tale, that Molly spent the remainder of her life near Fort Montgomery in New York, where neighbors knew her as "Dirty Kate." Rose's Captain Molly—most likely Margaret Corbin—eventually "died a horrible death from the effects of a syphilitic disease."[30] While earlier historians kept the Captain Molly of Monmouth distinct from Margaret Corbin at Fort Washington, Lossing, through his sources, merged them into a single character.

As damaging as these tawdry additions might seem, and despite the overall popularity of both Custis's and Lossing's volumes, numerous laudatory versions of the Captain Molly story continued to circulate in newspapers, magazines, and encyclopedias. Editors reprinted Custis's and Lossing's larger descriptions of the Battle of Monmouth, but none published the paragraphs about Molly as separate anecdotes the way they had excerpted positive depictions from other histories. This exclusion from the standard pattern of reproduction, the most basic measure of reader reception for anecdotes, suggests the growing strength of the collective memory of a bold, but virtuous, Molly.

Durivage released new editions of his *Cyclopedia* in 1841, 1842, annually from 1844 to 1852, and again in 1856, all containing his unchanged 1835 version of the Molly Pitcher story. In 1848 *Godey's Lady's Book* published an excerpt from Elizabeth Ellet's *The Women of the American Revolution* under the title "Heroic Women of the Revolution." In her introduction to the article on Deborah Sampson, Ellet briefly referred to Margaret Corbin and Molly Pitcher, identifying the actions of all three women as "instances . . . in which female courage was displayed by actions pertaining to the stronger sex."[31] Although Ellet did not provide a full sketch of Molly, she cited the work of another historian who did include a virtuous Molly in his history of the Mohawk Valley and who attributed the story to an eyewitness.[32]

Other contemporary authors included celebratory renditions of Molly's story in other collected histories targeted toward female audiences. Repeating the 1830s descriptions of Molly as an example for others, Jesse Clement, editor of the *Western Literary Messenger*, included her in his 1851 anecdote collection, *Noble Deeds of American Women*. Clement identified Molly Pitcher only as the wife of Mr. Pitcher. His Molly "fought partly, it may be, to revenge the death of her husband, but more, doubtless, for the love she bore for an injured country."[33] The common thread among all of Clement's stories was a noble bravery pushing women to patriotic or moral action. Molly's efforts at the cannon ranked her with valiant mothers who stoically sent their sons off to war and anecdotes like that of the "Faithful Little Girl" who reproved a fierce sailor for using foul language, ultimately leading him to salvation.

Following Clement's lead in balancing Molly's position as a wife and a patriot, several accounts of Molly in the early 1850s explicitly identified Pitcher, or variations such as Pritchard, as the heroine's surname and strengthened her connection to her soldier husband. By the mid-1850s the dominant representation of Molly Pitcher as a feminine, yet adventurous, heroine was complete. Expecting readers to know the story, advertisers and editors deployed Molly images to sell goods and to serve as a marker by which to describe other women's behaviors. Politicians and advertisers appropriated the image and reputations of many revolutionary heroes; Molly's transition into the cast of usable figures is evidence of the solidification of her story after more than two decades of negotiation. Despite the firsthand perspectives of Lossing's informants, and the seeming authority of Custis's accounts of Molly, other authors, historians, and newspaper editors repeatedly excluded all her negative qualities. As the story of the woman at Monmouth grew, only certain details remained attached to her image—when attributed words, she spoke with passion but rarely an accent; she carried water, but she had no obvious class position; and though her clothing was often damaged in battle, she remained feminine and virtuous.

A sanitized Captain Molly/Molly Pitcher appealed to readers for several reasons. Amid the conflicts over citizenship and challenges to gender norms and national unity during the antebellum era, she presented a comforting example of dramatic, but quickly contained, female patriotism. While the nation belatedly struggled to acknowledge aging and impoverished veterans, Molly's story inspired no guilt; her reward had come from Washington himself. Unlike accounts of Lydia Darrah or Deborah Sampson, anecdotes about Captain Molly lacked specific, identifying details about the heroine, making her an extremely malleable figure. Unattached to any particular location before or after her service at Monmouth, she was, by default, simply an American.[34]

Through repeated reprintings and adaptations, antebellum Americans embraced a Molly Pitcher whose work at the cannon reflected both patriotism and wifely devotion. Her example suggests that the appeal of collective memories that bolstered national identity and existing norms encouraged Americans to ignore contradictory accounts, even when provided by living witnesses. In contrast to elite-driven attempts to shape Revolutionary histories by silencing dissenting voices, the pattern of reprinting various versions of the Molly Pitcher story demonstrates the power of small, local newspapers in the consensus-building process. Tracing the variations in the early anecdotes of a Revolutionary character provides a unique lens into the methods both of exclusion and of incorporation that wove a range of individual experiences into standardized memories of the war.

NOTES

I would like to thank Patricia Biggs, Melanie Lewis, and the editors of this volume for their thoughtful readings and insightful critiques of this chapter.

1. For examples, see "A Tale of '76," *Baltimore Gazette and Daily Advertiser*, July 9, 1830; "A Tale of '76," *Charleston City Gazette*, July 15, 1830.
2. Alfred F. Young, *Masquerade: The Life and Times of Deborah Sampson, Continental Soldier* (New York: Vintage Books, 2004), 277–80.
3. On the Boston Tea Party, see Alfred F. Young, *The Shoemaker and the Tea Party: Memory and the American Revolution* (Boston: Beacon, 1999). On Deborah Sampson, see Young, *Masquerade*.
4. Michael Kammen, *A Season of Youth: The American Revolution and the Historical Imagination* (New York: Knopf, 1978), 16–21.
5. Eileen Ka-May Cheng, "Plagiarism in Pursuit of Historical Truth: George Chalmers and the Patriotic Legacy of Loyalist History," in this volume.
6. John and Rebecca Clendenin, pension file, records ser. W. 3223, National Archives, Washington, D.C., quoted in David G. Martin, *A Molly Pitcher Sourcebook* (Hightstown, N.J.: Longstreet House, 2003), 2–3.
7. Joel Fineman, "The History of the Anecdote: Fiction and Fiction," in *The New Historicism*, ed. H. Aram Veeser (New York: Routledge, 1989), 61; Catherine Gallagher and Stephen Greenblatt, *Practicing New Historicism* (Chicago: University of Chicago Press, 2000); Lee Schweninger, "Clotel and the Historicity of the Anecdote," *MELUS* 24, no. 1 (1999): 21–36.
8. Benjamin Franklin, *Poor Richard's Almanack: Selections from the Apothegms and Proverbs, with a Brief Sketch of the Life of Benjamin Franklin* (Waterloo, Iowa: U. S. C. Publishing, 1914), 22.

9. Freeman Hunt, *American Anecdotes: Original and Select*, vol. 2 (Boston: Putnam & Hunt, 1830), 275.
10. For work on the role of women and camp followers in the Revolutionary Army, see Holly A. Mayer, *Belonging to the Army: Camp Followers and Community during the American Revolution* (Columbia: University of South Carolina Press, 1996); Linda Grant De Pauw, "Women in Combat: The Revolutionary War Experience," *Armed Forces and Society* 7, no. 2 (1981): 209–26.
11. No contemporary records definitively authenticate the existence or actions of Molly Pitcher. This absence, however, has little bearing on the present discussion of a legend that developed unencumbered by factual constraints. Several works provide discussions of the known facts regarding Mary Hays McCauley and her family's claims that she was Molly Pitcher. The most thorough of these is Martin's *Molly Pitcher Sourcebook.* For others in this model, see Samuel Steele Smith, *A Molly Pitcher Chronology* (Monmouth Beach, N.J.: Freneau, 1972); Carol Klaver, "An Introduction to the Legend of Molly Pitcher," *Minerva: Quarterly Report on Women and the Military* 7, no. 2 (1994): 36–61; John Todd White, "The Truth about Molly Pitcher" in *The American Revolution: Whose Revolution?*, ed. James Kirby Martin and Karen R. Stubaus (Huntington, N.Y.: Krieger, 1981), 99–105; and David R. Wade, "Molly Pitcher Rediscovered," *Military History* 15, no. 2 (1998): 50.
12. Elizabeth F. Ellet, *The Women of the American Revolution*, 3 vols. (1848; repr., New York: Haskell House, 1969); Scott E. Casper, "An Uneasy Marriage of Sentiment and Scholarship: Elizabeth F. Ellet and the Domestic Origins of American Women's History," *Journal of Women's History* 4, no. 2 (Fall 1992): 10–35; Barbara Cutter, *Domestic Devils, Battlefield Angels: The Radicalism of American Womanhood, 1830–1865* (DeKalb: Northern Illinois University Press, 2003); Linda K. Kerber, *Toward an Intellectual History of Women: Essays by Linda K. Kerber* (Chapel Hill: University of North Carolina Press, 1997), 63–99. On Deborah Sampson, see Young, *Masquerade.*
13. "Female Heroism Rewarded," *Massachusetts Spy* (Worcester, Mass.), November 3, 1791, and *Morning Ray* (Windsor, Vt.), December 20, 1791.
14. *Acts of the General Assembly of the Commonwealth of Pennsylvania* (Harrisburg, Pa.: Clime, 1822), 32, quoted in Joseph Plumb Martin, *Private Yankee Doodle: Being a Narrative of Some of the Adventures, Dangers, and Sufferings of a Revolutionary Soldier*, ed. George F. Scheer (Boston: Little, Brown, 1962), 198–99; untitled article, *National Advocate* (New York, N.Y.), date unknown. Examples of reprints include "Legislative Acts," *Essex Patriot* (Haverhill, Mass.), March 2, 1822; "Molly Macauly," *Daily National Intelligencer* (Washington, D.C.), March 15, 1822.
15. "Advertisement," *Brattleborough (Vt.) Reporter*, October 20, 1804; *Boston Scourge*, November 9, 1811.
16. John Greenleaf Whittier, *Moll Pitcher: A Poem* (Boston: Carter & Hendee, 1832); Whittier, *Moll Pitcher and the Minstrel Girl* (Boston: Healy, 1840)
17. Francis A. Durivage, *A Popular Cyclopedia of History; Ancient and Modern . . .* (Boston: Broaders, 1835), 454.
18. "Molly Pitcher," *New-Jersey State Gazette* (Trenton, N.J.), December 1, 1837, quoted in Martin, *Molly Pitcher Sourcebook*, 8. Other examples include "Molly

Pitcher," *Baltimore Sun*, November 29, 1837; *New-Brunswick (N.J.) Times*, n.d. Like the "Tale of '76," the 1837 Molly likely originated in an anecdote book; however, the earliest traceable source is the attribution by the *Baltimore Sun* to the *New-Brunswick Times*.

19. "Mortuary Notice," *Portsmouth (N.H.) Journal of Literature and Politics*, May 8, 1841.
20. "Moll Pitcher," *Portsmouth (N.H.) Journal of Literature and Politics*, May 15, 1841.
21. William Huntting Howell, "'Starving Memory': Antinarrating the American Revolution," in this volume. See also Catherine Kaplan, "Theft and Counter-Theft: Joseph Plumb Martin's Revolutionary War," *Early American Literature* 41, no. 3 (2006): 515–34.
22. Martin, *Private Yankee Doodle*, 132–33.
23. George Washington Parke Custis, *Recollections and Private Memoirs of Washington* (New York: Derby & Jackson, 1860).
24. Seth C. Bruggeman, "'More Than Ordinary Patriotism': Living History in the Memory Work of George Washington Parke Custis," in this volume.
25. George Washington Parke Custis, "The Battle of Monmouth," *Daily National Intelligencer* (Washington, D.C.), February 22, 1840, quoted in Martin, *Molly Pitcher Sourcebook*, 11.
26. For additional commentary on the painting, see Martin, *Molly Pitcher Sourcebook*, 14–16.
27. George Washington Parke Custis, "The Headquarters: From the Custis' Recollections and Private Memoirs of the Life and Character of Washington," *Daily National Intelligencer* (Washington, D.C.), February 22, 1843.
28. John W. Barber and Henry Howe, *Historical Collections of the State of New Jersey* (New York: Tuttle, 1844), 16, quoted in Martin, *Molly Pitcher Sourcebook*, 16–17.
29. Benson Lossing, *The Pictorial Field-Book of the Revolution*, vol. 1 (1851; repr., New York: Harper & Brothers, 1859), 732.
30. Ibid., 2:155–56, quoted in Martin, *Molly Pitcher Sourcebook*, 19–21.
31. Elizabeth Ellet, "Heroic Women of the Revolution," *Godey's Lady's Book*, July 1848, 69, excerpt from Ellet, *Women of the American Revolution*, 2:122–35.
32. Jeptha Root Simms, *History of Schoharie County*, quoted in Ellet, *Women of the American Revolution*, 2:123–24.
33. Jesse Clement, *Noble Deeds of American Women* (1851; repr., New York: Arno, 1974), 238.
34. Laurel Thatcher Ulrich has described a similarly democratic appeal as part of the popularity of Betsy Ross, whose reputation as the maker of the first American flag emerged in the postbellum period. See "How Betsy Ross Became Famous," *Common Place* 8, no. 1 (October 2007), www.common-place.org/vol-08/no-01/ulrich/.

Part III

Dividing Memories

Forgetting History

Antebellum American Peace Reformers and the Specter of the Revolution

Carolyn Eastman

"A new era has commenced in history," wrote peace reformer William Ladd in the preface of his reform-minded children's book, *Adventures of a French Soldier* (1831), a radical retelling of a war memoir then circulating in the United States. In the past, Ladd explained, no one had questioned whether war was a necessity; history books commonly offered up heroic accounts of military officers and great battles. In doing so, however, "the death and sufferings of the privates are passed over in the aggregate, and no other account is made of them." Instead, war histories written by ordinary soldiers offered the reading public new truths about "all the disgusting forms of misery" experienced during war. Circulating accounts written by common soldiers would encourage children to reconsider heroic war histories in the light of the Gospel and "the great moral revolution which is to take place in the world, and which has already begun, when war shall be viewed in its true light; when that grim demon from the bottomless pit shall be bound a thousand years, and men shall seek the things that make for peace," Ladd reasoned.[1]

Adventures of a French Soldier was one of many books by earnest peace reformers that sought to revise historical narratives by leaving out events in favor of overwrought accounts of suffering, misery, and death:

> But where were the widows and orphans and the childless parents, whom this fatal victory had bereaved? Alas! they may retire and weep in secret; the gay and joyous crowd think little of their griefs. Where are the wounded? They are yet writhing in pain and anguish, their limbs amputated, and many of them dying a lingering and painful death. . . . And where are the souls of the departed? Who can draw aside the veil which hides eternity from our view, and say how many of them are already doomed to unutterable anguish?[2]

With strongly emotive passages like these, peace reformers sought not merely to revise history but to escape it. They filled their magazines and pamphlets not with discussions of the big events or sweeping historical change but with the minute, static moments of misery experienced by the widows and orphans, the wounded and dying. To counter the celebration of military heroes ubiquitous in popular media, advocates of peace described at length the ordinary individuals whose piteous suffering, they said, was required for commanding officers to rise to glory. In short, peace reformers attacked war by discussing it in melodramatic terms that took it out of time.

But if peace reformers found it expedient to condemn the suffering of individuals, it was politically hazardous to present the American Revolution in the same register or to criticize the generation of founders whose actions had wrought independence from Great Britain. The war had gained in popularity as a source for a muscular nationalism; by the 1810s public prints and speeches frequently invoked with pride the heroes and great battles of the Revolutionary War. Reformers knew that references to the war displayed models of manly patriotism and virtue and helped to establish a sense of shared national identity—making the war's memory all the more influential and difficult to challenge without fomenting public backlash. As a result, they could be eloquent and persuasive in denouncing war as an abstract concept, but they were compelled to express a conflicted view of the Revolution—alternately ignoring it and offering tepid criticisms mild enough to evade public opposition. Their conundrum demonstrates that the Revolution was not always easy to remember. For American peace reformers the battles that established the United States proved such an ideological minefield during the early nineteenth century that they usually opted to avoid the subject altogether—even as they held forth against war in the abstract.

Historians of the nineteenth-century peace movement have offered careful analyses of pacifists' opposition to war in general and have shown how influential they were among social reformers, but they have not explored peace reformers' specific treatment of the Revolution.[3] Nor have scholars dedicated much attention to the wide range of opinions about the Revolution held by antebellum social reformers across the board. Most reformers saw great benefit in draping themselves in patriotic memories of the war, claiming to be the worthy inheritors of the founders' Revolutionary vision and bravery, as Bruce Dorsey and others have shown.[4] But others took a riskier perspective. Some of the most fervent temperance reformers decried the founders' reliance on drink, and some abolitionists condemned their post-Revolutionary cautiousness on the slavery question.[5] Yet if reformers in general disagreed about the founders, peace reformers alone wrestled with whether to suggest that the Revolution never should have been fought. In effect they were the one reform movement dedicated to *not* remembering the war. Analyzing their conflicted and ultimately doomed attempts to turn people's minds from war as a source of national pride illustrates the overwhelming power of Revolutionary memory during the antebellum era.

American peace reformers took many years to cohere into a unified movement. It arose fitfully in the wake of the War of 1812 with the formation of a series of discrete peace societies—which knew little or nothing of one another's existence—in Massachusetts, New York, Rhode Island, and Ohio during 1815 and 1816. While most appeared content to meet quietly and intermittently without gaining much attention, the Massachusetts society set out to recruit large numbers of new members, create affiliate societies throughout New England, and publish a magazine, the *Friend of Peace*. By the early 1820s it had fostered nearly 50 local societies scattered throughout the United States, heavily concentrated in New England and dominated by Protestants, both laypeople and ministers. Only after a new leader emerged within the movement—William Ladd, a retired ship's captain in his forties with a seemingly inexhaustible eagerness to publish tracts and deliver speeches—did local societies combine their efforts. In 1828 Ladd created an umbrella organization, the American Peace Society, to which all local groups affiliated themselves. That event brought much more attention to the movement; ultimately at least 142 local societies and 18 international societies were founded during the 1820s and 1830s. At their most idealistic, leaders hoped the national society would give renewed energy to a movement that lagged behind the temperance and antislavery movements in membership numbers and social prominence.[6]

Enthusiastic leaders like Ladd believed that the peace movement could grow exponentially if it transmitted appealing ideas by means of the most modern movement-building technologies—specifically, print. Yet as they envisioned print diffusion facilitating social change on an unprecedented scale, they soon found themselves caught in a bind between popularity and ideological purity. Many peace leaders preferred presenting inspirational ideas rather than difficult ones. "The invention of printing has given wings to public opinion—wings which do not melt as they approach the source of heat & light," William Ladd wrote to Samuel J. May in 1827 with representative effusiveness. "With all these advantages, the progress of opinion is much more rapid than formerly, & we ought not to be accused of fanaticism if we predict that the next generation will be essentially different from the past."[7] Eager to expand the movement, these individuals found themselves loath to discuss ideas that might offend readers, believing that any controversy associated with the movement would be exacerbated by print's extensive dissemination. When the *Harbinger of Peace* commenced publication in 1828, it announced in its first issue, "We endeavour to avoid all 'doubtful disputation,' and to walk peaceably with all who will walk with us, whether they go further, or not so far, as the majority of the society; and we open the columns of our periodical publications to all."[8] Leaders' fear of alienating potential adherents led to a conservative approach to controversial subjects.

Topping the list of topics to be avoided was whether the peace reformers should celebrate the American Revolution as a justified war or decry it as a betrayal of Christian ideals. Their hesitance was justified, for, as the chapters in this volume clearly show, during the 1810s and 1820s a wide range of Americans invoked the Revolution in a variety of competing ways. Yet while they could express important disagreements on the meaning of the war, none suggested it was unimportant or that it had been fought for immoral reasons. In general, the public memory of the Revolution was used to emphasize that collective sacrifice had helped forge a shared national identity. Particularly after the passage of the 1818 Revolutionary War Pension Act, veterans were seen as exemplary citizen-soldiers rightly heralded by a grateful nation.[9] Men and women learned to celebrate the Declaration of Independence and the founding generation through the Fourth of July celebrations, toasts, and speeches that became so ubiquitous by the 1820s. Of the many arguments that took place over the war's memory—such as about whether the proper subjects for commemoration were officers or lay soldiers; over the recounting of local history, as James Paxton shows; in the difference between public memories and private ones, as Caroline Cox demonstrates; or in the insistence of powerful ideologues on one version of history, as Seth C. Bruggeman argues—all factions took for granted the fundamental importance of the war in history and culture.[10]

Yet even in such a cultural climate, some peace reformers did elect to question the morality of the war, even as they remained a tiny minority within the movement overall. These idealistic pacifists privileged individual inquiry and perfectionism rather than movement building and so did not seek to persuade a broad reading public. David Low Dodge, the early founder of the New York Peace Society, was one of these idealists. "Our object was not to form a popular society but to depend, under God, upon individual personal effort, by conversation and circulating essays on the subject." In his own life, Dodge had "struggled hard" in reading the Bible to query whether "defensive war, in extreme cases, might be tolerated by the Gospel; otherwise, the American revolution could not be justified." Answering that question was of particular urgency because Revolutionary heroes appeared as such "paramount" examples of piety and virtue that some believed their high-minded characters alone justified the war. Dodge could not agree. He deviated from William Ladd and other organizers such as Noah Worcester, who had created the expansionist Massachusetts Peace Society, believing that "they had a strong desire to justify the American Revolution, and this desire I have always found my greatest impediment in advocating the doctrines of peace."[11] From the perspective of Ladd and Worcester, however, high principles were useless if they achieved no measurable results. By 1827, when William Ladd visited New York eager to gain support for the new American Peace Society, he reported finding no one who knew a New York Peace Society existed—and due to its relative invisibility he felt confirmed in his conviction to avoid controversial denunciations of the Revolution.[12]

To be sure, Ladd would have been the first to insist on a critical difference between private principles and public positions. He agreed with Dodge that the central question of their movement was whether all war, or just wars of aggression, was unchristian. Ladd privately concurred with Dodge's conclusions. They differed only on publicity tactics: whether creating a popular movement was so important that they should suppress arguments about the Revolution lest they lose potential adherents. Ladd and his peers saw the Revolution as an unnecessarily controversial topic, one that sparked vitriolic debate, whereas criticism of other conflicts, such as the French Revolution and the Napoleonic Wars, created far less division within the ranks of reformers. On this question Ladd clashed with a young American Peace Society traveling agent, Henry C. Wright, when the younger man reported offending acquaintances by pronouncing that all war was a sin. "That is your opinion & mine also," Ladd told him, "but we neither of us adopted it at once & the world is not prepared for such a leap." Rather, he advised Wright to enlighten people gradually, gently, such that individuals would arrive at that view on their own. "It will be *his own* conclusion & he will foster it & endeavor to propagate it; but if you divine the conclusion for him, it is *your* conclusion & he feels but little interest in it."[13] Clearly, movement builders like Ladd believed that if reformers truly sought social change and world peace, they required a broad-based change in public opinion rather than a debate over the most divisive questions. Ladd himself penned numerous tracts that never referred to the Revolution at all.[14] Because pragmatic reformers published the vast majority of peace movement tracts and magazine articles, their views dominated the antebellum discussion of pacifism and kept the public's attention focused on the benefits of peace.

The subject of the Revolution did occasionally arise in peace literature, yet it always appeared in ways that focused not on the larger questions that animated the Revolution but on matters that appear strikingly marginal, thus revealing the authors' eagerness to contain the subject. In general, those rare peace-minded essays that discussed the Revolution opted for one of three possible ways of negotiating the subject. First, writers might describe a single, discrete historical moment to illustrate the antichristian decisions and actions that inevitably emerged during wartime. As disturbing as such a moment might be, the very specificity of such depictions never amounted to a full-blown denunciation of the Revolution. Second, they might assert that some of the nation's most prominent founders had actually been pacifists, often using the flimsiest of evidence. Finally, they composed thickly descriptive passages describing the suffering of individuals, demanding that readers step out of history to shed a tear on behalf of someone harmed by war. As rare as these mentions were, their authors' methods of raising the subject deserve detailed analysis, as they highlight reformers' strikingly tentative handling of the subject of the Revolution.

Illustrating the tendency to decry a single historical moment was an 1833 piece in the American Peace Society organ, the *Calumet,* that described angry and violent retributions by Revolutionaries against their loyalist neighbors in Brunswick, Maine. The essay explains that the minister had delivered a particularly patriotic sermon detailing British offenses against the colonies, especially during the Battle of Lexington, which exercised the Brunswick townspeople such that "those who before were luke-warm, now became ardent, & those who had been ardent were now excited to a phrenzy [*sic*]." This mob of patriots quickly became "lawless." When an even-tempered townsman objected that "such conduct was a disgrace to the community" and that "if this was their liberty, he had rather retain his allegiance to King George," the crowd threw him into a hastily dug grave, covered him with soil to the point of nearly suffocating, and told "him he should remain there until the day of resurrection." Backing up from this bleak portrayal of patriots' treatment of their neighbors, the author editorialized grimly, "There was no law to restrain them—and every one did that which was right in his own eyes."[15] Precedent like this biblical passage from Judges served to warn readers of how quickly warlike rhetoric could lead to antichristian behavior. Still, as much as this article might implicitly invite comparisons to other similar incidents of near civil war between Americans during that era, the author never did so explicitly.

One might argue that even if the author refused to extrapolate from one ugly incident to a broader criticism of the Revolution, readers might have made that leap on their own. After all, even if the author kept the moralizing to a minimum, the bare facts of the case offered ample opportunity for shock and dismay at patriotic zealotry. Yet we must be skeptical that such a treatment, however disturbing, implicitly begged for condemnation of the Revolution per se. The very specificity of the case probably delimited readers' responses—that it took place in a comparatively remote town far from the official theater of war and that it might be seen as an isolated incident—and permitted them to see such moments as regrettable while still maintaining their beliefs in the Revolution as a justified war overall. Certainly writers in peace-reform journals did not push the matter.[16]

A second frequent strategy was to offer a (mostly) counterfactual assertion: that the nation's Revolutionary heroes were actually pacifists and that they might well be claimed to be forefathers of the peace movement. The *American Advocate of Peace*, for example, cited inspiring yet cherry-picked antiwar anecdotes by Franklin, Washington, and Jefferson. "'God grant,' said Franklin, 'that we may never see another war; for in my opinion there was never a good war, or a bad peace,'" the magazine quoted with pride on the third page of its inaugural 1834 issue. In a subsequent year another author used the same method to claim that the writers of the Constitution were peace-loving men (thus carefully avoiding those men's participation during the war).[17] Likewise, the *Friend of Peace* reported that the pacifist comments of a Quaker, Warner Mifflin, had so powerfully lodged in the mind of the then general George Washington that years later Washington summoned Mifflin to the president's office for a more extensive conversation on the subject of peace. Anecdotes like this one seemed to imply that this great Revolutionary hero may have regretted his earlier actions or vowed to reform the nation for the future.[18] In these ways, writers circled around the subject of the Revolution, offering short pieces intended to chip away at readers' confidence in the morality of the war but never denouncing it outright.

The third method used by pacifist authors to broach the subject of the Revolution, and by far the most popular, was to view war purely through the lens of Christian sentiment rather than history. In these passages writers stepped outside time to focus on miniature pastoral moments of suffering brought about by war. Tract after tract contained detailed descriptions of soldiers losing life and limb, lying in battlefields after the armies had ceased fighting, dying ignominiously, and being buried without benefit of a coffin or service. Often lifting such accounts directly out of war histories, peace reformers believed they presented damning evidence of war's agonies. Quoting from a soldier's journal, the children's book *Howard and Napoleon Contrasted* described the miseries of a New Orleans army hospital:

> I crossed the river, to visit the sick soldiers in the barracks now converted into hospitals. There are 360 in the barracks. Some of them are dangerously ill. Five or six died the last night. I went into a number of the rooms containing each from thirty to forty sick. In one room, at which I called, there was a corpse, lying on the floor partially wrapped in a blanket. One person appeared to be in the agonies of death apparently insensible to every thing around him. Others were groaning and calling for assistance.

"These are the usual accompaniments of war and victory," one child explains to the other on the following page. "I suppose that not one recruit out of an hundred dies by the sword of the enemy, but the others are consumed by hunger, hardships, and disease."[19] If anything might persuade boys to change their minds about seeking military glory, reformers reasoned, it might be passages like these.[20] They resembled episodes in abolition and temperance literatures that sought to evoke sympathy for those who suffered from society's ills—the slave whipped and tortured by a cruel overseer or the distressed wife whose husband's intemperance drives her family to poverty and despair. To be sure, asking readers to sympathize with a suffering soul was standard fare in humanitarian writing of the era. Yet peace reformers went one step further: they expressed distrust of historians' hidden agendas.[21]

Asking readers to ignore the forest of history in favor of the trees of sentimentality was a deeply ahistorical perspective. Outside the peace movement, authors used similar scenes to very different and often historical ends. By the 1820s, for example, the figure of the wounded or dying soldier appeared in so many contemporary literatures (journalism, poetry, histories) that it amounted to a popular trope. Many writers made use of tear-jerking scenes of suffering to *underwrite* history—to suggest that soldiers' pain or death valorized the broader war and confirmed the multiple benefits of nationhood and independence. As Evert Jan van Leeuwen shows, early republic poets mobilized descriptions of wartime anguish or agony to muster patriotic feeling and a shared sense of faith in the larger cause for which Revolutionaries had sacrificed.[22] In other words, it had become common to use the trope of suffering soldiers to *sanctify* the historic change wrought by war.

But peace reformers used that trope differently. They took those scenes outside of time, removing them from the contexts they found so troubling: those vast panoramas of masculine military history offered up by such contemporary American historians as Jared Sparks, George Bancroft, and Francis Parkman. Instead, pacifist writers asked readers to emote in response to close-up, intimate portrayals of battlefield pain in an effort to persuade them that a soldier's suffering could never be justified by history. In short, they decried, rather than commemorated, individual anguish.

Passages like these, which emphasized sentiment rather than change over time, accorded with peace reformers' views of history. As one minister explained in an address before the Peace Society of Maine in 1827, the historian had a responsibility to "give a true account of the heart-rending scenes of war—its abominations and cruelties—its desolations and miseries. He has no right to employ the powers of rhetoric to give a false coloring to scenes of horror and death—to throw the shocking barbarities of war into the distance, and bring forward its 'pomp and circumstance' invested by unreal brilliancy."[23] Reformers complained that historians told only one kind of history, one that implicitly glorified war. The very least historians could do was describe its horrors to avoid glamorizing it for impressionable young minds; even better, they might tell other kinds of stories that avoided war altogether. Such complaints helped to align pacifists with a wider group of ministers writing about the past during this era in an effort to advocate Christianity. In a society that privileged highly masculinized, heroic histories, ministers offered a counternarrative: tales in which "nothing can happen, because there are no events, only objects and emotions—which increasingly merge together—on display," as Ann Douglas has written of clerical historians.[24] Pacifists were not the only ones who complained about the tendencies of popular histories of the day.

These highly melodramatic moments in "reformed" histories of war signified a radically new vision of the past in keeping with the Christian postmillennialism of the era: the belief that human beings could, through united effort, bring about one thousand years of peace culminating with Christ's return to Earth as predicted in the book of Revelation. Postmillennialism offered a distinct philosophy of history, premised on an optimistic view of humans' capacity for improvement. It promised that moral and rational cooperation among right-minded and purposeful Christians could ultimately bring about the thousand years of universal harmony—a millennium of peace absent of cataclysmic upheavals and clashes between leaders, and "the ultimate merger of the sacred and the secular, for it envisions a time when 'the kingdoms of this world are become the kingdoms of our Lord,' " as James Moorhead writes.[25] Thus, insofar as postmillennialism presented a Whiggish view of history necessary to achieve the millennium, its view of the millennium itself amounted to the *end* of history—a changeless era of peace—and beyond that, at the end of those thousand years, the end of human time altogether with the Second Coming. Thus, peace reformers' faith that world peace might be achieved had an antihistorical bent by imagining the end of time.

From its founding in 1815 until the early 1830s the peace movement mostly skirted around the question of the Revolution, offering antihistorical and misleading interpretations of the war or, at most, halfhearted criticisms. This trend was momentarily bucked by the South Carolina lawyer Thomas Grimké, who stunned the peace movement with a radical speech before the Connecticut Peace Society in 1832.[26] Grimké lambasted the movement for failing to denounce all war—and to make his point crystal clear he attacked the Revolution. "I know that, thousands and tens of thousands stand ready to charge me with ingratitude to the statesmen and patriots of 1776 . . . [insensitive] to the sufferings and triumphs of the glorious dead," he began. "But war and the warrior, violence and bloodshed in every form were instruments unworthy of a christian people." Americans should have adopted the position of complete Christian pacifism—"calmly, resolutely, self-devoted to martyrdom, returning good for evil, and blessing for cursing." Such a stance would surely have resulted in success, he claimed, in "conquering" the British parliament, king, and public: Americans could have liberated the United States without spilling a single drop of blood, much less declaring war. "Never was a nobler opportunity offered to a nation of christians . . . to vindicate the truth, power, and beauty of the principles of peace," he concluded. When Grimké's speech appeared in pamphlet form, the publication's editor demurred from such radical positions by insisting that "Mr. Grimké is to be considered responsible" alone for those opinions about the Revolution and that "various opinions exist in the minds of members of peace societies."[27] When Grimké argued that Americans could have "won" against the British by deploying pacifism, he went further than any other reformer to date in asserting the power of peace, and furthest yet in offering a counterfactual view of the Revolution.

For some, Grimké's bold view of the past liberated them to advance related, albeit less strident, complaints about the war. "We have serious doubts whether even *that* war can be reconciled with the principles of the gospel," wrote one contributor to the *Calumet*. "No doubt those who were engaged in it, thought they were doing right; but neither this consideration, nor the beneficial results which have followed it, are sufficient . . . [to rid] themselves of guilt."[28] But most disagreed on all counts. Peace periodicals were newly inundated with scholarly pieces, often written by ministers, insisting on the propriety of defensive war and demanding that the American Peace Society take an agnostic position on the topic of the Revolution. That war was "perhaps the most justifiable war which ever was waged," offered one writer, but "it is not for the Editors of the Calumet to give a casting voice either way on the question."[29] Reverend William Allen, president of Bowdoin College, presented the most sustained rebuke to Grimké in two successive essays in early 1834. Using highly detailed, scripturally based arguments, Allen ultimately avoided the subject of the Revolution to focus on what the earliest Christians—the *real* founders, in his opinion—had believed during an era so far in the distant past as to be nearly irretrievable. In other words, he followed in a peace movement tradition of avoiding the subject of the American Revolution—and failed to convince a majority of readers of his argument in the process.[30] Even the editor of the *Calumet* found it to be a side issue: "We could wish that the question of the lawfulness of Defensive War, might be discussed . . . without an appeal to ecclesiastical antiquity," he wrote.[31]

This conflict between Grimké's ideals and the mainstream peace movement soon spread to a wider group of social reformers whose radical beliefs had earned them the designation "ultra." His writings especially appealed to those abolitionists whose affiliation with the peace movement turned harshly antagonistic during 1837–38. A group led by William Lloyd Garrison took the ultra high ground on issues related to pacifism, not only by denouncing all war but by articulating what they termed "nonresistance": deploring all forms of human violence and coercion, including legal suits, self-defense, and jails, and declaring they would refuse allegiance to federal governments, as these were inherently coercive. Nonresistants expressed increasing disgust for the mainstream peace reform such that they began characterizing it as immoral, just as they had earlier demonized the American Colonization Society as even more abhorrent than slavery itself. Conflicts between the two groups flared at American Peace Society annual meetings and resulted in a formal split between them in 1838, a split that prefigured a similar divide within the abolition movement two years later.[32] Nonresistants believed the mainstream peace movement's unwillingness to denounce the Revolution and all war severely restricted its capacity to win public support. Such a conclusion might have been ironic if true, but in fact it was the peace movement, not nonresistance, that proved the popular and lasting institution.

Indeed, it was the split with the nonresistants that permitted the American Peace Society to set aside, finally, the problem of the Revolution. Just as the 1839 split within the abolition movement actually helped to expand the movement rather than hobble it, the divide in the peace movement gave Peace Society leaders license to proceed with a resolutely middle-of-the-road appeal to the public. Throughout the 1840s and 1850s peace publications continued to give the Revolution only glancing attention, thus displaying a reverence for the war matched by that in political culture more widely—and the society benefited in growing popularity.

Neither group escaped the conflict between political expedience and pacifist idealism, however, especially as political rhetorics of the 1850s grew more combative. Even nonresistants found it difficult to sustain their own philosophy. Having argued for years over whether to recommend that slaves resist their masters' tyranny, some increasingly felt that slaves were justified in using armed violence. "We are growing more and more warlike, more and more disposed to talk about 'finding a joint in the neck of the tyrant,' and breaking his neck," William Lloyd Garrison warned at the 1858 New England Anti-Slavery Convention.[33] By 1861 the American Peace Society voted to support the Union cause during the Civil War by reasoning that the war between the states was not a war at all but a criminal rebellion by a small group of influential figures in the South—a definition of the war that may have accorded with the one held by President Lincoln but which appeared tortured and legalistic to pacifists. The society's support for the war was joined by many nonresistants who believed the war would bring about an end to slavery—including those, like Garrison, who had previously preached disunionism and decried his group's own aggressive bombast.[34]

As tempting as it might be to dwell on the ironies or hypocrisies of pacifists' support for war, consider instead how much the society's views of the

Civil War reflected its long-standing antihistoricism. During those long stretches of the 1820s and 1830s when the United States had no war looming on its horizon, the society's leaders found it easier to split the baby between idealism and popularity. With their nation enjoying a long era of relative peace, readers might well entertain the suggestion to take a Christian view of the scene of a soldier dying on the battlefield; to ignore history's great shifts and tumults in favor of counterfactual scenarios like Great Britain releasing its American colonies without bloodshed; or to imagine human progress achieving its apex with a thousand years of changeless harmony. But faced with competing imperatives—the sense of urgency for ending slavery, the union split in two—peace reformers increasingly found that real-life historical events made it impossible to offer simple Christian solutions that would appeal to a wide public.

Pacifists' conflicts over the Revolution and the movement's eagerness to avoid the topic as much as possible testify to the significance of the war's memory in antebellum America. Peace reformers evaded the many debates that occurred over the memory of the war because they feared public backlash and because those debates opened up so many political rifts. Antebellum Americans fought over the war's memory as one means of questioning whether their nation was on the right path politically, if nonelites and ordinary soldiers could be celebrated for their war efforts alongside officers and great generals, and how the war's glory might be deployed for use in contemporary political causes. Determined to keep their organization separate from such partisan battles, the peace reform was the one group dedicated to *not* remembering the war. Yet, as we have seen, this avoidance bespoke a more thoroughgoing antihistoricism that applied to more than the memory of the Revolution; that war was unique only for its highly controversial nature in antebellum political culture. Peace reformers took on history not to retell it, but to escape it altogether by bringing about the end of time.

NOTES

1. [William Ladd], *Adventures of a French Soldier, by Philanthropos* (Boston: Loring, 1831), vi.
2. Ibid., 97. Although this book draws on C. O. Barbaroux's *Adventures of a French Serjeant* (Philadelphia: Carey & Lea, 1826), it has been erroneously attributed to

Barbaroux; Ladd's is an independent book that significantly condensed the original and overlaid a heavy moralism for reform purposes. Barbaroux's volume appeared in at least nine American and European editions.

3. The subject of pacifists' opposition to war during the early nineteenth century has been addressed in Peter Brock, *Freedom from War: Nonsectarian Pacifism, 1814–1914* (Toronto: University of Toronto Press, 1991); Merle Curti, *The American Peace Crusade, 1815–1860* (Durham, N.C.: Duke University Press, 1929); Charles DeBenedetti, *The Peace Reform in American History* (Bloomington: Indiana University Press, 1984), 32–58; Carolyn Eastman, "Fight Like a Man: Gender and Rhetoric in the Early Nineteenth-Century American Peace Movement," *American Nineteenth-Century History* 10 (September 2009): 247–71; James L. Tryon, "The Rise of the Peace Movement," *Yale Law Journal* 20 (March 1911): 358–71; and Valarie H. Ziegler, *The Advocates of Peace in Antebellum America* (Bloomington: Indiana University Press, 1992).
4. The literature on antebellum reform is vast; for scholars who reflect on reformers' views of the Revolution, see Bruce Dorsey, *Reforming Men and Women: Gender in the Antebellum City* (Ithaca, N.Y.: Cornell University Press, 2002), 130; and Ronald G. Walters, *American Reformers, 1815–1860* (New York: Hill & Wang, 1978), 101–21.
5. Following the pathbreaking scholarship of George B. Forgie, several historians of reform have termed this phenomenon a form of symbolic *patricide* of the founders. William Breitenbach, "Sons of the Fathers: Temperance Reformers and the Legacy of the American Revolution," *Journal of the Early Republic* 3 (Spring 1983): 69–82; Donald Yacovone, *Samuel Joseph May and the Dilemmas of the Liberal Persuasion, 1797–1871* (Philadelphia: Temple University Press, 1991), 105–17. See also Robert H. Abzug, *Cosmos Crumbling: American Reform and the Religious Imagination* (New York: Oxford University Press, 1994), 12, 174–75.
6. Curti, *American Peace Crusade;* DeBenedetti, *Peace Reform in American History*, 32–58; David Low Dodge, *Memorial of Mr. David Low Dodge* (Boston: Whipple, 1854), 99; Carolyn Eastman, "Speaking Peace to Fight War: Gender, Authority, and Rhetoric in William Ladd's Antebellum American Peace Movement" (master's thesis, University of New Hampshire, 1996), chap. 1; and Ziegler, *Advocates of Peace,* chap. 1. An additional society was founded in London in 1815, making the movement international.
7. William Ladd to Samuel J. May, July 5, 1827, William Ladd Letterbook, American Peace Society Records, Manuscript Division, Library of Congress, Washington, D.C.
8. "Circular Letter," *Harbinger of Peace* 1 (May 1828): 6–7.
9. John Resch, *Suffering Soldiers: Revolutionary War Veterans, Moral Sentiment, and Political Culture in the Early Republic* (Amherst: University of Massachusetts Press, 1999), chaps. 4, 5.
10. James Paxton, "Remembering and Forgetting: War, Memory, and Identity in the Post-Revolutionary Mohawk Valley," Caroline Cox, "Public Memories, Private Lives: The First Greatest Generation Remembers the Revolutionary War," and Seth C. Bruggeman, "'More than Ordinary Patriotism': Living History in the Memory Work of George Washington Parke Custis," all in this volume; see also

Michael Kammen, *A Season of Youth: The American Revolution and the Historical Imagination* (New York: Knopf, 1978), 37–58; Sarah Purcell, *Sealed with Blood: War, Sacrifice, and Memory in Revolutionary America* (Philadelphia: University of Pennsylvania Press, 2002), 144–70; and Alfred F. Young, *The Shoemaker and the Tea Party: Memory and the American Revolution* (Boston: Beacon, 1999).

11. Dodge, *Memorial*, 101, 79–80, 90.
12. William Ladd to Samuel J. May, June 11, 1827, William Ladd Letterbook, American Peace Society Records. New York Peace Society Records are contained within the American Peace Society Records in the Library of Congress. Ziegler, *Advocates of Peace*, includes a full account of the philosophical differences between these two groups.
13. William Ladd to Henry C. Wright, July 13, 1846, William Ladd Papers, Boston Public Library Rare Books and Manuscripts Department, Boston. Wright left the peace movement shortly thereafter to become one of the most idealistic, or "ultra," advocates in the abolition and nonresistance movements.
14. These tracts include William Ladd, *Essays of Philanthropos on Peace and War* (Exeter, N.H.: Burnham, 1825), and Ladd, *A Brief Illustration of the Principles of War and Peace* (Albany, N.Y.: Packard & Van Benthuysen, 1831). Meanwhile, his London-published *Letters from an American* (London: Ward, 1836), 1–2, discussed the Revolution solely with the intention of resolving lasting animosities between the two nations and fomenting pacifism in England.
15. "Revolutionary Scenes," *Calumet* 1, no. 12 (March–April 1833): 370–71. The magazine's name came from the long-stemmed peace pipe used on ceremonial occasions by some Indian tribes.
16. On a much more infrequent basis, an essayist might complain about the total cost of the war, presenting tallied columns of the massive dollar amounts spent during recent wars, likely to provoke readers oriented to economic common sense. For an example, see "Expenses of War," *Harbinger of Peace* 1, no. 4 (August 1828): 81–88.
17. "Jefferson on War," *American Advocate of Peace* 1 (June 1834): 7; "The Founders of the Constitution," *American Advocate of Peace* 1 (March 1836): 355. See also "Dr. Franklin's Views of War" and "Opinions of Washington," *Harbinger of Peace* 1 (November 1828): 160–61; and "Original Letter of Dr. Franklin," *Calumet* 1 (January–February 1832): 152–53.
18. "General Washington and Warner Mifflin," *Friend of Peace* 2, no. 7 (1821): 7–8.
19. [William Ladd], *Howard and Napoleon Contrasted in Eight Dialogues between Two Sunday School Scholars, by the Author of "The Sword, or Christmas Presents"* (Portsmouth, N.H.: Shepard, 1830), 84–86.
20. Such passages are ubiquitous in peace literature; see, for example, "An Estimate of Human Sacrifices in the Russian Campaign," *Friend of Peace* 1, no. 3 (1815): 24–25; "The Dead Soldier," *Harbinger of Peace* 1 (October 1828): 143–44; Calista, "Thoughts on War," *Calumet* 1 (May–June 1831): 28; and "The Execution of a Deserter," *American Advocate of Peace* 1 (December 1835): 310–16.
21. On the uses of scenes of suffering, see Frances M. Clarke, *War Stories: Suffering and Sacrifice in the Civil War North* (Chicago: University of Chicago Press, 2011); and Karen Halttunen, "Humanitarianism and the Pornography of Pain in Anglo-American Culture," *American Historical Review* 100 (April 1995): 303–34.

22. Evert Jan van Leeuwen, "The Graveyard Aesthetics of Revolutionary Elegiac Verse: Remembering the Revolution as a Sacred Cause," in this volume.
23. Rev. Charles Jenkins, "Sketch of an Address, Delivered at Portland," *Harbinger of Peace* 1 (July 1828): 56–57.
24. Ann Douglas, *The Feminization of American Culture* (New York: Knopf, 1977), 165–99, quotation on 199.
25. James H. Moorhead, *World without End: Mainstream American Protestant Visions of the Last Things, 1880–1925* (Bloomington: Indiana University Press, 1999), 8. See also Daniel Walker Howe, *What Hath God Wrought: The Transformation of America, 1815–1848* (New York: Oxford University Press, 2007), 288–89.
26. Grimké was the brother of Angelina and Sarah Grimké, who would thereafter rise to prominence and notoriety as abolitionists, inspired by their brother's example. They engaged in correspondence on behalf of the pacifist cause and authored magazine articles before turning most of their attention to abolition. Eastman, "Speaking Peace to Fight War," 76–83.
27. Thomas Grimké, *Address on the Truth, Dignity, Power, and Beauty of the Principles of Peace, and on the Unchristian Character and Influence of War and the Warrior* (Hartford, Conn.: Olmsted, 1832), 42–48. In addition, selections from this long speech and other Grimké writings were excerpted and circulated in peace periodicals. Grimké likely drew on the writings of the English pacifist Jonathan Dymond. See the review, "Dymond's Essays," *Calumet* 2 (July–August 1834): 49.
28. "Unchristian Patriotism," *Calumet* 1 (January–February 1832): 157.
29. "Editorial Comments by L. on 'Address on the Truth, Dignity, Power, and Beauty of the Principles of Peace,'" *Calumet* 1 (July–August 1832): 232–33.
30. [William Allen], "Defensive War Vindicated," *Calumet* 1 (January–February 1834): 524–32; [William Allen], "Defensive War Vindicated, No. II," *Calumet* 2 (May–June 1834): 12–23. See also Ziegler, *Advocates of Peace*, 44–47.
31. "Remarks," *Calumet* 2 (May–June 1834): 23.
32. Ziegler, *Advocates of Peace*, chap. 2; see also Eastman, "Fight Like a Man," 256–64.
33. Garrison quoted in Ziegler, *Advocates of Peace*, 140.
34. Ziegler, *Advocates of Peace*, 150. The American Peace Society continues to exist today with a prominent location in Washington, D.C., where it publishes *World Affairs*.

"Of Course We Claim to Be Americans"

Revolution, Memory, and Race in Up-Country Georgia Baptist Churches, 1772–1849

Daryl Black

Scholars have long recognized the connections between evangelical religion and colonial rebellion in British North America. The religious revivals of the mid-eighteenth century created among many colonists a powerful sense of local autonomy that helped drive the movement for political independence. During the Revolution, evangelical faith provided comfort that the patriot cause was God's cause. It remains less clear how local practices of evangelicalism merged with specific experiences of the American Revolution to shape communities of memory and make real the abstractions of nationalism.[1] Americans expressed and communicated national narratives in many forms—in parades, in pamphlets, in newspapers, and in public rhetoric.[2] But churches played a key role in shaping narratives too. This chapter expands our understanding of the embodiment of national imaginations by showing how white and black up-country Georgia Baptists fused their memories of the Revolution with the practices of racial slavery and evangelicalism to create social memories of the war's meaning and the nation's future.

Because of the limited nature of the sources, recovering the memory practices of these communities is not simple and exploring how they functioned can result in only tentative conclusions. In the two decades after the war's end, white preachers in the region produced just two texts and one short-lived newspaper that directly addressed the place of the Revolution in community memory. Unearthing the black memory of the Revolution is even more difficult because black Piedmont Georgia Baptists left no known written traces of how they remembered the rebellion. By examining how they worshipped, however, we can gain suggestive insights into how they used Baptist congregationalism as a means to claim autonomy and freedom. Indeed, as scholars such as Jacques Le Goff have pointed out, "the silences of history" must be studied and the "archives of silence" must be inventoried. Scholars should pursue the silence and "write history on the basis of documents and the absence of documents." Maurice Halbwachs provides an entry point into the archival silence that shrouds much of the social memory making that went on among Upper Piedmont Georgia Baptists. As he argues, every religion "reproduces in more or less symbolic form the history of the migrations and fusions of races and tribes, of great events, wars, establishments, discoveries, and reforms that we can find at the origin of the societies that practice them." And despite all its claims to exist outside of temporal society, religion "does not preserve the past but reconstructs it with the aid of the material traces, rites, texts, and traditions left behind by the past."[3] Thus, the forms of worship black Baptists in Georgia chose revealed an ongoing process of recalling and remaking both a biblical past and a past that emerged out of the Revolution.

Historians agree that Georgia Baptists were influenced by religious developments taking place in North Carolina and Virginia. But they disagree on how to characterize this influence. Whereas Rhys Isaac and Marjoleine Kars depict Baptist congregations furthering a radical dismissal of outside control that fed into independence, other scholarship focuses instead on the Baptists' conservative acceptance of social, racial, and gender hierarchies.[4] Neither can stand alone as an adequate characterization of the Baptist congregationalism that developed in the Georgia up-country. The white immigrants who introduced the Baptist Church to the state just before the Revolution and those who came in the years immediately after the war carried a complex of ideals and political visions that embraced the popular authority of congregationalism, opposition to the tax and property policies of the British Crown, and a dedication to patriarchal hierarchy and property in slaves.[5]

In Georgia the white Baptist Church developed late in the colonial era. Though a few Baptists may have been among the colony's early settlers, no permanent churches were organized until 1773, when a group of North Carolina Regulators, fleeing the royal backlash that followed the Battle of Alamance, moved to the Georgia up-country. They called their church Kiokee. Located a few miles from the backcountry trading center of Augusta, the Kiokee Church became the center of early Baptist life in Georgia. The immigrants' antiroyalist politics and belief in access to property in land also helped make the congregation a center for radical revolutionary politics. During the war nearly a half-dozen lay leaders and ministers from the church served as chaplains to Whig militia who helped link Revolutionary action with Baptist belief.[6]

After the fighting came to an end, Georgians and thousands of free and slave immigrants who poured into the state from South Carolina, North Carolina, and Virginia began to work out the meaning of independence. For many this was done within the context of Baptist congregations, where they forged a memory of the Revolution that melded Baptist faith and the meaning of national independence. Baptist theology and ecclesiology, as practiced by the white congregations, fit well into up-country society because they promised both hierarchical visions of social relations and assured local autonomy. The Baptist vision rested on the idea that their form of church represented the true apostolic church and that baptism was the only true rite. This claim, combined with the practice of absolute autonomy for local congregations, provided a powerful model for localized political and social imagination. Baptist Calvinism provided a theological means by which to draw social boundaries based on a hierarchical cultural politics that supported the growing centrality of racial slavery in the region.[7] At the same time Baptist leaders staked out a memory of the Revolution that linked American victory with the unfolding of biblical narrative.

At the war's close Baptist minister Silas Mercer published a densely written essay that wove a narrative placing the American independence movement within the eschatological framework of biblical ages.[8] He identified four empires that would be successively destroyed, until at last a fifth empire, embodying the "peaceable reign of *Christ*," would be established. Mercer based his argument on the idea that "kings were given for a *Curse* to the Lord's people" and that successive kings would be "broken to pieces" until replaced by the "*Kingdom* which the GOD OF HEAVEN shall set up which will stand for ever."[9]

The connection between the fifth kingdom and an independent United States was never far from the surface. Mercer noted that in the first biblical age the king "would first destroy their *liberty*, and then their *property*, and that he would become a *tyrant* and oppress them grievously by his despotic power" (4–5). Such oppression was enforced by an established church. In describing the second biblical kingdom, he claimed that the people gained only "tolerated liberty" (11–13). The king of the third kingdom " 'tore the book of the law which was in the temple and burnt it,' and set up his own arbitrary laws and worship" (16). The fourth kingdom was identified as the Roman Empire. Constantine embraced Christianity and "being replete with the spirit of liberty, thinking to secure the rights and liberty of his people, and to keep them from future persecutions, he 'established religion by law.' " But in so doing he made possible the rise of the antichristian assumption of power by the "Pope of Rome" (18–20). Only a remnant of the true church, identified by Mercer as the Waldenese and Albigenesses, "stood as a bulwark against Popery, through the whole reign of the Antichrist" (39). These "witnesses" maintained true religion and, in Mercer's reckoning, were the original Baptists. They helped keep true religion alive and kept the "abomination" of established religion from entirely enslaving the common populace by removing the scripture from the hands of the people. At the same time, the established clergy through "all their learning, worldly wisdom, and human reason" became "more profound deceivers" who helped maintain an unbiblical religion (31–33).

It was at this point that Mercer turned fully toward linking the American Revolution with the destruction of the Antichrist and with the establishment of the fifth kingdom. Using a mathematical formula that established a pattern for the length of the age of kingdoms, Mercer determined the late eighteenth century as the time when the fourth kingdom would fall and the fifth would rise. American Puritans and Baptists had stood as true witnesses who would not "be slain" and who, because of their congregational nature and their rejection of established religion, would help deliver the shock that would overthrow the Antichrist. That shock was the

Revolution (40–46). Britain, through a Protestant establishment, had become a nation of "wicked men" (53). God had led the Revolution and would continue to lead revolutions around the world against false, or established, religion. The true Christian duty had been to wage relentless war. "As long as these tyrannical nations will make war against an innocent free people to destroy their liberty, property and lives," Mercer wrote, "it must be the duty of these free people to resist them as long as they have power to resist." To Mercer "the civil government is the creature of the people, and originates with them, and it has nothing in view but their happiness." In the new United States "therefore every man is his own legislator, and in these free republic states, in all probability he will be properly represented by a delegate of his own choosing, so that the civil government will be managed in such a manner as to preserve the liberty of the inhabitants, and then their magistrates shall be God's ministers to the people for good" (62).

Over the course of the following decade and a half, the literary record remains blank. In January 1800 and then again in 1803, however, Henry Holcombe, a Georgia Baptist minister and editor of a short-lived denominational newspaper, produced two essays that helped give shape to a reactionary memory of the Revolution. In his 1800 "A Sermon Occasioned by the Death of Washington," Holcombe painted a picture of Washington that showed how the nation's first president had embodied "the sacred principles of liberty." Noting that Washington's participation in the Revolution was "too well known" to bear repeating, Holcombe instead emphasized Washington's practical knowledge and claimed him as an evangelical Christian who embodied Baptist notions of true religion. As Holcombe put it, "the essential advantages of religion, in a political light, were discovered clearly, and felt impressively by the American sage." Washington's "eagle eye distinguished plainly betwixt vain pretenders to religion, and its real possessors," and his "cool deliberative sagacity, discerned the difference between genuine religion, as delineated in the holy scriptures, and the empty forms, gross adulterations, and shameful abuses of it."[10]

Holcombe appealed directly to "*War-worn veterans!*" in his charge to action. They were called to "mourn with his venerable relict, sinking under stupendous grief for him who has slain your enemies, saved your country, and 'put on ornaments of gold upon your apparel.'" And they were charged to "do more." "You will," Holcombe demanded, "like the great and virtuous Washington, in your measure, increase the dignity and happiness of human nature; you will adorn by your solid, though private virtues, social life, of which you were intended to be the brightest ornaments." Washington's life, "his glorious example, both in the peaceful cabinet, and on the hostile plains," provided a constant reminder "of your special obligations to patriotic virtue, and genuine piety. He has taught you how to live and how to die." But it was not just in Georgia that Holcombe emphasized the lesson. The nation had lost a great man, and in mourning him the nation had come closer together—the "shock of Mount Vernon, trembling from the summit to its affrighted center, shakes the continent from New-Hampshire to Georgia!" For Holcombe's audience this memory of Washington and the lessons to be drawn from Washington's life represented the true national meaning of the Revolutionary era.[11]

In 1803 in the pages of the *Analytical Repository*, a short-lived Baptist newspaper, Holcombe expressed in greater detail the kind of Revolution he wanted his readers to recall. Responding, like many other clergy at the time, to the teachings of deists such as Thomas Paine and Elihu Palmer, Holcombe attacked the radically transformative social memory of the Revolution that might find foundation in the deist texts. Holcombe claimed that giving political power to ordinary people threatened the nation's future and subverted the real intent of the Revolutionary generation. He argued that "the fallacious orators of this '*Age of Reason*'" collapsed "essential distinctions" by artfully blending "natural and acquired rights." In this, they attempted to encourage "the very refuse of society to rise up under the influence of an imaginary equality and treat their superiors with the most brutal insolence and barbarity." Holcombe countered that in a slave society there existed a clearly articulated social hierarchy that affirmed order because it excluded the "lower orders of society" from exercising public authority. Were the degraded, both black and white, "enfranchised, they would come to control the government and 'knavish demagogues [would] . . . find the means of rearing a despotism upon the ruins of such a democracy.'" Holcombe's remembered Revolution rested not on the promise that all men were created equal but on the confidence that God had created humanity unequal, that all rights were acquired, and that both the apostle Paul and Jesus commanded "subjection to the constituted authorities."[12] Holcombe's essay built both on his earlier assertions in "A Sermon Occasioned by the Death of Washington" and on

Mercer's typological construction of the Revolution to present a memory of the war as fulfillment of revelation unfolding over thousands of years of biblical history.

The emerging community of memory also can be glimpsed in the pages of a widely circulated biographical essay of early Baptist preacher Sanders Walker. The narrative arc of the biography provided a way to remember the Revolution as both personal and community transformations that merged faith into a form of character expressive of Revolutionary freedom. Walker's conversion "transformed him from a person of unmanageable temper and addiction to vices to such meekness and gravity that he became known as 'the meek.' "[13] His preaching and his work organizing the Kiokee Church linked his evangelizing efforts to the up-swelling of revolutionary fervor.[14] His service as a chaplain in Elijah Clarke's patriot militia command confirmed his status as a model American, while the memory of his work in organizing community after the war established a model of faith and patriotism to be emulated by the new American citizens. When viewed together, the texts produced by post-Revolutionary white Georgia Baptists provided a basis for a community memory of the transitions wrought by the war. They established a providential remembrance of the conflict as the unfolding of biblical ages, a reactionary memory of the war's results, and a personal remembered life that provided a model for living out a patriot's life.[15]

For African American slaves the creation of Baptist congregations came at the same time that conversations increasingly turned to the crisis in self-determination. Such timing is vital in understanding the ways that black Baptists claimed the Revolution. As historian Ira Berlin points out, enslaved African Americans were able "to listen in on the debate between white Americans and their British overlords." They understood tyranny well and took advantage of Revolutionary conflict to assert independence.[16] Such an opportunity presented a dramatic change in the religious and political world in which black Georgians lived. During the first decades of Georgia slavery, which was legalized in 1751, white owners forbade slaves from becoming Christian because they believed that conversion might provide a basis for resistance to slavery.[17] Planters such as Jonathan Bryan, looking for a way to alleviate the guilt they felt over the treatment of the enslaved, began providing opportunities for their slaves to hear sermons and to create religious societies led by enslaved lay preachers in the slave quarters.[18] On this foundation emerged the structures of a black-controlled church. In 1773 a congregation called Silver Bluff Baptist Church organized on the South Carolina side of the Savannah River in Aiken County. By 1778 the church had grown to about 30 members, some of whom lived in Georgia. The church disbanded that year as members fled to British-controlled Savannah seeking freedom. Some of the dispersed congregation, however, returned to the Silver Bluff area and reorganized the church in 1782 after patriot forces reestablished control. Led by Jesse Galphin, the church grew to 180 members by the early 1790s. In 1793 the congregation relocated to Augusta and began calling itself the Springfield Baptist Church.[19] This church, arguably the oldest African American congregation in the United States, grew quickly and by the end of the eighteenth century ranked as the largest Baptist Church—black or white—in the up-country.[20]

African American Baptists' deployment of a Revolutionary memory remains difficult to pinpoint and, as Halbwachs affirms, requires a suggestive reading of the ways that ritual performances expressed a community memory. The first bit of evidence that helps illuminate the memory practices of African American slaves comes from Methodist leader William Capers. He observed that Georgia's African Americans preferred "the economy and doctrines of the Baptist church and could choose pastors and deacons, and sacraments, and discipline all their own."[21] Caper's observation suggests that choice and local autonomy in selecting pastors and in enforcing church discipline enabled black Georgians to express independence and act as free people. Slave Baptists thus claimed one of the essential elements of the liberty promised by the Revolution. Going to church, controlling a congregation, and acting freely became both religious and political, involving congregants staking public claims to a memory of the Revolution that included freedom for all.

At the all-black Springfield Church in Augusta, preachers and the church deacons, selected from among the congregation, provided control over their own rites, enforced their own discipline, and extended their own methods of accepting new members into their community. The Springfield congregation met in their own church and controlled their own disciplinary activity and governing structures. One white observer described the congregation as "numerous and respectable." In "their large house of worship . . . the pews, the aisles, the galleries, stair and lobbies were all crowded to their utmost capacity."[22] They had ritually staked a claim on a Revolutionary heritage that promised to erase the legal and social limits of slavery and establish freedom for all. Springfield's black pastor Jacob Walker summed up this claim in 1829. At the time some white Augustans had begun to encourage black Georgians to emigrate to Africa. When Walker was asked if his congregation would prefer to resettle in Liberia, he replied "most of us were born in this country, and of course we claim to be Americans."[23]

Despite the success of the Springfield Church, all-black churches remained rare during the first decades of independence. From the 1780s through the onset of the Civil War, most black and white Baptists worshiped in biracial settings. Yet such an observation tells only part of the story. While black and white up-country Georgians met in the same room, the built space of the church building visually communicated the dominant ideal that forbade intermingling and showed the exclusive nature of white up-country Georgians' version of the independent nation. The specific arrangements varied from church to church, but each physically segegated black and white members. At some churches slaves sat in shed additions. At others, black members sat in a gallery overlooking the white worshipers or in the rearmost pews, having entered the church through side doorways that led only to the all-black seating area. Thus, church architecture provided visual evidence of the hierarchical narrative white Georgians applied to Revolutionary freedom even in ordinary comings and goings. When the congregations conducted church business, African American members remained silent unless they were called on to answer charges.[24] In some churches ministers delivered special short sermons directly to black members that demanded they uphold their biblical responsibility to remain obedient to their masters and to look for freedom only in heaven.

Such practices provided a pageant in which black and white Baptists embodied the hierarchical society that white Baptists sought to build. Yet these attempts to dominate rural African American Baptists through overt forms of marginalization failed to silence African Americans who looked to the Revolutionary heritage to stake their claim to autonomy. By the 1820s African American church members in the rural districts began to assert congregational independence. At the Kiokee Church in 1822 the black members attempted to incorporate an exclusively African American church. The state refused to grant a legal charter; however, independent worship practices persisted. Following revivals in 1828 the church at Washington, Georgia, established separate meetings for black and white members. The African American members selected black deacons L. William Hoxey and "Brother David" to lead their congregation. Through the 1830s and into the 1840s the Washington congregation held quarterly conference meetings and received and excluded members. They also organized prayer meetings, granted the privilege to members to exhort and lead prayer, selected representatives to the Georgia association's general meeting, and in 1839 began building their own church building.[25]

In 1844, at the same time that white Georgia Baptists were promoting the creation of the proslavery Southern Baptist Convention, slave Baptists at Penfield, the home of the denomination's Mercer College, created the Penfield African Church. Between 1844 and 1846 blacks held separate meetings in the white church building. In 1846 "the church secured the use of a house for the blacks' religious services, where twice a month white ministers led worship services for blacks, and four times a month slaves assembled for prayer meetings 'chiefly conducted by blacks themselves.'" Two years later, the slave members of the Penfield Church celebrated the dedication of a new building for their exclusive use. After this "the African Church had its own leadership, worship service, communion, and church conferences." By the early 1850s, the slave church even had hired an African American pastor. The performance of independence embodied in the creation of a largely self-regulating institution shows that in their own practices African American Baptists had created a physical space that embodied the essence of self-regulation and Revolutionary autonomy.[26]

Behind these peaceful performances, however, lay real threats of revolutionary action. At no time did this become more apparent than in the weeks and months following Nat Turner's 1831 rebellion. When white Georgians received news of the revolt in Southside Virginia and reports of Turner's religious inspiration, they acted quickly to forestall any religiously inspired revolutionary action. Marshals closed the Springfield Church in mid-October. As Augusta resident Susan Nye Hutchison put it, "the excitement continue[d] through the country," and many whites deemed "it a needful measure to compel the coloured people to worship with the whites."[27]

In the rural districts white Baptists acted similarly. On October 15, 1831, the Bethesda Church "resolved . . . that she disapproves of any meeting of the Black, by night for religious exercises of any kind." Turner's rebellion had exposed underlying suspicions that the slave community's religious practice contained within it a spark of revolutionary potential. Even during daylight hours no slave was to be granted liberty "under a view of Preaching or other religious exercise." African Americans could exhort "only at some public meeting of the whites at this church." The church "required of the Deacons of this church (as corporate authorities) to make some effective provision for the good order among the black People and especially for their dispersing immediately after the religious exercise of the day."[28] The Goshen congregation likewise acted to create a new set of rules for "the better regulation of the colored members." Planter Thomas W. Murphy drafted a statement "that any colored of this church during divine worship shall be found engaged in company with other on the way to the spring or at the spring in the woods adjacent to the meeting house having not the worship of God in view or after being regularly dismissed does not promptly and speedily return to the service of their owners but found in crowds with other of their color without the best of excuses, to be judged by the church, shall also be expelled."[29]

Such drastic responses suggests that the white community understood that the independence African Americans performed in their Baptist worship threatened the future of the hierarchical narrative and the godly social order that had become fused in white Baptist minds as the essential meaning of the Revolution. The interpretation of freedom embraced by African American church members—the community of memory performed within the walls of independent black churches and the impulse toward using that memory to achieve freedom implicit in independent religious practice—threatened the coherence of the memory that white Baptists held up as the universal inheritance of the Revolution. African American slaves' embrace of the practices of liberty embodied in Baptist worship showed an alternative social and cultural model that staked claims to autonomy and freedom promised in the Revolution. This image confounded the Baptist antiblack rhetoric that defined slaves as incapable of participating in republican self-rule and provided irrefutable evidence that black men and women could and indeed did exercise autonomy. Recalling their own violent rebellion had used religious imagery and justifications, white Baptists understood that the radical implications of congregationalism, and the autonomy that came from it, could easily be used against them. They had for a generation and a half watched as black Baptists performed freedom by claiming social space and their own religious destinies within the context of Baptist churches, and they feared that the memory of legitimate armed rebellion would serve as the foundation for physical resistance to the region's oppressive slave system.

When the crisis of disunion erupted in 1860, up-country Georgians' responses were predictable. White leaders, many of the same men who had created the proslavery Southern Baptist Convention, invoked Revolutionary ideals to support a slaveholder's nation. God, they claimed, was on their side. With their faith and cultural politics firmly established in proslavery theology, they felt well armed to strike for political independence. In claiming the 1770s as their own, white Georgia Baptists connected the cultural politics they helped articulate in the late eighteenth and early nineteenth centuries and extended into their constructions of secession an understanding of the Revolution that accorded with their hierarchical constructions of the imagined nation. They cloaked their political rebellion as a second, authenticating chapter that realized the real Revolution. The Revolution they claimed had resulted from a conscious set of remembrances forged to create and maintain a version of Revolutionary freedom that rested on the right to enslave.

In contrast, African American Baptists' emancipationist memory, which they expressed in rituals and church organizations, provided the means by which to invoke the Revolution's liberating potential and lay claim to national citizenship. The results of the war provided African American up-country Georgians a new space in which to operate and new opportunities to participate in the free political system. As one officer from the Freedman's Bureau, speaking at the Springfield Church, put it, "They know what freedom is as well as I do."[30] They knew because three generations of black Baptists remembered the freedom achieved by Revolution. A new struggle for memory, however, emerged in the decades after the Civil War, as Americans, black and white, struggled to control the meaning of Confederate defeat and the legal end of slavery. And once again the churches became a primary space in which race and national futures were created.

NOTES

1. Patricia U. Bonomi, *Under the Cope of Heaven: Religion, Society, and Politics in Colonial America* (New York: Oxford University Press, 1986); Nathan O. Hatch, *The Democratization of American Christianity* (New Haven, Conn.: Yale University Press, 1989); Jon Butler, *Awash in a Sea of Faith: Christianizing the American People* (Cambridge: Harvard University Press, 1990); Ruth Bloch, *Visionary Republic: Millennial Themes in American Thought, 1756–1800* (New York: Cambridge University Press, 1985); Christine Leigh Heyrman, *Southern Cross: The Beginnings of the Bible Belt* (Chapel Hill: University of North Carolina Press, 1998); Dee E. Andrews, *Methodism and Revolutionary America, 1760–1800* (Princeton: Princeton University Press, 2000); Jon Butler, *Becoming American: The Revolution before 1776* (Cambridge: Harvard University Press, 2000); T. H. Breen, *American Insurgents, American Patriots: The Revolution of the People* (New York: Hill & Wang, 2010).
2. Benedict Anderson, *Imagined Communities: Reflections on the Origin and Spread of Nationalism* (London: Verso, 1991); David Waldstreicher, *In the Midst of Perpetual Fetes: The Making of American Nationalism, 1776–1820* (Chapel Hill: University of North Carolina Press, 1997).
3. Jacques Le Goff, *History and Memory*, trans. Steven Rendall and Elizabeth Claman (New York: Columbia University Press, 1992), 182–83; Maurice Halbwachs, *On Collective Memory*, ed. Lewis A. Coser (Chicago: University of Chicago Press, 1992), 84, 86–99, 119.
4. Rhys Isaac, *The Transformation of Virginia, 1740–1790* (New York: Norton, 1988); Marjoleine Kars, *Breaking Loose Together: The Regulator Rebellion in Pre-Revolutionary North Carolina* (Chapel Hill: University of North Carolina Press, 2002); Jewel L. Spangler, *Virginians Reborn: Anglican Monopoly, Evangelical Dissent, and the Rise of the Baptists in the Late Eighteenth Century* (Charlottesville: University of Virginia Press, 2008), 8, 215; Randolph Ferguson Scully, *Religion and the Making of Nat Turner's Virginia: Baptist Community and Conflict, 1740–1840* (Charlottesville: University of Virginia Press, 2008).
5. Jon F. Sensbach, "Before the Bible Belt: Indians, Africans, and the New Synthesis of Eighteenth-Century Southern Religious History," in *Religion in the American South: Protestants and Others in History and Culture*, ed. Beth Barton Schweiger and Donald G. Mathews (Chapel Hill: University of North Carolina Press, 2004), 5–30.
6. Waldo P. Harris III, *Georgia's First Continuing Baptist Church* (Appling, Ga.: Kiokee Baptist Church, 1997); Robert G. Gardner et al., *A History of the Georgia Baptist Association, 1784–1984* (Atlanta: Georgia Baptist Historical Society, 1988); Harvey H. Jackson, *Lachlan McIntosh and the Politics of Revolutionary Georgia* (Athens: University of Georgia Press, 1979), 102–3; Leslie Hall, *Land and Allegiance in Revolutionary Georgia* (Athens: University of Georgia Press, 2001); Breen, *American Insurgents*, 10, 242.
7. Thomas A. Tweed, *Crossing and Dwelling: A Theory of Religion* (Cambridge: Harvard University Press, 2006), 110–11; Anthony L. Chute, *A Piety above the Common Standard: Jesse Mercer and the Defense of Evangelistic Calvinism* (Macon, Ga.: Mercer University Press, 2004); Daryl Black, "'The Excitement of High and Holy Affections': Baptist Revival and Cultural Creation in the Upper-Piedmont

Georgia Cotton Belt, 1800–1828," *Georgia Historical Quarterly* 87 (Fall–Winter 2003): 329–58.

8. Paul Connerton, *How Societies Remember* (New York: Cambridge University Press, 2008), 46.
9. Silas Mercer, *Tyranny Exposed, and True Liberty Discovered: Wherein Is Contained the Scripture Doctrine concerning Kings; Their Rise, Reign, and Downfall: Together with the Total Overthrow of Antichrist* (Halifax, N.C.: Davis, 1783), 4 (hereafter cited in text).
10. Henry Holcombe, "A Sermon Occasioned by the Death of Washington," in *Political Sermons of the American Founding Era, 1730–1805*, ed. Ellis Sandoz, 2nd ed. (Indianapolis: Liberty Fund, 1998), available at oll.libertyfund.org/title/817/69454.
11. Ibid.
12. Henry Holcombe, "Address to the Friends of Religion in the State of Georgia on Their Duties in Reference to Civil Government," American Periodical Series, *Analytical Repository* 1, no. 4 (September–October 1802).
13. J. R. Huddleston and Charles O. Walker, *From Heretics to Heroes: A Study of Religious Groups in Georgia with a Primary Emphasis on the Baptists* (Jasper, Ga.: Pickens Tech Press, 1976), 35.
14. Harris, *Georgia's First Continuing Baptist Church*, 255.
15. The Walker narrative appears in Huddleston and Walker, *From Heretics to Heroes*, 34–36; Jonathan M. Bryant, *How Curious a Land: Conflict and Change in Greene County, Georgia, 1850–1885* (Chapel Hill: University of North Carolina Press, 1996), 14–16; Eric Hobsbawm, "Introduction: Inventing Traditions," in *The Invention of Tradition*, ed. Eric Hobsbawm and Terence Ranger (Cambridge: Cambridge University Press, 1983), 7; and Connerton, *How Societies Remember*, 40, 63, 86–87.
16. Ira Berlin, *Many Thousands Gone: The First Two Centuries of Slavery in North America* (Cambridge: Belknap Press of Harvard University Press, 1998), 140–41; Sylvia R. Frey, *Water from the Rock: Black Resistance in a Revolutionary Age* (Princeton: Princeton University Press, 1992).
17. Sylvia R. Frey and Betty Wood, *Come Shouting to Zion: African American Protestantism in the American South and British Caribbean to 1830* (Chapel Hill: University of North Carolina Press, 1998).
18. Alan Gallay, *The Formation of a Planter Elite: Jonathan Bryan and the Southern Colonial Frontier* (Athens: University of Georgia Press, 1989), 164–65.
19. Gardner et al., *History*, 17.
20. Edward J. Cashin, *Old Springfield: Race and Religion in Augusta, Georgia* (Augusta, Ga.: Springfield Village Park Foundation, 1995).
21. Christopher H. Owen, *The Sacred Flame of Love: Methodism and Society in Nineteenth-Century Georgia* (Athens: University of Georgia Press, 1998), 10. William Capers quoted in Frey and Wood, *Come Shouting to Zion*, 160.
22. Cashin, *Old Springfield*, 20–30; Gardner et al., *History*, 168–69; Albert J. Raboteau, *Slave Religion: The "Invisible Institution" in the Antebellum South* (New York: Oxford University Press, 1978), 48, 52–54, 177; Mechal Sobel, *Trabelin' On: The Slave Journey to an Afro-Baptist Faith* (Westport, Conn.: Greenwood, 1979), xxi; Charles Joyner, "'Believer I Know': The Emergence of

African American Christianity," in *African American Christianity: Essays in History*, ed. Paul E. Johnson (Berkeley: University of California Press, 1994), 36; Walter F. Pitts Jr., *Old Ship of Zion: The Afro-Baptist Ritual in the African Diaspora* (New York: Oxford University Press, 1993), 59; Albert J. Raboteau, *A Fire in the Bones: Reflections on African American History* (Boston: Beacon, 1995), 143–44.

23. Douglas R. Egerton, *Death or Liberty: African Americans and Revolutionary America* (New York: Oxford University Press, 2009); Jacob Walker quoted in Cashin, *Old Springfield*, 33.
24. C. D. Mallary, *Memoirs of Elder Jesse Mercer* (New York: Gray, 1844), 144. See also Stephanie McCurry, *Masters of Small Worlds: Yeoman Households, Gender Relations, and the Political Culture of the Antebellum South Carolina Low Country* (New York: Oxford University Press, 1995).
25. Minutes of the Kiokee Church and the Washington Church, quoted in Gardner et al., *History*, 125–26.
26. Jonathan Bryant, "Notes and Documents: 'My Soul An't Yours, Mas'r': The Records of the African Church at Penfield, 1848–1863," *Georgia Historical Quarterly* 65, no. 2 (Summer 1991): 403–12, quotations on 408, 410.
27. Susan Nye Hutchison, diary entries, April 7 and 10, 1829; December 4, 1829, Manuscript Department, Louis Round Wilson Library, University of North Carolina, Chapel Hill.
28. Minutes of the Bethesda Baptist Church, October 15, 1831, Greene County, Ga., Georgia Department of Archives and History, Atlanta; J. William Harris, *Plain Folk and Gentry in a Slave Society: White Liberty and Black Slavery in Augusta's Hinterlands* (Middletown, Conn.: Wesleyan University Press, 1985), 44–45.
29. Thomas W. Murphy quoted in Minutes of the Goshen Baptist Church, October 14, 1831, Lincoln County, Ga., Georgia Department of Archives and History.
30. Cashin, *Old Springfield*, 45.

"A Strange and Crowded History"

Transnational Revolution and Empire in George Lippard's Washington and His Generals

Tara Deshpande

> The children of the Revolution and countrymen of Washington, are thronging the vallies, darkening the mountains of this land, bearing in their front amid a tide of sword and bayonet the Banner of the Stars, which they have determined to plant on the Hall of Montezuma and Cortez, thus establishing in the valley of Mexico, a new dominion—THE EMPIRE OF FREEDOM.[1]

In the midst of the U.S.-Mexican War George Lippard published a weighty volume of fictionalized historical tales of the American Revolution, which he ended with this call to arms. With this image and the accompanying promise of a sequel set in Mexico, *Washington and His Generals; or, Legends of the Revolution* ensured that its readers would connect the ongoing war with their nation's history and interpreted the American Revolution as a patriotic example that they should strive to live up to as they took its ideals to new lands. His efforts connected with a great many Americans. Lippard was an extremely popular, prolific, and commercially successful writer of scandalous fiction and sensational journalism, whose works reached a substantial working-class audience.[2] Although he is now virtually unknown to the wider reading public and very few of his works are in print, scholars have established his significance to antebellum popular culture, including his important role in celebrating and sanctifying

Washington and his fellow founders and his works' imaginative support for the annexation of Mexican land.[3]

Lippard's writing made an important contribution to the many invocations of the American Revolution in support of the U.S.-Mexican War that appeared in fiction, histories, and paintings during the 1840s. Modern scholars have identified a surge in popular interest in the Revolution then, which included frequent comparisons of the two conflicts. For many Americans, the war had the potential to reinvigorate the ideals of the Revolution and thereby stimulate contemporary patriotism and national virtue. This was the case for volunteers—some of whose surviving writings refer to the Revolution—and also for those removed from the fighting.[4] Michael Kammen, for example, argues that patriotic poems during this period aimed to justify expansion.[5] Karsten Fitz's analysis of the Revolution in visual art has identified celebratory analogies in paintings such as Caton Woodville's *Old '76 and Young '48* (1849), which depicts a young man's return home from the U.S.-Mexican War, where he is reunited with his family, including his grandfather, a veteran of the Revolutionary War.[6]

Yet the cultural context that prompted such celebrations simultaneously engendered anxieties about the Revolution's meaning and about the nation it had produced. As Kammen points out, works like John Greenleaf Whittier's poem "Yorktown" commemorate the Revolution to inspire Americans to continue its work, in this case by abolishing slavery and extending freedom to all.[7] But slavery was not the only evil that appeals to the Revolution sought to combat: "Yorktown" goes on to condemn the war in Mexico in a similar mode, asking rhetorically, "Where's now the flag of that old war?" and answering, "Where Mexic Freedom, young and weak / Fleshes the Northern Eagle's beak."[8] For Whittier, the war too is a failure of Revolutionary promise, the subjugation of a new republic, rather than its fulfillment.[9]

For Lippard as well, there was a reforming impulse in his representations of the Revolution. He was a labor activist and drew frequent analogies between eighteenth-century British tyranny and the depredations of the nineteenth-century American capitalist elite. In his writing, the Revolution therefore becomes part of an ongoing struggle by the common people to throw off oppression.[10] But there is much more to his representations of the Revolution than that. In this chapter I focus on the largely unexplored tension and complexity of the vision that Lippard created, which both contributed to the construction of the war with Mexico as an opportunity to revive Revolutionary ideals and simultaneously problematized the idealization of the war as the Revolution's sacred and inevitable consequence.

Lippard constructed this vision in particular in his "legends," which were fictionalized histories intended to show what he called the "spirit" of an age. This literary form gave Lippard great license to shape and revise the events he described to heighten their effect and is thus extremely telling about his political concerns. In a short period he published *Washington and His Generals*, a second volume of "Legends of the Revolution,"and one on the U.S.-Mexican War, although viewing these texts as about either the Revolution or the war is artificial.[11] *Washington and His Generals; or, Legends of the Revolution* (1847) ends anticipating a future volume about the U.S.-Mexican War, effectively if not subtly representing it as the Revolution's sequel. In turn, when it appeared later the same year, *Legends of Mexico* invoked the Revolution, as did a novel set during the same conflict, *'Bel of Prairie Eden* (1848).[12] What is most interesting about Lippard's texts is that rather than establishing a straightforward correlation between the two events, they locate the Revolution within a much broader transnational context, comparing it to other insurrections, nations, and empires. Their representations thereby challenge the direct identification of the American Revolution with the contemporary United States and begin to question the exceptional status of both.

It should not be surprising that cultural products of the 1840s contained both celebration and challenge. The very idea that the U.S.-Mexican War could *reinvigorate* the Revolution inevitably contains at least a hint that the Revolution's legacy had been lost or betrayed. There were many reasons why Americans of this period questioned and contested the meaning of the Revolution for national identity. By this time, the founding generation had died, severing the nation's most obvious connection to the Revolutionary era.[13] Increasing the sense of alienation that some Americans felt from the past were the social and cultural changes of Jacksonian commercialism. At the same time, revolutions in Europe were raising questions about how desirable revolution really was and what position the United States should take in response to popular uprisings beyond its borders.[14] Perhaps most important for this chapter's concerns, though, this was also a period of rapid territorial expansion and the doctrine of manifest destiny, according to which white U.S. Americans were seen to be divinely ordained to populate the entire North American continent on account of their superior civilization. In preceding decades, formal policies of "Indian removal" had enabled westward settlement by white Americans. The admission of Texas to the United States in 1845 and subsequent war with Mexico would culminate in the annexation of substantial territories in 1848.[15] Although this appropriation of Mexican land was celebrated by many as both inevitable and virtuous, to its critics it looked like empire building, which was incompatible with republican virtue.[16] Never one to favor moderation in his writing, Lippard engaged with all these anxieties, most dramatically in book 5 of *Washington and His Generals.*

Book 5 is titled "The Fourth of July, 1776" and opens with the story of that day before proceeding to locate it within a transnational and transhistorical context. This story of "The Day" is Lippard's most enduring contribution to the popular memory of the Revolution and represents the signing of the Declaration of Independence. Like much of the material in *Washington and His Generals,* this tale had been published previously, with versions appearing in various newspapers in 1846. What is most interesting about this story is how it functions within the context of the book as a whole. The story begins at the State House in Philadelphia, where an old man rings the bell to announce independence to the waiting people. The scene then moves to inside the building, where we learn what has prompted this proclamation: Jefferson, Franklin, and Adams present the Declaration of Independence to their fellow founders, after which an unidentified congressman gives a rousing speech. Then, suitably inspired, they all rush to sign the document and free themselves of British tyranny. The most important element of the story is the "Speech of the Unknown," which, the author explains in a footnote, is intended "to embody in abrupt sentences, the very spirit of the Fourth of July, 1776" (397).[17] Despite its factual inaccuracy, the narrative of "The Fourth of July" found longevity as well as popularity when it was repeated by historians during the nineteenth and the early twentieth centuries.[18] The influence it had over the popular imagination was no doubt due in part to Lippard's considerable fame but also to the fact that it was published at a time when its construction of an idealized national history, animated by a commitment to liberty, was bound to resonate.

From the beginning, Lippard represents the American Revolution not only as the foundation of a virtuous nation but also, and most emphatically, as an event of transnational significance: the Declaration of Independence is adopted by "fifty-six traders, farmers and mechanics [who] had assembled to shake the shackles of the *world*" (393; emphasis added). This is not, however, a simple narrative of U.S. global influence. The meaning of the Revolution itself is constructed through a context that goes beyond the geographic and temporal limits of the individual nation state. After recounting the American Revolution, the text flits between the colonization of the Americas, the French Revolution, the British Empire, the nineteenth-century United States, and scenes from the Bible. In adopting a broad perspective that transcends the nation state, Lippard draws attention to discourses of nationhood. When he examines the American Revolution through this frame, he makes the nation the subject of discourse, holding it out as an idea that is imaginatively constructed by culture and through interactions with different geographies and cultures. The comparisons that he draws between the American and French Revolutions, and between the expansionist United States and the Spanish Empire, engender possibilities for viewing the nation—and particularly the legacy of the American Revolution—as fluid and mutable rather than as a coherent paradigm that contains and constrains cultural production.[19]

Book 5 of *Washington and His Generals,* however, is simultaneously unequivocal in its reverence for what it constructs as the spirit of the Revolution through the men who signed the Declaration of Independence and other heroic revolutionaries throughout history. It therefore suggests a distinction between the ideal bequeathed to the United States and what that nation has become. In its emphasis on the spirit rather than the precise events of the Revolution, it also introduces the possibility that even in 1776 the new nation was failing to live up to its promise. Yet where it is fearful or critical of the way the state is, was, or could be, it is certain that the solution lies in the Revolution's truth. Consequently, while the transnational and historical contexts allow Lippard to reexamine the nation from outside the assumptions of celebratory exceptionalist narratives, the ideals of such narratives are to a great extent reinscribed—albeit in modified form—when he appeals to the spirit of the Revolution for further reform.

The volume's opening story begins by insisting on the inextricability of nation and empire and sanctifies the propagation of the American

Revolution beyond national borders. While the Liberty Bell "awoke a world, slumbering in tyranny and crime," the narrator claims that the Declaration of Independence will become "the Text-book of Freedom—the Bible of the Rights of Man forever!" (393, 396). As both "Text-book" and "Bible," it will serve as an example to the rest of the world, asserting the unique political virtue of the United States and its moral right to leadership. As the American eagle "spreads its wings, full-grown, over a whole Continent," the republic is identified with the whole of North America and thus Lippard implicitly supports the continental expansion of the 1840s as a benevolent and "natural" consequence of the events of 1776 (393). Independence therefore announces future territorial expansion in North America and a broader political influence born of a truth that transcends national boundaries.

This language of righteousness and freedom, reminiscent of the Declaration of Independence, continues in the "Speech of the Unknown," which is characterized as "the very *spirit* of the Fourth of July, 1776" (397; emphasis added). But the speech also invokes Thomas Paine's *Common Sense* (1776) and its terrifying representation of tyranny and thereby prepares the way for the text to highlight the vulnerability of the ideal nation state imagined implicitly in the Declaration.[20] The orator uses gothic imagery to denounce tyranny and assert the rights of the oppressed. He accuses kings generally, declaring, "You have waded on to thrones over seas of blood—you have trampled on to power over the necks of millions—you have turned the poor man's sweat and blood into robes for your delicate forms, into crowns for your anointed brows" (395). Typical of Lippard's outraged descriptions of oppressors, from kings to conquerors to corrupt priests, this description forcefully recalls Paine's images of violence and excess and his claim that "monarchy and succession have laid . . . the world in blood and ashes."[21] This works not only as a rallying cry against the British king and an affirmation of the Revolution's aims, but also serves to present an uncanny double for the image of the virtuous nation created by the Revolution, reasserting the frightening qualities that cannot be acknowledged as part of the Revolution's legacy.[22] It vividly represents tyranny, suggesting the vulnerability of civic virtue and providing an alternative, cautionary model against which to measure the Revolution's inheritors.

As the volume progresses, further images of tyranny and violence reflect on the opening story, modifying its idealized image from a complacent celebration to a challenge. The story of "The Day" is followed immediately by a number of other short pieces, each of which tells of a noble truth that has been corrupted, implying that the "spirit" of the American Revolution has also been subverted. The text's most specific challenge to U.S. expansion immediately follows its account of the nation's founding. This section, subtitled "The Apostle to the New World," challenges the earlier rhetoric of virtuous exceptionalism, by revealing and problematizing its reliance on imperialism. Lippard takes his reader back two hundred years to provide a context for the preceding narrative; he chooses William Penn's arrival in North America and compares it to the foundation of the Spanish Empire in the Americas.

Penn's historical representation as the instigator of a positive relationship between white and indigenous peoples made him a significant figure in the 1840s, when the nation's westward expansion relied on policies of Indian removal.[23] Here, Lippard exploits Penn's reputation for diplomacy and integrity to the full, to represent both tolerance and Christian destiny as central elements of the nation's spirit:

> That Apostle built a Nation without a Priest, without an Oath, without a Blow. Yet he never wronged the poor Indian.
>
> That Apostle reared the Altar of Jesus, on the Delaware shore, and planted the foundations of a Mighty People, amid dim old forests. Yet he never wronged the poor Indian.

Yet Lippard goes on to relate how "the Indian Mother" has now been "driven far beyond the Mississippi, driven even from the memory of the Delaware" (402). Herself forgotten, she nonetheless passes on the story of Penn to her child, preserving his history. Now the accusation implicit in the repeated statement "*he* never wronged the poor Indian" becomes a direct challenge to the more recent policies of Indian removal that allowed white Americans to settle further west. This is more than a call for the nation to recognize the rights, or even existence, of indigenous peoples. Removal was a prerequisite for the realization of manifest destiny. The previously positive image of the U.S. eagle "spread[ing] its wings . . . over a whole Continent" consequently becomes tainted by the fate of the "poor Indian" (393, 402).

Lippard encourages an identification of removal, figured in law as a matter primarily affecting lands and peoples within the United States, with international imperialism by depicting a historical moment prior to the foundation of the nation state and by introducing a comparison of Penn with Spanish imperialists.[24] The use of Spain as a negative Other is an important trope that recurred in literary constructions of the United States throughout the late eighteenth and nineteenth centuries.[25] While it could serve to emphasize U.S. virtue through contrast, this comparison could also undermine exceptionalism by producing Spain as an uncanny double, implicitly associating its worst excesses with the United States. Penn's message of religious "toleration" is contrasted with a summary of the more worldly concerns of "Columbus, with his eye fixed on land—the land of the New World—Pizarro gazing on the riches of Peru, [and] Cortez with the Temples of Montezuma at his feet" (401). Lippard invokes the "Black Legend" of Spanish atrocities in the Americas by asserting Penn's superiority to "the butchers of the human race, called CONQUERORS" (402).

Although Penn is more benevolent than the Spaniards, his arrival is portrayed as substantially similar to theirs. Like them, he is associated with images of boats and discovery. When he disembarks, he greets an Indian, who is repeatedly described as "kneeling" (400, 401). The meeting is represented as a tableau: the description focuses on the visual, and it is called both a "scene" and a "picture." This mode brings the encounter into direct comparison with the "mighty pictures" and "historic image" of the Spanish explorers and holds them up for scrutiny. Penn's position relative to the "kneeling Indian" resonates with "Cortez," who has "the Temples of Montezuma *at his feet*" (401; emphasis added). The parallels blur the distinction between Penn and the others and suggest that his virtuous colonization could easily degenerate into a conquest. Indeed, the references to Indian removal and the fact that in the 1840s the United States was seeking to annex parts of the land of Montezuma suggest that perhaps it has already.[26] European imperialism generally, and the Spanish empire specifically, work as uncanny doubles, which are both like and—the narrator anxiously insists—unlike the United States.

The suggestion that the Revolution's spirit might be betrayed is drawn out further in the biblical episodes that follow. The narrative moves even further back, to the time of Jesus Christ, who is described as being "the origin of the noble words contained in the Declaration of Independence" (403). This section picks up explicitly on contemporary labor politics:

Jesus is insistently described as poor and represented as a revolutionary mechanic.[27] Significantly, though, this section also represents his motivating spirit of revolution as being under a direct threat. Lippard uses the story of Jesus' temptation in the wilderness, with Satan taking on the role previously performed by the British monarch and Spanish conquerors. Satan exhorts Jesus: "Forsake this dream of Good—a beautiful Dream it may be, yet still only a dream—which tells thee that thou canst lift up the toiling Millions of the human race, and the glory of all ages, the grandeur of all empires shall be thine!" (412). Jesus of course refuses, but at this point the narrator warns the reader directly that "there will come a time in your life, when like Jesus, you will . . . have the good things of this world spread out before you, you will hear the voice of the Tempter." Interestingly, Satan encourages readers to "*crush the voice . . . which bids you go out and speak boldly and act bravely for the rights of man*" (413). Christ's dream is translated into a discourse of the rights of man, underlining its link with the Revolution's spirit, even while its vulnerability is emphasized.

As in the New Testament, the specific images that Satan conjures are images of earthly power. But Lippard's version is also shaped by the book of Revelation. On one level this works to intensify the effect created by his gruesome representations of kings and conquerors: Revelation supplies more blood, torment, and destruction than any of the Gospels' accounts of Christ's temptation. Lippard's use of Revelation, however, does more than simply augment his gothic imagination. First, it introduces the expectation of the judgment, and the related possibility of damnation, that the book predicts. The text suggests that those to whom Jesus' mission has been entrusted might choose power over virtue and be damned for it. Second, the allusions to Revelation engage with constructions of contemporary U.S. virtue in terms of millennialism. According to the book of Revelation, judgment will be preceded by a period of a thousand years, the millennium of Christ's rule on earth, which will end in Satan's defeat and a new creation. In the antebellum United States, which saw a surge in millennialist beliefs, most Protestants subscribed to a postmillennial interpretation of this prophecy. That is, they believed that Christ would return to earth at the end of the millennium, rather than to instigate it; humans would help to create the millennium without direct divine intervention. For the many who believed the millennium was imminent, this belief complemented and reinforced their confidence in the sanctity of U.S. "progress" and the doctrine of manifest destiny.[28]

Lippard invokes postmillennialism through Revelation but then undermines some of his contemporaries' confidence in the role of the United States in building the new millennium by locating Revelation in a representation of Christ's temptation. More specifically, he challenges the association of national expansion with righteous progress by embedding empire within Satan's visions. These show "the Romes of all ages," including "Nineveh of old," "Imperial Rome," and "Papal Rome." Subjugation is implicit in all of them, as, for example, in the description of imperial Rome's "unconquered banner . . . floating over the heads of kneeling millions" (411). They are followed by an unnamed empire, personified as female, which is more overtly oppressive: "above gorgeous empires, whose names have been lost in the abyss of ages, there rose another Empire, terrible to behold in her bloody beauty." This empire's "temples were built upon the skulls of millions, her power was fed on human flesh, her Red Cross Flag was painted with the blood of martyrs" (412). These lines echo the "Speech of the Unknown" and its indictment of monarchs generally and George III specifically; its mention of the flag recalls the first book of *Washington and His Generals,* in which the red-cross banner is a prominent motif in the arrival of the British in Philadelphia.[29] At first glance, this empire could be identified with that of the British and appear to function as a straightforward invocation of British tyranny to bolster American Revolutionary virtue.

It is significant, however, that this empire is not named. Like the unidentified congressman whose "Speech of the Unknown" encapsulates the spirit of revolution, she is unidentified and therefore able to capture the essence of empire through the ages, without being tied to a specific time or place. As Satan's vision of what might be, she is also the prophecy of an empire to come. Since she is the temptation of Jesus, who has been called "the origin of . . . the Declaration of Independence" and is the source of other revolutions through the ages, this empire suggests a perpetual struggle between corrupt imperialism and virtuous revolution and posits an American empire of the future, to be realized if and when Revolutionary ideals are abandoned (403). As a female embodiment of empire tempting masculine virtue, the figure also echoes common representations of Mexico as bride to the U.S. groom. As Shelley Streeby has shown convincingly, this image was variously deployed to support the war, by figuring conquest as consent, and to oppose it, by suggesting Mexico as an unsuitable match.[30] Here Lippard's text resonates with the latter camp, demonstrating that it is not Mexico but imperialism that the United States is set to embrace, with all the bloody consequences that empire entails.

With this in mind, the details of the empire's representation engender a different set of associations. Lippard writes that "her banners were fanned by every breeze that swept the earth, the ice-wind of the north, the hot blast of the tropics, the summer gales of more lovely climes" (412). Instead of referring just to the British Empire, this claim to global influence recalls and twists the earlier claims that Philadelphia's bell "awoke a world" (393). The images of temples built on the "skulls of millions" and "power fed on human flesh" resonate with a common trope in U.S. writing about Mexico: both histories and war fiction of the 1840s made much of Aztec human sacrifice. In William H. Prescott's influential *History of the Conquest of Mexico* (1843), for example, the ritual killing of numerous victims, cannibalism, and "immense heaps of human skulls" feature prominently in his description of Aztec society.[31] For the U.S. soldiers who visited Mexico City's national museum—many of whose expectations had been informed by Prescott—one of its more striking artifacts was the stone altar on which such sacrifices had been made.[32] In Lippard's *'Bel of Prairie Eden,* though, human sacrifice would function as a trope for Aztec barbarity, which is then matched first by Spanish, then by U.S., cruelty. Rather than construct a dichotomy between U.S. freedom and others' savagery, this image therefore encourages an identification. Similarly, in *Washington and His Generals* Satan's vision of bloody empire's human sacrifices is overlaid with Aztec tyranny, the Spanish conquest, and the U.S.-Mexican War. If Jesus, or the contemporary United States, were to succumb to temptation, each would fall into a pattern of bloody empire that haunts history.

Lippard concludes his historical survey with the revolutions in France, which he constructs as an illustration of the consequences that arise when revolutionary impulses yield to the temptations of power. Here the horrors that have featured previously in allusions (as in the "Speech of the Unknown") or in visions (as in Christ's temptation) erupt in the narrative's foreground, realized as historical fact. There are many examples of what are by now familiar images of bloody tyranny. The French kings have "waded up to thrones, through rivers of blood," "built their thrones upon islands of dead bodies," and are "clothed with the groans, the tears, the blood of fifteen million people" (431). The difference here is that these horrors are not *ended* by revolution but *perpetuated* by it: the French Revolution is clearly identified with monarchy in its embodiment as "King Guillotine," who is, perhaps unsurprisingly, accompanied by another "pile of human heads" (434).

What is significant about these scenes is that Lippard does not construct them as evidence of a specifically French depravity or as the product of a false revolution, either of which would have allowed a reassuring comparison with the United States. Instead, he takes "truth from the carnage" and considers "the Principle of the French Revolution," declaring that "it was for this same principle that Jesus toiled" (434). Its degeneration therefore constitutes proof that even the most noble and sincere commitment to liberty and equality does not guarantee the realization of a free and fair society.

After this terrifying subversion of Christ's dream, the final chapters of book 5 return to the nineteenth-century United States. They represent the deaths of several important members of the Revolutionary generation, with the concluding pages focusing on the peaceful death of "the last of the signers," Charles Carroll (457). In many ways these scenes provide a relief from the relentless horror of the preceding chapters: there is no physical violence here. This section, however, is far from complacent. Alongside Carroll, Jefferson, and Adams, Lippard also shows Robert Morris and Thomas Paine spending their final days in obscurity and poverty, neglected by a nation that fails to acknowledge and perpetuate their Revolutionary heroism. Furthermore, their placement at the end of what Lippard describes as "a strange and crowded history" means that, despite their relatively gentle and much less sensational tone, all these death scenes posit an urgent challenge to U.S. citizens (449). Although it defies chronology, the sequencing of historical incidents in the book constructs a logical trajectory that follows the sacred spirit as it inspires a Revolution and is subsequently tempted and tested by the desire for power, then corrupted, defeated, and transformed into tyranny. In these deaths can be read the possible demise of the Revolution's spirit and corresponding ascendancy of its opposite, empire.

After the war there remained an appetite for patriotic writing that viewed conquest in Mexico through an imagined Revolutionary past.[33] What Lippard's text illuminates, however, is the possibility for a narrative that, rather than using the Revolution to strengthen and sustain exceptionalism, uses it to decenter U.S. experience and thereby challenge its claims to be unique. His representations are of particular interest because of their huge popularity and importance in developing the triumphalist narrative linking the Revolution to expansion. That a deeper reading of his work reveals anxieties—not just about the nineteenth century's ability to live up to the Revolution but about the Revolution's ability ever to embody its ideal spirit—suggests that the meaning of the Revolution and the cultural work it performed could be challenging and conflicted in nineteenth-century mainstream popular culture and far from complacent. It points to a need to reexamine popular manifestations of Revolutionary memory with an eye to the ways in which a war of conquest problematized both the nation's self-image and its interrelated perception of other states and empires.

NOTES

1. George Lippard, *Washington and His Generals; or, Legends of the Revolution* (Philadelphia: Zieber, 1847), 524 (hereafter cited in text).
2. On Lippard's career and the reception of his work, see David S. Reynolds's introduction to George Lippard, *The Quaker City; or, The Monks of Monk Hall: A Romance of Philadelphia Life, Mystery, and Crime* (Amherst: University of Massachusetts Press, 1995), vii–xli.
3. David S. Reynolds, *George Lippard: Prophet of Protest, Writings of an American Radical, 1822–1854* (New York: Lang, 1986); Shelley Streeby, *American Sensations: Class, Empire, and the Production of Popular Culture* (Berkeley: University of California Press, 2002).
4. Robert W. Johannsen, *To the Halls of the Montezumas: The Mexican War in the American Imagination* (Oxford: Oxford University Press, 1985).
5. Michael Kammen, *A Season of Youth: The American Revolution and the Historical Imagination* (New York: Oxford University Press, 1980), 126.
6. Karsten Fitz, *The American Revolution Remembered, 1830s to 1850s: Competing Images and Conflicting Narratives* (Heidelberg: Universitätsverlag Winter, 2010), 70–71.
7. Kammen, *Season of Youth*, 122.
8. John Greenleaf Whittier, "Yorktown," in *Poems* (Boston: Mussey, 1849).
9. Although largely beyond the scope of this chapter, debates about annexing Mexican territory were deeply involved in discussions about slavery and its extension to any new territories and states. See Daniel Walker Howe, *What God Hath Wrought: The Transformation of America, 1815–1848* (Oxford: Oxford

University Press, 2007), 762–70; and Lyon Rathbun, "The Debate over Annexing Texas and the Emergence of Manifest Destiny," *Rhetoric and Public Affairs* 4 (2001): 459–93.

10. Reynolds, *George Lippard* (1986), 29–33; Timothy Mason Roberts, *Distant Revolutions: 1848 and the Challenge to American Exceptionalism* (Charlottesville: University of Virginia Press, 2009), 87–88.
11. George Lippard, *Washington and His Men: A New Series of Legends of the Revolution* (New York: Stringer & Townsend, 1850).
12. George Lippard, *Legends of Mexico* (Philadelphia: Peterson, 1847) and *'Bel of Prairie Eden: A Romance of Mexico* (Boston: Hotchkiss, 1848).
13. Lippard, in *Washington and His Generals,* describes several of these deaths, testifying to their cultural significance.
14. Michael A. Morrison, "American Reaction to European Revolutions, 1848–1852: Sectionalism, Memory, and the Revolutionary Heritage," *Civil War History* 49 (2003): 111–32; Roberts, *Distant Revolutions.*
15. James M. McPherson, *Ordeal by Fire: The Civil War and Reconstruction*, 2nd ed. (New York: McGraw-Hill, 1992), 57–62.
16. For example, traditional republican thought attributed such warnings to Thomas Coles's series of paintings *The Course of Empire* (1833–36). The paintings follow a society through five stages, showing, as Cole wrote to his patron, "how nations have risen from the Savage State to that of Power & Glory & then fallen & become extinct." Thomas Cole to Luman Reed, September 18, 1833, quoted in *The Art of Thomas Cole: Ambition and Imagination,* ed. Ellwood C. Parry (Newark: University of Delaware Press, 1988), 140. The series' original audience interpreted it variously as a pessimistic judgment on their nation's excessive expansion and commercialism or as a celebration of the unique virtue that would allow the United States to escape the cycle. See Streeby, *American Sensations,* 57; and Alan Wallach, "Thomas Cole: Landscape and the Course of American Empire," in *Thomas Cole: Landscape into History,* ed. William H. Truettner and Alan Wallach (New Haven, Conn.: Yale University Press, 1994), 23–111, esp. 95.
17. On the differences between this version and earlier published ones, see David S. Reynolds, *George Lippard* (Boston: Twayne, 1982), 65.
18. Reynolds, *George Lippard* (1982), 65.
19. My reading of Lippard resonates with Wai Chee Dimock's use of "deep time" to understand American literature as "weaving in and out of other geographies, other languages, other cultures." But whereas Dimock uses "deep time" to move away from the primacy of the nation state in thinking about culture, I argue that Lippard's perspective facilitates an analysis of the nation. *Through Other Continents: American Literatures across Deep Time* (Princeton: Princeton University Press, 2006), 6.
20. Paine is represented directly later in the volume, as Lippard seeks to rehabilitate his memory as a Revolutionary and excuse his deism as an understandable but regrettable error of judgment. This theme continues in the chapter "The Violator of the Grave: A Sequel to the Fourth of July, 1776."
21. Thomas Paine, *Common Sense* in *Rights of Man, Common Sense and Other Political Writings,* ed. Mark Philp (1776; repr., Oxford: Oxford University Press, 1995), 18.

22. My use of the term "uncanny" here is derived broadly from Freud's thesis that the uncanny is produced when the familiar, having been either repressed or surmounted, reasserts itself. Sigmund Freud, "The Uncanny," in *The Standard Edition of the Complete Psychological Works of Sigmund Freud,* trans. and ed. James Strachey, vol. 17 (London: Hogarth/Institute of Psychoanalysis, 1955), 217–52. It is also indebted to the work of several scholars who have argued that in U.S. culture the construction of citizen subjectivities has relied on the exclusion of others from full citizenship and that this act of disavowal has produced these others as uncanny. See, for example, Toni Morrison, *Playing in the Dark: Whiteness and the Literary Imagination* (Cambridge: Harvard University Press, 1992); Priscilla Wald, *Constituting Americans: Cultural Anxiety and Narrative Form* (Durham, N.C.: Duke University Press, 1995); Renée L. Bergland, *The National Uncanny: Indian Ghosts and American Subjects* (Hanover: University Press of New England, 2000).
23. On Penn's appearance to spiritualists at this time, as well as the frequent appearances of Native American spirits, see Bridget Bennett, *Transatlantic Spiritualism and Nineteenth-Century American Literature* (New York: Palgrave Macmillan, 2007), 83–113. Penn's significance is also evident in the essays that Jeremiah Evarts, secretary to the American Board of Commissioners for Foreign Missions, wrote to protest against removal in 1829 and 1830 under the pseudonym "William Penn." See Francis Paul Prucha, ed., *Cherokee Removal: The "William Penn" Essays and Other Writings* (Knoxville: University of Tennessee Press, 1981).
24. For example, see the language of the Removal Act (1830), which provides for the president to "exchange" land "belonging to the United States" in the West for "territory claimed and occupied by such tribe or nation, within the bounds of any one or more of the States or Territories." *U.S. Statutes at Large,* vol. 4 [1830], 21st Cong., 1st sess., ch. 148, p. 411. Chief Justice John Marshall's judgment in *Cherokee Nation v. State of Georgia* (1831) found the Cherokee to be a "domestic dependent nation." *Cherokee Nation v. State of Georgia,* 30 U.S. (5 Peters) 1 (1831). In doing so he rejected the Cherokee Nation's assertion that it was a foreign nation entitled to bring the case. The case of course also testifies to the alternative view held by representatives of the Cherokee Nation and others.
25. María DeGuzmán, *Spain's Long Shadow: The Black Legend, Off-Whiteness, and Anglo-American Empire* (Minneapolis: University of Minnesota Press, 2005).
26. References to Montezuma were common in the discourse of the U.S.-Mexican War. See, for example, George Lippard's *Legends of Mexico* (Philadelphia: Peterson, 1847).
27. David S. Reynolds again sees this episode as a critique of the wealthy. See *Faith in Fiction: The Emergence of Religious Literature in America* (Cambridge: Harvard University Press, 1981), 137–38.
28. Howe, *What God Hath Wrought,* 285–89.
29. Book 1 of *Washington and His Generals,* "The Battle of Germantown," begins with a section titled "The Red Cross in Philadelphia."
30. Streeby, *American Sensations,* 76, 82–84.
31. William H. Prescott, *History of the Conquest of Mexico, with a Preliminary View*

of the Ancient Mexican Civilization, and the Life of the Conqueror, Hernando Cortés, vol. 1 (New York: Harper & Brothers, 1843), 54–89 and 399.

32. Johannsen, *To the Halls*, 157. On visits to historical sites where sacrifices might have taken place, see pages 156 and 158.
33. See, for example, James Fenimore Cooper's additions to his preface to *The Spy* when it was reissued in 1849 (New York: Putnam, 1849).

"The Sacred Ashes of the First of Men"

Edward Everett, the Mount Vernon Ladies Association of the Union, and Late Antebellum Unionism

Matthew Mason

Decades ago, in what is today an unjustly neglected work, scholar George B. Forgie illustrated how two cults that assumed gigantic proportions in the 1850s—those of domesticity and of George Washington—came together in the activities of Edward Everett. From the late 1850s into 1860 Everett traveled the country delivering his oration on "The Character of Washington," donating the proceeds from these lectures to the purchase of the dilapidated Mount Vernon estate to preserve it as a national treasure. Americans' enthusiastic response to Everett's oration suggests a widespread demand for its message in the very late antebellum United States. Forgie interpreted this fascinating cultural moment as evidence of Americans' "sentimental regression from politics to domesticity." He painted Everett, who retired from the Senate in the wake of the blistering debate over the Kansas-Nebraska Act in 1854, as merely the most influential of a whole series of "counterpolitical sentimentalists uncomfortable with ideology" on the American scene in this crisis decade.[1]

But Everett and his many fellow travelers would have scratched their heads at this attempt to separate the cultural and the political. They embraced the Unionist cause with unbounded sentimentalism for the Union and its founders (none more so than Washington), but theirs was no escapism. At all ranks they articulated a targeted political purpose: saving the Union. And they continued and refined an ideology of Union that compared the national compact to a family united by ties of feeling. While the moderate political platform Everett represented went down in defeat in 1860, the Unionism it represented remained a force to be reckoned with during the Civil War.

Everett's crusade intensified a long hagiography of Washington that cast a patriotic hue over Mount Vernon. Unionist patriots had long imagined Mount Vernon as a haven from sectional turmoil and invited their compatriots to "come to this hallowed spot, and, around this sacred sarcophagus, promise to live together like brothers, for he was the Father of you *all.*" Washington had embodied the Union during his military and political careers and had urged its preservation against partisan and sectional threats in his famous Farewell Address, so the hope was that pilgrimages to Mount Vernon would make plain the folly and apostasy that disunion would involve.[2] Everett's Mount Vernon activities thus tapped into deep existing wells of civic religion. But Unionists drew this water in a panic, fighting a host of fires threatening to gut the nation's house.[3] And never was their appeal to Washington to advocate unconditional commitment to the Union more powerful and urgent—and defensive—than in the late 1850s.

By a happy coincidence, in the 1850s the material decline of the Mount Vernon property became intolerable to many Americans. Proposals that the Virginia or federal government purchase the estate failed amid sectional and constitutional squabbles that typified how Americans used Washington as a club as much as a shield. Women, playing their role as paragons of patriotic virtue, stepped into the breach. In 1853 Louisa Bird Cunningham and her daughter Ann Pamela launched a ladies' fund-raising campaign, eventually incorporated in 1856 as the Mount Vernon Ladies Association of the Union (MVLAU). As the name suggests, the idea was to sway Unionist sentiment to save Mount Vernon, while leveraging Washington to save the Union. By 1858 the MVLAU had succeeded spectacularly, purchasing the estate from the family for two hundred thousand dollars.[4]

Everett was a natural choice as the lead fund-raiser for the MVLAU. He enjoyed the reputation as the greatest living exemplar of the orator's art of linking the rational to deep emotionalism.[5] Moreover, his devotion to both Washington and to the Union was a decades-long theme in his public career. His MVLAU activities only confirmed that devotion. By Everett's own estimate, in 1859 alone he gave the speech 129 times. The nationwide travel posed great expense and inconvenience to a man in his sixties and of indifferent health, and multiple repetitions of the orations took their toll in concentrated mental labor. Everett refused to mingle any other business with the address, be reimbursed for his expenses, or even to indulge in recreational excursions while on this consecrated trail. He donated all the proceeds—nearly ninety thousand dollars all told—exclusively to the MVLAU.[6]

Part of what attracted Everett to the MVLAU was the fact that it bid fair to unify sympathizers "in every part of the land." His oration travels allowed him to cultivate contacts with dignitaries in all parts of the Union and confirm them in the faith. For both these elites and grassroots donors, acting to save Mount Vernon promised to give coherence and concreteness to previously unfocused Unionism. As the nation walked through the valley of the shadow of sectional strife, Everett confidently expected that "all persons must admit" this cause was of pressing importance.[7]

Indeed, for Everett this was a holy cause. In 1860 Everett sent a copy of one of Washington's letters to a local leader to acknowledge her followers' contributions. He was sure she would be grateful for this thank-you gift, for the letter gave "insight into the affairs of one who" to Americans was "a sort of demi-god, lifted alike above human needs and passions." Nor did he espouse this sort of pseudoreligious veneration of Washington in private alone. His appeal for the Mount Vernon Fund spoke of the need to restore "paths, once pressed by feet which consecrated the soil on which they trod." Moreover, the restored Mount Vernon would house "a collection of all the personal relics and memorials of" the sainted founder and would feature a mausoleum "to enshrine the sacred ashes of the First of Men." For Everett every artifact or antiquarian detail connected with Washington constituted holy relics in this civic religion. He invited his readers to "dwell upon" the scenes of the founding "in reverent contemplation" and rendered the dates of Washington's life with a level of detail reminiscent of biblical chronologies. God had plainly raised up Washington—"THE GREATEST OF

GOOD MEN AND THE BEST OF GREAT MEN"—to effect the founding of the American Union, Everett argued. And perhaps the crowning achievement of his efforts was his Farewell Address, with its prescient rebuke of sectionalism that spoke so directly to the 1850s. Not long after the popes had claimed infallibility, Everett claimed for the address "marvellous discernment and unerring wisdom."[8]

"The Character of Washington" oration itself, of course, was his central text in his emotional preachments against sectional passion. To study Washington's career, Everett taught, was to learn that he was "the greatest man of our own or of any age," "a man toward whom affection rises into reverence, and reverence melts back into childish, tearful love." In evangelical tones he bore witness that "I believe, as I do in my existence, that it was an important part of the design of Providence in raising him up," to give Americans "a living example" of the sort of public and private virtues that could save the Union. And "O," cried Everett the preacher, "that his pure example, his potent influence, his parting counsels," or ideally his voice "from the heavens to which he has ascended," could unite Americans again in "one bond of constitutional Union!" But if Everett's church of Washington did not hope for actual intervention from this patron saint, it did have a mecca in Mount Vernon, and "while it stands the latest generations of the grateful children of America will make this pilgrimage to it as to a shrine." Everett also proposed that this sect "make a national festival and holiday of his birthday," which would unite congregants as they realized that their "fellow-citizens on the Hudson, on the Potomac, from the Southern plains to the Western lakes, are engaged in the same offices of gratitude and love." Finally, this cult of Washington had a sacred text in the Farewell Address, to which parishioners must give "practical deference" by "the preservation of the Union of these States." Should Americans forget the address, boats on "the Potomac may toll their bells with new significance as they pass Mount Vernon; they will strike the requiem of constitutional liberty for us,—for all nations. But it cannot, it shall not be. . . . No, by the sacred dust enshrined at Mount Vernon; no, by the dear immortal memory of Washington,—that sorrow and shame shall never be."[9]

Multitudes responded enthusiastically to this powerful oration and its cause. Throngs paid a minimum of fifty cents each to hear the oration. In some towns Everett had to deliver it twice to accommodate demand. One contemporary asserted plausibly that more people heard this oration than any other speech "since the beginning of time." Railroad companies gave Everett free passes for his travel to deliver it, and when in New York he stayed at a new hotel named in his honor. In late 1858, realizing what hot property Everett had become, Robert Bonner, editor of the *New York Ledger*, offered to donate ten thousand dollars to the fund if Everett authored a year-long weekly series on topics of Everett's choosing. This was an offer Everett could not refuse, both for the fund's sake and because it gave him a weekly audience of as many as a million readers for his Unionist gospel.[10] The Mount Vernon Papers series generated laudatory reactions and a huge number of small contributions to the Mount Vernon Fund from every part of the country. And even aside from Everett's activities, the MVLAU used remarkably modern-sounding fund-raising techniques to reach thousands upon thousands of donors, most at the dollar level.[11]

This level of popularity for both Everett and his cause bespoke Americans' enormous reverence for the Union in the late 1850s. As Elizabeth Varon has shown, even as disunion rhetoric and programs became more commonplace, attacking one's enemies as disunionists remained an appealing and winning political tactic. Even abolitionist militant John Brown, she demonstrates, "struggled with the issue of disunion" and seems to have believed that his raid on Virginia was aimed in part at "defending the Union from slavery."[12] Southern reaction to Brown's October 1859 invasion of Harpers Ferry, Virginia, of course, did not bode well for the peace and harmony of that Union.

But while Northern abolitionists' praise for Brown garnered headlines especially in the South, another Northern response to Harpers Ferry was to call mass meetings to reassure Southern Unionists (and warn those abolitionists) that Northerners would stand by the sacred Union. Citizens organized Union meetings in Bangor, Maine; Portsmouth, New Hampshire; Brighton, Lowell, and Barnstable, Massachusetts; Bridgeport, Hartford, and New Haven, Connecticut; Rochester, Albany, and Troy, New York; Newark and Morristown, New Jersey; Harrisburg, Pennsylvania; and Cincinnati, Ohio. Upper South Unionists conducted meetings in their own accent in Washington, D.C., and Knoxville, Tennessee. Published reports pointedly remarked on the enthusiasm as well as the size of the Unionist throngs, asserting that they represented the vast silent majority.[13] Boston,

New York, and Philadelphia hosted "Monster Meetings," whose turnout refuted the notion that old-school Unionism with its emotional appeals to Washington and the founding was limited to a few fossilized patricians.[14]

These meetings tapped the masses' deep emotional attachment to the Founding Fathers' Union. At the Philadelphia gathering, held December 7, 1859, a series of speakers lauded the Constitution as "our sovereign without mortal frailty. It should have a life everlasting." Its blessings should never be measured in crass material terms, for it was nothing less than "a divine revelation for the political regeneration of man." "Let the Union," urged one, "formed by the wisdom of sages and patriots, and sanctified by the breath and blood of sainted heroes, be guarded like the holy altar of the temple." And as if all these echoes of the Mount Vernon cause were not enough, a number of Philadelphia's ladies joined—and thus helped to consecrate—the cause by sending a flag emblazoned with suitable Unionist sentiments to Virginia's governor.[15]

As extravagant as these expressions were, they would not outdo the next day's meeting in Everett's hometown of Boston. From the opening prayer forward, the blessings of the Union were a constant theme in this gathering. The meeting resolved "that the advantages and privileges, through the blessing of Divine Providence, enjoyed by the people of this country, are unparalleled in the history of nations." Thus, "with the deepest emotions of veneration" for its author, the meeting's final resolution reiterated the Farewell Address's warning against sectionalism. Everett, one of the headline speakers, received an enthusiastic response from both the crowd and his fellow orators. He led by recounting his involvement in the Mount Vernon cause, wherein he found the "congenial" and "useful" work of "seeking to rally the affections of my countrymen North and South, to that great name and precious memory which is left almost alone of all the numerous kindly associations, which once bound the different sections of the country together." Everett's predominant purpose here, as with the Mount Vernon lectures, was "to inculcate the blessings of the Union," consecrated as they were by "the memory of our Fathers," who had passed them to the next generations. Those who could not attend but who sent letters participated fully in such histrionics, such as one who thanked "God we have Everett . . . and a host of others, fit priests to serve at altars, whose fires were lighted by pilgrim hands." Should someone strike up "a grand chorus to the tune of the 'Constitution and the Union,'" he continued, it would "find a response in more hearts than you dream of." A newspaper reporter remarked on "the frequent tears in the eyes and on the faces of multitudes touched by a common sympathy, as some patriotic emotion was awakened by the sentiments of the several speakers." Indeed, attendees' "hearts were swelling with pent-up emotions, longing to find adequate expression."[16] The memory of Washington may have been one of the few threads holding the Union together, but this meeting testified that it was tied tightly to countless heartstrings.

The New York Unionists met in the Music Hall, whose owners traditionally prohibited political assemblies but made an exception for this gathering, which represented something much higher and holier than mere politics.[17] Speakers and letter writers repeatedly exhorted the roughly thirty thousand attendees that "the voluntary affection and loyalty of the people" must be yielded to the Union not simply for its commercial benefits but as "the greatest political blessing ever conferred upon mankind." Such citizens would "ever resist the ruthless and sacrilegious efforts to rend asunder those grand communities which the great Architect of nations has so graciously joined together." This meeting was especially fruitful in such rhetoric equating the Union to the sacrament of marriage.[18] A banner on the hall's stage excerpted the Farewell Address, as did the last of the resolutions. One speaker pointed out that after a national separation, "the dividing line would take from us the grave of Washington." It would be a poor trade, he gibed, to "lose the grave and lose all connection with the name of Washington" and be left only with the "memory of John Brown in its place."[19] These meetings amply illustrated the impact of the melding in the Mount Vernon campaign of Washington's political principles with sentimentalism and domestic analogies to create a more powerfully affecting Unionism than ever.

But these Unionists' attempt to carry that appeal into electoral politics met with mixed results. Well-wishers predicted that these meetings would awaken "honest men everywhere," who would in future elections "frown down all attempts to sunder those whom a beneficent Providence has joined together." They would open "a new era in the political history of the country . . . by kindling the flames of enthusiasm" for a "conservative and Union ticket" as an alternative to the morally bankrupt Democratic and treasonable Republican parties.[20]

Given his association with Washington and the Union, Everett was a natural choice for the vice presidential nomination of the resultant Constitutional Union Party. After a brief struggle to nominate John Bell of Tennessee as president, the convention nominated Everett as his running mate by acclamation. Convention delegates recognized Everett's connection with Washington as a universally acknowledged Unionist talisman. The party convention met in May 1860 in Baltimore underneath a full-length portrait of Washington. It was an emotional meeting, where delegates broke into loud and prolonged cheers at every mention of party shibboleths. Speakers knew the Washington hagiography by heart and argued that to reject the Union would be to "scatter the sacred dust of Washington ('Never,' 'never,'), teach your boys to forget his name, and never let the pilgrim's foot tread the consecrated groves of Mount Vernon."[21] As for Everett himself, one supporter recorded that his nomination "heaved the breast; it kindled the cheeks; it broke from the eyes in warm, gushing, irrepressible tears." His association with both Washington and the ladies was the touchstone for this response. Because Everett "has studied the character of Washington," a delegate from Mississippi enthused, his patriotism "is enough of itself to save the Union." His Mount Vernon activities also rendered Everett wildly popular with the ladies in the galleries, and another Mississippian cracked that "the delegates were mostly married men, and must know very well that it was no use to oppose the ladies." A delegate from Tennessee invoked the aid of ladies who had "participated with the illustrious gentleman who has just been nominated by such loud acclaim, in that great work of redeeming the grave of Washington." He assumed they were "to the last man, 'Everett men.'" More seriously, he continued, "if we have domestic discord and civil war, does it not visit the household? Does it not overspread the hearthstone?"[22] In such formulations, Everett as avatar of domesticity epitomized the nightmare of disunion as well as the virtues of the Union.

Party rallies and literature thereafter also wielded the double-edged sword of sentiments associated with the Mount Vernon cause. Both Constitutional Unionist mass meetings and those aiming at fusion with other anti-Republicans in the North were large, emotional affairs on the order of the December 1859 Union meetings. Their speakers laid direct claim to the legacy of Washington's Farewell Address by charging the Republicans with trampling on its warning against sectionalism. At a Constitutional Unionist meeting in Mississippi, when a speaker appealed to "our battle-fields, . . . our heroes, . . . our statesmen, and . . . the Father of his Country," it "warmed every heart and gave inspiration to those who have enlisted for the war." "Few could have failed to record a vow to Heaven that come weal come woe we will stand by the glorious Union of our fathers," the newspaper account concluded. Party faithful in North Carolina resolved that the party platform that had been "approved and recommended by the illustrious Washington and his compeers, is National and broad enough for all true patriots."[23] The old-time religion was good enough for Washington, and therefore good enough for them.

Party publications also highlighted Everett's Mount Vernon activities, which gave both "popularity" and "nationality" to "his fame" and made him better-known and better-loved by women, even in the Upper South, than Bell. Indeed, Harvard students campaigned for their old president under the slogan "Bell and the Belles." Everett's candidacy thus embodied all the disinterested patriotism associated with the ladies. But the party also claimed to represent "the courage and the manliness to stand firm" and defend the damsel in distress that was the Union. One of Everett's fans at the party convention came close to this idea when he proclaimed that his state was "in love with Edward Everett." Still, in the rough and tumble of electoral politics with all its masculine posing for exclusively male voters, a candidate might not benefit from being so closely tied to "feminine" ideals.[24]

These limits to the electoral power of these ideals in 1860 derived from more than gender. Unionism was also so widely accepted a creed that it seemed maddeningly nebulous as a platform in 1860. It produced great enthusiasm in masses of voters, and in the election it appealed to their noblest aspirations, as opposed to the sectional parties' appeal to their anger and fear. Even while acknowledging the difficulty of assaulting both the "Ladies of the Union" and "that spirit of patriotism which claims something of respect even in its most eccentric manifestations," abolitionists, radical Republicans, and fire-eaters alike sneered at Everett, the MVLAU cause, and the Union meetings.[25] Even worse, most of Everett's Southern comrades in the Constitutional Unionist cause—including Bell himself—sided with the Confederacy once war broke out. So did Ann Cunningham, who created another ladies' association—for the benefit of the Confederate Navy.[26]

But if secession and war represented the utter failure of the sectional compromise tradition, the Unionism associated with that tradition was far from dead, even in the secession winter of 1860–61. Yearning for the old formula of compromising to save the Union showed in local election returns, together with scores of procompromise Union meetings in Northern cities. In Boston alone, some twenty-two thousand people signed a procompromise petition to the Senate, and Everett served as a member of the delegation to take it to Washington. One observer of such movements encouraged compromiser John J. Crittenden that his "great measure of reconciliation strikes the *popular heart.*" Even—perhaps especially—in the secession winter, support for sectional compromise to preserve the Union was alive and well, at least in the abstract. It was at the level of the concrete—whether to coerce or conciliate the South—that this plurality broke down. Unionism, then, was dazed and confused, not dead.[27]

When compromise finally failed and war commenced, Everett's brand of affective Unionism came to the fore with greater clarity. Everett's biographer stated that the Confederacy's attack on Fort Sumter struck Everett "as though his mother, or wife, or a member of his family had been struck!"[28] It was an apt analogy given Everett's linkage of domesticity and Union, and he plunged into the Union cause with earnestness of purpose. Millions joined him in this. When Northern soldiers marched south, they did so with a holy zeal for preserving the Union uppermost in their minds. And the "religious feeling, that this war is a crusade for the good of mankind," to be wrought by putting down "this hell-begotten conspiracy," sustained those who stayed through four bloody years of conflict at least as much as did hatred for the South.[29] The fact that they were willing to fight for so long was in part a testament to the cultural work people like Edward Everett had done in perpetuating and increasing a deeply emotional attachment to the Union.

Their leader, President Abraham Lincoln, framed the issues of secession and war in terms reminiscent of the Mount Vernon cause and the Union meetings. On his way from Springfield to Washington, he complained that those who balked at forcibly upholding the Union treated it as nothing "like a regular marriage at all, but only as a sort of free-love arrangement." More soberly in his first inaugural address, he again compared the Union to matrimony and appealed to disgruntled Southerners to consider not only the "benefits" but also the "memories" associated with the Union. "Though passion may have strained, it must not break our bonds of affection," he implored in his peroration. "The mystic chords of memory, stretching from every battle-field, and patriot grave, to every living heart and hearthstone, all over this broad land, will yet swell the chorus of the Union, when again touched, as surely they will be, by the better angels of our nature."[30] Readers familiar with the first inaugural may be inclined to think Everett had waxed Lincolnesque in his poetic and emotional outbursts about the Union resting on sacred bonds of memory. But in truth, it was Lincoln who waxed Everettesque in these passages.

Lincoln and Everett also converged more than physically when they arrived to dedicate thousands of new patriot graves in Gettysburg, Pennsylvania, in November 1863. In his address Everett framed the significance of the Battle of Gettysburg by the struggle to save the sacred and beloved Union. July 1–3 were "days on whose issue it depended whether this august republican Union, founded by some of the wisest statesmen that ever lived, cemented with the blood of some of the purest patriots that ever died, should perish or endure." He appealed to "the bonds that unite us as one People," including "a common history; a common pride in a glorious ancestry." That history, when added to by "these martyr-heroes" buried at Gettysburg, united "the heart of the People" to exclaim, "God bless the Union."[31] To be sure, Everett's repeated invocations of the Union of the Founding Fathers demonstrated that it was not for him, as it was for Lincoln when he followed him on the program, to call for a "new birth of freedom." He had never seen the Union of Washington as flawed, so he and Lincoln spoke in different accents at Gettysburg.

But they spoke to the same purpose of giving high meaning to the battle, as well as to the larger war. Everett's expressions as to the stakes involved, the illegitimacy of secession, and the need for a "vigorous prosecution of the war" mirrored Lincoln's own thinking on secession and policy on the war, and he appreciated the heft that the prestigious ex-doughface Everett brought to their discussion. The day after the service, Lincoln wrote Everett that while he "knew Mr. Everett would not fail" in his oration, "there were passages in it which transcended my expectation. The point made against the theory of the general government being only an agency, whose principals are the States, was new to me, and, as I think, is one of the best arguments for the national supremacy."[32]

Other observers mirrored Lincoln's judgment of what Everett brought to the Union cause at Gettysburg and elsewhere. When Everett died in January

1865, one eulogist remembered that "no person who came under the influence of" his "Character of Washington" oration "can imagine that he failed in rekindling the fire of patriotism on a thousand, thousand altars; that he failed in . . . preparing many noble hearts to offer themselves in generous sacrifice for its preservation and perpetuity."[33] With all due allowance for eulogistic hyperbole, this speaker captured the truth that Everett's mobilization of the memory of Washington belied Robert Penn Warren's famous argument that "the Civil War is our only 'felt' history." On the contrary, the Mount Vernon campaign constituted affective Unionism feeding consciously on the memory of Washington. So nourished, it could not stave off secession, but it helped assure that secession meant civil war.[34]

NOTES

1. George B. Forgie, *Patricide in the House Divided: A Psychological Interpretation of Lincoln and His Age* (New York: Norton, 1979), 159–99, 255–56, 271.
2. Jean B. Lee, ed., *Experiencing Mount Vernon: Eyewitness Accounts, 1784–1865* (Charlottesville: University of Virginia Press, 2006), 21, 65, 102, 104–5, 128, 135, 139–42, 146–52, 169–74, 174–82, 186, 190–96, 203, 206–7; quotation on 182. See also Lee, "Historical Memory, Sectional Strife, and the American Mecca: Mount Vernon, 1783–1853," *Virginia Magazine of History and Biography* 109 (2001): 255–300; François Furstenberg, *In the Name of the Father: Washington's Legacy, Slavery, and the Making of a Nation* (New York: Penguin, 2006); and Scott E. Casper, *Sarah Johnson's Mount Vernon: The Forgotten History of an American Shrine* (New York: Hill & Wang, 2008), 32–33.
3. Forgie, *Patricide in the House Divided*, 14; Paul C. Nagel, *One Nation Indivisible: The Union in American Thought, 1776–1861* (New York: Oxford University Press, 1964); Robert Penn Warren, *The Legacy of the Civil War: Meditations on the Centennial* (New York: Random House, 1961), 3–13.
4. *The Illustrated Mount Vernon Record: The Organ of the Mount Vernon Ladies' Association of the Union . . .*, vol. 1 (Philadelphia: Devereux & Co., 1859), 1; Casper, *Sarah Johnson's Mount Vernon*, 63–71; Lee, "Historical Memory," 299; Elizabeth R. Varon, *We Mean to Be Counted: White Women and Politics in Antebellum Virginia* (Chapel Hill: University of North Carolina Press, 1998), 10–70, 124–36.
5. Daniel Walker Howe, *The Political Culture of the American Whigs* (Chicago: University of Chicago Press, 1979), 219–31; Garry Wills, *Lincoln at Gettysburg: The Words That Remade America* (New York: Touchstone, 1992), 42–52.
6. Stuart J. Horn, "Edward Everett and American Nationalism" (PhD diss., City University of New York, 1973); Everett to Ticket Agent of the Wilmington and Baltimore Railroad, April 28, 1860, Edward Everett Papers, New York Public Library; Everett to A. B. Merriam, April 2, 1857, and Everett to Mrs. Pellet,

October 19, 1857, Edward Everett Letters, 1816–63, Massachusetts Historical Society, Boston; Everett to Samuel Souther, July 20, 1858, and Everett to Charles Deane, December 7, 1858, Rare Books and Manuscripts, Boston Public Library, Mass.; Everett to "My Dear Sir," November 16, 1858, Edward Everett Papers, Phillips Exeter Academy Library, Exeter, N.H.; Paul Revere Frothingham, *Edward Everett, Orator and Statesman* (Boston: Houghton Mifflin, 1925), 373–407; Varon, *We Mean to Be Counted,* 130; Edward Everett, *The Mount Vernon Papers* (New York: Appleton, 1860), 53–71; Edward Everett, *Orations and Speeches on Various Occasions,* vol. 4 (Boston: Little, Brown, 1868), 3–17; Ronald F. Reid, *Edward Everett: Unionist Orator* (New York: Greenwood, 1990), esp. 1–3, 79–85, 214–15.

7. Everett to Governor Wise, March 4, 1856, and Everett to Truman Smith, January 16, 1859, Phillips Exeter Academy Library; Everett, *Mount Vernon Papers,* 3–4, 6, 8.
8. Everett to Mrs. William Eve, July 2, 1860, Edward Everett Letters, New-York Historical Society, New York; Everett, *Mount Vernon Papers,* 4, 6, 81–97, 106–14, 124–34, 155–62, 221–47, 327–51, 427, quotes on 4, 124; Edward Everett, *The Life of George Washington* (New York: Sheldon, 1860), 99–103, 211–22, 262–72. Everett put the "greatest of good men" epitaph for Washington on cards bearing his signature, which he gave to admirers; see Everett, autograph, n.d., Phillips Exeter Academy Library; Everett, autograph, November 15, 1861, New York Public Library; Everett, note card, March 3, 1862, Edward Everett Papers, 1832–65, American Antiquarian Society, Worcester, Mass.
9. Everett, *Orations and Speeches,* 4:20–51.
10. Everett to William Dickinson et al., April 18, 1856, and Everett to A. B. Merriam, April 2, 1857, Massachusetts Historical Society; Everett to Ticket Agent, April 28, 1860, New York Public Library; Frothingham, *Edward Everett, Orator and Statesman,* 375; Everett, *Mount Vernon Papers,* iii–v, 1–2, 9, 293–309, 485–86, 489–91; Forgie, *Patricide in the House Divided,* 171.
11. For the truly impressive lists of both sets of donors, see Edward Everett Papers, 1675–1910, Massachusetts Historical Society, reels 16–17, microfilm; *Illustrated Mount Vernon Record,* passim.
12. Elizabeth R. Varon, *Disunion! The Coming of the American Civil War, 1789–1859* (Chapel Hill: University of North Carolina Press, 2008), 9–11, 128, 151, 174, 208–9, 227–28, 263–64, 273–87, 327–28, 344, quotes on 327–28.
13. *Bangor (Maine) Daily Whig and Courier,* January 4, 1860; *Lowell (Mass.) Citizen and Daily News,* December 29, 1859; *Charleston Mercury,* December 19, 1859; *Fayetteville (N.C.) Observer,* December 19, 1859; *Newark (Ohio) Advocate,* December 16, 1859; *Daily National Intelligencer* (Washington, D.C.), December 24, 1859; January 26, February 3, 1860; *New York Herald,* December 24, 29, 30, 1859; January 1, 7, 8, 13, 1860; *Weekly Raleigh (N.C.) Register,* December 28, 1859; January 11, 1860; *Daily Constitutionalist* (Georgia), November 3, 1859; John B. Stabler, "A History of the Constitutional Union Party: A Tragic Failure" (PhD diss., Columbia University, 1954), 273–300.
14. *Great Union Meeting, Philadelphia, December 7, 1859: Fanaticism Rebuked* (Philadelphia: Crissy & Markley, 1859), 3–7; *Boston Courier Report of the Union Meeting in Faneuil Hall, Thursday, Dec. 8th, 1859* (Boston: Clark, Fellows,

1859), 3–8, 10, 12, 13, 20, 22, 24–26, 30; *Official Report of the Great Union Meeting Held at the Academy of Music, New York, December 19, 1859* (New York: Davies & Kent, 1859), 3, 41, 43–44, 86–89, 93–176; *North American and United States Gazette* (Philadelphia), December 8, 1859; *Frank Leslie's Illustrated Newspaper* (New York), December 31, 1859.

15. *Great Union Meeting, Philadelphia*, 14–21, 27, 34, 42–43, 46–47, 55–59.
16. *Boston Courier Report*, 10–17, 23–24, 28–30. One newspaper printed Everett's Boston speech on the same page as an advertisement for "Full Length Steel Engravings of Washington and Everett, including a View Mount Vernon [*sic*]." *Newark Advocate*, January 13, 1860.
17. *New York Herald*, December 13, 1859.
18. *Official Report*, 47–48; see also 6, 14–15, 21–27, 36–39, 49, 55, 60, 62–64, 67–70, 73, 76–77. For crowd estimates (ranging from twenty thousand to forty thousand), see *Daily National Intelligencer*, December 21, 1859; *Fayetteville Observer*, December 22, 1859; *Dover (N.H.) Gazette and Strafford Advertiser*, December 24, 1859.
19. *Official Report*, 9–10, 19, 27–28.
20. *North American and United States Gazette*, December 8, 1859; *Daily National Intelligencer*, December 9, 1859; *New York Herald*, December 21, 23, 1859.
21. William B. Hesseltine, ed., *Three against Lincoln: Murat Halstead Reports the Caucuses of 1860* (Baton Rouge: Louisiana State University Press, 1960), 121–22, 127, 135–39, 140; Joseph H. Parks, *John Bell of Tennessee* (Baton Rouge: Louisiana State University Press, 1950), 349–55; Stabler, "History," 416–40, 465–68.
22. *Union Guard* (Washington, D.C.), July 12, August 23, 30, 1860; Hesseltine, *Three against Lincoln*, 131–34, 137–39; Stabler, "History," 465–68.
23. *New York Herald*, February 5, September 17, October 7–8, 25, 28, November 3, 1860; *Daily National Intelligencer*, September 19, October 10, 1860; *Weekly Raleigh Register*, July 11, September 26, October 17, 31, November 7, 1860; *Hinds County Gazette* (Raymond, Miss.), March 21, 1860; *Virginia Free Press* (Charlestown, Va.), August 30, 1860.
24. *Address of the National Executive Committee of the Constitutional Union Party to the People of the United States* ([1860]), 1, 4; *The Life, Speeches, and Public Service, of John Bell, Together with a Sketch of the Life of Edward Everett* (New York: Rudd & Carleton, 1860), 97–101; Varon, *We Mean to Be Counted*, 144–46; "A Graduate's Lament," Nathan Appleton Jr. Scrapbooks, Massachusetts Historical Society; *Union Guard*, August 23, 30, 1860. For more on gendered rhetoric and the sectional crisis, see Varon, *Disunion!*, 186–91, 196, 201, 203, 221.
25. *The South* (Richmond, Va.), January 26, February 1, 10, 11, 1858; *Daily Morning News* (Savannah, Ga.), December 13, 1859; *Daily Mississippian* (Jackson, Miss.), January 19, 1860; *Freedom's Champion* (Atchison, Kans.), January 28, 1860; Samuel May Jr. to Richard Davis Webb, March 11, 1856, and Stephen Barker to Mrs. M. W. Chapman, January 24, 1860, Boston Public Library; *Liberator* (Boston), December 30, 1859; *Bangor Daily Whig and Courier*, December 10, 1859; January 4, 12, 1860; *Boston Daily Advertiser*, December 16, 1859.
26. *Daily Constitutionalist*, December 7–8, 11, 13, 16, 24, 1859; Casper, *Sarah Johnson's Mount Vernon*, 82–84; Parks, *John Bell of Tennessee*, 389–407; Don Green, "Constitutional Unionists: The Party That Tried to Stop Lincoln and

Save the Union," *Historian* 69 (Spring 2007): 238–39; David I. Durham, *A Southern Moderate in Radical Times: Henry Washington Hilliard, 1808–1892* (Baton Rouge: Louisiana State University Press, 2008), 137–50; Daniel W. Crofts, *Reluctant Confederates: Upper South Unionists in the Secession Crisis* (Chapel Hill: University of North Carolina Press, 1989), 104–29, 134, 153, 289–352.

27. Peter B. Knupfer, *The Union as It Is: Constitutional Unionism and Sectional Compromise, 1787–1861* (Chapel Hill: University of North Carolina Press, 1991); Russell McClintock, *Lincoln and the Decision for War: The Northern Response to Secession* (Chapel Hill: University of North Carolina Press, 2008); Kenneth M. Stampp, *And the War Came: The North and the Secession Crisis, 1860–1861* (Baton Rouge: Louisiana State University Press, 1950), 123–78; Mrs. Chapman Coleman, *The Life of John J. Crittenden*, 2 vols. (Philadelphia: Lippincott, 1871), 2:254; *Memorial of Edward Everett, Lemuel Shaw, Robert C. Winthrop . . .*, broadside, January 23, 1861 (Boston, 1861), Massachusetts Historical Society.

28. Frothingham, *Edward Everett, Orator and Statesman*, 416–72, quotation on 416.

29. James M. McPherson, *For Cause and Comrades: Why Men Fought in the Civil War* (New York: Oxford University Press, 1997), quotation on 13.

30. Abraham Lincoln quoted in Roy P. Basler, ed., *The Collected Works of Abraham Lincoln*, vol. 4 (New Brunswick: Rutgers University Press, 1953), 195, 235–36, 239–44, 266, 269, 271.

31. Everett, *Orations and Speeches*, 4:622–59.

32. Everett, *Orations and Speeches*, 4:640–57; Lincoln to Everett, November 20, 1863, Loose Mss. Lincoln, Massachusetts Historical Society.

33. Wills, *Lincoln at Gettysburg*, 51; *Tribute to the Memory of Edward Everett, by the New-England Historic-Genealogical Society, at Boston, Mass., January 17 and February 1, 1865* (Boston: New-England Historic-Genealogical Society, 1865), 3–6, 66, 72–74, 82–83, 93–95, quotations on 5, 95.

34. Warren, *Legacy of the Civil War*, 4. For a powerful book-length illustration of how deeply antebellum Americans "felt" Revolutionary history, see Forgie, *Patricide in the House Divided*.

Martyred Blood and Avenging Spirits

Revolutionary Martyrs and Heroes as Inspiration for the U.S. Civil War

Sarah J. Purcell

On June 25, 1861, the volunteers in the Second Vermont Regiment stopped in New York City on their way to be mustered into federal service in Washington, D.C. After dining at the Park Barracks, where troops from many Northern states were gathering in the opening days of the Civil War, the Vermonters assembled in front of city hall at 2 p.m. for a formal ceremony and flag presentation from the "sons of Vermont." Despite the heat, the ten companies wore their full dress uniforms with gray wool coats and caps, each of which displayed an evergreen sprig that signaled Vermont pride and referenced the Revolutionary heritage of the Green Mountain State.

Erastus Culver, a Brooklyn judge and former Congressional representative who had graduated from the University of Vermont, addressed the men and sought to stir their courage for the coming fight. The *New York Times* reported that Culver's speech expressed "confidence that they would not dishonor Vermont, for . . . their countenances reminded him of those who, eighty-four years ago, stood by JOHN STARK at Bennington, by ETHAN ALLEN at Ticonderoga, and by SETH WARNER."[1] As the crowd cheered, Culver urged these Vermonters to fight "to preserve and hold fast to that which the men at Bunker Hill, Lexington, Monmouth, Valley Forge and Yorktown preserved for them . . . that heritage of freedom which came down hallowed with the blood of their forefathers!"[2] Culver linked the cause of these Vermonters joining the Union Army directly to the memory of Vermont's heroes of the Revolutionary War, and he called on them to view the Civil War as a chance to uphold the blood sacrifice of the founding generation in battles from Vermont to Virginia.

Culver was not the only one that day who used memories of the Revolutionary War to motivate the Vermonters as they marched off to this new war. After several more speeches, the regiment marched through New York City streets lined with well-wishers who cheered and gave the volunteers flowers. Vermont's official Civil War historian, George Grenville Benedict, reported in 1886 that among the offerings from the crowd "was a basket with the following note: 'Will the Colonel of the Second Vermont Regiment please accept for his regiment the accompanying basket of evergreens, from a Vermont lady, who has trimmed them with the scissors with which her mother, Millicent Barrett, cut the papers for the first cartridges that were used at Concord, Mass., and Bunker Hill, in 1775.' "[3] After the Revolution Barrett had married James Swain and moved to Vermont.[4] Now, her daughter offered evergreens cut with these historical shears as a material link between the Revolutionary past and the call for new sacrifice in war. The men of the Second Vermont could not have misperceived that the public expected them to live up to the legacy of Revolutionary heroes. Less than a month later the Second Vermont fought bitterly at Bull Run and inaugurated what would be a bloody four years for their own ranks.[5]

The offering of evergreens and the speech by the former representative were just two examples of a widespread common phenomenon—the use of Revolutionary War memory to motivate military action in the early days of the Civil War. Public memory of Revolutionary martyrs and heroes fed the *rage militaire* in both regions, as images of past sacrifice were pressed into duty in ways that fitted the present conflict.

Images of martyrs and heroes from the Revolutionary War stirred enlistments and shaped reactions to the initial deaths of the Civil War. Popular culture in both the Union and the Confederacy styled early Civil

War volunteers in the mold of previous Revolutionary heroes, and they held up images of Revolutionary martyrdom to glorify Civil War deaths. Scholars have examined how the Revolution informed early Civil War political rhetoric, especially in the battle over secession and discussions of the Constitution.[6] Starting in the 1850s Fourth of July speeches, novels, editorials, and political commentaries on both sides viewed the rising regional conflict as a test of Revolutionary "liberty."[7] But public memory of the Revolution actually spread much more widely to provide a cultural context for military conflict, especially once people started dying. In the first months of the Civil War, an outpouring of popular culture likened the casualties to those of the men who had sacrificed themselves in the Revolutionary War.

Public memory of the Revolutionary War, particularly praise for Revolutionary martyrs and heroes, had been an important part of American national identity since the time of the Revolution itself. A particular strain of Revolutionary memory—often repeated in Fourth of July orations, battlefield commemorations, monument dedications, and political speeches—stressed how the blood of those killed in the Revolution had consecrated the United States as a sacred nation. Public commemorations of national martyrs such as Joseph Warren, killed at the Battle of Bunker Hill in 1775, provided a common point of reference for nationalist celebrations in all different regions of the United States. At the same time Warren also became a special hero to New Englanders through the years, just as a host of other, more local Revolutionary heroes bolstered other versions of regional pride. For example, William Jasper, the hero of the Battle of Sullivan's Island that took place near Charleston, South Carolina, and who had died later at the Battle of Savannah, received particular praise across the South, especially as part of the annual Palmetto Day celebration in Charleston. Seth Warner, hero of the Battle of Bennington, stood out to Vermonters.

For the most part, up until the 1830s praise for regional Revolutionary heroes and martyrs grew alongside and reinforced the nationalism inspired by national figures such as Joseph Warren, Richard Montgomery, and George Washington. But by the end of that decade, regional uses of Revolutionary War memory became increasingly polarized in some notable instances.[8] Abolitionists as different as William Lloyd Garrison and Henry Highland Garnet cited Revolutionary memory to bolster their cause.[9] Rival South Carolinians contended over whether Revolutionary memory rightly justified nullification or federal union during the Nullification Crisis of the 1830s.[10] Jonathan B. Crider has shown how during the 1850s the pages of the most popular Southern magazine, *De Bow's Review*, often invoked the heroic memory of Revolutionary Southern slaveholders like George Washington and Henry Lee to boost regional pride and to downplay Northern heroism.[11] The Revolutionary War, while still the subject of an overarching American national identity, started to become usable also in regional contest.

At the outset of the Civil War, the stakes were raised, and military memory took on a special urgency. The national identity created by public memories of Revolutionary War sacrifice during the early national period had never been unitary or uncontested, but it *had* provided a solid set of symbols intended to inspire unity in the American public. By the spring of 1861, however, with armies mobilizing and secession fully underway, the same set of symbols turned, and the traditions of Revolutionary heroism and martyrdom that had once held the nation together now helped to split the nation apart. Images of Revolutionary martyrs and heroes such as Joseph Warren, George Washington, and William Jasper—once the cornerstones of national identity (albeit sometimes with a regional accent)—were now used to animate sectionalist military fervor. Even as many, including a correspondent for the *Newark Daily Advertiser*, worried that "the panorama of our country's greatness, from the small seed of Bunker Hill" seemed to be crumbling, the same spirit of Bunker Hill sacrifice urged others into the fray.[12]

This chapter focuses on how public memories of the early battles in the Revolutionary War provided a familiar nationalist vocabulary that was, in the military context of 1861, used in particularly divisive ways. The specific regional associations of Revolutionary War symbols—such as the heroes of the Battle of Bunker Hill or the Battle of Sullivan's Island—also played new roles in 1861. Supporters of the Union and the Confederacy both tried to lay claim to Northern and Southern military symbols. They used martyrs and heroes as symbols of national honor, and they tried to exclude their rivals from the legitimacy granted by Revolutionary memory. By using martyrs and heroes to motivate the fight in 1861, politicians, editors, and orators also engaged in a fight for custody of some of the most hallowed national symbols. In the first months of the Civil War, each side looked back to the opening days of the Revolutionary War and concluded that historic sacrifice both hallowed their own cause and delegitimated their opponents as they took up arms.

Public memories of the June 1775 Battle of Bunker Hill—the first large battle in the Revolutionary War—played a particularly clear role in this process. Bunker Hill, and the memory of its most notable hero martyr, Joseph Warren, provided one of the strongest points of inspiration at the outset of the Civil War. Warren was the first American officer killed in the Revolutionary War, and he occupied a central place in both national and regional Revolutionary memories. Through the first half of the nineteenth century, Warren's fame had persisted as Bunker Hill itself grew in national esteem as a tourist destination and the site of the country's most impressive Revolutionary War monument. Warren's memory also seemed to prove the worthiness of sacrificing life in the interests of preserving political values, as he was styled as a glorious martyr to liberty. Many commentators invoked Warren in the opening days of the Civil War both to motivate men and to offer them an example to emulate—even unto death. Bunker Hill stood as a great national symbol and as a particular symbol of New England strength in public memory, and both themes would play into its influence in 1861.

Joseph Warren's memory was used throughout the Revolutionary War to call for soldiers to "avenge his death" by fighting hard, a fact that seemed newly relevant in the spring of 1861.[13] One anonymous Southern Unionist pamphleteer looked to Warren for motivation as he wrestled with the painful fact that the beginning of the war meant that men like him would have to fight their fellow Southerners—something he knew they would be loathe to do. He searched for a way to offer both comfort and resolve to Unionists gearing up for the fight. The 1861 pamphlet *The Trial of Faith* reprinted Barnabas Binney's broadside poem "Lines Sacred to the Memory of Joseph Warren" that had rallied Americans to the Revolutionary cause in July 1775. The poem painted Warren as a republican hero, lavished praise on him for "nobly" bleeding for freedom, and advised those who remembered Warren's bravery to "Banish hence your ev'ry Fear." The 1861 pamphleteer told his readers, "Behold the faith that bore the mighty soul of Warren . . . up to the Bunker Hill baptism! That Faith is here to-day! There is here to-day power enough to meet this emergency." He told his readers that Warren had no American martyrs to welcome him into heaven when he sacrificed himself for the cause of liberty in 1775, "But now the ministering angels at the side of Warren are a legion of heavenly hosts . . . smiling on the American Union. And shall not the men of to-day keep the Faith?" According to the anxious pamphleteer, the memory of the Revolutionary martyr should spur loyal Southerners to fight for the United States in the Civil War, and if they sacrificed their own lives to protect the Union, Warren would greet them in "immortal glory."[14] Bloody sacrifice for Unionism thus became equated to Warren's foundational heroism that had first helped to create the Union.

Northern commentators also picked up this theme and urged emulation of Joseph Warren's sacrifice for the American union. When four Massachusetts troops were killed in rioting in Baltimore on April 19, 1861—the anniversary of the Battles of Lexington and Concord—many Northern newspapers and orators likened them to the early martyrs of the Revolution, including Warren. William Burleigh wrote in a newspaper poem that the dead soldiers from the Sixth Massachusetts had shed "Blood of the martyrs! Holily imbued With power redemptive for our periled land" just like Warren and those killed at Lexington and Concord.[15] A newspaper in Bangor, Maine, commented, "Southerners have foolishly believed that our northern troops would not fight, but they had at Baltimore a small specimen of the pluck of Yankee boys. If they have forgotten Bunker Hill, they now have something else to remember."[16] At the funeral of Corporal Sumner Needham, one of the Massachusetts volunteers killed in Baltimore, drums used at Lexington and at Bunker Hill sounded the funeral roll, as, in the words of an Illinois newspaper report, he was "tenderly laid beneath the soil which smoked with the first sacrificial blood of the Revolution."[17]

The first Union officer killed in the Civil War one month after the Baltimore riots invited even closer comparison to Joseph Warren. Colonel Elmer Ellsworth, a former law student of Abraham Lincoln who had organized a highly publicized Zouave unit of New York City firefighters, was killed in Alexandria, Virginia, on May 24, 1861, the day after Virginia seceded from the Union. After Ellsworth's men had easily secured the city, he entered the Marshall House Hotel, intent on removing the large Confederate flag displayed there by the hotel's owner, James W. Jackson. After Ellsworth cut down the flag, Jackson shot him and was, in turn, killed by Ellsworth's aide, Corporal Francis Brownell. Although some newspapers called Ellsworth's sortie against the Confederate flag a folly,

Ellsworth was immediately hailed as the first great martyr to the Union cause.[18]

The 1861 skirmish in Alexandria was quite different from the pitched battle at Bunker Hill in June 1775, but Ellsworth immediately stood out in Northern popular culture as an analogue to Joseph Warren. One of several popular portrait engravings of Ellsworth paired him with Joseph Warren above the caption "The First Officer Killed in the Revolution, Warren—The First Officer Killed in the Present Rebellion—Ellsworth."[19] Newspapers across the North lamented Ellsworth's death but praised his ability, as a martyr, to motivate enlistments—just as Warren's martyrdom had inspired generations of Americans before. The *Daily Citizen and News* in Lowell, Massachusetts, for example, commented,

> The fall of the gallant Colonel Ellsworth . . . is one of those sad incidents of war which are to be looked for where the bravest men, seemingly self-forgetful, eagerly rush to the defense of their country's flag. But how terrible is the retribution which is sure to follow the sacrifice of such a man in so noble a cause! The public mind turns at once to another young leader, whose blood moistened the soil of Bunker Hill in the opening battle-scene of the revolution. Ellsworth was the idol of his command as was Warren in the other conflict.[20]

Ellsworth, who had gained fame by training a company of National Guard cadets before the war, wrote a popular military drill manual that was now republished for Civil War soldiers with a biography of its author appended. The brief biography told its soldier readers that Ellsworth's "memory will be revered, his name respected, and long after the rebellion shall have become a matter of history, his death will be regarded as a martyrdom, and his name will be enrolled upon the list of our country's patriots, by the side of Warren and others who fell among the first in the Revolution in defense of their country."[21] Heroic death would never be forgotten.

The impetus behind linking Ellsworth's sacrifice to the memory of the Revolutionary War and to Joseph Warren was to move the public to action. Ellsworth, like Warren, must inspire men to fight. The New Jersey Atlantic Democrat editor claimed, "The death of Col. Ellsworth will mark an era in the history of this war, and his name will hereafter stand by the side of Warren, and others who fell among the first in the Revolution in defense of their country. . . . The effect of his murder will be to intensify the war feeling in the North, and to furnish a battle-cry in future conflicts!"[22] A paper in Sandusky, Ohio, added that Ellsworth's name would be "enrolled by the side of that of Warren and the other braves who died upon the altar of Human Liberty," because he became a "sacrifice, that in his wicked death the cause might be sealed and the people be aroused to avenge his blood.—And truly they will do it."[23] A quick biography of Ellsworth published a few months after his death commented on his power to motivate the fight, in the mold of Warren: "The death of Ellsworth, like that of Warren on Bunker Hill, will send a thrill of indignant rage throughout the land. His blood will cement the covenant to which our armed hosts have sworn, to count their lives as nothing in support of their cause."[24] Evidence indicates that at least some members of the Northern public responded to such calls: a newly formed company of Zouaves dubbed themselves "The Ellsworth Avengers," and two popular songs and a recruiting pamphlet went by the same name.[25]

The thirst for vengeance continued when other Union officers killed early in the war also drew comparisons to Warren. In particular, Nathaniel Lyon and Senator Edward Baker became martyrs similar to Warren in the eyes of their eulogists and in public memory. Lyon, who had controversially ordered his men to fire on secessionist rioters in Saint Louis in May 1861, was brigadier general in charge of Union troops in Missouri when he was killed at the Battle of Wilson's Creek on August 10, 1861. Lyon's actions at Wilson's Creek were credited with helping to prevent Missouri from joining the Confederacy. Baker, meanwhile, had been elected to the U.S. Senate from Oregon in 1860 and was serving as a major general with the Pennsylvania Volunteers when he was killed at the Battle of Balls Bluff on October 21, 1861.[26] Both men were commemorated in a manner specifically intended to draw political support for the Union and enlistments.

Neither Lyon nor Baker called Bunker Hill to mind as extensively as Ellsworth had, but nevertheless they too seemed to offer the possibility of motivating revenge and enlistment. Kansas senator Samuel Clarke Pomeroy eulogized Lyon on the floor of the U.S. Senate by calling him "the Warren of this war."[27] When Lyon was buried in Connecticut, Pennsylvania Congressman Galusha A. Grow compared him to another Bunker Hill officer, Connecticut hero Israel Putnam, before assuring mourners that Lyon's memory would demand "vengeance" against secessionists.[28] The fiery political preacher Thomas Starr King officiated at

Baker's burial service in California, where he told the crowd not to despair because a great man "is a seed. . . . It germinates thus in this world as well as in the other." Like Joseph Warren, Baker's "seed" would bear the fruit of public inspiration: "Was Warren *buried?* . . . No; the monument that has been raised where his blood reddened the sod . . . is a feeble witness of the permanence and influence of his spirit among the American people."[29] The linking of past and present martyrs was similarly made in visual representations. For instance, a Currier and Ives print titled *Death of Col. Edward D. Baker, at the Battle of Balls Bluff* closely resembled John Trumbull's 1786 history painting, *The Death of Dr. Warren at the Battle of Bunker Hill,* which had also been reproduced in many popular nineteenth-century engravings.[30] Just as Revolutionaries had looked to emulate Warren, a new generation could now gaze on Baker's martyrdom as an inspiration to march off to war.

Confederate supporters did not as widely invoke memories of the martyred Joseph Warren to bolster their own cause, but they were not content to let Unionists and Northerners monopolize the memory of Bunker Hill. As a symbol of Revolutionary military defiance, the battle could occasionally be used to boost the Confederate cause, and sometimes Confederates and Democrats used Bunker Hill references to label New Englanders as fanatics. The North Carolina correspondent to the Democratic *New York Herald,* for example, argued in January 1861 that New England was a "cancer" that "must be severed" from the Union because of its antislavery radicalism. The correspondent assured readers that Southerners would "always honor" the memory of "Bunker Hill, and Concord, and Lexington, and the graves of her great and noble patriots, whose devotion to the constitution [New England] has ceased to imitate."[31] In this Southern Democratic formulation, New Englanders' radicalism had led them to forfeit the right to monopolize Bunker Hill memory.

The Revolutionary memory of Bunker Hill remained a national symbol, available to mobilize both Northerners and Southerners. But the traditional nationalist purpose of Bunker Hill—to motivate military action against a tyrannical foe—instead split the regions in this new civil war. Confederates sometimes used Bunker Hill as a national symbol of defiance, even when they simultaneously argued for Southern exceptionalism. Virginia senator James Murray Mason famously remarked early in 1861 that he would never visit Bunker Hill again "unless I come as an ambassador."[32] During the bombardment of Fort Sumter, a Virginia correspondent to the *Charleston Courier* wrote a piece called "The Plain Truth," using memories of Southern heroism in the Revolutionary War to stir readers to action in the impending conflict. The writer assured Charlestonians that "George Washington and the brave men who co-operated with him" had not hesitated to prove to the British which side would win in a fight between "a government resolved on despotism and a people determined on freedom." Northerners' emphasis on Bunker Hill irked him, since "the people of Virginia, we know, won their freedom and independence without the assistance of a Northern army. . . . While Virginia bones whitened every battlefield from Charleston to Bunker Hill, when we were invaded, we received not the aid of a man from the Northern States."[33]

The New Orleans *True Delta* similarly likened the beginning of the Civil War to the outset of the Revolution by assuring readers that Confederates were playing the role of the patriots at Bunker Hill. The first blood of the Civil War shed in the Baltimore riots, the editor wrote, "has as effectually separated the slave from the free states as the battle of Bunker Hill did that of the old thirteen colonies from the mother country."[34] Bunker Hill, in this formula, signaled a break from domination, seemingly appropriate to secessionists, even as they mobilized men to fight to protect the dearly held tradition of slavery. The national symbol took on a paradoxically regional function.

Public memory of heroism in an early Southern Revolutionary battle—the Battle of Sullivan's Island—showed a similar pattern, but with the regional roles reversed. Residents of Charleston, South Carolina, had long celebrated the anniversary of the June 28, 1776, battle as a regional holiday, Palmetto Day. Until the 1850s celebrations of the battle, in which American forces had repulsed British assault on Fort Moultrie, had mixed regional pride and nationalist themes, but the celebration had become increasingly sectionalist and belligerent in the years immediately preceding the Civil War.

Sergeant William Jasper, who had kept the Palmetto flag flying over Fort Moultrie in the midst of the battle, had been hailed as both a regional and national hero.[35] Since Sullivan's Island was in sight of Fort Sumter in the Charleston harbor, it was only natural that public memory of Jasper and his heroism should play a role in the reactions to the opening of the Civil War.[36] Just as Southerners tried to claim the mantle of Bunker Hill, some Northerners fastened on Jasper's memory to both ennoble their own cause and bash the Confederacy. For example, one Philadelphia newspaper poem claimed that Elmer Ellsworth's "fame" would exceed William Jasper's because, while the latter had heroically saved a flag, Ellsworth had "torn down Disunion's Rag."[37] One San Francisco newspaper published a "Song for the Volunteers" that claimed Union soldiers could "glory . . . in a sergeant Jasper story" because he "was true to the Union in Dixie Land."[38] Just as some Southerners had used Warren and Bunker Hill, some Northerners used Jasper and Fort Moultrie to delegitimize the military choices of their rivals.

Southerners did not give up Jasper's name without a fight, however. *New York Times* correspondent and native Charlestonian George Salter signed his pro-Southern dispatches from Charleston in late 1860 and early 1861 under the penname of "Jasper." The name took on a cruel irony in the days surrounding Fort Sumter, when General P. G. T. Beauregard arrested Salter as a "federal spy," jailed him, and then expelled him from the city because he worked for a Northern newspaper.[39] Southerners fought to maintain control of Jasper as a symbol of Southern pride. The *Richmond Daily Whig* wrote of James W. Jackson, the man who shot Elmer Ellsworth: "The name of Jackson shall be enshrined in the heart of Virginia, as the name of Jasper in South Carolina, and recorded upon the brightest pages of her history."[40] Southern newspapers could not let go of Jasper as a symbol of Southern resistance, because his memory was needed to stir Confederate fighting spirit.

The battle over Revolutionary military memory was a symbolic struggle with real-world stakes in the first months of the U.S. Civil War, as the conflict claimed its first victims. The part of American national identity predicated on the sacrifice of Revolutionary heroes appealed to both Northerners and Southerners, and invoking Revolutionary sacrifice proved an effective way to fan patriotic flames in both regions. The uses of Revolutionary memory contained several layers of irony, as national symbols such as Bunker Hill were used by people on both sides of the conflict to justify their own military sacrifices and to delegitimize their opponents. The same image could be used to justify mobilization for exactly opposite causes. Beyond justifying rival politics, these uses of Revolutionary public memory inspired violence. As the men of the Second Vermont Regiment marched through New York City and were reminded of their Revolutionary forebears in speeches and with evergreen tributes, they were marching off to kill and be killed.

By likening their own martyrs and heroes to William Jasper or Joseph Warren, both Southerners and Northerners linked themselves to a long history of American national identity. But by using nationalist symbols of Revolutionary memory to justify their own causes, Union supporters and Confederates now drove a strong wedge between the sections as they mobilized for war. Memories of Revolutionary bloodshed in the early months of the Civil War begat not unity, as they had in the early days of the republic, but more bloodshed.

NOTES

1. "News of the Day," *New York Times*, June 26, 1861; "Local Military Movements; Arrival of the Second Vermont Regiment . . . ," *New York Times*, June 26, 1861; Paul G. Zellner, *The Second Vermont Volunteer Infantry Regiment, 1861–1865* (Jefferson, N.C.: McFarland, 2002), 17. On Culver, see "Culver, Erastus Dean (1803–1889)," *Biographical Directory of the United States Congress*, http://bioguide.congress.gov/scripts/biodisplay.pl?index=C000978.
2. "Arrival and Departure of the Second Regiment of Vermont," *New York Herald*, June 26, 1861.
3. George Grenville Benedict, *Vermont in the Civil War: A History of the Part Taken by the Vermont Soldiers and Sailors in the War for the Union, 1861–1865*, vol. 1 (Burlington, Vt.: The Free Press Association, 1886), 67–68.
4. James P. Swain, presentation letter, March 24, 1875, quoted in "Historic Sources on the Concord Fight," *Concord Magazine*, January–February 2000, www.concordma.com/magazine/janfeb00/barrett.html; Frederic C. Detwiller, *Col. James Barrett Farm Historic Structure Report* (Georgetown, Mass.: New England Landmarks, 2008), 49, 64–65.
5. Benedict, *Vermont in the Civil War*, 72–80.
6. James M. McPherson, *Battle Cry of Freedom: The Civil War Era* (New York: Oxford University Press, 1988), 241–45; William W. Freehling, *The Road to Disunion*, vol. 2 (NewYork: Oxford University Press, 2007), 346–47; Robert P. Sutton, *Revolution to Secession: Constitution Making in the Old Dominion* (Charlottesville: University Press of Virginia, 1989); William A. Link, *Roots of Secession: Slavery and Politics in Antebellum Virginia* (Chapel Hill: University of North Carolina Press, 2003), 226–27, 230, 246; Robert E. Bonner, *Mastering America: Southern Slaveholders and the Crisis of American Nationhood* (New York: Cambridge University Press, 2009), 255–64.
7. Charles S. Watson, "Simms and the Civil War: The Revolutionary Analogy," *Southern Literary Journal* 24 (March 1992): 77–78; Bonner, *Mastering America*, 155–58.

8. Sarah J. Purcell, *Sealed with Blood: War, Sacrifice, and Memory in Revolutionary America* (Philadelphia: University of Pennsylvania Press, 2002).
9. William Lloyd Garrison, "I Will Be Heard," *Liberator*, January 1, 1831; Henry Highland Garnet, "An Address to the Slaves of the United States of America, Buffalo, N.Y., 1843," *Electronic Texts in American Studies* 8, http://digitalcommons.unl.edu/cgi/viewcontent.cgi?article=1007&context=etas.
10. Bonner, *Mastering America*, 151–52.
11. Jonathan B. Crider, "De Bow's Revolution: The Memory of the American Revolution in the Politics of the Sectional Crisis, 1850–1861," *American Nineteenth Century History* 10 (September 2009): 321–24.
12. *Newark (N.J.) Daily Advertiser*, May 27, 1861; Jeremiah Burns, *The Patriot's Offering; or, The Life, Services, and Military Career of the Noble Trio, Ellsworth, Lyon, and Baker* (New York: Baker & Godwin, 1862), 27.
13. Hugh Henry Brackenridge quoted in Purcell, *Sealed with Blood*, 33.
14. *The Trial of Faith* (n.p., 1861), in the collection of the American Antiquarian Society, Worcester, Mass.; Barnabas Binney, *Lines Sacred to the Memory of the Late Major-General Joseph Warren* (Providence: John Carter, 1775).
15. William Burleigh, "April 19, 1861," *Daily Citizen and News* (Lowell, Mass.), May 23, 1861. See also Stephen M. Klugewicz, "The First Martyrs: The Sixth Massachusetts and the Baltimore Riot of 1861," *Southern Historian* 20 (1999): 17.
16. *Bangor (Maine) Daily Whig and Courier*, May 8, 1861.
17. "The Funeral of Corporal Needam," *Pittsfield (Mass.) Sun*, May 9, 1861; "In Memoriam," *Illinois Journal* (Springfield), May 15, 1861.
18. Ruth Painter Randall, *Colonel Elmer Ellsworth: A Biography of Lincoln's Friend and First Hero of the Civil War* (Boston: Little, Brown, 1960); William C. Winter, "The Zouaves Take St. Louis," *Gateway Heritage* 19 (1999): 20–29.
19. J. C. Upham, "The First Officer . . . ," in *The Union Image: Popular Prints of the Civil War North*, ed. Mark Neely Jr. and Harold Holzer (Chapel Hill: University of North Carolina Press, 2000), 28.
20. *Daily Citizen and News*, May 25, 1861.
21. Elmer Ellsworth, *The Zouave Drill . . . with a Biography of His Life* (Philadelphia: Peterson & Brothers, [1861]), vi.
22. *Atlantic Democrat* (Egg Harbor, N.J.), May 25, 1861. See also *Newark Daily Advertiser*, May 25, 1861.
23. *Daily Commercial Register* (Sandusky, Ohio), May 25, 1861.
24. *Biography of Col. E. E. Ellsworth* (Cincinnati: Mumford, 1861).
25. A. S. Hudson, "Ellsworth Avengers!" (Baltimore: Doyle, [1861]), Archive of Americana, American Antiquarian Society.
26. "Nathaniel Lyon," Civil War Trust, 2011, www.civilwar.org/education/history/biographies/nathanial-lyon.html; Ashbel Woodward, *Life of General Nathaniel Lyon* (Hart-ford, Conn.: Case, Lockwood, 1862); "Baker, Edward Dickinson (1811–1861)," *Biographical Directory of the United States Congress*, http://bioguide.congress.gov/biosearch/biosearch.asp.
27. *Obituary Addresses of Messrs. Pomeroy, Dixon, and Foster on the Death of Brigadier General Lyon: Delivered in the Senate of the United States, December 20, 1861* (Washington, D.C.: Congressional Globe Office, 1861).
28. Galusha A. Grow quoted in Burns, *Patriot's Offering*, 51, 54.

29. Thomas Starr King quoted in Burns, *Patriot's Offering*, 80–81.
30. *The Death of Col. Edward D. Baker, at the Battle of Balls Bluff near Leesburg VA, Oct. 21st 1861* (New York: Currier & Ives, [1861?]).
31. "Our Raleigh Correspondent," *New York Herald*, January 12, 1861.
32. *Virginia Free Press and Family Journal*, February 7, 1861; "Mason and Winthrop," *Daily Citizen and News*, January 22, 1861.
33. "The Plain Truth," *Charleston (S.C.) Courier*, April 13, 1861.
34. "The Union For Ever Dissolved," *Daily True Delta* (New Orleans, La.), April 21, 1861. For a similar view that the civilians killed in Baltimore violated the spirit of Bunker Hill, see "War," *The American Farmer, a Monthly Magazine of Agriculture and Horticulture*, May 1861, 338.
35. Purcell, *Sealed with Blood*, 44–48, 211–12.
36. Comments on the proximity of Sullivan's Island and Fort Sumter feature in "Latest Details from Charleston," *Sun* (Baltimore), January 1, 1861.
37. M. D. O., untitled poem, *Press* (Philadelphia, Pa.), May 28, 1861.
38. "We'll Never Give up Dixie!," *Bulletin* (San Francisco), September 20, 1861.
39. *New York Times*, March 12, April 9, 12, 15, May 5, 1861. Other papers followed the story of "Jasper's" arrest; see *Inquirer* (Philadelphia, Pa.), April 16, 1861; *Liberator*, May 3, 1861; J. Cutler Andrews, *The North Reports the Civil War* (Pittsburgh: University of Pittsburgh Press, 1955), 18.
40. "The Martyr Jackson," *Richmond (Va.) Daily Whig*, May 30, 1861.

Old-Fashioned Tea Parties

Revolutionary Memory in Civil War Sanitary Fairs

Frances M. Clarke

In early 1864 an invitation was issued to visitors at the Northern Ohio Sanitary Fair to attend a "Continental tea-party" in the "costume and style of 1776." Invitees entered a room with ten lavishly decorated tables, around which sat men dressed to represent well-known Revolutionary figures, from Jefferson, Madison, and Monroe, to an assortment of generals, all accompanied by their wives. A performer in the guise of George Washington occupied the center table, along with his ersatz spouse and mother. Punch bowls, silverware, china, and a variety of treasured heirlooms—some of them said to have been used by the great man himself—covered the tables, which were waited on by liveried black servants. Frozen in place at first, the actors came alive to mingle among the guests as the evening wore on, keeping in character as they held conversations and answered questions about their Revolutionary roles. There were no rowdy mobs to disturb the proceedings, such as those that had gathered at the original Boston Tea Party. But to spice up their tableau, the performers did include several white men dressed as Indians, who were probably employed (as they were in other fair performances) to run through the room occasionally, whooping menacingly to add an element of surprise to an otherwise genteel spectacle.[1]

This "tea party" performance was one of the many evocations of the Revolution on display at the dozens of sanitary fairs held in the North in the last year and half of the Civil War. Organized to raise money for sick and wounded soldiers, these events transfixed wartime audiences, drawing tremendous crowds to their unique panoply of temporary buildings, decorated stalls, art exhibitions, gigantic floral displays, curiosity departments, armories, period rooms, and costumed performances.[2] Fair organizers routinely used memories of the Revolution in their opening speeches and parades. They massed Revolutionary-era items and images in their displays of weapons, artwork and "relics." And they paid obeisance to the founding generation in colonial-themed kitchens, theatricals, and tableaux.

These fairs consolidated two trends in memorialization discussed elsewhere in this collection. As Sarah J. Purcell notes in the preceding chapter, both Unionists and Confederates relied on memories of the Revolution to give their war efforts the stamp of tradition. Fair organizers similarly drew on a patriotic lineage to generate loyalty for their cause by donning the dress and manners of their forebears and surrounding themselves with items from the past. Constantly referring to the founders' threatened legacy and self-sacrifice, they worked to establish the Union as a sacred entity—a task made all the more pressing given the extent to which their enemies drew on the very same heritage to authorize their rebellion. Likewise, their visions of the past reflected the domestication of Revolutionary memory charted by Michael A. McDonnell, James Paxton, and others.[3] Erasing a complex Revolutionary history of plebeian uprisings and loyalist struggles and of shifting landscapes of power occupied by Native Americans, slaves, and women, fair organizers imagined instead a conflict-free past of elite founders dedicated to creating and maintaining a unified republic.

Yet beneath this filiopietism, strong countercurrents were evolving during the war years, working to minimize the significance of the Revolution as America's founding moment—cutting its heroes down to size and rendering their achievements less inspiring than they had once seemed. Scholars have noted this transition in memory, suggesting that the Revolution had come to seem a distant event by the postbellum era, still seen as worthy of grateful remembrance, to be sure, but not as formative in its political impact as the Civil War. Criticisms of the founders (especially their failure to deal adequately with the issue of slavery) were now voiced openly. Bumping Washington from his pedestal, Lincoln would become the most celebrated icon of the newly reunified nation, with works dedicated to his memory outstripping those of the nation's first father two to one by the 1870s.[4]

In some ways this revisionism was determined by the extent of the Civil War, which dwarfed the Revolution in absolute terms in both size and impact, drawing in millions of men and leaving hundreds of thousands killed or maimed. But privileged Unionists also quite consciously remade the Revolution at this time, sanitizing their heritage and portraying their own efforts as grander and more crucial than those of their predecessors. At the center of these efforts were middle-class Northern women. Contributing to the domestication of Revolutionary memory that began in the antebellum era, they focused on the private virtues of men like Washington—always pictured now, as he was in the tea party described earlier, together with his wife or mother (who had also become a commemorative focus by this time). Their tea drinking was not an entirely serious business; it contained more than a hint of parody.[5]

Pioneering novel ways of performing and experiencing Revolutionary memory, fair organizers helped to create a long-dead era when oddly named men and women dressed in unfashionable outfits and made their own food and clothing, where slaves were safely off to the political sidelines, and Native Americans merely added picturesque color to colonial life. Inviting citizens to participate in the past as spectators and purchasers, they imagined a Revolution that was safe and consumable in its quaintness and oddity—quite distinct and remote from the war in which they participated. Simultaneously emulating and distancing themselves from the past, they set up their own period as one of modernity and transformation, a "second founding" that was grander than their forebears' achievements.

Attitudes toward the past were ambivalent and contradictory in antebellum America. On the one hand, reverence for the founders reached its zenith in the 1850s, as middle-class educators, biographers, and families sought to create a "useable past" by focusing on the character of Revolutionary elites to inculcate civic virtue and morality in the nation's youth.[6] On the other hand, public discourse celebrated the nation as young and novel, a country lacking in history, with only a present and a future. "In America, each generation is a new people," and "no one cares for what occurred before his time," wrote Alexis de Tocqueville in 1831. Believing they had banished the dead weight of precedent, Americans expressed little reverence for their history. The subject was not a required part of most educational curricula; landmark buildings were torn down or fell into disrepair; and attempts to erect monuments honoring Revolutionary events or individuals foundered time and again on the shoals of indifference or local disagreement.[7]

This willful public forgetfulness and simultaneous hero worship of forebears were intricately connected, according to historian George B. Forgie. For if filiopietism was needed to consolidate the nation by providing a unifying set of symbols, it also established America's elite founders as peerless and supreme, generating hostility as well as reverence. The children and grandchildren of Revolutionary participants were a "post heroic generation" in Forgie's analysis, destined to safeguard the legacy handed down by their predecessors but incapable of measuring up to their achievements and reaping similar respect—a generation doomed "to *preserve*, and not to create," to use the words of Charles Francis Adams. Seeking to escape "the father's debt," agrees historian David Lowenthal, Americans "denigrated the past more intensely . . . than any culture before or since," even as they held up the founders as incomparable individuals.[8]

The Civil War marked a transformation in public celebrations of the Revolutionary past. In wartime fairs the Revolution would become a long-gone era, its memorabilia newly worthy of collecting and putting behind glass, but no longer a time that evoked tacit hostility alongside respectful obeisance. Sanitary fairs contributed greatly to this transformation. Most of the scholarship on Revolutionary memory focuses on men's public pronouncements and celebrations. But as Keith Beutler's chapter points out, women played a crucial part in shaping memory in this period.[9] As moral mothers they were supposed to nurture connections between the living and the dead, preserving memory and transmitting it to subsequent generations in their roles as chief mourners, custodians of family heirlooms, and educators of the young. Their wartime fairs would presage a rage in the postbellum years for Martha Washington tea parties and historical preservation efforts of the kind charted in Matthew Mason's chapter for the prewar years.[10]

The first large-scale sanitary fair was held in Chicago over a two-week period beginning in late October 1863. Months of planning preceded the event, with solicitations sent out far and wide requesting financial donations and organizational assistance, handmade goods for sale, and curiosities, artworks, and items for display. Combining the charity bazaar format, featuring tables stocked with ladies' handiwork, and that of regional fairs and international expositions, showcasing machinery, produce, and livestock, the Northwestern Fair successfully drew in a broad cross-section of the population, far exceeding expectations by clearing seventy-eight thousand dollars in profits. This marked the beginning of what the press called "fair mania." Approximately two dozen mammoth sanitary fairs took place over the next year and a half in cities from Saint Louis to New York. Most ran for a number of weeks, with several earning proceeds that ran into the millions (the New York Metropolitan Fair, for instance, made more than two million dollars), most of which filled the coffers of the United States Sanitary Commission—a wartime voluntary organization that lent the fairs its name. Middle-class women did the bulk of the fair organizing. Keeping a close eye on their counterparts elsewhere, they traveled to fairs in neighboring cities and towns or corresponded with their organizers, copying their methods as well as adding their own innovations.[11]

Revolutionary memory was not particularly prominent in the first Chicago fair. Yet it would take up increasing space in later events, as women organizers gained knowledge of the kinds of entertainment, amusements, and exhibits with greatest public appeal. In 1864 both the Albany Army Relief Bazaar and the Brooklyn and Long Island Sanitary Fair fixed on the anniversary of Washington's birth to stage their inauguration galas. Reminders of the Revolution were everywhere at both of these events. In his opening speech, George Thacher, president of the Albany bazaar, asked assembled visitors to think about how Washington would have felt about the current crisis before reminding them that they owed it to his memory to "do all in your power to cheer the hearts and nerve the arms" of Union soldiers who now held "the destiny of our country in their hands." After listening to his address, fairgoers could wander through exhibits that connected them in more tangible ways to the Revolutionary past, moving past a Yankee Booth, with women in Revolutionary-era dress standing alongside a model of the Bunker Hill monument made of parched corn, for instance, or examining the Military Trophies Room that housed a range of flags and weapons used in the Revolutionary War.[12]

Visitors to the much grander Brooklyn and Long Island Sanitary Fair entered two buildings specially erected for the purpose: a two-story-high structure, one hundred by sixty-eight feet, housing a restaurant called Knickerbocker Hall and a single-story building of one hundred square feet containing the Hall of Manufactures and a sizable room called the New England Kitchen. In the first building they were greeted with a mass of evergreen boughs interspersed with flags and bunting that covered every available inch of wall or column. At the end of the hall, a large portrait of Washington hung on the back wall surrounded by miniature flags.[13] More images and items from the Revolutionary era were displayed in the Art Gallery and Curiosity Shop as well. Replicating many of these attractions, subsequent fairs typically contained period rooms, exhibitions of art and armory, elaborate floral halls, curiosity shops, and themed booths decorated to represent particular national groups—with wigwams and Yankee booths being especially ubiquitous.

Fairs offered audiences a rare opportunity to wander among the traces of the past. In the prewar years ordinary people had access to scattered items of historical interest—at P. T. Barnum's famous New York museum, for instance, or at George Washington Parke Custis's Arlington estate, described in Seth C. Bruggeman's chapter—but museums dedicated to Americana did not yet exist.[14] The curiosity departments and armory exhibits in wartime sanitary fairs signaled a new interest in collecting and displaying items from the country's past. Organized in the midst of another war and at a moment of intense nationalism, Revolutionary-era curiosities were among the most common and popular fair exhibitions. Most came from private individuals, in response to flyers sent out by fair organizers. Those in charge of the New York Metropolitan Fair's Curiosity Shop, for instance, requested "relics of old, the historical and revolutionary times, and of the rebellion," as well as seeking "Indian curiosities and manufactures . . . personal or household ornaments; minerals and shells, stuffed birds and animals," and a jumble of other material valued either for its "beauty" or "grotesqueness."[15] Items from the Revolutionary War were thus framed by a hodgepodge of old and new, natural and human made, inexpensive and valuable. Visitors to the Albany fair's Curiosity Shop could examine a lock of Washington's hair, his camp chest, tent, writing case, razor, fire shovel, pistol, sword, and coat; a musket used at Bunker Hill; Madison's cane; Revolutionary-era currency; and dozens of similar items. Scattered among them were more venerable and bizarre objects: lava from Mount Vesuvius; a pebble from the Dead Sea; nails from a house in Pompeii; a pistol brought over on the Mayflower; an Indian skeleton; a witch's death warrant; coins and linen from ancient Egypt; petrified fish remains, and so on.[16]

Commentators recognized that the opportunity to examine so many Revolutionary-era objects all at once was a unique experience. Boasting about the Albany fair's Curiosity Shop, one article in the fair's daily newspaper noted, "There is no museum like it in the country, and we probably never again will have so rare and valuable a collection. The Washington memorials, of priceless value and great national interest, are alone worth the price of admission." Another commentator was struck with equal force by the novelty and popularity of a similar display at the Metropolitan Fair's Curiosity Shop. Marveling that no "shrewd Yankee" had previously thought to put together such a collection, he concluded that it was exactly "what a true museum should be."[17] As these writers acknowledged, the fairs' innovation did not lay simply in exhibiting a host of curious items. Indeed, early American museums tended to be organized in precisely this way, showcasing "collections of random and unconnected objects."[18] What *was* novel, however, was the volume and variety of the Americana gathered. Generating immense crowds, these fairs demonstrated the value and appeal of Revolutionary-era objects and imagery in particular.

There was little to guide fairgoers in interpreting this material. Some fairs had printed catalogs listing each object displayed in curiosity departments alongside a brief note on the item's provenance or historical association to justify its inclusion. Several also hired ushers dressed in Revolutionary-era garb to answer patrons' questions.[19] But there were no accepted modes of categorizing historical objects or additional explanatory texts beyond these minimal aids to facilitate or guide understanding. Given the legendary status of fakes and hoaxes in antebellum culture, it is likely that many fairgoers retained a healthy dose of skepticism when it came to confronting an alleged lock of Washington's hair or a set of his fire tongs. Lacking a well-established museum culture to lend its imprimatur to what they were seeing, viewers could never be sure that what they were examining was genuine—a fact that might well have added to the appeal of these displays.

The fair organizers who put these collections together and the writers who commented on them usually referred to Revolutionary items as "relics," a word that held sacred, wistful, and disparaging connotations. A "relic" in this period could suggest a fragment of the past, suggestive but incomplete; a rare surviving trace of a long-ago time; or a "residue of a nation or people." In a more derogatory sense, a "relic" implied something outmoded and unfashionable, a person or thing "left over from an earlier era." Yet it might also denote an object invested with hallowed associations, "sanctified by contact" with someone considered holy or worthy of adulation.[20] There is no way to know precisely which of these definitions fairgoers brought to the "relics" they examined. What is clear is that curiosity departments placed objects from the Revolutionary past in such a way that all eras were conflated—with Washington's breeches placed on a par with ancient Egyptian coins or the Mayflower voyage, rendering them all equally anachronistic.

Fairgoers were a mere few generations removed from their Revolutionary forebears. In collapsing this more recent past into a single category, fair organizers fixed the Revolution as a long-ago era, far removed from the present—as distant as the landing at Plymouth Rock or the Salem witch trials. Enhancing this sense of historical remoteness, visitors passed by exhibitions of gleaming new machinery before entering curiosity departments, for many fairs displayed the latest advances in American manufactures, ranging from sewing machines to ploughs. Appearing alongside this evidence of technological progress, Revolutionary-era relics, merged in with petrified fish remains or specimens of ancient porcelain, could not but appear ancient and quaint, despite their comparatively recent vintage.

A similar conflation of American history existed in the New England kitchens or period rooms set up in wartime fairs. Offering visitors an opportunity to live vicariously in the past, these rooms were among the most well attended and widely discussed fair attractions.[21] Many were specifically designed to represent Revolutionary life, as organizers for the

Brooklyn fair made explicit. A circular sent by the planning committee to potential donors informed them of the intent to "reproduce the manners, customs, dress, and if possible, the idiom of the time; in short to illustrate the domestic life and habits of the people, to whose determined courage sustained by their faith in God, we owe that government, so dear to every loyal heart. The period fixed upon is just prior to the throwing overboard of the tea in Boston Harbor."

Two long tables ran down the center of this New England Kitchen. The wall on the far right was taken up with a massive fireplace, topped by a mantle containing a large Bible. Around the room were various items of historical interest, such as a table once belonging to Plymouth colony governor William Bradford, a clock with a face smashed by a British bullet during the Revolution, and an antique dresser holding wooden bowls, pewter mugs, and old iron pots.[22] Much like curiosity departments, period rooms thus fused together the entirety of American history, establishing equivalence between the distant Puritan era and that of the Revolution.

Adding to the sense that they had stepped back into a long-ago time, diners were surrounded by women performing the household functions or wearing the clothing of their colonial forebears. At a platform at the front of the kitchen, one woman in period dress sat at a spinning wheel, evoking an age of homespun cloth. Two others were engaged in knitting stockings by the hearth, while another, dressed in a homespun pinafore, checkered apron, pointed shoes, and woolen stockings, with her hair held up in a high comb, stood cooking at the fireplace. Some eight to ten hundred visitors per day paid fifty cents to sit down at tables appointed with "old fashioned china" and two-tined forks to eat what was billed as the plain fare of earlier times—from pork and beans to doughnuts and apple cider—served by costumed attendants.[23]

In the evenings, the middle-class women involved in setting up this fair held a range of performances that similarly evoked the nation's past. On opening night they staged a series of readings, musical recitals, and *tableaux vivants* at the Brooklyn Athenaeum, most of which revolved around Washington. The New England Kitchen provided the stage for a number of additional entertainments, including a "spinners frolic," an "apple-paring frolic," and a "quilting party," followed by a "donation party," which sought to illustrate the way "pastors of the early days" raised money by visiting congregants' homes. The festivities culminated in a mock New

England wedding, "according to the form and usages of the Puritans," succeeded by a dance "after 'ye ancient fashion of our fathers.' " Elements of the Puritan era were once again merged with those of Revolutionary times into a seamless past that fair organizers dubbed "ye olden tyme."[24]

There was as much parody as homage in these representations. Serving their visitors in a variety of shapeless outfits with their hair done up in fantastical styles, the middle-class women who dominated New England Kitchens deliberately intended their outfits to be amusingly dour—the antithesis of their usual tastefully decorative outfits. Male performers also donned a variety of wigs, the more outlandish the better, to accompany their knee breeches and buckled shoes. This fact was not lost on reporters, one of whom described the Brooklyn fair performers' evening wear as even more "preposterous" than their daytime attire. Both male and female participants gave themselves a variety of obsolete or ridiculous names, such as Dorcus, Jerusha, Dr. Calomel, or Reverend Jedediah Poundtext. At their old folks' concert in Brooklyn, they sang traditional tunes in "low metre in a high key through their noses," according to one onlooker, that is, slowly and in high-pitched, nasally voices, parodying the Puritan style of hymn singing. They rounded out their performances with scripted dialogues liberally sprinkled with imitation Puritan or Quaker vernacular, referring, for instance, to "thou," "ye," or "thee." Gently mocking the concerns of the past, they made up imaginary scenes where men talked politics and women recounted local gossip ("Ezeciah Cute was making up to Mehitable Jones, and Deacon Jones was dead sot agin it").[25] Visitors did not fail to perceive these satirical undertones, with one complaining that the kitchen was "a stage caricature of New England," and numerous outraged clergymen denouncing the counterfeit wedding as a travesty on the holy estate of marriage.[26]

Fair organizers represented the Revolution primarily in terms of domestic activities that took place in kitchens or parlors, not in war councils, congresses, or battlefields, as did the speech makers who opened their events, speaking of how Washington's mother and wife nurtured his lofty character, and the tableaux performers who staged living reproductions of popular prints that depicted Washington courting his future wife or seeking his mother's blessing as he left for war.[27] Reflecting an intensive Victorian idealization of motherhood and domesticity, such representations were commonplace by midcentury, drawing from histories such as

Elizabeth Ellett's *The Women of the American Revolution* (1848) or hagiographies such as Margaret Conkling's *Memoirs of the Mother and Wife of Washington* (1850), which focused on the importance of women's patriotism during the Revolution.[28]

It was this decidedly middle-class, domestic version of Revolutionary memory that organizers drew from in staging their fair performances. Their remembrances served both to blunt the Revolution's radicalism and to erase the participation of ordinary people in this history. In the words of one contemporary, fair performances were mostly staged by the "wives of congressmen, professional men, clergymen, editors, merchants, bankers, [and] millionaires."[29] They drew their costumes from the "attic trunks and camphor-scented boxes" that middle-class women kept "on hand for chance *tableaux* and theatricals."[30] And the historical props that surrounded performers—much like the items on display in curiosity shops, armories, and art exhibitions—typically came from the homes of wealthy families. Performing roles and displaying material objects that connected them directly to the Revolutionary past, elites maintained a powerful ability to demonstrate personal connections to iconic founders that was unavailable to the mass of ordinary people, who did not own valuable antiques to pass down or "camphor-scented boxes" to protect perishable items. Nonelites now participated from the sidelines, assuming they could afford the price of a ticket.

Other historical actors from the Revolutionary past were rendered equally passive. Representations of colonial life in wartime fairs often included Indian characters as props to amuse crowds or add picturesque detail to historical scenes. Dressed as Indians, white male and female performers helped to transform a history of warfare between Anglo-Americans and Native cultures into harmless fun, much as their "Continental tea parties" reimagined a sanitized Revolution free of violence and social divisions. At the Northern Ohio Sanitary Fair, whites in redface sat in wigwams among the massive floral exhibitions. Others, "hideous in horns and paint," were employed to "stalk solemnly" among the diners at the Brooklyn fair's New England Kitchen.[31] During at least one of the entertainments in this kitchen, another counterfeit Indian made an appearance, evoking screams from the women on stage. Similarly, the fictitious pastor at this fair's donation party entertained the assembled crowd by reading out a record of marriages, births, and deaths, ending up with a "cheerful account" of the demise of himself and his family "prematurely knocked on the head and scalped."[32] At a safe remove from the violent confrontations between Native Americans and white settlers that were ongoing in the West, fairgoers could imagine the still-threatening figure of the stalking Indian as an impotent jester, capable of producing a delightful shock that turned quickly to laughter.

Conflating the colonial and Revolutionary eras, fair organizers collapsed a complex history of wars, alliances, and treaties between Native Americans and white settlers, imagining instead a single Native culture that had long since disappeared. Most fairs had wigwams like the one at the Albany fair, which contained a dozen local white men and women dressed to represent Indian figures from history or literature. Various decorations—a canoe, bows and arrows, beadwork, and baskets—adorned the walls of their abode, while the performers inside presented standard caricatures of Native Americans, representing "the character, habits of life . . . listless inactivity, pride and fondness for dress and display of the tribes they personate."[33] Distinctions between "tribes" actually mattered little for either fair organizers or their patrons. Most exhibitions made no effort to represent the diversity of Native cultures, instead merging artifacts, customs, and "characters," both real and fictional.[34] As one fair history jauntily noted, "Most Americans know in reality so little about the original possessors of their soil, that any insight into the Indian ways and appearances, comes with all the charm of novelty."[35]

Appropriating Native American dress, customs, or symbols had long been popular among Anglo-Americans, involving both vilification and idealization of cultures that had been, or were in the process of being, dispossessed.[36] Sitting comfortably in wigwams surrounded by beads and basketwork, imagined Indians could represent an attractive preindustrial lifestyle that compared well to the stresses of modern living. But in gazing on "savages" whose "listless inactivity" could never have produced the gleaming machinery in the halls beyond, fairgoers could simultaneously lament their decline and celebrate a seemingly predestined dispossession that had made way for the modernity that surrounded them. Adding to the sense of a changeless, singular Indian culture existing only in the past, Native American skeletons and items dug up from burial sites were on display in many of the fair's curiosity shops.

Representations of African Americans and the history of slavery at sanitary fairs were Janus-faced in a different sense. All of the large-scale fairs were held after the passage of the Emancipation Act and the enlistment of black soldiers into the Union army. They typically celebrated this fact, gesturing to the North's racially enlightened attitudes compared to those of their enemy. The original Emancipation Proclamation was put up for sale at the first Chicago fair, and elaborately engraved copies were available either for display or sale at subsequent fairs. Plentiful evidence of slavery's brutality also confronted fairgoers in curiosity shops, with one circular for the second Chicago fair requesting "articles connected with the institution of slavery and its marts, from the *block* to the *driver's lash!*"[37]

Whereas fair organizers were ready enough to celebrate emancipation in the abstract, however, their treatment of both African Americans and the history of slavery tended to compound rather than challenge racial stereotypes. Black workers were invariably employed at fairs in ways that sanctioned racial hierarchies and minimized the horrors of slavery. Most participated either in low-paid service roles, as waiters serving white diners, or as colorful "darkies." As one perceptive reporter noted in relation to the Brooklyn fair's New England Kitchen, elite women in period costumes maintained the illusion that they were cooking over an open hearth much as their foremothers had done, although in reality the food was prepared by an army of black workers in a back room, sweating over a kitchen fitted out with "all the modern improvements."[38] Likewise, fair histories and newspapers heaped praise on the middle-class white women who acted as hosts in this period room, while remaining silent on the "corps of colored waiters" who served much of the food.[39] The only black characters given visible roles were those hired to play the fiddle or sit by the fire in scarlet coats and breeches, representing a particularly sanitized version of slavery in New England's past. Bloodgood Cutter, the self-styled "Long Island poet" described these workers in a verse written for sale at one of the fairs:

> An old darkey stood in fire-place [*sic*],
> To represent that ancient race,
> That was once there in slavery,
> But the good people made them free.[40]

Fair organizers interpreted emancipation as a sign of national progress, depicting blacks as either victims of Southern slavery or grateful recipients of a freedom bestowed by Northern benevolence. But when it came to social relations between the races they ensured that black participants maintained their roles as servants or faithful "old darkeys."

There was little opportunity for African Americans to participate in fairs in ways that might have challenged these representations. As the Ladies Sanitary Committee of the Saint Thomas Colored Episcopal Church in Philadelphia complained in one of its reports, the railway cars of the city refused admittance to African American passengers, making it difficult for them to attend that city's fair.[41] Black women's organizations had also been barred from participating in the event itself and were forced to hold their own fair six months later.[42] Nor were black organizations invited to participate in the New York Metropolitan Fair—an event held less than a year after the draft riots had exposed a vicious racism at the heart of the city's culture. There were stalls dedicated to "all nationalities, except '*poor bleeding Africa*,' " complained one black commentator, "but we are swallowed up in this great White sea—no identity yet." Black schools had held concerts and black citizens had contributed to the fair, he went on, but they worked without recognition.[43] This silence extended to fair histories, which typically omitted any mention of black benevolence.[44]

Fair organizers did not seem to notice the incongruity in celebrating emancipation while representing African Americans as cheerful servants or passive objects of charity, anymore than they detected the irony of middle-class women parodying the domestic labor of their foremothers while black men and women were in the back rooms doing much of the work. Yet their caricatures of a conflated colonial-Revolutionary era of self-sufficient women, comical Indians, contented slaves, and genteel tea parties revealed more than a little ambivalence toward the past. Any act of parody simultaneously mocks and pays homage to its subject. Women were doing both in their uses of the past. Those who sat working at spinning wheels or knitting by the fire evoked histories of the Revolution in which women had made substantial contributions by renouncing luxuries, practicing self-sufficiency, and accepting hardships. Yet the women involved in these performances did not actually need to follow their lead. The majority of fair organizers were middle class, with enough money to purchase clothing and household necessities and probably the help of servants as well.

In reality, their fairs provided the occasion to forsake deprivation for spending and merry making. In the midst of untold suffering, these women were effectively urging people to buy and enjoy, to engage in guilt-free fun in the name of the troops. But was rampant consumption really appropriate at such a moment? Did it really reflect a Revolutionary spirit?[45] At least one reporter for the *Brooklyn Daily Eagle* tacitly posed this question in a column headed, "The Patriotism of Eating," archly noting, "Everyone seems willing to brave the terrors of surfeit, nightmare or even chronic dyspepsia for the benefit of our suffering soldiers."[46] The sheer luxury and profusion of these events inevitably raised uncomfortable questions about whether or not fair organizers measured up to women of the past.

In raising this question, however, middle-class fair organizers managed to hide another. Performing the roles of Revolutionary foremothers whose suffering had been idealized by a generation of printmakers, publishers, and speechwriters, they linked their work to a glorified history in ways that obscured the reality of their undertakings. Their fairs were massive fund-raising ventures that involved thousands of women in managing and organizing, staging performances, and making money. As historian Beverly Gordon points out, one of the main items they were selling was domesticity itself.[47] Most of the products they displayed were items of ladies' handiwork; women used their beauty and charm to entice customers; and their fairs were purposefully designed to showcase the taste and ingenuity that ladies typically devoted to parlors and outfits. In the most obvious ways, these fairs turned middle-class women into merchants and domesticity into profit. In this context the Revolution served as a stable anchor in what was essentially a novel project: a series of large-scale, female-run public endeavors designed to generate huge profits and further national war aims. By parodying a past of homespun simplicity—simultaneously paying homage to and mocking their forebears—female organizers could stamp their actions with the imprint of tradition, all the while subtly gesturing to their own modernity and marking the distance they had come from a long-gone era when women could demonstrate their patriotism only by spinning by the fire.

Memory is always as much about the present as it is about the past. Sanitary fair organizers used history to speak to their current context. The Civil War witnessed an epic transformation in race relations. It produced an upsurge in class conflict and an unprecedented mobilization of women. And it led to increasing violence on the western frontier, becoming a prelude to the Indian wars that quickly followed in its wake. In the midst of such dramatic changes, middle-class fair organizers evoked a particular version of their past—one that focused on sedate tea ceremonies and harmless quilting parties while mystifying the possibility of violent upheaval. Their fairs also emphasized that the founders' work was finally done. This point was nicely encapsulated by a lithograph on sale at the Brooklyn fair, which pictured a tree of liberty along one border, marked at the trunk with "1776" and at the top with "1863." This tree bore the fruit of the Emancipation Proclamation, with Abraham Lincoln's face dominating the frame.[48] Represented as distant and marginal, the Revolution had become merely a precursor to the Union's far grander achievements—the roots but not the flourishing tree.

The Civil War marked a subtle transformation in Revolutionary memory. Often termed America's "second revolution," this conflict laid to rest much of the ambivalence described by the contributors to this volume—ambivalence rooted in the changing nature of America's republic, fears about whether the union could endure, questions about the founders' intentions regarding slavery, and concerns about whether subsequent generations could measure up to the deeds of their celebrated ancestors. Revolutionary icons were not so much replaced during this period as fossilized—consigned to a past filled with characters so lofty and unreal that they could serve equally well as a source of uncritical anecdote or burlesque. Having been transformed into empty symbols of a long-dead era in which all questions had been answered and all debates resolved, the founders could now become the inspiration for groups that ran the gamut from civil rights activists to Tea Party conservatives.[49]

NOTES

1. [Mary Clark Brayton], *Our Acre and Its Harvest: Historical Sketch of the Soldiers' Aid Society of Northern Ohio* (Cleveland: Fairbanks, Benedict, 1869), 195–97.
2. The best study of these fairs is Beverly Gordon's *Bazaars and Fair Ladies: The History of the American Fundraising Fair* (Knoxville: University of Tennessee Press, 1998).
3. See Sarah J. Purcell, "Martyred Blood and Avenging Spirits: Revolutionary Martyrs and Heroes as Inspiration for the U.S. Civil War," Michael A. McDonnell, "War and Nationhood: Founding Myths and Historical Realities," and James Paxton, "Remembering and Forgetting: War, Memory, and Identity in the Post-Revolutionary Mohawk Valley," all in this volume.
4. Barry Schwartz, "Social Change and Collective Memory: The Democratization of George Washington, *American Sociological Review* 56, no. 2 (1991): 224.

5. Costumed performances were played for laughs more at some wartime fairs than they were at others. Organizers of the tea party mentioned earlier, for instance, emphasized the seriousness of their enactment, but they obviously worried about being associated with more lighthearted events of a similar nature. Their history thus emphasized the "dignified carriage and careful personation" with which performers depicted "the distinguished men and women of '76," adding, "Nothing was caricatured." Brayton, *Our Acre and Its Harvest*, 197.
6. François Furstenberg vividly details how this process began in the post-Revolutionary era, when Americans began to venerate Washington as the nation's common father. *In the Name of the Father: Washington's Legacy, Slavery, and the Making of a Nation* (New York: Penguin, 2006).
7. Michael Kammen, *Mystic Chords of Memory: The Transformation of Tradition in American Culture* (New York: Knopf, 1991), 11–12, 34–52; David Lowenthal, *The Past Is a Foreign Country* (Cambridge: Cambridge University Press, 1985), 105–13. Alexis de Tocqueville, *Democracy in America*, ed. Thomas Bender (1831; repr., New York: Modern Library, 1981), 115.
8. George B. Forgie, *Patricide in the House Divided: A Psychological Interpretation of Lincoln and His Age* (New York: Norton, 1979); quotations from Lowenthall, *Past Is a Foreign Country*, 118, 122.
9. Keith Beutler, "Emma Willard's 'True Mnemonic of History,'" in this volume.
10. Matthew Mason, "'The Sacred Ashes of the First of Men': Edward Everett, the Mount Vernon Ladies Association of the Union, and Late Antebellum Unionism," in this volume; Karal Ann Marling, *George Washington Slept Here: Colonial Revivals and American Culture, 1876–1986* (Cambridge: Harvard University Press, 1988).
11. Figures for the Northwestern Fair taken from Sarah Edwards Henshaw, *Our Branch and Its Tributaries: Being a History of the Work of the Northwestern Sanitary Commission* (Chicago: Sewell, 1868), chap. 10. See also Gordon, *Bazaars and Fair Ladies*, chap. 3; and William Y. Thompson, "Sanitary Fairs of the Civil War," *Civil War History* 4 (1958): 64.
12. Descriptions of this fair and its opening can be found in various issues of *Canteen* (Albany, N.Y.), February 22 to March 5, 1864, as well as in Frank B. Goodrich, *The Tribute Book: A Record of the Munificence, Self-Sacrifice and Patriotism of the American People during the War for the Union* (New York: Derby & Miller, 1865), 210–13.
13. *History of the Brooklyn and Long Island Fair, February 22, 1864* (Brooklyn: Union Steam Presses, 1864), 26–27, 67.
14. Seth C. Bruggeman, "'More Than Ordinary Patriotism': Living History in the Memory Work of George Washington Parke Custis," in this volume. Private citizens undoubtedly cherished material objects that linked them to their ancestors, but Kammen and Lowenthall confirm that the few individuals who collected Americana in the decades before the war found it impossible to generate public interest in their exhibits. Kammen, *Mystic Chords of Memory*, 53, 74–76; Lowenthal, *Past Is a Foreign Country*, 111.
15. *A Record of the Metropolitan Fair in Aid of the U.S. Sanitary Commission Held at New York, in April 1864* (New York: Hurd & Houghton, 1867), 73.
16. The items are listed under the title "Curiosity Shop" in consecutive issues of the *Canteen*, February 29 to March 3, 1864.

17. *Canteen,* March 2, 1864; *Record of the Metropolitan Fair,* 74.
18. Gary Kulik, "Designing the Past: History-Museum Exhibitions from Peale to the Present," in *History Museums in the United States,* ed. Warren Leon and Roy Rosenzweig (Urbana: University of Illinois Press, 1989), 6.
19. "The Great Sanitary Fair: The Opening Night," *Brooklyn Daily Eagle,* February 23, 1864.
20. *The Oxford English Dictionary Online,* s.v. "relic, n.," www.oed.com/view/Entry/161910.
21. Period rooms varied somewhat in their historical associations, with Philadelphia's fair honoring the state's Quaker heritage with a "William Penn Parlor," and fairs in cities such as Saint Louis or Milwaukee focusing instead on Dutch-themed colonial kitchens. See, for instance, *Report of the Dutchess County and Poughkeepsie Sanitary Fair, March 13 to March 19, 1864* (Poughkeepsie: Platt & Schram, 1864); and Thomas Izod, ed., *Pennsylvania Sanitary Fair Catalogue and Guide* (Philadelphia: Magee Stationer, 1864).
22. *History,* 73, 76–78.
23. "Great Sanitary Fair"; "The New England Kitchen," *Brooklyn Daily Eagle,* February 22, 1864; "Who Started the Fair and the Result," *Brooklyn Daily Eagle,* March 7, 1864.
24. "Great Sanitary Fair"; see also *History,* 75, and "New England Kitchen."
25. "The Donation Party," *Brooklyn Daily Eagle,* February 26, 1864; see also "Visit to the Yankee Kitchen," *Daily Countersign* (Saint Louis, Mo.), May 27, 1864.
26. "Who Started the Fair"; "The Religious Press on the Mock Marriage," *Brooklyn Daily Eagle,* March 11, 1864.
27. "Great Sanitary Fair."
28. E. F. Ellet, *The Women of the American Revolution* (New York: Baker & Scribner, 1848); Margaret C. Conkling, *Memoirs of the Mother and Wife of Washington* (Auburn, N.Y.: Derby, Miller & Co., 1850).
29. Goodrich, *Tribute Book,* 162.
30. *Record of the Metropolitan Fair,* 73–74.
31. Brayton, *Our Acre and Its Harvest,* 183; *History,* 75.
32. "The Donation Party," *Brooklyn Daily Eagle,* February 26, 1864.
33. "The Wigwam," *Canteen,* February 27, 1864.
34. The majority of fairs made do with whites in redface, but Native Americans themselves participated in at least one fair as both spectators and exhibits. An article in the *New York Times* noted that a large contingent of Native Americans were in town visiting the Metropolitan Fair. "Indian Visitors," *New York Times,* March 29, 1864. At the same event Indian performers were also employed by Albert Bierstadt, the renowned German-born painter of western landscapes who had just returned from a trip out west as part of a U.S. government survey expedition to map a new transcontinental route to California. Fair organizers hired Bierstadt to direct their "Indian Department," which encompassed an enormous wigwam in front of a painted backdrop, with a stage on which Native American performers sang and danced to sold out crowds. Obviously interested in distinguishing his exhibition from the generic displays of "savagery" elsewhere, Bierstadt emphasized his "undoubted acquaintance" with the cultures he pictured and stressed that he was "above suspicion of charlatanry." This emphasis on presenting authentic knowledge of Native American cultures made Bierstadt's

department unique among sanitary fairs. But he was not above playing to the crowds by offering fictitious details about his performers' backgrounds. They "were from the Rocky Mountains, or from the wilds of Mackerelville, [a slang term for New York's Lower East Side] according to the spirit of the narrator," explained the fair's history, adding in a later chapter that they were actually "a party of Iroquois Indians." *Record of the Metropolitan Fair*, quotes on 49–50, 200, 250–51.

35. *Record of the Metropolitan Fair*, 50.
36. Philip J. Deloria, *Playing Indian* (New Haven, Conn.: Yale University Press, 2006).
37. Stella S. Floor Coatsworth, *The Loyal People of the North-west, a Record of Prominent Persons, Places, and Events, during Eight Years of Unparalleled American History* (Chicago: Church, Goodman & Connelley, 1869), 234.
38. "Great Sanitary Fair."
39. *History*, 70–71.
40. Bloodgood H. Cutter, *A Poem on the New England Kitchen* (privately printed and published for the Benefit of the Metropolitan Sanitary Fair, 1864).
41. *Report of the Ladies Sanitary Committee of the St. Thomas Colored Episcopal Church Fair Auxiliary to the United States Sanitary Commission* (Philadelphia: Crissy & Markley, 1864).
42. "For the Sick and Wounded Soldiers. St. Thomas' Church" (flyer advertising a fair), Library Company of Philadelphia, SM Am 1864 St. Tho Ch.
43. "Brooklyn Correspondence," *Christian Recorder*, April 16, 1864.
44. In Goodrich's *Tribute Book*, for instance, there is only a single mention of one elderly black woman donating to a fair. Likewise, *Record of the Metropolitan Fair* refers in an appendix to a "colored school" that donated more to the fair than any other school in its ward, but there is no further mention of African American contributions to this event (212).
45. "American Women," *Spirit of the Fair* (New York), April 20, 1864.
46. "The Patriotism of Eating," *Brooklyn Daily Eagle*, February 26, 1864.
47. Gordon, *Bazaars and Fair Ladies*, 5.
48. "Brooklyn News," *New York Times*, March 5, 1864.
49. On the transformation of the Revolutionary generation into empty symbols capable of supporting diverse political positions, I've drawn from Alfred F. Young, *The Shoemaker and the Tea Party: Memory and the American Revolution* (Boston: Beacon, 1999); and Jill Lepore, *The Whites of Their Eyes: The Tea Party's Revolution and the Battle over American History* (Princeton: Princeton University Press, 2010).

Notes on Contributors

PETER BASTIAN is an adjunct professor of history at the Australian Catholic University. He has published widely in many forms, including electronically, and is the author of several books, including *A Century of Celebration: RSL LifeCare, 1911–2011* (2011), *Andrew Fisher: An Underestimated Man* (2009), *John F. Kennedy and the Historians* (2008), and *Bearing Any Burden: The Cold War Years, 1945–1991* (2003). He was also the editor of the *Australasian Journal of American Studies* from 1986 to 1990 and again from 2000 to 2006. He was the recipient of university teaching awards in 1998 and 2005 and is a former president of the Australian and New Zealand American Studies Association.

KEITH BEUTLER holds a PhD from Washington University and is an associate professor at Missouri Baptist University. He has written and researched extensively on memory and history, especially the historicization of memory in the period from the Revolution to the Civil War. He is the author of the forthcoming *George Washington's Hair: How Early Americans Remembered the Founders.*

DARYL BLACK received a PhD from the University of California, Irvine, and is now the executive director of the Chattanooga History Center. He has published articles on southern evangelicals and material culture and the making of Civil War memory. He is currently completing a major museum exhibit design and construction project in Chattanooga.

SETH C. BRUGGEMAN earned a PhD at the College of William and Mary and is an associate professor of history and American studies and public history coordinator at Temple University. He is the author of *Here, George Washington Was Born: Memory, Material Culture, and the Public History of a National Monument* (2008) and the editor of *Born in the USA: Birth, Commemoration, and American Public Memory* (2012).

W. FITZHUGH BRUNDAGE received a PhD from Harvard University and is now the William B. Umstead Professor of History at the University of North Carolina, Chapel Hill. He has published extensively on memory, history, and the South. His most recent book, *The Southern Past*, received the Southern Historical Association's Charles Sydnor Award for distinguished work in southern history. His other major work on the topic includes a widely cited edited collection of essays on historical memory and regional identity in the American South (2000) and articles in *Journal of American History* and *Journal of Southern History*, among others. In addition he has published an acclaimed study of utopian socialism and a dual prize-winning book on lynching in the American South (1993).

EILEEN KA-MAY CHENG earned a PhD at Yale University and is an associate professor at Sarah Lawrence College. She has written articles on loyalism and American historical writing and a book titled *The Plain and Noble Garb of Truth: Nationalism and Impartiality in American Historical Writing, 1784–1860* (2008). Her current book project is on loyalist historians of the American Revolution and their legacy.

FRANCES M. CLARKE received a PhD from Johns Hopkins University and now lectures at the University of Sydney. Her research interests center on the American Civil War and Reconstruction, postwar memorialization, wartime gender relations, and the history of war-induced trauma. She is the author of *War Stories: Suffering and Sacrifice in the Civil War North* (2011).

CLARE CORBOULD is an Australian Research Council Future Fellow in Monash University's History Department. Her publications include

Becoming African Americans: Black Public Life in Harlem, 1919–1939 (2009).

CAROLINE COX is a professor of history at the University of the Pacific. She is the author of numerous articles about the Revolutionary era. Her first book, *A Proper Sense of Honor: Service and Sacrifice in George Washington's Army* (2004), received the LTG Richard G. Trefry Award from the Army Historical Foundation. She is currently completing her second book, *Boy Soldiers of the American Revolution.*

TARA DESHPANDE received a PhD from the University of Leeds and has taught at the University of Leeds and Leeds Metropolitan University. A literary historian, she works and publishes on eighteenth- and nineteenth-century American literature, including George Lippard, the fiction of the early republic, and Civil War memoirs.

CAROLYN EASTMAN holds a PhD from Johns Hopkins University and is an associate professor of history at Virginia Commonwealth University. She has published widely on gender, nationalism, and the media in early American history, including most recently *A Nation of Speechifiers: Making an American Public after the Revolution* (2009), which received the James Broussard Best First Book Prize from the Society for Historians of the Early American Republic. Her current book project is titled "Learning to See: Gender in the Eighteenth-Century Atlantic World of Print."

WILLIAM HUNTTING HOWELL received a PhD from Northwestern University and is an assistant professor of English at Boston University. He has published articles in the *William and Mary Quarterly, Early American Studies, Journal of the Early Republic,* and *American Literature.* He is currently working on a book on imitation, emulation, and literary culture in the early United States.

EVERT JAN VAN LEEUWEN is a lecturer in English and American literature at Leiden University. He has published articles in various journals and collections on British and American gothic fiction, graveyard poetry, and popular culture and is the author of the book *Alchemical Construction of Genders in Anglo-American Fiction, 1799–1852* (2011). He is currently compiling and writing the introduction for an anthology of eighteenth- and nineteenth-century Anglo-American graveyard poetry and developing a new research project that involves the textual as well as empirical study of popular supernatural fiction's potential to facilitate readers' spiritual quests.

EMILY LEWIS BUTTERFIELD is a doctoral candidate in history at Arizona State University. Her dissertation, "'The Patriot Blood of Our Fathers Runs through Our Veins': Revolutionary Heritage Rhetoric and the American Woman Suffrage Movement, 1848–1880," explores women's rights advocates' use of Revolutionary memory and heritage as rhetorical tools in their arguments for social and political equality.

DANIEL MANDELL is a professor of history at Truman State University. He has published widely on Native American and African American history. His books include *Behind the Frontier: Indians in Eighteenth-Century Eastern Massachusetts* (1996), the two *New England Treaties* volumes in the series Early American Indian Documents: Treaties and Laws, 1607–1789 (2003), and *Tribe, Race, History: Native Americans in Southern New England, 1780–1880* (2008), which was awarded the Lawrence W. Levine Prize by the Organization of American Historians for the best book on American cultural history. His most recent book is *King Philip's War: Colonial Expansion, Native Resistance, and the End of Indian Sovereignty* (2010).

MATTHEW MASON is an associate professor of history at Brigham Young University. He has published numerous articles on the politics of slavery in the early American republic. He is the author of *Slavery and Politics in the Early American Republic* (2006) and the coeditor, with John Craig Hammond, of *Contesting Slavery: The Politics of Bondage and Freedom in the New American Nation* (2011).

MICHAEL A. MCDONNELL earned a DPhil in history at Oxford University and is an associate professor at the University of Sydney. He has published articles on the American Revolution in the *Journal of American History*, *William and Mary Quarterly*, and *Journal of American Studies*. His first book, *The Politics of War: Race, Class, and Conflict in Revolutionary Virginia* (2007) received the New South Wales Premier's History Award in 2008. He won the Lester Cappon Prize for the best article published in the *William and Mary Quarterly* in 2006, and his work was featured in the Organization of American Historians' *Best American History Essays* (2008). He is currently working on a book-length project, "The Founding

Syndrome," and finishing a book titled "Beyond Borders: Michilimackinac and the Making and Unmaking of the Atlantic World."

JAMES PAXTON holds a PhD from Queen's University, Kingston, Ontario, and is an associate professor of history at Moravian College. His research centers on the Haudenosaunee in eighteenth- and nineteenth-century New York and Upper Canada. He is the author of the book *Joseph Brant and His World: Eighteenth-Century Mohawk Warrior and Statesman* (2008).

SARAH J. PURCELL is professor of history at Grinnell College, where she is director of the Rosenfield Program in Public Affairs, International Relations, and Human Rights. She has published extensively on the topic of war, memory, and national identity. Her books include *Sealed with Blood: War, Sacrifice, and Memory in Revolutionary America* (2002) and *The Early American Republic: An Eyewitness History* (2004). She is currently working on a book on public memory and spectacular political funerals of the Civil War and Reconstruction.

Index

abolition, 41–53; and Baptist Church, 240–45; and pacifism, 228–29. *See also* slavery
Adams, John, 9, 44–45, 59, 61–66, 69–70, 156, 181, 252, 260
Adams, John Quincy, 110, 170
Adams, Samuel, 58, 64–65, 69, 89
African Americans: and Baptist Church, 234–45; emancipation of, 8–9, 41–53, 240–45; identity and the American Revolution, 8–9, 41–53; representation of in historical reenactments, 305–7
Albany Army Relief Bazaar, 298–99, 300, 305
Allen, Ethan, 93, 281
Allen, William, 228
American Peace Society, 220, 222–23, 228–29, 233n34
André, Major John, 114, 118
anecdote, 198–211
anti-Indian sublime, 180, 192, 194–95. *See also* Native Americans; Indian removal
antinarrative, 98–99, 106–7, 145, 157.
Arlington House, 128, 133, 136–40, 299. *See also* Custis, George Washington Parke
Arlington National Cemetery, 128–29, 139
Arnold, Benedict, 93, 114
Artis, Isaac, 120–21
Augusta, Georgia, 236, 241–43

Baker, Edward, 287–88
Balls Bluff, Battle of, 287–88
Baltimore, Massachusetts, 137, 164, 205, 272, 285, 289

Bancroft, George, 59, 144–47, 154–57
Banister, John, 25
Baptist Churches, 234–45
Barber, John W., 208
Barlow, Joel, 76–81; "Elegy on the Late Honorable Titus Hosmer, Esq.," 78–81
Barrett, Millicent, 281
battles. *See entries for individual battles*
Beardslee, John, 187
Beauregard, P. G. T., 290
Bell, John, 272–73
Benedict, George Grenville, 281
Benezet, Anthony, 49
Bennington, Battle of, 112, 118–20, 280–82
Benton, Nathaniel, 186–87, 191
Bethesda Church, 244
Binney, Barnabas, 284
Blake, A. M., 169
Blake, J. L., 167
Blatchford, John, 115
Bonner, Robert, 269
Borst, Joseph, 193
Boston, 11, 20, 43–46, 49–52, 54n8, 56n35, 76, 199, 269–70, 274, 294, 302
Boyer, Paul, 21
Brandon, Josiah, 121
Brandywine, Battle of, 120, 203
Brant, Joseph, 189
Brooklyn, Battle of, 95
Brooklyn and Long Island Sanitary Fair, 298–99, 301–6, 309
Brown, John, 269, 271
Brown, John M., 183, 193
Bull Run, Battle of, 281
Bunker Hill, Battle of, 282–90
Burgoyne, John, 23, 118–19
Burleigh, William, 285
Bush, George W., 1, 20, 107

Campbell, William W., 179, 181, 183–86, 188, 191, 193–94
Capers, William, 241
"Captain Molly." *See* Pitcher, Molly
Carroll, Charles, 260
cemeteries. *See* graveyards
Chalmers, George: *Political Annals*, 144–49; plagiarism of, 144–57
Charleston, South Carolina, 23, 282, 289–90
Chaney, John, 117
Chicago. *See* Northwestern Fair
christianity: and abolition, 42, 44, 47–48, 50, 240–41; Joseph Brant, 189; and elegiac verse, 77, 79–80, 83, 88; George Lippard, 255; and pacifism, 220–24, 226–28, 230. *See also* Baptist Church; eschatology; millennialism; postmillennialism
Civil War, 2–3, 10, 229–30, 245, 266–69, 274–76, 280–91, 294–309
Clement, Jesse, 209–10
Clendenin, Rebecca, 200
Cogswell, Nathaniel, 111, 121–22
Colonial Williamsburg, 11, 127–28
Concord, Battle of, 46, 281, 285, 288
confederates, 288–89, 291. *See also* Civil War; loyalists
Connecticut, 26–28, 47, 81, 97, 101, 119, 206, 227, 269, 287
Connecticut Peace Society, 227
Conner's Prairie, 127
Constitution, the, 2, 20, 32–33, 148; John Dickinson's support of, 52, 59, 65; pacifists and, 224; and Unionism, 270–71, 282; Hugh Williamson's support of, 148
Constitutional Convention, 33, 64, 148
Constitutional Union Party, 271–73
Continental Army, 23–25, 47, 63, 78, 95, 97, 102–3, 106, 113, 116–17, 119–20, 130; animosity toward the Continental Congress, 28–29; mobilization problems, 26–27; mutiny of, 32. *See also* Continental Congress; Martin, Joseph Plumb; pensions
Continental Congress, 26–29, 33, 58, 62

Cooper, James Fenimore, 95–96, 188
Corbin, Margaret, 203–4, 208–9
Cornwallis, Lord Charles, 23, 93
Cowpens, Battle of, 93
Cox, Allyn, 131
Crittenden, John J., 274
Culpeper's Rebellion, 149–50, 152, 155–56, 160n26
Culver, Erastus, 280–81
Cunningham, Ann Pamela, 266, 273
Cunningham, Louisa Bird, 266
Custis, George Washington Parke, 8–10; childhood and early life, 129–31; commemoration of George Washington and the American Revolution, 128–40, 299; description of Captain Molly, 207–8; political career, 132–33
Custis, Nelly, 129–30

Declaration of Independence, 20, 33, 41, 52, 62–63, 65, 72n23, 73n41, 181, 221, 252–54, 256, 258
Delany, Martin, 51
Delaware, 22–23, 60, 63, 67–69. *See also* Kent County
Delaware River, 47, 255
Dickinson, John, 7, 9–11, 58; and John Adams, 61–66, 69–70; early life and education, 60; marriage and home life, 61, 63, 67–69; political career, 59–67; self-promotion, 59–60, 66, 69–71
Dickinson, Mary, 59, 61, 63, 67–69
disunion, crisis of, 245, 269, 274. *See also* Civil War; secession; Unionism
Dodge, David Low, 221–22
domesticity: in rhetoric of Edward Everett, 265, 271–72, 274; in sanitary fair displays, 295–96, 302–4, 307–8
Duane, James, 32, 63–64
Duncan, Robert, 111
Durivage, Francis Alexander, 205, 209
Dutch settlers, 186, 192

Easton, Hosea, 51
education. *See* pedagogy
elegiac verse, 75–90
Ellet, Elizabeth, 203, 209, 304
Ellsworth, Elmer, 285–87, 290
Equiano, Olaudah, 42, 48
Erie Canal, 180, 183–84, 186–87
eschatology, 236–38
Everett, Edward, 10; "The Character of Washington," 265, 268, 276; and Civil War, 274–76; and Constitutional Union Party, 271–73; hagiography of George Washington, 266–68; and Abraham Lincoln, 274–75; and MVLAU, 267, 269–70; popularity of, 268–69, 272–73; preservation of Mount Vernon, 265–68, 270, 273; on sectionalism, 270, 274–75

Fairhill, 61, 66, 68
fairs, 127, 294–309
Farewell Address, 20, 33, 266, 268, 270–72
First Peoples, 184, 187–88, 195. *See also* Haudenosaunee; Mohawks; Oneida; Six Nations Confederacy
Fletcher, Ebenezer, 115
Fort Moultrie, 289
Fort Sumter: attack on, 274, 289, 290
Fourth of July, 110–12, 145, 221, 252, 254, 282. *See also* Independence Day
Fox, Ebenezer, 115
Franklin, Benjamin, 59, 69, 91n14, 201, 224, 252
Fredericksburg, Virginia, 172
Freeman, Elizabeth, 47
Freneau, Philip, 76, 84; "The British Prison-Ship," 84–89; "George the Third's Soliloquy," 86, 89–90; "The House of Night," 85–90; "The Rising Glory of America," 84, 86
French Revolution, 65, 135, 222, 253, 259–60
Fries's Rebellion, 51

Galloway, Joseph, 61–62
Galphin, Jesse, 241
Garnet, Henry Highland, 51, 282
Garrison, William Lloyd, 228–29, 282–83
George III, King, 80, 83–85, 87, 89–90, 93, 223, 258
Georgia, 10–11, 29, 234–45. *See also* Savannah
German settlers, 181, 185–86
Germantown, Battle of, 120
Gerry, Elbridge, 62
Gettysburg, Battle of: consecration of graves, 275
Gilmore, William, 119–20
Grant, Jehu, 116–17
graveyards: poetry, 77–85. *See also* tombs
Graydon, Alexander, 24
Great Tree of Peace, 181, 194
Greenfield Village, 127
Grimké, Thomas, 227–28, 233n26
Grow, Galusha A., 287

Hall, James, 167–68
Hall, John, 169
Hall, Prince, 41, 43, 50–52; anti-slavery petition, 41, 46–47, 50–52
Hamilton, Alexander, 32, 59, 73n39, 91n14, 208
Hammond, Jupiter, 49
Hansyerry, 193
hardship. *See* suffering
Harpers Ferry, 269
Haswell, Anthony, 112
Haudenosaunee, 179–81, 188–89, 193–94. *See also* Mohawks; Oneida; First Peoples; Six Nations Confederacy
Haynes, Lemuel, 42, 52
Herkimer, Nicholas, 186
Hervey, James, 81
historical reenactment, 127, 134–35, 138, 294–96, 302–8
Holcombe, Henry, 238–40
Hollis, James, 121
Holmes, Abiel, 148
Hosmer, Titus, 78; representation of, in poetry, 78–80, 82
Howe, Henry, 208
Humphreys, David, 76; "Addressed to the Armies of the United States of America," 81; "Elegy on Lieutenant De Hart," 81–84; "On the Happiness of America," 81
hunger, 96–105, 107, 111, 117–18
Hunt, Freeman, 204–5
Hutchison, Susan Nye, 243

imperialism: American, 255–56, 259; Spanish, 253, 255–57, 259. *See also* U.S.-Mexican War
Independence Day, 4, 110, 117. *See also* Fourth of July
Indian removal, 188–89, 251–52, 255–56. *See also* Native Americans; anti-Indian sublime

Jackson, Andrew, 188–89
Jackson, James W., 285, 290
Jacobs, Eli, 117
Jameson, David, 25
Jasper, William, 282–83, 289–91
Jay, John, 32, 63–64
Jefferson, Thomas, 32, 39n40, 111, 132, 140, 156, 167, 181, 224, 252, 260, 294; relationship with John Dickinson, 64–66, 70

Kames, Lord, 77–78, 83
Kammen, Michael, 3, 76, 200, 250
Keeler, Cornelia, 163
Kent County, Delaware, 60, 138
King, Thomas Starr, 287–88
King's Mountain, Battle of, 121
Kiokee Church, 236, 240, 242–43
Kip's Bay, Battle of, 95, 101
Knox, Henry, 21, 24, 32
Knoxville, Tennessee, 269
Kosciuszko, Tadeusz, 93

Ladd, William, 217–22

Lafayette, Marie Joseph Paul Yves Roch Gilbert Du Motier, marquis de, 8, 25–26, 93; tour of the United States, 95, 138, 169–70, 173, 182, 192
Lee, Richard Henry, 65, 283
Lee, Robert E., 129, 139
Lexington, Battle of, 46, 223, 281, 285, 288
Lincoln, Abraham, 173, 229, 274–75, 285, 196, 309
Lippard, George, 249–52; *'Bel of Prairie Eden*, 251, 259; *Legends of Mexico*, 251; *Washington and His Generals*, 249, 251–61
living history. *See* historical reenactment
local history: of Mohawk Valley, 8–9, 180–86, 188–89, 190–92, 194
localism: and African American identity, 42–43, 51; during the Revolutionary War, 21–24, 26–29
local memory theory, 164–65, 167–68, 170–71. *See also* physicalism
Longfellow, Henry Wadsworth, "Paul Revere's Ride," 75–76
Long Island, New York, 29, 168, 306. *See also* Brooklyn and Long Island Sanitary Fair
Lossing, Benson, 208–10
loyalists, 29–30, 118, 121, 38n32; and Native Americans, 179–81, 186, 189–92, 194, 223, 295. *See also* loyalist historians
loyalist historians: plagiarism of, by nationalist historians, 9, 144–57
Lyon, Nathaniel, 287–88

Madison, James, 23, 32, 59, 64, 204, 294, 300
Maine, 11, 94–95, 223, 226, 269, 285
Marshall, John, 145–47, 150–57; *Life of George Washington*, 150–54
Martin, Joseph Plumb, 9–11, 28–29; biographies of, 106; *Narrative of Some of the Adventures, Dangers and Sufferings of a Revolutionary Soldier*, 94–107, 117; and Molly Pitcher, 206–7
Maryland, 24–25, 147. *See also* Baltimore
Massachusetts, 8, 21, 27, 41, 43–47, 50–52, 110, 116, 119, 203–4, 219, 221, 269, 285–86. *See also* Boston
Massachusetts Peace Society, 221
Mason, James Murray, 288
McCauley, Mary Hays, 203–4, 212n11
memoirs, 94–107, 115–17
memory: African Americans, 41–53; processes of, 113–14; public versus private, 110–12, 118–19, 121–22; and sectionalism, 282–92; soldiers, 94–107, 111–22. *See also* fairs; historical reenactment; physicalism
Mercer, Silas, 236–38
Mexican War. *See* U.S.-Mexican War
millennialism, 75–78, 80–81, 226–27, 257–58. *See also* postmillennialism
Mississippi, 272–73
Missouri, 287
mnemonics, 163, 165–66. *See also* physicalism
Mohawks, 181, 183, 189, 190, 194. *See also* Oneida; Haudenosaunee; First Peoples; Six Nations Confederacy
Mohawk Valley, 11, 146, 179–95, 209
Monmouth, Battle of, 120, 198–99, 200–202, 204–11, 281. *See also* Pitcher, Molly
monuments: Arlington House, 128, 133, 136–40, 299; of Crispus Attucks, 52; at Bunker Hill, 170, 284; of the Marquis de Lafayette, 170; of George Washington, 136, 164; of Mary Washington, 172; of Emma Willard, 163–64. *See also* Mount Vernon; physicalism
Montgomery, Richard, 111, 282
Morris, Robert, 32, 64, 260
Morse, Jedidiah, 148
Mount Vernon, 129–30, 132–33, 137–38, 168–69; campaign to preserve, 265–76

Mount Vernon Ladies Association of the Union (MVLAU), 265–70, 273
Murphy, Thomas W., 244
Murrin, John, 32–33, 39n41
museums: Charles Willson Peale's, 134, 136; early, of Revolutionary War artifacts, 299–301. *See also* fairs
MVLAU. *See* Mount Vernon Ladies Association of the Union

national identity and the American Revolution, 19–34. *see* also localism; sectionalism
nationalist historians: plagiarism of loyalist histories, 9, 144–57
Native Americans, 179–95; in historical reenactments, 304–5, 311n34
Nat Turner's Rebellion, 243–44
Needham, Sumner, 285
Nell, William Cooper, 52
New England, 23–25, 42–43, 45–50, 52, 58, 147–48, 153, 184, 219, 229, 282, 284, 288; New England Kitchen fair display, 299, 301–4, 306. *See also* Connecticut; Maine; Massachusetts; New Hampshire; Rhode Island; Vermont
New Hampshire, 32, 47, 269,
New Jersey, 28, 66, 104–5, 202, 205, 269, 286–87
New Orleans, 225, 289
New York, 8–9, 24, 30–31, 37n19, 114, 117–19, 130, 162–64, 168, 172, 202–3, 209, 269–71; peace movement, 219, 221–22; sanitary fairs, 298–307, 309, 311n34. *See also* Mohawk Valley; New York City; Utica
New York City, 97, 111, 280–81, 285, 290–91
New York Metropolitan Fair, 298–99, 307
New York Peace Society, 221–22
nonresistance, 228–29
Norris, Isaac, 61, 68
North, Lord Frederick, 93
North Carolina, 25, 29, 38n30, 121, 148–49, 155, 235–36, 273, 288
Northern Ohio Sanitary Fair, 294–95, 304
Northwestern Fair, 298, 306

Obama, Barack H., 19–20
Ohio, 219, 269, 287, 294, 304
Oneida, 190–92. *See also* Mohawks; Haudenosaunee; First Peoples; Six Nations Confederacy
Oregon, 287
Otis, James, 44

pacifism, 63, 222, 227–28; and abolition, 228–29. *See also* peace movement; peace societies
Paine, Thomas, 78, 91n14, 239, 254, 260
Painter, Thomas, 117
Palfrey, John, 148
Palmetto Day, 282, 289
Parkman, Francis, 226
Parrish, Cyprian, 117
peace movement, 217–30. *See also* pacifism
peace societies, 219–23, 226–29
Peale, Charles Willson, 134, 136
pedagogy, 166–73
Penfield African Church, 243
Penn, William, 255–56
Pennsylvania, 23–26, 28, 58, 60–63, 67, 70, 111, 121, 203, 269, 275, 287. *See also* Philadelphia
pensions, 42, 95, 108n19, 111–17, 119–22, 200, 202–4, 221
petitions, 31, 41–42, 44–53, 62, 163, 172, 181, 203, 267, 274. *See also* pensions
Philadelphia, 11, 23, 28, 32, 43, 52, 58, 60, 62, 64, 67–69, 93, 103, 130, 134–35, 137, 169, 202, 252, 258–59, 269–70, 290, 307, 311n21
physicalism, 8, 76–77, 162–73
Piedmont, Georgia, 11, 235
Pitcher, Molly, 8–9, 11, 157, 198–211

plagiarism: of loyalist history, 144–57, 200
Plimoth Plantation, 127
Plumb, J. H., 13n5, 112, 146
poetry, 49–50; elegiac verse, 75–90
Porter, Ebenezer, 168
postmillennialism, 226–27, 257–58. *See also* millennialism
Prescott, William H., 259
presidential addresses, 1, 19–20, 33, 34n2, 274–75. *See also* Farewell Address
Pulaski, Casimir, 93
Putnam, Gen. Israel, 98–99, 287

Ramsay, David, 96, 148
Reed, Joseph, 64
reenactment. *See* historical reenactment
relics, 8, 12, 76, 130, 136–39, 163, 167–69, 173, 176n27, 267, 295, 299, 301. *See also* monuments; museums; physicalism
Renan, Ernest, 34
Rhode Island, 32, 116, 219
Rush, Benjamin, 33, 62, 70

Saint Louis, Missouri, 287
Salter, George, 290
Sampson, Deborah, 199, 203–4, 209–11
Sancho, 48
San Francisco, 290
sanitary fairs. *See* fairs
Saratoga, Battle of, 23, 93, 119
Savannah, Georgia, 241
Savannah, Battle of, 282
Schoharie, 181–83, 185–86, 192–93, 195n2. *See also* Mohawk Valley
Scott, Sir Walter, 135
secession, 245, 273–76, 282–83, 287, 289. *See also* Civil War; disunion; sectionalism; Unionism
sectionalism, 6, 10, 24–25, 266–68, 270, 272–74, 283, 289. *See also* Civil War; disunion; localism; secession
segregation in Baptist worship, 242–43
sensibility, 77, 85, 88, 90
Sewall, Samuel, 43–44
Shays's Rebellion, 51, 56n34
Shi, David Emory, 20–21
Shurtliff, Robert. *See* Sampson, Deborah
Sigourney, Lydia H., 171
Silver Bluff Baptist Church, 241
Simmons, Sybilla, 169–70
Simms, Jeptha, 182–85, 187, 191–92, 194
Six Nations Confederacy, 179, 184, 188, 190–91. *See also* First Peoples, Haudenosaunee; Mohawks; Oneida
Skansen Museum, 127
slavery, 2–3, 68, 219–20, 229–30, 234, 236, 240, 242–43, 245, 250, 261n9, 269, 288–89, 296, 305–6, 309; John Dickinson's attitude to, 68; Georgian Baptist Church, 234–36, 239–45; petitions against, 41–53. *See also* abolition; slaves
slaves: George Washington Parke Custis's ownership of, 133, 138; Thomas Jefferson's ownership of, 66; representation of, at sanitary fairs, 305–7; service of, in Revolutionary War, 24, 36n14, 46, 116–17. *See also* abolition; slavery
Somerset decision, the, 44–45, 48, 55n16
soldiers: desertion, 121; friendship, 119–20; hardship, 21, 96, 117–18; memory of, 94, 107, 111–22, 217–18; neutrality, 29–30; suffering, 224–26, 307–8
South Carolina, 23, 31, 117, 227, 236, 241, 282, 289–90
Southern Baptist Convention, 243, 245
Sparks, Jared, 148, 226

Springer, Uriah, 120–21
Springfield Baptist Church, 241–43, 245
Stamp Act Congress, 44, 58
Stark, John, 118, 281
Steuben, Baron von, 26
Stillé, Charles J., 59
Stone, William Leete, 187, 189
Stoney Point, siege of, 120
suffering, 25, 77, 79, 84, 86–88, 90, 95, 103, 108n8, 108n9, 110, 217–18, 223–27, 307–8; as threat to national unity, 30–31
Sullivan, William, 167
Sullivan's Island, Battle of, 282–91
Swain, James, 281

Tarleton, Banastre, 93
Taylor, Isaac, 164–65
textbooks, 20–21, 76, 78, 164–70
Thomson, Charles, 32, 64
Ticonderoga, Battle of, 281
Tindall, George Brown, 20–21
Tocqueville, Alexis de, 297
tombs, 77; of George Washington, 76, 78, 139, 168–70; of Mary Washington, 172. *See also* graveyards
Trenton, Battle of, 93, 134
Troy Female Seminary, 164–65. *See also* Willard, Emma
Trumbull, John: *The Death of Dr. Warren at the Battle of Bunker* Hill, 288; *George Washington before the Battle of Trenton*, 134–36, 138
Tyler, Bishop, 116–17
Tyler, Moses Coit, 59

Unionism, 266–76, 281, 283–88, 290–91, 295–96, 298, 309; antiunion feeling during Revolutionary War, 26. *See also* Civil War; disunion; localism; sectionalism; secession
U.S.-Mexican War, 249–51, 259. *See also* Lippard, George
Utica, New York, 182–83, 192

Valley Forge, 20, 95, 281
Valley Forge National Historic Park, 20
Vanishing Indian, myth of, 188–90
Vermont, 52, 112, 119, 280–82, 290–91
veterans, 4, 7–8, 28, 47, 111–22, 169, 173, 182–83, 186, 192, 194, 210, 221, 238–39, 250
Virginia, 22, 28, 30–31, 46, 101, 117, 120–21, 127, 129, 131–32, 136, 147, 172, 235–36, 243, 266, 269–70, 281, 285, 288–90

Walker, David, 52
Walker, Jacob, 242
Walker, Quock, 47
Walker, Sanders, 240
Walton, William, 117
Warner, George, 192–93
Warner, Seth, 118, 280–82
Warren, Joseph, 282–88, 290–91
Warren, Mercy Otis, 70, 96
Warren, Robert Penn, 276
Washington, Bushrod, 133
Washington, D.C., 136, 269, 280
Washington, George, 1, 11, 21, 23–24, 26, 32–33, 46–47, 59, 63, 69, 81, 84–85, 91n14, 93, 128–30; commemoration of, 76, 78, 95, 111, 128–40, 164, 167–70, 238–39, 266–68, 270–73, 276; Farewell Address, 20, 33, 266, 268, 270–72; in George Lippard's *Washington and His Generals*, 249, 251–61; and pacifism, 224; and Molly Pitcher, 199–200, 202, 205, 207–10; and Unionism, 282–83, 289; representations of, at sanitary fairs, 294, 296, 298–99, 300–303; Mary Ball Washington, 171
Washington, Martha, 129–33, 138, 298
Washington, Mary Ball, 170–72
Watts, Garret, 121
Wells, Austin, 119–20
Weem, Mason Locke, 96
Wheatley, Phillis, 48–50

Whipple, Prince, 47
Whiskey Rebellion, 51
White Plains, Battle of, 95
Whittier, John Greenleaf, 204, 250
Willard, Emma, 162–66, 170–73
Williamsburg, Virginia, 22. *See also* Colonial Williamsburg
Williamson, Hugh, 145–50, 152–57
Wilson's Creek, Battle of, 287
women: fundraising campaign to save Mount Vernon, 266; patriots, 199, 203–5; pensions, 202–4; role in preserving memory, 162–63, 170–73, 272, 296, 297–99, 302–4, 307–9. *See also individual entries*
Woodbridge, William Channing, 164–66
Woodville, Caton, 250
Worcester, Noah, 221
Wright, Henry C., 222

Yale University, 77, 81, 83
Yerks, John, 114, 117–18
Yorktown, Battle of, 93, 95, 129, 135–36, 281
Younglove, Samuel, 120

CPSIA information can be obtained
at www.ICGtesting.com
Printed in the USA
BVHW080957060922
646306BV00006B/81